D0627386

The Audubon Society Field Guide to the Natural Places of the Northeast: Coastal

The Audubon Society Field Guide to the Natural Places of the Northeast: Coastal

Stephen Kulik
Pete Salmansohn
Matthew Schmidt
Heidi Welch

A Hilltown Book
Pantheon Books, New York

Staff for this volume

Editor:	Caroline Sutton
Reporters:	Diane DeLuca
	Stephen Kulik
	Pete Salmansohn
	Matthew Schmidt
	Heidi Welch
Cartography:	Rebecca Lazear Okrent
	Gene Gort
Essays:	Edward Ricciuti
Consultants:	Edward Ricciuti
	Tudor Richards

Library of Congress Cataloging in Publication Data

Main entry under title:
The Audubon Society field guide to the natural places of the Northeast.

    Bibliography: v. 1, p.
    Includes index.
    Contents: Coastal—Inland.
    1. Natural areas—Northeastern States—Guide-books.
I. Kulik, Stephen. II. National Audubon Society.
QH76.5.N96A93   1984   917.4'0443   83-23629
ISBN 0-394-72281-7 (v. 1)
ISBN 0-394-72282-5 (v. 2)

Text design: Clint Anglin

Manufactured in the United States of America
First Edition

The National Audubon Society

For more than three-quarters of a century, the National Audubon Society has provided leadership in scientific research, conservation education, and citizen-action programs to save birds and other wildlife and the habitat necessary for their survival.

To accomplish these goals, the society has formally adopted the Audubon Cause: TO CARRY OUT RESEARCH, EDUCATION, AND ACTION TO CONSERVE WILD BIRDS AND OTHER ANIMALS, TREES AND OTHER PLANTS, SOIL, AIR, AND WATER, AND ALSO TO PROMOTE A BETTER UNDERSTANDING OF THE INTERDEPENDENCE OF THESE NATURAL RESOURCES. To carry out the Audubon Cause, the society's programs are structured around five specific missions that encompass the tremendous scope of the organization:

—Conserve native plants and animals and their habitats
—Further the wise use of land and water
—Promote rational strategies for energy development and use
—Protect life from pollution, radiation, and toxic substances
—Seek solutions for global problems involving the interaction of population, resources, the environment, and sustainable development.

Our underlying belief is that all forms of life are interdependent and that the diversity of nature is essential to both our economic and our environmental well-being.

Audubon, through its nationwide system of sanctuaries, protects more than 250,000 acres of essential habitat and unique natural areas for birds and other wild animals and rare plant life. The sanctuaries range in size from 9 acres around Theodore Roosevelt's grave in New York State to 26,000 acres of coastal marsh in Louisiana. Most of the sanctuaries are staffed by resident wardens who also patrol adjacent natural areas not owned by Audubon.

Audubon's 500,000 members provide the underpinning for all the society's programs and activities. Two-thirds of our members also belong to local Audubon chapters, now numbering more than 480, which serve in their communities as focal points for conservation, nature education, and citizen action on environmental issues.

We also maintain ten regional offices, each staffed by two or more full-time professional conservationists who advance Audubon programs throughout the fifty states.

Our staff conducts wildlife research to aid such endangered species as the bald eagle, whooping crane, eastern timber wolf, and bog turtle and to provide knowledge of the ecologically sound management of our sanctuaries. The society also publishes the award-winning *Audubon* magazine and *American Birds* magazine.

For further information about the society, write or call:

National Audubon Society
950 Third Avenue
New York, N.Y. 10022
(212) 832-3200

Contents

**Long Island, Cape Cod, and the Islands:
The Sandy Fringe**   1

Cape Cod National Seashore   97

Long Island Sound's North Shore and the Rhode Island Coast: Sound and Bay   133

Cape Cod to Portland: Rocky Beginnings   211

Portland North: Rough and Rocky Ramparts   277

Acknowledgments

A project as ambitious and as comprehensive as these *Audubon Society Field Guides to the Natural Places of the Northeast* has required the expertise and assistance of dozens of people throughout New York and New England. Foremost thanks must go to Dan Okrent, who conceived and developed the idea for this series, and to the National Audubon Society for recognizing the need for the series and sponsoring its publication.

I cannot say enough about the dedication, enthusiasm, and knowledge that the contributors to the Northeast volumes brought to their work. Pete Salmansohn, Matt Schmidt, and Heidi Welch spent many months traveling through the Northeast, hiking, researching, and writing major portions of the books. Diane DeLuca also contributed to many of the New York and Connecticut site descriptions. I am very grateful to them all.

Many naturalists, both amateur and professional, served as advisors at various stages of this project. Foremost among them is Ed Ricciuti of Connecticut, who wrote the four regional essays in each volume. Tudor Richards, of the Audubon Society of New Hampshire, was a great help in the latter stages of the research. Their thorough knowledge of natural history served not only as a valuable resource but as an inspiration.

Many other individuals and organizations provided help in identifying and evaluating natural areas for inclusion, providing guided tours and special knowledge of specific sites, reviewing manuscripts, and checking site descriptions for accuracy. I want to thank all of the following people: Gary Van Wart, Anthony Boutard, Steven Bassett, Philip Truesdell, Doug Cross, and James Dodge of the Trustees of Reservations in Massachusetts, a private, nonprofit organization that serves as a national model for land conservation efforts; Richard Enser of the Rhode Island Natural Heritage Program; Jan McLure of the Society for the Protection of New Hampshire Forests; Erik Kiviat of the Hudsonia Institute; Bob Moeller; Marshall and Jean Case of the Northeast Audubon Center; James Gibb, Clifford Emanuelson, Tom Carrolan, and Whitney Beals of The Nature Conservancy; Art and Sue Gingert; Dave Rosgen; Bill Kolodnicki; Larry Penny; Les Mehroff; Scott Sutcliffe; Joanne Chandler; Susan Cooley; Gordon Loery; Allison Beall; Elsa Bumstead; Thelma Haight; Steve Maslansky; Phil Schaeffer; Ted Gilman; Rick Ryder; Margo Myles; Bill Paterson; Allan Lindberg; Lois Lindberg; Carol Ryder; Paul Stoutenburgh; Steve Englebright; Gil Bergen; Russell Hoeflich; Schuyler Horton; Frank Burzynski; Roger Spaulding; Terry Schreiner; Jim Rod; Dave Beglin; Bob Devine; Ann Pesiri; Nick Shoumatoff; Michael Pochan; Bernard Kane; Dean Bouton; Bob Brandt; Ted Fink; Tom French; Sid Quarrier; Ed Kirby; Hobson Calhoun; Don Ritter; Lois Kelley; Robert Craig; Dianne Mayerfield; Michael Bell; Carl Helms; Mary Lamont; Marty Strong; Louise Harrison; Herb Mills; Ed Zero; Ed Rufleth; Steve Resler; Bill Norton; Ed Reilly; Kate Dunham; Fred Johnson; Lauren Brown; Chip David; Ron Rosza; Heinz Meng; Hans Weber; Jim Stapleton; Rob Smith; Neil Jorgensen; Lincoln Page; Margaret Watkins; Fred Steele; Sarah Fried; Ann Vick; Dr. Peter Rosen; Dr. Hubert Vogelmann; Rod MacDonald; Jonathan Tucker; and Steve Johnson.

In a state as large and diverse as Maine, whose natural areas constitute a large portion of these volumes, special thanks are due from Heidi Welch to a number of people: Joyce Harms, for making the original connection; Hank Tyler of the Maine Critical Areas Project for helping to ferret out information; and Bill Drury of the College of the Atlantic for being there to answer questions. The following people were wonderfully helpful in many ways: Doug Miller of Moosehorn National Wildlife Refuge; Jean Hockwater Gordon; Gerald Merry of Baxter State Park; Karen Gustafson of the Maine Chapter of The Nature Conservancy; Pam Truesdale of Wolf Neck Woods State Park; Leslie Van Cott of Maine Audubon; Pat Welch for being the first editor and a captive audience; Diana Cohen for invaluable advice and encouragement; Than James for a typewriter; and the Maine Geologic Survey for providing maps. In addition, many thanks are due to: Jerry Bley of the Maine Natural Resources Council; Lois Winter and Bob Rothe of Acadia National Park; Ron Davis and Sally Stockwell of the University of Maine; Nora Davis; Steve Kress of the

Audubon Ecology Camp in Maine; Craig Greene and Janet Andrews of the College of the Atlantic; and Howard Richard, Bill Towsend, and Paul Favour.

My thanks and appreciation goes out to the editors and staff at Pantheon Books, and especially to David Frederickson for his painstaking work with the directions for the entries. I am grateful to Becky Okrent and Gene Gort for their practical and artistic maps, which add so much to the site descriptions.

In a project such as this, there is usually one person without whom it just would not have happened, and these guidebooks are no exception. Caroline Sutton served in the invaluable role of editor, liaison, and coach throughout the two-year process of producing these volumes. Her sensitive, direct, and incisive editing improved both the content and style of the entries, and I believe that all of us are better writers today for having worked with her. I cannot thank her enough.

Finally, I want to thank my wife, Suzanne, and my son, Sam, who was born in the middle of this project, for their patience and support during the long months spent traveling and writing. The books are for them, and I now look forward to revisiting many of these natural places of the Northeast together.

—Stephen Kulik
Worthington, Massachusetts
January 1984

How to Use This Book

The aim of the Audubon Nature Guides is to enable the reader to explore and enjoy the natural history and ecology of selected natural areas in the United States. Unlike any other guide to the outdoors, this series describes the interaction of plants, animals, topography, and climate so that the hiker, birder, or amateur naturalist will be able to understand and more fully appreciate what he sees. Today, almost all the sites presented in these guides, whether in public or private ownership, are maintained for public education and enrichment. All offer geological, botanical, or biological points of interest, as well as the beauty, excitement, and tremendous variety of the outdoors.

This guide is one of an initial set including a Northeast inland volume, a Mid-Atlantic coastal volume, and a Mid-Atlantic inland volume. The areas covered in each guide have been determined, as often as possible, according to geological rather than governmental boundaries. The separation of coastal and inland volumes in the Mid-Atlantic series, for example, is clearly indicated by the "fall line." This roughly north/south demarcation running from New York City into Georgia occurs where the flat coastal plain rises to meet the rolling hills of the piedmont. In the Northeast, there is no such distinct dividing line between coast and interior but rather a gradual blending of one into the other. Here, the coastal region has been determined by both ecological and social factors, a region where the landscape and outlook of the people reflect the proximity of the sea.

Each guide contains descriptions of over 100 natural areas, and each site description pinpoints what is most significant, intriguing, or unusual about that area. More importantly, it explains *how* the site came to look as it does, and *why* certain species of vegetation and wildlife can be found there. Thus, while one narrative unravels the geological history of a region as it is revealed in the rock outcrops along a trail, another centers on a rare and ancient stand of Atlantic white cedar, and still another highlights the waterfowl that gather in an area, explaining their feeding, breeding, and migratory habits. Indeed, if the diverse entries about a particular area such as Cape Cod are read as a group, the visitor can reach a fuller, more in-depth understanding of both the existing biotic climate and the workings of human and natural history. Furthermore, the sites have been organized by geological and ecological regions, each prefaced by an introductory essay providing a general look at the geology, vegetation, and wildlife in that region and the human influence on it.

In this volume, the essays and site descriptions are arranged from south to north, reflecting the northward retreat of the great glaciers at the end of the Pleistocene Ice Ages. The first essay introduces natural sites from Long Island through Block Island, Martha's Vineyard and Nantucket to Cape Cod. This region is characterized by sand, rubble, and gravel left behind by the retreating glaciers. The second region moves north and west to Connecticut and southeastern Massachusetts, a section of the coast similar in many ways to Long Island and the Cape Cod islands, while also reflecting glacial action of the mainland. Cape Cod marks a biological boundary, dividing warm-water marine fauna of the south from animals tending to cold water north of its long, sandy hook. Furthermore, the stretch of coast just north of the Cape, the third region, displays the physical impact of the glaciers, though sand and rubble left by the ice begins to decrease. Finally, north of Portland, Maine, the coast is raw and younger than to the south because it was relieved of the burden of the glaciers later than they. Here rocky cliffs jut up from the sea and ragged inlets and bays carve the coastline.

All sites in this guide are numbered, and a system of cross-referencing throughout enables the reader to locate the most thorough discussion of a particular species of geological formation. For example, ospreys may be mentioned briefly in one description, but there will also be a reference to a fuller discussion elsewhere in the book. Each site opens with precise directions to the area and ends with a section called *Remarks*. Here is included such practical information as the length and difficulty of a recommended walk; what equipment to bring; possible activities such as swimming, fishing, and

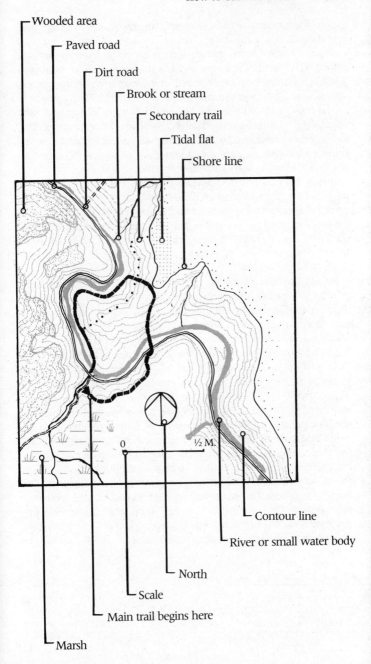

Wooded area

Paved road

Dirt road

Brook or stream

Secondary trail

Tidal flat

Shore line

Contour line

River or small water body

North

Scale

Main trail begins here

Marsh

0   ½ M.

skiing; the availability of boat rentals; nearby places to camp; and best times of the year to visit.

Most site descriptions include a map, keyed by letter to the narrative, which leads the visitor along a suggested walk or boat trip. There is a sample map on page xvii, along with a key to the various symbols which appear throughout the book.

The back of each guide includes a brief glossary, a thorough bibliography of works on related subjects, and an extensive index. The index is cross-referenced to enable the reader to find a particular site of interest, whether because of a species or geological formation or because of certain sports and other activities.

It may be useful to read about a site before visiting to learn the length of the trip and what equipment to bring. For example, while principal species of vegetation or wildlife are identified in the entries, others are mentioned in passing. The amateur birder or botanist may therefore wish to bring along a field guide to birds, trees, or wildflowers. Recommended supplementary guides are listed in the bibliography.

Finally, it is important to remember that natural sites are never unchanging places, rather always in flux. Wind and wave action alter the profile of the coast; bogs fill in with vegetation; some animals learn to adapt to the influx of civilization while others vanish. Many natural areas reflect the human impact of the past two centuries, be it the draining of marshes or re-seeding of forests. No such change is an isolated event. As an old field returns to forest, for example, pioneer seedlings give way to mature forest, and the birds of prey that once hunted the open field are replaced by their forest counterparts. Similarly, our knowledge about such phenomena is interdisciplinary, and forever changing as further observations are made and past theories uprooted. In these volumes we have attempted to present the most widely accepted geological and ecological theories. We do not presume to be comprehensive, nor to judge the validity of other recent theories and conclusions. Our aim is to introduce some of the processes botanists, biologists, and geologists believe to be at work in the natural world, thereby offering the reader a deeper appreciation and understanding of the complexity, beauty, and vulnerability of our natural areas.

Long Island, Cape Cod, and the Islands: The Sandy Fringe

From the sandy outliers of its southernmost shores to the raw, rocky headlands of northern Maine, New England has many coasts. Each is unique, created by different combinations of geological processes. All, however, share a common birth because the mixtures of forces that shaped them ultimately resulted from the flow and ebb of the glaciers.

Rising from the sea along the coast of southern New England stand the heights of a drowned prehistoric world. These remnants of a realm lost beneath the waves at the end of the ice ages are today bounded on the west by New York City's landscape of concrete, glass, and steel. Their eastern march is the hook of sandy terrain terminating at Provincetown, Mass. Doubtless the various clans of indigenous hunters and fishermen who populated them in earlier times called them by myriad names. But for the present, at least, maps identify them as Long Island, Fisher's Island, Block Island, Martha's Vineyard, Nantucket, and Cape Cod.

Like the New England mainland, this fragmentary edge of the continent rests on underpinnings of primal granite and its offspring by heat and pressure, gneiss. Unlike the bedrock to the north, however, that of the Cape and the islands is buried hundreds of feet deep. Over it are layered clays, sands, and in some cases lignite, partly formed coal. Atop these materials are heaped more sand together with rocks and gravel.

Some of the layers over the bedrock were deposited as sediment when the Cape and islands were under water,

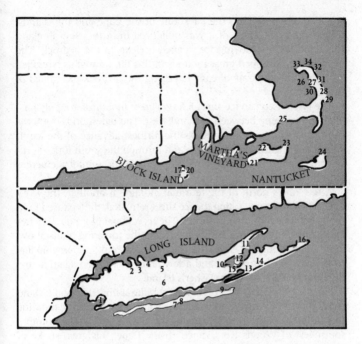

long before the ice ages. Others, such as lignite, were formed when the sea level was much lower than it is today, and the Cape and islands were not just above water but were part of a broader terrestrial landscape.

Throughout geologic time the sea has made repeated assaults on New England, only to retreat, sometimes far beyond the present shoreline. When the Pleistocene Ice Age began about a million years ago, the sea had ebbed and the Cape and islands were low hills on a vast coastal plain that rimmed the eastern margin of the continent. The Atlantic Coastal Plain south of Long Island is the unflooded inner border of that ancient flatland, little changed because the ice-age glaciers that reshaped the landscape to the north never reached it.

The southernmost advance of the glaciers ended along a front from Long Island to Cape Cod, including Nantucket, the Vineyard, and the other islands. All owe their present configuration to the halt of the glaciers, particularly those of the last ice age, the Wisconsin, which ended 11,000 years ago.

A rubbly mix of rocks and sand deposited when the ice sheets came to rest makes up the backbone of the Cape and the islands. Called *glacial till,* most of it was bulldozed from the New England mainland, as the moving ice scraped it clean to the bedrock. The glaciers then dropped great mounds of this till, known as *moraines,* atop the ancient strata already overlying the bedrock just ahead of the ice front.

The last Wisconsin ice sheet left two great moraines, roughly parallel and running between east and west. The oldest and southernmost, a *terminal* moraine, marks the furthest advance of the ice. It runs along the middle of Long Island through the south fork, disappearing under the water beyond Montauk Point, until it reemerges atop Block Island, then on the Vineyard and Nantucket.

A few miles north of the terminal moraine is another, the *recessional.* It was formed when the ice sheet retreated, then paused for a while before continuing to shrink. The recessional moraine stretches along Long Island's north shore, creating the towering bluffs above Long Island Sound. It extends through Orient Point, popping up just to the east as Plum Island and a few other islets, then again across the mouth of the sound at Fisher's Island.

For a brief stretch the recessional moraine skims the Rhode Island coast, then loops toward the Cape. Just before the Cape, the moraine can be seen as the small chain of the Elizabeth Islands, pointing southwest of Woods Hole. Once on the Cape, this great snake of glacial debris runs north across the base of the peninsula, then along the north shore in the form of great sandy bluffs above the water's edge.

Along the southern edge of the moraines is another landscape formed when the glaciers rested. These are *outwash plains,* which are just what the name implies. Streams of meltwater leaking from the glaciers washed out gravel, cobble, sand, and mud and spread it at the foot of the moraines, where it was smoothed into terrain that is gentle and level. On Long Island, the Southern State Parkway lies on an outwash plain. Such plains cover the southern tiers of the Vineyard and Nantucket, as well as, scientists believe, the hook of the Cape north of its elbow. The puzzle is that there is no moraine associated with the outwash plain of the lower Cape. Presumably it was devoured by the waves or simply slipped below the water line as the ocean rose.

When the water locked up in the glaciers was released, the sea rose quickly against a landscape that had been pressed down and tilted seaward by the weight of the ice. The ocean flooded Nantucket Sound, Long Island Sound, Block Island Sound, Cape Cod Bay, and other depressions that had been valleys on the Coastal Plain. The islands and the Cape were sundered.

Waves and winds continue to eat at their shores, whose broad, sandy beaches, scarce in the rest of the New England region, are products of moraines. Scientists estimate that on parts of the Cape's eastern shore, Martha's Vineyard, and Block Island, land is vanishing at the rate of a yard a year as sand is blown away or swept out to sea.

The largely sandy content of the soils of the Cape and islands makes them less than fertile, incapable by and large of supporting the hardwood forests of interior southern New England. For the most part, the vegetation of these glacially shaped lands resembles that of the Atlantic Coastal Plain to the south, even though their geological history differs. Where not destroyed by human agency, a scraggly mix of pitch pine and scrub oak, rather like the Pine Barrens of New Jersey, covers much of the country. Near the beach, the oaks and pines shrink to dwarfs, mixing with heath and holly, bayberry, and juniper. Hickories, red maples, and locusts grow with the pines and scrub oaks in a few places where sand is blended with other soils, richer and better able to hold water than till and outwash. Mainly, however, the vegetative aspect of the countryside is dominated by a green sea of conifers sprinkled with the gnarled forms of oaks.

An exception are moors, which cover wide expanses of some islands, notably Nantucket and Block. Windswept and desolate, evocative of Baskerville settings, they were once covered by forest. The trees were cut to make pastures for sheep grazed by colonial farmers and those who followed. Long abandoned because the flocks overgrazed the vegetation, the moors remain treeless, testifying to the impoverished nature of the soil.

The animals that inhabit the fields and forests of the Cape and the islands belong to the same groups that live on the mainland. In some cases, however, isolation has shaped some species into subspecies subtly different from the mainland types that were their ancestors. The short-tailed shrew that originally invaded the Cape, Martha's Vineyard, and Nantucket after the ice retreated and the land greened was the same species as on the mainland. Since, it has diverged into a separate subspecies in each place.

Of all animals inhabiting the Cape and islands, the birds of the sea and shore attract the most attention. Some—such as various gulls—throng year-round. Spring brings a burgeoning of species, particularly during late May, when within the space of a few weeks immense numbers of shorebirds pass through on their way to breeding grounds in the Arctic. Enough of them—especially snowy egrets and others of the heron family—peel off to stay and make things interesting for the first half of summer, and by August, northern nesters are straggling back on migration that lacks the urgency of the pell-mell rush to breeding grounds.

The birders who flock to the Cape and islands may be exceeded in enthusiasm only by the anglers lured by fish. The sand-rimmed lands built up by glaciers offer superb fishing from shore, certainly the finest in New England. Fish rove the inshore waters in great variety, largely because this is a transitional zone between the frigid boreal waters north of Cape Cod and warmer seas to the south.

Cod, for instance, are fish of the cold sea. Bluefish are rather tropical in habitat. Cod inhabit the waters of the region year-round, but in winter, when there is little temperature difference in the sea north and south of the Cape, they move in from the deeper water, where in summer they hide from the warming temperatures inshore. Bluefish are absent during the winter, when they rove the ocean far to the south. But by summer, as the water around the Cape and islands warms to a level that verges on the semitropical, the bluefish arrive in great silvery schools that, chasing bait, churn the water to a froth. Very few bluefish filter north of the Cape because even in summer the water there is too cool.

The Cape is a well-defined boundary for many other forms of marine life, particularly that of the seashore. Although a few may stray beyond its sandy hook, Cape Cod constitutes the northern limit of the blue crab. Similarly, the chip crab, flat-browed mud shrimp, hairy sea cucumber, and several species of beach flea reach the northernmost part of their range there. On the other hand, Cape Cod is the southernmost point attained by the mud-star, silky sea cucumber, and, in shallow water, the green sea urchin. Other examples of creatures that do not pass the Cape in one direction or another fill the pages of field guides to seashore animals.

The coasts of the Cape and islands have changed vastly in the few centuries since Europeans arrived to settle them. As anyone who visits the seashore knows, few of the alterations have been for the good. The environmental degradation visited upon the coastline has been well documented. Still, as the sites described in this section demonstrate, great natural treasures remain, and with dedication and understanding, others, now lost, can perhaps be restored.

—Edward Ricciuti

1.

Jamaica Bay
Wildlife Refuge

Directions: **New York, N.Y. Take the Belt Parkway to Exit 17S. Take Cross Bay Blvd. south for 3.6 miles. The entrance to unit headquarters is on the right, marked by a sign that is somewhat difficult to see. The refuge is also accessible by public transportation: take the IND A or CC train to Broad Channel and walk north to the refuge.**

Ownership: **Gateway National Recreation Area, National Park Service.**

Within New York City limits, and less than 2 miles from Kennedy Airport, lies one of America's most unique wildlife refuges: Jamaica Bay. An important stopover for migrating birds along the Atlantic flyway, this pocket of wildness amid urban sprawl is well known for attracting many unusual species. Over 315 different kinds of birds have been recorded, many pausing here on their long migratory journeys in the spring and fall. And although the accessible parts of the refuge make up only about 250 acres of the unit's 9,100 total acres, there is an excellent variety of habitats in which you may walk. Salt marsh, mudflats, freshwater ponds, upland woods, and cultivated gardens all greet the visitor with their abundant birdlife and surprising beauty.

Behind the visitors' center is a 1¾-mile trail encircling West Pond. Begin by turning right from the back door of the center and walking about 75 yards to a small dirt path that leads you to an overlook (**A**). Although this spot is only 17½ feet above sea level, it provides a good view of the property and, in the distance, the landmarks of New York City. Jamaica Bay, consisting of 25,000 acres of marshlands, has been extensively dredged since the late 1800s, so that only 13,000 marshland acres remain. (Kennedy Airport, in fact, lies on top of some of this dredged material.) The bay originally averaged just 3 feet in depth, but now averages 16 feet due to the dredging.

Once the sandy outwash plain of melting glaciers, Jamaica Bay flooded as global sea levels rose and slowly assumed its marine configuration (see **Long Island, Cape Cod, and the Islands**). Today a great barrier beach at Rockaway to the south protects the entire bay from open ocean but allows the waters to circulate through

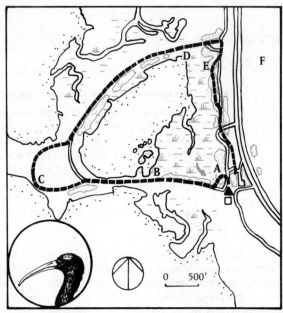

Inset: Glossy ibis

an inlet to the southwest of here. The hill you are standing on is man-made, built from dredge spoils when nearby West Pond was created in the early 1950s. From this point, you can look out over the salt marsh that stretches into Jamaica Bay. As is typical of salt marshes, the salt-meadow cordgrass (*Spartina patens*) gives way to the salt-marsh cordgrass (*Spartina alterniflora*) (see **#77**) near the water's edge, marking the extent to which the tides periodically flood the land.

In the midst of the country's most densely populated region, this salt marsh is engaged in a constant battle against pollution. Rubbish floats into the marshland; less obvious substances work their way unseen into the system. Yet the salt marsh persists and life abounds. Snails climb grass leaves to avoid the flooding tides, fiddler crabs burrow in the mud, clapper rails move secretively through the grass. Notice the osprey platform on top of a thick pole, a solitary high point on the level expanse of the marsh. Ospreys tend to build their large nests of sticks in dead trees near the water in which they fish. Platforms are often erected where no natural nesting site exists. No ospreys have nested on this one yet, however. (See **#22, #50,** and **#99** for more on ospreys.)

The southeast edge of West Pond (**B**) is an excellent place to see a number of different ducks. American wigeons, teal, shovelers, mallards, and black ducks are usually present, their numbers varying with the seasons. These are all dabbling or marsh ducks, which feed primarily along the surface of the water or just below by upending and dunking their heads under water. They eat aquatic plants, seeds, grasses, and small pond animals. Diving ducks, such as canvasbacks, buffleheads, and greater scaups, feed in the deeper sections of the 45-acre West Pond. In order to take flight, they patter along the surface to get under way, whereas dabblers spring into the air immediately.

West and East Pond (across Cross Bay Blvd.) were created by the New York Transit Authority through an agreement with the city Parks Department when they dredged the bay to construct a railroad embankment here. Both contain brackish water and are partially drained at certain times of the year to encourage shorebird use. West Pond's water level is lowered in the spring as shorebirds pass through the area on their way to their northern breeding grounds. Originally fresh water, the pond has become increasingly brackish from infiltrating seawater. This change in salinity has caused changes in the bird population—it seems that freshwater-marsh-nesting birds, such as the least bittern and pied-billed grebe, no longer breed here. The National Park Service is working to restore the impoundment to its intended freshwater state. Many birds make use of the pond, particularly wintering waterfowl. Part of the ice is kept open to provide access for Canada geese, brant, and a variety of ducks such as black, bufflehead, canvasback, ruddy, mallard, and wigeon. Other wintering birds you might see include sandpipers, dunlins, dowitchers, ruddy turnstones, greater yellowlegs, and many others along the muddy shores of the entire wetland complex.

All of the vegetation here was originally hand-planted, including over a million clumps of American beach grass, which help stabilize the sand (see **#79**). Species were chosen that could survive in the sandy soil and severe weather conditions, thus providing food and shelter for wildlife throughout the seasons. For example, the black willows on the northwest edge of the pond provide a windbreak for wintering waterfowl on the water, in addition to nesting areas for small songbirds. Common dune vegetation also grows here: bayberry, Virginia creeper, poison ivy, salt-spray rose, seaside goldenrod, and little bluestem grass. In 1982 volunteers and park personnel planted salt-marsh cordgrass (*Spartina alterniflora*) along this badly eroded storm beach in the hope of stabilizing the shoreline. The results, as you can see, have been very encouraging.

Snowy and great egrets frequent the extensive stretches of salt-marsh cordgrass on the north side of the refuge during the warmer months (**D**). Other wading birds such as great blue herons and glossy ibis are also seen here, searching the mudflats and low-tide zone for fish and other marine life.

Beyond the western end of the pond is the Tern Nesting Area (**C**). It is closed to visitors from April to August in an attempt, as yet unsuccessful, to lure common terns to nest here. Decoys and tape recordings of tern calls are being used to try to reintroduce this species, which left the beach about 20 years ago due to human interference, excessive vegetation, and predation by rats and gulls.

For those more interested in songbirds, the North Garden (**E**) is probably the best spot on the grounds to observe warblers and other varieties, especially during the May migration when nearly thirty species have been recorded, (see **#96** for more on migration.) Many different trees and shrubs have been planted here with wildlife in mind. Black cherry, autumn olive, hawthorn, and multiflora rose are among the better-known food sources for songbirds. The entire property is managed to provide for a maximum of wildlife diversity. In fact, almost all the larger trees and shrubs you see on the refuge have been planted since the early 1950s. Certain species, such as the ever-present phragmites, Virginia creeper, and tree-of-heaven, tend to crowd out other varieties more valuable to wildlife, and their growth patterns are closely monitored.

Remarks: *The walk takes about 1½ hours. Bring binoculars and, if possible, a spotting scope. Photographers should bring telescopic lenses. During spring and summer, take along insect repellent. The 100-acre East Pond (**F**) is usually less popular than the West Pond only because of its location across the highway. It is a superb birding area, especially during the fall migration when it too is partially drained. Rubber boots are highly recommended for those venturing out on the mudflats. Gateway National Recreation Area has three other units—Breezy Point, Staten Island, and Sandy Hook—within its 26,000 acres. There are a wealth of interpretative programs and activities to explore. Hours here are generally from 8:00 a.m. to 5:00 p.m., although the area is open until 7:00 in the summer and 6:00 in the fall. The visitors' center has a number of interpretative exhibits, saltwater tanks, live reptiles, and a small bookstore. A permit (free) must be obtained here before using the grounds. Hiking is permitted only on the gravel paths as the vegetation is very fragile. For further information, contact the visitors' center at (212) 252-9286.*

2.

Welwyn Preserve

Directions: **Glen Cove, N.Y. From New York City, take the Belt (Cross Island) Parkway to Exit 30. From there go east about 8 miles on the Long Island Expressway (Route 495) to Exit 39. Go north on Glen Cove Rd. 6.2 miles, bearing left at a major fork near the end. Turn north (right) onto Brewster; go 0.5 mile. Turn north (left) onto Dosoris Lane; go 0.7 mile. Go left for 0.4 mile on New Woods Rd. At Crescent Beach Rd., proceed for about 0.1 mile to the Welwyn gate on the right. Park at the left of the main house.**

Ownership: **Nassau County Department of Recreation and Parks.**

On the stately grounds of the former Pratt estate grows one of the finest stands of old-growth tuliptrees on Long Island. A small stream valley, laced with several other tree species unusual for the region, leads to a salt marsh and sandy beach on Long Island Sound. Waterfowl, wading birds, and shorebirds as well as woodland varieties may be seen here in the many habitats.

From the parking lot walk along the driveway back toward the entrance and pick up the trail on the left, just past the staff building. Once into the woods, the visitor is immediately dwarfed by the enormous tulip and hemlock trees that dominate the rich and moist terrain (**A**). One four-trunked specimen, with a girth of approximately 22 feet, is reputed to be the largest tuliptree on Long Island. Tulips are the tallest of eastern hardwoods, and here their height approaches 100 feet.

Tuliptrees are a southern species, usually found in the southeastern and Mid-Atlantic states. Here, however, they grow along with several prominent northerly types, especially hemlock and yellow birch, largely because of extreme climatic changes thousands of years ago. After the glaciers receded from the area 12,000 to 15,000 years ago, the first pioneer vegetation was lichens, followed by a succession of other plants that slowly migrated here from the warmer south. Since the climate was still cool thousands of years after the glaciers melted, the first trees were cold-tolerant varieties such as hemlocks. As the climate moderated, conditions became too warm for most of the northern species and they died out, except in isolated cool pockets. Southern varieties like the tuliptree have been slowly and continually advancing northward as the climate continues to moderate, so that now in certain areas of the northeast one finds representatives of two regions growing together. The fact that Long Island has no really significant differences in elevation or latitude, two of the factors that commonly define species distribution, supports this theory.

This southern section of the preserve is situated in an area where seepage from a high water table is quite obvious. Spicebush, a shrub commonly associated with streambank communities, grows here. Look for its dense clusters of small yellow flowers along the stems in early to middle spring. Arrowwood, another deciduous shrub frequently found along the edges of swamps and wet thickets, is also found here. Its leaves are sharply toothed with prominent veins underneath. Small white flowers bloom in clusters in spring.

At **B** the woods open up a bit and large white oak trees become evident. This is probably due to the increased slope of the stream valley where sandier and better-drained soils replace the wetter types.

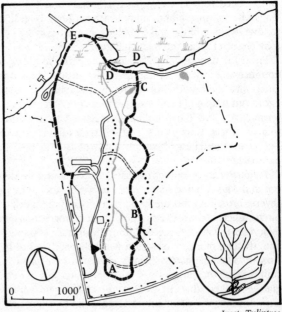

Inset: Tuliptree

Striped maple and sassafras grow close to the trail. Canada may-flower, starflower, and true Solomon's seal bloom in spring. Japanese knotweed, an alien and a member of the buckwheat family, is dense in a wet thicket to the left.

Some of the trees and shrubs at Welwyn are here as the result of extensive landscaping carried out in the earlier parts of the century. Members of the Olmsted family, whose famous patriarch, Frederick Law Olmsted, designed Central Park, were hired by the Pratts to do this. It is possible that they planted the river birch (**C**) that stands beside Turtle Pond. This species, with its distinctive frayed and peel-ing reddish-brown bark, is extremely rare on Long Island. It gener-ally prefers low elevations beside rivers and ponds, or marshy wood-lands along the southern Coastal Plain and through the Mississippi and Ohio river basins.

Snowy egrets and great blue herons are commonly seen during warm months wading through the salt marsh in search of food (**D**). An osprey nesting platform, erected in 1982, is situated in the marshy area to the left of the trail. Although ospreys, commonly known as fish eagles, used to breed along the shoreline of Long Island, they have become scarce because of human interference, loss of habitat to development, and pesticide levels in the food web. Nesting plat-forms have been successful in other areas, and Welwyn naturalists hope that ospreys will once again nest in Glen Cove. (See **#22, #50,** and **#99** for more on ospreys.)

A stand of Austrian black pines, planted by the Olmsteds, lies between the marsh and the beach. Its needles, 3 to 5 inches long, grow in clusters of two and resemble those of red pine, but are far more rigid. In this country, the Austrian pine is cultivated as an ornamental and is sometimes used in the reforestation of denuded woodlands. In Europe, its hard and very durable wood is used for building.

The beach is sandy, rather than stony as one would expect, simply because the Pratts had the rocks removed (**E**). The visitor can enjoy a wonderful view of Long Island Sound, with Connecticut on the opposite shore to the right. Several wild beach plants, including beach plum, rosa rugosa (wrinkled rose), and prickly-pear cactus, grow nearby. Found from Massachusetts south to Florida, prickly pear is the only cactus native to the northeast. It produces a showy yellow flower in early summer (see **#24**). Its thick skin is an adap-tation for holding water in the windy, desiccating environment of a sandy beach.

Remarks: *Walking time is about 1½ hours.*

3.

Muttontown Preserve

Directions: **East Norwich, N.Y. From New York City, take the Belt (Cross Island) Parkway to Exit 30. From there, go east about 13 miles on the Long Island Expressway (Route 495) to Exit 41. Go north on Route 106 (which becomes Jericho–Oyster Bay Rd.) about 4 miles to East Norwich. Turn west (left) on Route 25A (North Hempstead Turnpike); after 0.3 mile turn south (left) onto Muttontown Lane. Go 0.2 mile into the preserve headquarters and parking lot.**

Ownership: **Nassau County Department of Recreation and Parks.**

Once the property of several estate holders, Muttontown Preserve is now 500 acres of woods, fields, and wetlands. Among the interesting glacial features here in northern Nassau County are kettle ponds, morainal hills, and a kame. A significant stand of persimmon trees, highly unusual for Long Island, can also be found on the grounds. Indigo buntings nest here, and a large variety of other birds have been recorded by staff naturalists.

At the rear of the nature-center building go left on trail 1 for a short distance until it meets trail 2. Proceed on this route until you see a prominent hill, or *glacial kame,* to the left (**A**). A side path will take you to the top of this pebbly and sandy deposit, created approximately 10,000 years ago during the last ice age. A kame is formed by material that collected in openings in stagnant or wasting ice. The material built up, and when the glacier finally melted, a mound was left standing (see **#28**). This kame is composed primarily of quartz pebbles and sand, with some chert and quartzite. According to a local geologist, most of this rock debris was carried here from the northwest, especially from the Hudson River valley area, by the advancing glacier. Granites and gneisses were ripped, plucked, and ground about by the thick ice until the most resistant minerals, such as quartz, became concentrated in the glacial sediments. A scooplike depression on the west side of the kame is evidence of gravel mining.

Continue along trail 2. The brushy field to the right was farmed as recently as the late 1950s to early 1960s.

A scattering of vernal kettle ponds throughout the immediate area is further proof of glaciation (**B**). The kettles are shallow depressions

formed when small chunks of ice became isolated from the receding glacier and were partially or completely buried in rock and sand left behind as the glacier melted (see **#99**). These chunks of ice then melted, creating ponds, which filled in during the spring when rain, snowmelt, and a rising water table combined to flood them. Deposits of clay under the kettles are believed to help keep the water from draining.

Pick up trail 6 as trail 2 turns right. Beside one kettle to the right of the trail is a small grove of persimmon trees (**C**). Irregular, dark, bumpy, and armor-plated bark identifies this tree. Persimmons are a distinctly southern species, most abundant in the lower Ohio basin. Only a few trees occur on Long Island, all in the western section. They thrive in the plentiful sunlight of fields and open woods and produce the well-known ocher-orange-colored fruit—a favorite of humans, raccoons, skunks, and especially opossums, which are thus attracted to this area. The persimmon fruit matures over the summer, but it is not edible until after the first frost. Before that time, it is too tart. Freezing induces a chemical change that makes it more palatable.

The translucent pink petals of winged euonymus *(Euonymus alata)* blaze with color in the fall (**D**). Notice the unusual winglike projections on the twigs and branches, a growth form whose function, if any, is unknown. This shrub is a native of northeastern Asia and China and was probably planted along the former estate driveway here, between sugar and Norway maples. The name *euonymus* means "good plant," but certainly must not refer to its edibility—deadly toxins are contained in the seeds, leaves, and twigs of many of the members of the different euonymus species!

Indigo buntings, which are rare to uncommon on Long Island, according to ornithologist John Bull of the American Museum of Natural History, have nested in this brushy successional field for several years (**E**). The dazzlingly colorful male can frequently be heard singing from the top of the highest trees in the area, staking out territory during the June-to-July nesting season. Look for a sharply blue-colored bird, about the size of a house sparrow, singing a lively, high, and strident song, with notes usually paired *(sweet-sweet, chew-chew)*. The females are plain brown with a pale breast, and are usually quiet during this period. Buntings are insect eaters and build their nests on saplings and bushes from 20 inches off the ground to about 4 feet high. Approximately seven to eight pairs nest in this area and among the shrubby undergrowth by the nearby ruins of the old walled garden.

Continue past the old garden area and onto a dirt path leading into a mature conifer-hardwood forest. The forest floor is quite hilly, owing to the material left here on the terminal moraine (**F**). The Harbor Hill Terminal Moraine, as it is properly called, is the line marking the edge of the continental glacier. Accumulation of rock debris along this front, which stayed for some time and then receded, formed the irregular ridge that extends the length of Long Island. The Ronkonkoma Terminal Moraine, several miles to the south, marks the southernmost limit of glaciation. The reason there are two morainal ridges on the island is because the glacier eventually receded from the Ronkonkoma position into the Harbor Hill location and stayed there for a time (see **Long Island, Cape Cod, and the Islands**).

Dark Norway spruces with their long, sweeping, pendulous branches create a peaceful mood here. These conifers were probably planted by former owners of the preserve. The tree is a European species, commonly cultivated throughout the northern part of the country.

Chestnut oak, red oak, white oak, and black birch are also present. Look for goldfinches and other songbirds feeding on seeds in the small fruiting cones of the black birch. Saw-whet owls have been sighted here, and wood warblers pass through during their May migration (see **#96** for more on migration).

Take trail 5 and head north through catbriers, oriental bittersweet, and mixed hardwoods. Pass out of the forest, along successional fields to trail 1. Go right, parallel to a shrubby hedgerow. On the left, a field cut about 25 years ago is reverting to woods, except for some areas that are purposely mowed. Continue on trail 1 to the nature center.

Remarks: *The walk is about 1¾ hours. The grounds are open 7 days a week, from 9:30 a.m. to 4:30 p.m., but the nature-center building is open from Monday to Friday only. Horseback riding is permitted, as is cross-country skiing.*

4.
Caumsett
State Park

Directions: **Lloyd Neck, N.Y. From New York City, take the Belt (Cross Island) Parkway to Exit 30. From there, go east about 20 miles on the Long Island Expressway (Route 495) to Exit 49. Go north on Route 110 (New York Ave.) about 6 miles to Huntington. Turn west (left) on Main St. (Route 25A), then turn north (right) onto West Neck Rd. (opposite Chemical Bank); go 5 miles to the park entrance on the right.**

Ownership: **Long Island State Park and Recreation Commission.**

Open space on Long Island is hard to find, especially in the western section, close to the New York City border. Caumsett State Park, lying within 30 miles of the Queens County line, is notable for its huge open fields set within an exceptional 1,500-acre parcel of woods, beaches, high cliffs, and salt marshes. The site of Marshall Field's once-glorious estate, Caumsett is laced with miles of scenic hiking trails and bridle paths. Birdlife abounds, and marsh hawks commonly hunt for prey over both tidal and inland areas.

The brushy areas that parallel the fields here in the south and southeast portions of the property near the parking area make up an *ecotone* (**A**), or border area between one distinct ecological com-

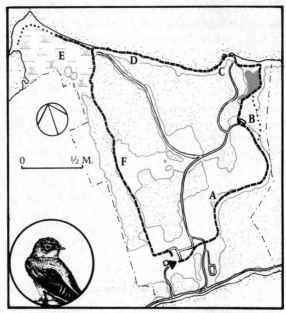

Inset: Bank swallow

munity and another. In this case the ecotone is an impenetrable mass of catbriers, honeysuckle, various vines, shrubs, and small trees that stands between the fields on one side and a mixed hardwood forest on the other. These habitats are known to be especially attractive to birds and small mammals, as they provide a source of seeds and fruits and a tangled refuge from predatory hawks, owls, and foxes. In time, the forest will encroach, and the ecotone will shrink and finally disappear.

Brown thrashers, catbirds, and mockingbirds, all members of the family Mimidae (for "mimics"), nest here, and all can be heard chattering noisily during the warmer months. Their ability to mimic other members of the bird world is quite uncanny. The mockingbird usually repeats his succession of phrases and notes at least six times in a row, while the catbird doesn't repeat, and the brown thrasher repeats at least once. Although the exact reasons for mimicry are unknown, it is true that these complex vocalizations serve the birds in several ways. Since all three birds are rather drab in color and frequent thick, shrubby vegetation, their highly evolved songs tend to supplement their low visibility and aid in courtship and territorial behaviors. All three species are year-round residents of Long Island, but some winter further south. They eat a variety of fruits and also insects.

To get to the beach, you must pass the imposing 108-room Georgian mansion of the late Marshall Field III (**B**). In 1921 Field bought the property and cleared nearly 30 percent of the woods in order to make room for his dairy farm and numerous buildings. By opening up so much of the land, he created new habitat for mammals and birds, particularly bobwhite quail and ring-necked pheasants. Field originally stocked the pheasants, but today they flourish here in the wild. The mansion is currently being used by an environmental-science program from Queens College. From the side and back of the house are superb views of Long Island Sound, with the Connecticut shoreline about 6 miles away.

In front of the mansion is a man-made freshwater pond, where bass and sunfish thrive. Pass the pond and continue to the sandy path and dunes that separate it from the sound. Beach plum, bayberry, poison ivy, and catbriers grow in abundance.

At the water's edge you can gaze across miles of salt water and watch the sailboats that often bob along these waters. Underfoot, the beach is mostly quartz gravel with some sand. Several tide pools occur nearby, where a group of large boulders border the intertidal zone (see **Cape Cod to Portland**).

The bluffs of sand and gravel that slowly rise to heights of about 30 feet behind you (**C**) are perfect locations for tunnel nests of the bank swallow. A small bird with a brown back, white breast, and dark breastband, the bank swallow uses its bill and feet to excavate the nest chamber. Here, a few feet from the top of the cliff, you can see a number of their holes, circular in shape and between 2 and 4 inches in diameter. Researchers have found that the nest tunnel can be anywhere from 9 inches to 6 feet long, but is usually between 2 and 4 feet. The end chamber is slightly enlarged and lined with grasses. Bank swallows lay four to five eggs in late spring, and both sexes incubate them for 2 weeks, until the eggs hatch. About 3 to 4 weeks later the babies fledge. Bank swallows feed primarily on insects, catching them while in flight.

Caumsett's bluffs are among the highest in western Suffolk County and were formed as massive accumulations of previously deposited glacial outwash material were pushed up between newly advancing lobes of ice (**D**) (see **Long Island, Cape Cod, and the Islands**). The many yards of this mixture of sand, silt, pebbles, and boulders rest on top of much older silts and clays dating from the Cretaceous period, 60 to 135 million years ago. The entire assemblage is being attacked by the combined erosional forces of wave action, especially during winter storms, and rainfall. Portions of the bluffs look as if they could be part of the western badlands, a weathered and ravaged face of earthen debris.

The beach continues around to the west, where it takes the shape of a sandspit that protects a salt marsh behind (**E**) (see **#29**). Great and snowy egrets, green and great blue herons, terns, gulls, and assorted shore and marshbirds can usually be seen here. Although the outer beach looks like an excellent spot for terns to nest on, local observers report that heavy boating traffic and the associated landing parties who bring their dogs ashore have kept the terns away. Common and least terns are breeding, however, on nearby Eaton's Neck, a few miles to the east. You can walk out to the end of the spit if you wish. (See **#23** for more on terns.)

As you walk back toward the entrance gate, be sure to pause along the shady road for a last-minute look at the mudflats—if it is low tide. This is a good spot from which to see birds, which are drawn to the bountiful food supplies of the mudflats.

Another large field, (**F**) parallels the left side of the road and is usually a fine spot to look for meadowlarks, indigo buntings, field sparrows, goldfinches, and various swallows in May through mid-September. It is important to wildlife survival that a field such as this be mowed only in the fall, so as to allow nesting areas for birds and refuge for rabbits and rodents. The hawks of the area, mainly red-tails, kestrels, and marsh hawks, depend upon the availability of mice, rats, voles, shrews, and other rodents that live in the grasses and weeds. Cutting this field during late spring and summer reduces the habitat for those creatures, and the whole food chain suffers.

Remarks: *Walking time is about 4 hours. Bring a canteen. The park is open from 8:00 a.m. to 4:30 p.m. daily, and there is an entrance fee of $2.50 per automobile from Memorial Day through Labor Day. Water and sanitary facilities are available at the entrance only. Horseback riders, call (516) 673-5533 for information. The park sponsors nature walks; call (516) 423-1770 for information. Bicycling is permitted, as is surf fishing, but be advised that the beach is a 2-mile walk from the parking area. A scope is advised for serious birders who visit the salt marsh. Cross-country skiers, call (516) 423-1770 for conditions.*

5.

Nissequogue River
State Park

Directions: **Smithtown, N.Y. From New York City, take the Belt (Cross Island) Parkway to Exit 30. From there, go east about 27 miles on the Long Island Expressway to Exit 53N. Go north about 3 miles on the Sunken Meadow Parkway to Exit SM3, then go east on Route 25 (Jericho Turnpike). There are a number of access points to the river. Fly fishermen only can fish the river within the confines of Nissequogue River State Park, about 2.5 miles east of Exit SM3. Canoeists can put in on the south side of Route 25 where it meets Route 25A, about 1 mile further east. Both canoeists and hikers can get to the river's mouth by driving north on Route 25A for 1.7 miles from the intersection with Route 25, to St. Johnsland Rd. Bear right and proceed for 1.8 miles to Old Dock Rd. Turn right and follow to dead end, adjacent to Kings Park Bluffs and parking area. Both the canoe rental service and the Greenbelt Trail are here. (Residents of Suffolk County can use Blydenburgh Park, about 6 miles from the mouth, while residents of the town of Smithtown may use Short Beach and Landing Avenue parks.)**

Ownership: **Many owners—state, county, town, and private.**

The lovely Nissequogue River was designated a Scenic and Recreational River by New York State in 1982, and stringent land-use measures now protect its natural integrity. Flowing north for approximately 9 miles, it crosses the two terminal moraines present on Long Island (see **#3** and **Long Island, Cape Cod, and the Islands**), and contains freshwater, brackish, and saltwater portions. Countless numbers of fish, birds, mammals, and other living creatures, from trout to terns, live in and near the river.

The Greenbelt Trail runs perpendicular to the end of Old Dock Rd. and along the western shore of the river for a short distance. General access to the river is limited due to local topography and the different land uses in the area. You can walk north, or upstream, for perhaps an eighth of a mile until the trail turns inland; it does not parallel the river again for at least a half-mile. Or you can walk downstream for about a hundred yards into a small park and then follow the trail up steep bluffs that afford a spectacular view of the river's mouth and Long Island Sound.

The dramatic and beautiful scene at the Kings Park Bluffs is quite surprising, given this major river's proximity to the suburbs of Smithtown. The river is several hundred feet wide and flows out to the sound between two sandspits. To the north are bluffs 75 feet high and to the east, across the channel, is Short Beach Park, a federal and state sanctuary for breeding least and common terns (see **#23**). The impact of man is noticeable in the presence of boats and a restaurant and parking lot nearby, but it does not detract from the primal immediacy of sky, sun, sand, and moving water.

The Nissequogue is one of four major rivers on Long Island, (the others being the Peconic, Carman's, and the Connetquot) and is known for its beauty, its variety of vegetational communities due to the different zones of fresh and salt water, its adjacent archaeological sites, and its colony of approximately 300 nesting pairs of least terns, the largest such colony in New York.

The river begins in a series of small tributaries, fed by groundwater and runoff, about 9 miles south from here; it then flows into the second largest lake on Long Island, New Millpond. Bordered by a mixed oak–pitch-pine forest, New Millpond is home to trout, bass, sunfish, and catfish, and is the site of an 1802 earthen dam and a nineteenth-century gristmill, now being restored. New Millpond is contained within the 675 acres of Suffolk County–owned Blyden-burgh Park.

The river flows over the dam and enters a narrow channel running through the property of Nissequogue River State Park. Access to the river here is limited to fly fishermen with a permit obtained at the state park office, and to participants in regular guided natural history walks. A team of environmental analysts studying the waterway calls this section "the most untouched area," because the river corridor is densely wooded and "there is no indication that a town with a population of 123,000 exists nearby." Black tupelo, red maple, sassafras, black walnut, and other lowland types grow here, along with many ferns, club mosses, wildflowers, and shrubs. The state stocks this stretch with brook, brown, and rainbow trout.

Tidal flow extends upriver roughly to the point where the Nissequogue winds under Route 25. Canoeists putting in on the south side of Route 25 begin their paddle in fresh water, past pickerelweed, arrowhead, and marsh marigold, but soon notice the first salt-tolerant plants, such as spartina grasses. Wood ducks, mallards, and black ducks nest nearby.

Meandering through a heavily vegetated corridor, the Nissequogue slowly changes from brackish to saline, and salt-marsh cordgrass becomes the most common plant. Mudflats and marsh islands appear as the channel widens. Marine-associated birds such as herring and greater black-backed gulls are common, though many songbirds are present along the shoreline and neighboring upland woods. The last several miles or so of the river is saline, though fresh water enters the almost half-mile-wide channel through numerous feeder streams, creating an estuarine effect. Spartina grasses are found, along with spike-grass and glasswort. Shore and wading birds such as green herons, snowy egrets (see #74), and killdeer are often seen searching the low-tide areas for food.

The archaeological sites discovered along the river corridor include the remains of an Indian village, seasonal camps, flaking stations (points and arrowheads), and fishing and hunting areas. Collected material may be seen in local and county museums.

As the river flows past this vantage point at the end of Old Dock Rd., one cannot but be impressed by its vitality and its healthy community for birds and other life. The water is largely untouched by industrial contamination and suffers only from nonpoint pollution (runoff from storm sewers). Canoeing is obviously the best way to see the Nissequogue, but if weather conditions prohibit, spend some time walking the Greenbelt Trail. It will give you good but intermittent views of a very special natural area.

Remarks: *Hikers on this northern section of the Greenbelt Trail need a permit (free) and a map, obtainable by calling (516) 265-1054, or by visiting Nissequogue River State Park (closed on Mondays). Permits cannot be mailed. You may rent canoes by calling (516) 544-9708, or you may bring your own. Check the tide charts and make sure you are paddling downstream about an hour and a quarter after high tide, or upstream an hour or so after low tide. Dress warmly, as temperatures and winds near the mouth are apt to be cool. Make sure you have transportation back to your car.*

6.

Connetquot River
State Park Preserve

Directions: **Oakdale, N.Y. From New York City, take the Belt (Cross Island) Parkway to Exit 25A. From there, go east about 34 miles on the Southern State Parkway to Exit 44. Turn onto Sunrise Highway going east; the park entrance is 1.3 miles further east, on the left.**

Ownership: **Long Island State Park and Recreation Commission.**

The largest state park on Long Island, 3,473-acre Connetquot is a historic and scenic oasis amid surrounding suburban clutter. Pitch pines and oaks line the tranquil river and fill the adjacent woodland. You may very well see white-tailed deer browsing among the trees and many species of waterfowl feeding on and near the large mill-pond. The Long Island Greenbelt Trail, part of the National Recreational Trail System, passes through the preserve for a distance of about 4 miles.

Cross the dam on a blacktop road and turn left about 150 yards further onto the red trail. After a short walk find an overlook at the pond's edge (**A.**). This 15-acre body of water was created in about 1750 as a reservoir to power a grist and cloth-fulling mill. The mill, located downstream a bit, is listed on the National Register of Historic Places and is open to the public. Since the pond is only a few miles from Great South Bay, many bay ducks, such as canvasback, redhead, greater and lesser scaup, and bufflehead are common. That well-known dabbling duck the mallard is also found here. Listen for its different noises. Only the females can make the familiar quacking sound. The males, distinguished by their shiny green heads, have two calls: a nasal *rhaeb* sound, and a short whistle that is associated with courtship displays. The whistle will catch most bird-watchers unaware, because of its nonducklike quality. The mallards and other ducks eat pond vegetation and are also fond of freshwater amphipods—small shrimplike crustaceans found in many ponds and marshes.

A small fishing dock marked with a number 8 leads a few yards into the Connetquot River itself (**B.**). A layer of glacial pebbles covered with dark silt makes up the shallow bottom. The Connetquot

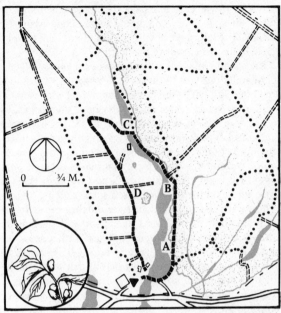

Inset: Spicebush

begins as a spring-fed seep several miles to the north. As the water is a cold 52 degrees when it emerges from the underground aquifer, it is particularly well suited for trout. Brook trout are native, but browns and rainbows have been introduced. Although rainbows are native to the western United States, they are now fairly successful as hatchery-raised trout here in the east. They are known to be quite tolerant of the intensive feeding procedures and crowded conditions in hatcheries and are also able to withstand warmer winter temperatures than the brook trout. The people you may see angling here are required to use fly-fishing equipment only—a throwback to earlier traditions when the Southside Sportsmen's Club owned the property in the 1860s.

Notice the typical forest along the red trail. Pitch pines and white oaks are the dominant trees in this sandy soil, which is characteristic of the glacial outwash plains (see below). Pitch pines are considered by some ecologists to be indicator plants for the so-called sand-plain community. Their especially deep root system penetrates the dry, porous ground to help them extract as much moisture as they can. They are the prevailing tree in the pine-oak barrens of Suffolk County, which extend from here all the way to the eastern end of Long Island (see **#9**). However, white oaks are perhaps the most common tree found on Long Island, according to the Long Island Horticultural Society. The larger specimens are found not here but almost exclusively in the richer soils of the north shore.

The continental glaciers that descended upon New England stopped a few miles north of Connetquot, leaving their mark in a jumble of small hills known as the Ronkonkoma Terminal Moraine. The area south of the glacial edge on which Connetquot is located is known as an *outwash plain*, a gently sloping flattish zone composed of sand and gravel deposited by the glacier's meltwater. As these meltwater streams lost their velocity, they dumped enormous loads of debris, which became the broad plain that makes up the southern half of Long Island (see **Long Island, Cape Cod, and the Islands**).

Continue on the red trail, past a small building on the left, to the yellow trail. Go left toward the river and the trout-hatchery complex. Continue to the right along a small pond as the yellow trail cuts left. Cross a wooden bridge, marked 20a (**C**), that separates an upper and a lower pond. If you are here in the fall, winter, or early spring, you may well see the great blue herons that winter at the far end of the upper pond. Approximately thirty to forty individuals spend the colder months in this spot where fish are plentiful before leaving for breeding grounds in late April and early May. Exactly where these herons go is not known. However, one can be fairly sure they do not nest on Long Island. None have been known to do so since 1900, and those nesting here then were actually found on Gardiner's Island. Today the blue herons' scattered and secluded colonies along the East Coast range from Florida to southern Nova Scotia. It is not unusual to find more than a hundred pairs in a single nesting colony. The birds are quite wary, so approach quietly and slowly.

Cross another bridge to a sandy road and walk left toward a trailer and buildings. Pick up a dirt path that parallels the paved road just past the last structure.

The terrain changes quite dramatically at **D,** for here the area looks barren, desolate, scrubby, and open. In 1977 a fire swept through 600 acres here, decimating all but a few of the hardier, taller pitch pines. Young white, black, scarlet, and scrub oaks and high- and low-bush blueberries are rising from the poor soil. Notice also the small pitch pines trying to regain their lost territory. Pitch-pine seeds are unusual in that they can germinate on sterile mineral soil containing no humus at all. The ability to sprout from dormant buds at the base of burned trunks also allows these hardy trees to regenerate after a fire (see **#87**).

An osprey nesting platform on top of a telephone pole is the westernmost breeding site on the south shore of Long Island for ospreys. The pole was put up in 1977 after the original nest tree burned down. The birds used the artificial nest for a few years, but in 1982 they moved to a nearby pine tree. That tree, however, blew down in a fall storm, and it is unclear whether the ospreys will reuse the platform or find a more natural site (see **#22**, **#50**, and **#99**). Notice the aluminum flashing around the lower section of the pole: its purpose is to prevent raccoons and other predators from climbing into the nest and destroying the eggs or young. Flashing was also used on the nest tree.

Continue along the path until you meet a paved road, with a large open field to the left. Go a short distance and take the left fork toward the buildings and the millpond.

Remarks: *Walking time is about 1¾ hours and is relatively easy. There are many other trails that cover different areas in this large preserve. There are also 25 miles of bridle paths. Fly fishing is on a fee basis—$5 for each 4-hour session. Admission to any part of the park is by permit only, which can be obtained by calling (516) 581-1005 or by writing to the Connetquot River State Park Preserve, P.O. Box 505, Oakdale, N.Y. 11769. There is a small daily-use fee. Hours are from 6:00 a.m. to sunset from April through October, and 8:00 a.m. to sunset during the winter. The park is closed on Mondays during the warmer months, and Mondays and Tuesdays in the winter. Camping facilities are available at nearby Hecksher State Park in East Islip. For information contact Hecksher State Park, East Islip, N.Y. 11730; (516) 665-3759.*

7.

Fire Island National Seashore: Smith Point

Directions: **Shirley, N.Y. From New York City, take the Belt (Cross Island) Parkway to Exit 25A. From there, go east about 50 miles, first on the Southern State Parkway to Exit 44, then on the Sunrise Highway (Route 27). Take Route 46 (William Floyd Parkway) south for about 10 miles, crossing Smith Point Bridge to Fire Island. There is ample parking on county property, ($2 fee, summers only), and signs direct you to National Park Service property.**

Ownership: **National Park Service**

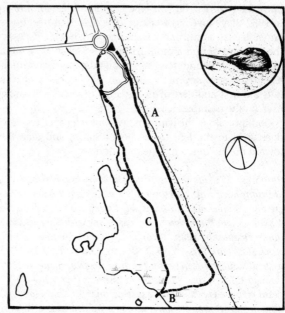

Inset: Horseshoe crab

Seven miles of sandy beach, dunes, swales, and pockets of hardy vegetation create a unique natural area along this stretch of Fire Island from Smith Point west to Watch Hill. The sole federally designated wilderness area in New York State, these 1,400 acres of barrier beach are accessible only by foot (with the exception of a boardwalk trail for the handicapped) to allow for a rich and relatively undisturbed coastal exploration. During migration periods, the ocean beach affords views of humpback and rare northern black right whales, along with numerous species of waterfowl and shorebirds. In fall, falcon migration can also be spectacular. In addition, the dunes and swale (interdunal areas) offer protection to such diverse animals as the brown thrasher, Fowler's toad, red fox, and whitetailed deer. The mudflats and salt marshes along the bayside add yet another dimension to this coastal jewel.

Begin walking along the beach at the ocean's edge (**A**). Fire Island is a barrier beach, formed within the last 3,000 years by constant wave action on the sandy substrate. Originally a long sandspit that stretched for more than 50 miles, it was separated by storms that caused the beach to give way to an open channel, which is now Moriches Inlet to the east. The beach can be a wild place—with the

Atlantic Ocean stretching endlessly toward the horizon, the air is filled with the sound of crashing waves that slowly alter the shoreline. Behind you an extensive dune system lines the upper edge of the beach and protects another unique community behind from the destructive force of the beating surf (see **Long Island, Cape Cod, and the Islands**).

Take a closer look at the deep, soft sand that you trudge through and that helps build the 30- to 40-foot dunes. It is generally light in color, a clue to its chief mineral component: quartz. Yet strong winds may expose other minerals, and portions of the windblown upper beach are frequently covered by crystals of black magnetite and red garnet.

The sand is host to numerous marine organisms like fiddler crabs during some phase of their life cycle. Although the beach may look empty and barren, aside from the empty shells and organic debris deposited by the waves, some individuals survive beneath its protective cover, especially in the intertidal zone, which the seawater inundates twice a day. Certain creatures, such as the horseshoe crab, come to the beach only once a year to lay their eggs and then return to the ocean.

Late spring and early summer are times when you may have the rare opportunity to witness one of these landward breeding migrations. The horseshoe crab, a remarkable ancient arthropod related to spiders and mites, begins crawling ashore in early summer. Those individuals that brave the strong ocean waves can be seen along the beach here. The majority, however, will crawl up in the gentler surf of the bay. Shaped like a horse's hoof with a long barbed tail and two pairs of eyes, it is a living fossil that has remained virtually unchanged for 200 million years. The female molts up to sixteen times and lives for almost 9 years before reaching breeding age. With the smaller male in tow in a semi-piggyback style, she scrapes out a depression just below the high-tide line and lays up to a thousand eggs. She then drags her mate across the nest while he deposits sperm. The next wave or tide covers the tiny round light-green eggs with sand. The eggs hatch in a matter of weeks, and tailless larvae crawl out and head for the water. During their short journey many will be intercepted and consumed by crabs, mollusks, and shorebirds.

One of the shorebirds that might take advantage of this meal is the sanderling. Look along the water's edge for this plump, light-colored, starling-sized sandpiper with its dark shoulder patch and black legs and bill. Seemingly tireless, sanderlings play a feverish kind of tag with the broken waves as they follow the advancing and receding water, searching for small food organisms. In flight, the little birds flash a broad and bright white wing-stripe. Sanderlings nest on the upland tundra in the high Arctic, where they subsist on buds and berries until the appearance of fly larvae in ponds. They are commonly seen along Fire Island beaches during fall and spring migrations (August to September and April to May).

In addition to the sanderling, the migration (see **#96**) may bring considerable numbers of other shorebirds here, including black-bellied plovers, ruddy turnstones, dunlins, dowitchers, least and semi-palmated sandpipers. But as summer draws near, most head north to breed, leaving only a few inconspicuous residents, such as the piping plover. Common and least terns also nest in the area and can be seen feeding offshore, swooping and skimming the surface of the water (see **#23**).

Although birds are among the most visible creatures here, they are not the only migrants. Other offshore travelers that can be seen occasionally along the beach are whales. These mammals have evolved into the largest animals alive, with blue whales measuring up to 100 feet long. Whales are superbly adapted to a marine existence, with their streamlined bodies, insulating blubber, and complex respiratory system. They are lung breathers, and their nostrils have moved to the top of the head as a "blowhole," to allow breathing with maximum submersion. The force of exhalation is such that a whale's "blow," composed of moist lung air and droplets of an oily emulsion important to nitrogen absorption during deep dives, can be seen from considerable distances and is useful in identification (see **#64**).

During March, the rare northern black right whale is sometimes seen from here. This whale gained its name because after being harpooned it floated easily on the surface, unlike some other whales that tended to sink before the whaling ship could secure them. Hence it was considered the best or "right" whale to catch commercially. Subsequently it was hunted almost to extinction, and estimations are that only about two hundred individuals now exist after several years of international protection. The large finback whales, reaching up to 70 feet in length and weighing some 50 or 60 tons, may also be spotted far offshore as they move toward more productive feeding grounds in northern waters. The waning of summer in late August and September may bring the acrobatic humpback whales to Long Island as they return south to the warm Caribbean waters to breed.

Continue up the beach past two walkways that pass up over the dunes and head north into the swale. These walkways were erected to protect the fragile dunes, which can be severely damaged by trampling. Beach grass predominates on the outer edge of the dunes (see #79), with seaside goldenrod, beach pea, and dusty miller scattered throughout. Dusty miller looks as though it had been dusted with powder—actually it is covered with woolly white fibers that help protect it from heat and desiccation.

The third walkway you come to offers benches and a white compass painted along the boards to show wind directions. This boardwalk takes you up over the dunes, through the swale, to the marshy bay areas along the Old Inlet (**B**). Follow it all the way to get a good comparison of bay and ocean habitats.

As you near Great South Bay, the vegetation changes drastically from the low plants and shrubs of the dunes and swale. Phragmites 8 to 10 feet high line the inner edge here, creating a thick barrier and obstructing views. This plant grows along the upper areas of the marsh where the soil has built up enough so that it is no longer inundated by tides. An exotic, meaning it was not a native species here, it has spread like wildfire along both fresh and salt waterways. But closer to the bay, still washed by the sea, salt-marsh cordgrass (*Spartina alterniflora*) has a hold (see #14 and #77). Glasswort and sea blite may also be nestled along the upper edge.

The Old Inlet was created as waves broke through the barrier island's interior, but since the early 1800s, has filled in with sand and mud to create this marsh (see #29 on marsh formation). Loons, grebes, and brant are just a few of the larger waterbirds that may be resting just offshore in the usually calm bay waters. Whimbrels, willets, spotted sandpipers, and greater yellowlegs can be seen feeding along the marsh edge in spring and early fall.

Retrace your steps to the sand path that winds east through the swale (**C**). This walk is a rare opportunity to examine the beautiful, well-developed community that grows in the protection of the dunes. The swale is perhaps the most severe beach environment, because the dunes cut off cooling sea breezes and the concave topography radiates heat toward the center. The plants and animals living here are well adapted to survive in this desertlike environment.

The vegetation is noticeably different from that along the marsh and the ocean side of the dunes. Low, sprawling beach heather (*Hudsonia tomentosa*) dominates the area and is well suited to survive the dryness and heat with its thick, woolly, scalelike leaves. Scattered patches of thick-leaved bayberry and beach plum line the swale. Pitch-pine stands can be seen along the bay side (see #9). The deep sand and clumps of vegetation offer protection to a few hardy animals that carve out an existence here. White-tailed deer, red fox, cottontail rabbit, long-tailed weasel, and smaller rodent species make their homes here. Birds are numerous, and even reptiles and amphibians, such as the hognose snake and Fowler's toad, survive. Listen for the droning, buzzy, penetrating call of this toad in late spring and summer.

The sand trail eventually joins the boardwalk and leads back to the parking area.

Remarks: *The walk takes at least 4 hours. Bring lunch and water. Fire Island is magnificent at all times of the year, but some of the most exciting wildlife can be seen in the spring, fall, and winter. National Park Service interpretive activities include walks, talks, and the nature trail for the handicapped. The numbers painted on different portions of the boardwalk refer to a National Park Service guidebook, which describes the ecology of the swale and can be purchased at the visitors' center. Guided walks are given more frequently in the summer. Access to the Watch Hill Visitor Center and beach to the west of here can be gained by ferry service, which departs from Patchogue during May through November. Camping is also available there during the warmer months, from May through October. Call (516) 597-6633. Please observe all signs to keep off the dunes, as they are very sensitive to trampling.*

8.

Fire Island National Seashore:
Sunken Forest at Sailor's Haven

Directions: **Sailor's Haven, N.Y. Sunken Forest can be reached only by a May-through-November ferry from Sayville, N.Y. From New York City, take the Belt (Cross Island) Parkway to Exit 30. From there take the Long Island Expressway (Route 495) east about 36 miles to Exit 59. From the service road turn right at the first light and go south on Route 93 (Ocean Ave., then Lakeland Ave.). At the fifth light, Lakeland Ave. is no longer called Route 93; continue south to the eighth light (about 6.5 miles from Exit 59). At Main St., follow the green-and-white signs to the Fire Island Ferry terminal; for a fee, park at the commercial lot. Take the ferry to Sailor's Haven.**

Ownership: **National Park Service.**

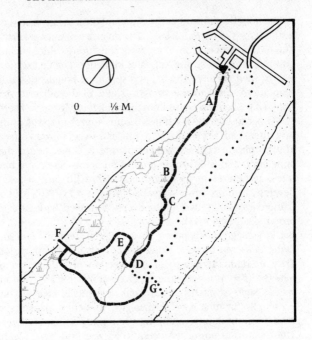

Fire Island harbors many unique and fascinating habitats, but one of the most enchanting is the Sunken Forest. The largest maritime forest on the island, it earns its name from its location down behind the dunes. Tucked between Great South Bay and the Atlantic Ocean, this unusual woodland is composed primarily of American holly, shadbush, tupelo, and sassafras. The height of the gnarled trees rarely exceeds 30 feet, although many of the specimens are known to be more than 150 years old—this is testimony to the pruning effect of the constant salt spray.

The air is invigorating and the scenery spectacular as the ferry heads out toward distant Fire Island. More than 3,000 years ago this body of water was contiguous with the Atlantic Ocean, but as Fire Island formed, it cut off these inshore waters and created Great South Bay. The island protects the bay from the open-ocean forces and creates a shallow lagoon of more than 100 square miles, which slopes so gradually from shore that one can wade out quite a distance. The bay's sheltered waters allow many migrating waterfowl, including brant, scaup, black duck, and red-breasted merganser, to congregate. Flounder, fluke, and blackfish flourish, and the fishing here is renowned.

The boardwalk through the Sunken Forest begins just to the right of the ferry slip on Fire Island. The diversity of trees is fairly limited due to the combination of growing conditions, which include mineral-poor soil and strong saltwater influence. The first section of the trail is lined with the twisted and spreading boughs of shadbush, a dramatic contrast to the straight trunks of the adjacent American holly (**A**). Shadbush (also known as Juneberry or serviceberry) is so called because its thick white blossoms appear in spring at the same time that shad ascend the New England rivers to spawn (see **#43**). The purple, berrylike fruit will mature in June, hence the name Juneberry, and is a favorite food of numerous species of birds. The tree is recognized by its smooth gray bark with dark stripes; it often develops in a group of several stems (see **#25**). You will also see scattered sassafras here, with deeply furrowed bark of a reddish-brown color (see **#45**).

Old scraggly pitch pines, an occasional, tenuous redcedar, and dying oaks can be seen along the boardwalk at various locations. They are remnants of a past forest type in which they used to dominate (see **#9**). But over time, as succession (see **#38**) continued and species such as pitch pine and oaks eventually created conditions unsuitable for their own further growth, better adapted species of trees began to flourish and give way to the present-day forest types. Thick stands of poison ivy seem to grow everywhere, regardless of conditions; caution is advised. Where the sun filters through to the forest floor, wildflowers such as starflower and wild sarsaparilla can be seen in spring.

Along with the flowers and tree blossoms of spring, the area is alive with winged migrants, some of which will stay to nest, while others head much further north (see **#96**). Brown thrashers, catbirds, rufous-sided towhees, yellowthroats, yellow warblers, and American redstarts all make their summer homes in and around the Sunken Forest, gorging on the abundant insect population and the berries of holly, shadbush, and other fruiting shrubs. The chuck-will's-widow, recently expanding its range northward into New York, is also thought to spend summers here. During the spring and fall these birds are joined by countless others using the area to rest and refuel during their long journeys. Flickers (by the hundreds), flycatchers, swallows (by the thousands in the fall), and warblers of all kinds pass through in good numbers.

One of the most colorful and animated avian summer residents is the American redstart. The male is black with bright-orange patches on the wings and tail, while the female is olive brown with yellow patches in the same pattern. To capture insects, their prime source of nutrition, they jump into the air with drooping wings and fanned tail. The redstart builds a nest of bark shreds and grass, often bound with spider web, in the crotch of a tree or shrub.

The first real break in the canopy comes as you enter a small wetland (**B**). Here the groundwater table reaches the surface and forms a community similar to that found in an inland bog. Because the sandy soil is low in nutrients and drainage is poor, acidic conditions exist and bog-adapted plants take hold (see **#56**). Sphagnum moss, cattails, and ferns are rimmed by highbush blueberry. This wetland area is quite beautiful, with species of even height casting a wide range of colors.

Continuing just a bit further, the trail winds upward and ascends a short flight of stairs (**C**). One can now get a spectacular elevated view of the forest. The open ocean is off to the east, across the dunes, while the maritime forest trees line the bayside. In spring the dark green of scattered pitch pine, the kelly green of holly, the white of shadbush blossoms, and the pinks and purples of many blooming shrubs combine to create a classic impressionist setting. The uniformity of height is evident from here and reveals that the canopy of the Sunken Forest lies level with the dune tops. The constant salt spray keeps the trees pruned, and they can grow only as long as they remain in the protective shadow of the dunes. The ocean salt provides essential nutrients, such as calcium, magnesium, potassium, and phosphorus, but the salt can also kill foliage if sufficiently concentrated. As the limbs reach up into the zone above the dunes, they are susceptible to high salt concentrations and die back.

Small redcedar, some of which are more than one hundred years old, and bearberry are plentiful as you come to the edge of the forest, evidence again of earlier successional stages and the tenacity of redcedar (**D**). Approximately 250 years ago this area of the forest was barren sand. Eventually, beach grass (see **#79**) and other pioneer dune species, such as beach heather and seaside goldenrod, took hold. The stabilization and added nutrients provided by these plants paved the way for taller, more woody species such as the redcedar and pitch pine, which then took hold. The Sunken Forest is the result of continued successional stages over the last couple of hundred years.

Continue up to an even more exhilarating view and then back down into the forest. Canada mayflower lines the trail as you descend the dune edge. Back in the heart of the woods you come to an enlarged section of the boardwalk complete with benches (**E**). The largest trees thus far, American hollies, grow up through cutout sections of the walkway. The smooth, gray-green trunks, often covered with cone-shaped growths, grow tall here and support crowns nearly 40 feet high. American holly is found along the Atlantic

Coast, from Massachusetts to Florida, and through the Mississippi valley. A few sassafras may also be seen here, eking out an existence, along with an understory of catbrier, wild grape, and poison-ivy vines.

The trail winds around and comes out to a platform that overlooks the bay and its marshy shoreline (**F**). Phragmites, a roughly 5-foot-tall weed that grows in dense stands, dominates, although salt-marsh cordgrass still has a hold along the water's immediate edge. Erosion has eaten away at the marsh, and little remains to protect the forest vegetation now.

The boardwalk heads through the woods again and out into the open swale (the area between the dunes) (**G**). You can continue along a cement walk that leads down the center of the swale and back to the ferry dock. Or you can follow the wooden boardwalk that climbs up over the primary dunes and follow the beach back. Both choices offer a chance to explore new barrier-island communities.

Remarks: *The entire walk takes about 1½ hours, but you will probably want to explore further. The ferry runs from May through November, and hours and other information can be obtained from the Sunken Forest Ferry Company, River Rd., P.O. Box 626, Sayville, N.Y. 11782. The National Park Service operates a small museum and bookstore by the ferry dock, and a lunch concession is nearby. A picnic area is available, complete with outdoor hearths, and lifeguards staff the ocean beach during the summer. You may dock your boat here at the small marina. For camping nearby, see #7.*

9.

Quogue
Wildlife Refuge

Directions: **Quogue, N.Y. From New York City, take the Belt (Cross Island) Parkway to Exit 25A. From there go east about 62 miles, first on the Southern State Parkway to Exit 44, then on the Sunrise Highway (Route 27). At Exit 64, go south on Route 104 for 2 miles. Turn right onto Old Country Rd.; go 0.7 mile to the entrance, on the right.**

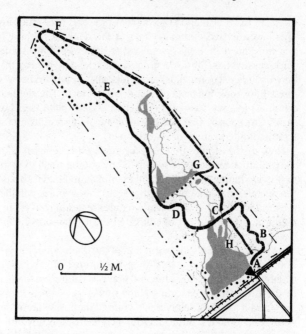

Ownership: **Southampton Township Wildfowl Association, managed by the New York State Department of Environmental Conservation.**

One of the most uncommon habitats on Long Island is the dwarf-pine plains, a scrubby forest where full-grown pitch pines seldom reach heights above 10 feet and are usually less than that. Quogue Wildlife Refuge contains a portion of this intriguing woodland, along with the headwaters and dammed ponds of Quantuck Creek. A rehabilitation center for animals, including a golden eagle, great horned owls, and turkey vultures, is also located here.

The pens that hold the injured and orphaned wildlife are located at the pedestrian gate, and one has to pass this area to gain access to the hiking trails (**A**). Refuge manager Carl Helms cares for the animals, some of which are eventually released, while others remain indefinitely if they are not able to live on their own. The 28-year-old resident golden eagle has never lived outside captivity. There is a deer yard, where two does presently reside. The food for all of the animals is paid for through public donations.

Begin walking to the right of the rehabilitation complex on the so-called main trail and enter a pitch-pine and bear-oak forest (**B**). These are the two dominant trees of the Long Island pine barrens and are joined here by several white oaks and some scarlet- and black-oak hybrids. Shrubs associated with the pine barrens that grow here include bayberry, blueberry, huckleberry, and inkberry. On the forest floor look for bearberry and wintergreen. The sterile quartz-dominated sandy soils of the glacial outwash plain (see **Long Island, Cape Cod, and the Islands**) are of low fertility and support a rather limited variety of vegetation.

Note the brushpiles that have been placed here in an effort both to open up areas of dense woodland by cutting small trees and also to provide hiding places for small mammals and birds. This is part of the overall management plan that seeks to maximize wildlife use of the grounds. In other parts of the refuge are nesting boxes, an osprey platform, and a number of cultivated shrubs that provide food and cover for birds.

As one approaches the north end of the main pond, the ground is noticeably moist, and a small bog has formed (**C**) (see **#56**). The acidity of the underlying sand and gravel is conducive to the growth of the unusual insectivorous plant sundew (see **#58**), sphagnum moss, wild orchids, leatherleaf, young Atlantic white-cedars (see **#30**), and a modest but lush crop of cranberries. A tiny pink flower forms on this creeping shrub during May through July and is followed by the familiar juicy red berry later in the fall (see **#31**).

The trail crosses over the main pond and leads north through undisturbed pine-oak woods toward the dwarf-pine plains (**D**). If you are here after late April and before early September, you'll most likely hear the penetrating and distinct song of the prairie warbler. Listen for the steadily ascending notes of *zee-zee-zee-zee-zeet!* This little yellow-olive insect-eating bird has a series of small black lines along its side. It is particularly numerous in the pine and oak barrens of the East Coast and—unlike most wood warblers—it is more abundant on Long Island and coastal New Jersey than farther inland. Some suggest that scrub warbler would be a more appropriate name, since the bird builds its nest in low shrubs and trees, from 1 to 10 feet above the ground.

Continuing through these peaceful woods, you reach the high point of the refuge, 45 feet above sea level. From here gaze over a sea of low pitch pines and even scrawnier bear oaks (**E**), a strikingly unique forest whose average height is only about 5 feet. In the distance, to the northeast, is a low rise of hills; this is the Ronkonkoma Terminal Moraine, or the southernmost point of glacial advance (see **Long Island, Cape Cod, and the Islands**).

The dwarf-pine plains range over about 875 acres of land on Long Island. Their origin is under debate. Naturalists and ecologists have been theorizing about their existence since the 1800s. Some believe the pine plains are just young trees growing up in an area that was formerly burned. Others suggest that a greater-than-average distance from the water table is the cause of their stunted condition. A recent synthesis of ideas focuses on two key variables: the role of fire and the quality of the soil. The theory states that because the soils here contain more coarse sand than surrounding areas, they are excessively drained and have poor moisture and nutrient retention. Thus they are subject to drought stress and less able to withstand the ravages of fire. After a fire passes through the area, and it does so with some regularity (although this particular spot hasn't been burned since 1931), the soil becomes even more leached and impoverished than before. The trees, then, have evolved to their present state from coping with these long-term stressful influences. Researchers call this process natural selection, and it ensures the survival of the population.

Upon reaching the fence, turn right and then right again along the eastern fence perimeter (**F**). A housing development is being planned for the forest on this side of the refuge, though local residents are fighting the project. If it is built, it would drastically reduce the region's so-called wildlife reservoir zone and almost certainly lead to the disappearance of certain species that need a large territory.

North Pond is the second man-made body of water on refuge grounds, and one can walk along the earthen dam at its southern edge (**G**). You may hear the short, nasal *car* or *ca* of the fish crow, a tidewater species that breeds along the East Coast and along some major river valleys. Look for a slightly smaller bird than the much more common American crow, which has a less nasal, more distinct *caw* voice.

Main Pond is larger than North Pond and was created in 1913 by the Quogue Ice Company for the purpose of supplying ice to their customers (**H**). The company ceased ice harvesting with the advent of refrigeration, and the property was sold in the 1930s to a local waterfowl association. The pond is now home for breeding Canada geese, mallards, black ducks, and wood ducks. Pickerel, bullhead, bass, sunfish, and other warm-water species are found swimming in these waters, as well as snapping, painted, and spotted turtles. The pond averages 3 feet in depth, with a maximum of 5 feet. Quantuck Creek flows over a spillway at the south end of the pond and into Quantuck Bay, eventually reaching the Atlantic.

Remarks: *Walking time is about 1¾ hours. The refuge is not open to hunting, fishing, or picnicking. The hours are from 9:00 a.m. to 5:00 p.m., 7 days a week, and the nature-center building is open on Tuesdays and Thursdays from 1:30 to 4:00 p.m. and for special programs as adver-*

tised. Call (516) 653-4771 for information. There is no charge for admission to the refuge, but any donations you may choose to make for the care and feeding of the animals would be appreciated. The upland sandpiper, a bird on New York State's List of Special Concern Species, nests at the adjacent Suffolk County Airport. Permission to bird-watch there can be obtained at a firehouse near the airfield's control tower. For camping nearby, see #7.

10.

Penny Pond and Hubbard Creek Marsh

Directions: **Flanders, N.Y. The parklands are spread out, and there is no main entrance or main sign. From New York City, take the Belt (Cross Island) Parkway to Exit 25A. From there go east about 68 miles, first on the Southern State Parkway to Exit 44, then on the Sunrise Highway (Route 27) to Exit 65. Go northwest on Route 24 (Riverhead-Hampton Bays Rd.) about 2 miles to Red Creek Rd. Go right for 1.1 miles, staying to the right at the fork. An iron pipe between two stone pillars to the right of the road marks the path to Penny Pond. To find the Hubbard Creek Marsh, continue past this point to the first intersection with Upper Red Creek Rd. and go left. About 0.5 mile farther a driveway loop will be on the right. Park there.**

Ownership: **Suffolk County Parks Department.**

A kettle pond and an extensive salt marsh/tidal creek are among the features at little-known Hubbard County Parkland. Many hiking trails and dirt roads cut through the woods to other ponds, creeks, and marshes, making this large tract of land and adjacent Sears-Bellows County Park an intriguing place to explore.

The narrow road to Penny Pond winds through a mixed-oak and pitch-pine forest. Situated in an intermediate zone between the terminal moraine and the outwash plain (see **Long Island, Cape Cod, and the Islands**), the soil is just slightly richer than the poorest Long Island grades, where scrub oak (*Quercus ilicifolia*) grows abundantly. Here, however, black, white, and scarlet oaks predominate, with occasional scrub oaks.

The soil types in this part of Long Island are known as the Plymouth-Carver series. They are characterized as deep, excessively drained, and coarse-textured. They form in a mantle of loamy sand over thick layers of glacial gravel and sand. They are also quite acidic and low in natural fertility. It comes as no surprise, then, to find that almost all the shrubs and subshrubs along the path are members of the heath family—a group of frequently evergreen plants that have adapted to growing in acidic soils (below 4.5 pH). Notice the particularly dense growth of wintergreen on the forest floor and the blueberry bushes above, both of which are heaths.

Penny Pond itself is a relatively unspoiled representative of the hundreds of kettle ponds left on Long Island by small chunks of glacial ice melting in depressions (see **#99**). Its sources are underground seepage and rainfall. The pond is shallow, has a sandy bottom, and is populated with largemouth bass, pumpkinseed, and eastern chain pickerel. Pumpkinseeds and largemouth bass are both members of the sunfish family, a group that also includes crappies, bluegills, and rock bass. Pumpkinseeds are one of the most common

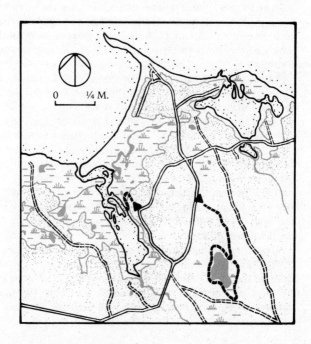

fish in New York State, along with perch and bullheads. Surprisingly, they live for an average of 8 to 9 years, rarely growing any bigger than about 10 inches. Largemouth bass, on the other hand, are known to live up to 15 years and have been caught in New York at weights greater than 10 pounds.

A walk around the pond begins at the right of the first clearing along the water's edge. It goes through both open and very brushy areas, and one particularly soggy spot. Eventually it loops around to the entrance path.

At several places close to the water are small stands of Atlantic white-cedar (see **#30**). Formerly more common on Long Island, this swamp-loving species has been eliminated by man from much of its range. Its wood is very durable in contact with soil and was used extensively for fence posts. House shingles were cut from the larger trees.

Another member of the heath family makes a noticeable appearance on the backside of the pond: sheep laurel. Look for its oval evergreen leaves, light green above and whitish beneath. Sheep laurel is a common shrub, growing not only in moist areas such as this but also along the edges of dry fields. Its nickname, lambkill, refers to the fact that its leaves contain chemicals toxic to livestock.

Several kinds of lichen grow throughout (see **#88**). British soldiers, reindeer moss, pixie cup, and a foliose variety can be found by the keen observer. Because lichens do not grow in polluted air, their presence may attest to a clean atmosphere just 80 miles east of New York City.

Hubbard Creek Marsh is a classic example of the transition from pine-oak upland to salt marsh. The brief walk from the impromptu parking lot to the marsh leads through pitch pines, white oaks, redcedars, and greenbriers to a very different array of vegetation. Groundsel-tree can be found at the marsh edge, while marsh elder grows about 40 to 50 feet in. Sea lavender flourishes in the heart of the marsh, among acres of salt-meadow cordgrass (*Spartina patens*) and spike-grass. All of these plants are able to withstand salt spray, but only those in the high-tide zone can tolerate the inundation of their roots by salt water (see **#14** and **#77**). If you spend some time here with a wildflower field guide, you will undoubtedly be able to identify more species.

A walk to the end of the sandy road brings you to Hubbard Creek flowing north to Flanders Bay. Notice the long sandbar in the distance, to the right, which allowed the marsh to develop away from the open surf (see **#29** for salt-marsh development). The marsh is a favorite among local hunters—you will probably see duck blinds scattered throughout the area. When the hunting season is not in full swing, this is an excellent spot for waterfowl and wading birds.

Remarks: *The trail to Penny Pond takes about 15 minutes. The walk around it takes about 30 minutes. Wear rubber-bottomed shoes if you decide to take that route. A spotting scope is useful at Hubbard Creek Marsh, as the area is quite large. Fishing is permitted at both locations. Access to this entire park and all other parks owned by Suffolk County is officially restricted to residents and property holders of Suffolk County and their guests. Nonresidents, however, may visit the park by calling the park-system headquarters in West Sayville at (516) 567-1700. Camping is available at Wildwood State Park, about 15 miles north of Penny Pond in the town of Wading River. For information contact Wildwood State Park, Wading River, N.Y. 11792; (516) 929-4314.*

11.
Orient Beach
State Park

Directions: **Orient, N.Y. From New York City, take the Belt (Cross Island) Parkway to Exit 30. From there, take the Long Island Expressway (Route 495) east about 64 miles to Exit 72. Continue east, now on Route 25, about 35 miles; the park entrance is on the right, about 9 miles beyond Greenport.**

Ownership: **New York State.**

A resident of the North Fork describes the Orient area, with its lovely colonial-style villages and seascapes of Gardiner's Bay and Long Island Sound, as "the most New England piece of real estate on Long Island." The 4-mile-long barrier spit known as Orient Beach is definitely reminiscent of parts of Cape Cod—a place where wind, water, and shifting sands have come together to create a special natural environment. Waterfowl, shorebirds, gulls, and a variety of landbirds join an elusive deer herd and an occasional red fox on the 363-acre parkland. A walk to the end of the point leads through scrub forest, salt marsh, and open beach.

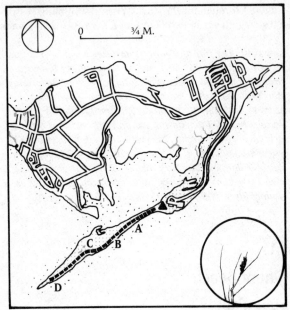

Inset: Spikegrass

Drive along the entrance causeway to the bathing beach, snack bar, and parking lot. Begin walking along the sandy Jeep road to the right.

The beach (**A**) affords fine views of Gardiner's Island and the Montauk peninsula in the distance. Orient Beach is a product of littoral drift, or the movement and accumulation of sand and gravel by tides, currents, and waves (see **#29**). In this case, the drift is to the west, and over a period of thousands of years it has formed a narrow spit subject to changes in size and form. The beach is steadily eroding along this side, as is evidenced farther down the peninsula by the bleached stumps of once-healthy and -protected redcedar trees. The moving sand is slowly being added on to the western tip of the point.

East of Orient Point is a chain of islands beginning with Plum Island, just a mile away, and continuing on to Great Gull and Fisher's Island. Geologists theorize that at one time these islands were connected in a ridge of glacially deposited material that formed the eastern boundary of Long Island Sound when it was a vast freshwater lake of glacial meltwater at the end of the Wisconsin glacial period about 10,000 years ago (see **Long Island, Cape Cod, and the Islands**). When the waters eventually burst through that boundary and the ocean came in, most of the land disappeared, except for the islands still visible from the beach today.

The spit widens enough here within its relatively narrow confines to include a salt marsh (**B**). High flood tides usually enter from the north, or Orient Harbor side, and maintain the shallow levels of water. Redcedars line the perimeter, while salt-meadow cordgrass (*Spartina patens*) and spike-grass grow in the marsh itself. Ospreys (see **#22, #50,** and **#99**), kestrels, and various ducks can frequently be seen in the area.

According to local authorities, the reddish-purple color of the sandy road is due to the remains of crushed brick and other materials used to stabilize the track when the spit supported a fish factory years ago (**C**). Remains of the old factory, including concrete slabs and piles of weathered fishbones and by-products, can be found a little farther along the trail. The red road leads to an oasis of Japanese black pine (*Pinus thunbergii*) and post oak. A small brackish pond to the right is the main source of water for the tiny resident herd of white-tailed deer. Also in this area are at least two other well-known beach plants: prickly-pear cactus (see **#24**) and bayberry.

All of the vegetation here except the pines occurs naturally. The state decided to plant Japanese black pines largely because these trees are the hardiest and most durable evergreen along ocean-front properties. Their irregularly placed, wide-open branches allow them to survive in windy places. The tree is easily transplanted and can be placed with other seedlings as close together as 5 to 6 feet. As the tree gets older and taller, its lower limbs stay healthy and green, even if in the shade of other members of the stand. Notice that the bright needles are in clusters of two.

As the spit narrows to its end, the trees get smaller and smaller until they are shrub size and then disappear (**D**). Seaside goldenrod and other "weeds" are apparently the only vegetation hardy enough to withstand the winds and desiccation of such an exposed place. At the very end of the walk, the concrete and steel remains of an old lighthouse stick out of the water. The lighthouse, which burned in an arsonist's fire, can be approached during low tide.

Remarks: *Walking is slow because of the sand and glacial pebbles. Allow approximately 4 hours round-trip. In the summer the area is thick with mosquitoes and poison ivy. Bring water if you attempt the walk during the warmer months. Binoculars will also be useful, as will a scope for serious waterfowlers. In winter the park is open from 8:30 a.m. to 4:30 p.m.;*

*closed on Tuesdays and Wednesdays. Beginning April 1, the grounds stay
open a bit later. In midsummer the gates are closed at 8:00 p.m. The ferry
to New London, Conn., is nearby. Private camping facilities are located in
the nearby town of Greenport.*

12.

Mashomack Preserve

Directions: **Shelter Island, N.Y., in Gardiners Bay, between
the North Fork and South Fork of Long Island. Call the
preserve office for information on access and directions
before visiting; (516) 749-1001.**

Ownership: **The Nature Conservancy.**

Justifiably known as the "jewel of Peconic Bay," Mashomack ranks
among the most pristine and spectacular natural environments on
Long Island. Its 2000 acres, encompassing about a third of the land
area of Shelter Island, is a wonderland of salt marsh (see **#29**),
coastline, kettle ponds, open fields, and oak forest. Thirteen pairs of
osprey nested here in 1982, making it the second largest Long Island
colony. An unusual white-pine swamp in the western part of the
preserve has been designated of "unique local importance" by New
York State's Department of Environmental Conservation.

The walk begins a short distance from the small parking lot near
the entrance gate. Proceed to the nature hut and pick up the trail on
the right side of the road.

Several small kettle ponds (see **#99**) occupy low areas in an
otherwise dry oak-beech forest (**A**). When the water table is high,
usually in spring, the kettles take on a swampy appearance. Notice
trees and shrubs growing within the kettle itself. Summersweet, or
sweet pepperbush, rims the little wetland with its small white, clustered blossoms in middle to late summer. Highbush blueberry and
winterberry are also common in and around the kettles, along with
the other shrubs of the wooded swamp community. Wood ducks
nest in the hollow cavities of trees in this area.

After the first warm rain of early spring, salamanders and frogs
crawl from their underground winter hiding spots to breed in these
shallow waters. Spotted salamanders and spring peepers are abundant, but both amphibians are difficult to observe directly, though

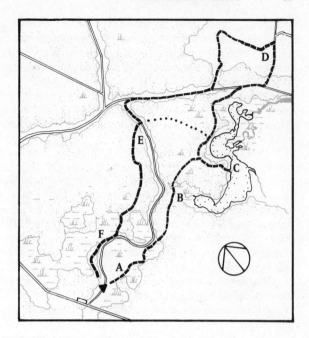

for different reasons. The salamanders, upon laying and fertilizing their eggs, return to the damp soils and rotting logs of the woodland floor, only venturing out to eat during the night. Peepers are quite small (about ¾ to 1⅜ inches); they blend into the woods through their brown coloration and are very sensitive to the presence of human beings, whose voice and step usually cause the little frog to stop calling. In recent years low pH levels, associated with the increasing incidence of acid rain, have destroyed the eggs of many amphibians. In some locations, the spotted salamander population appears to be dying out.

Switch grass and salt-marsh cordgrass (*Spartina alterniflora*) are two common plants at the edge of Miss Annie's Creek (**B**) (see **#14** and **#77**). Probes and corings of this salt marsh have found layers of salt peat over freshwater peat, indicating that the area was once freshwater swamp that was eventually flooded by the postglacial rise in sea level.

A side trail goes down to the water's edge; from here you can see an osprey nest to the right on top of a small dead tree (**C**). (See Great Swamp, **#22, #50,** and **#99** for more on ospreys.) Since most

of the other osprey nests on the preserve are on off-limits Mashomack Point, this may be your only opportunity to witness these
inspiring birds of prey soaring overhead or swooping down over the
water in search of fish. Across Shelter Island Sound is the peninsula
of North Haven.

As the trail cuts along the edge of the marsh, several high spots
provide good territory from which to scan the waters for birds. Black
ducks are a frequent sight, as are glossy ibis, great blue herons, and
great and snowy egrets.

At **D** is a large field, which was once farmed for potatoes but now
exists primarily for wildlife and human enjoyment. Little bluestem,
a native prairie grass, covers the 40-odd acres with its blue-green
hues in summer and its golden tones in fall and winter. Its root
system is especially thick, enabling it to capture far more of the
available moisture than other competitive species. Small black-cherry
trees, an occasional redcedar, bayberry, huckleberry, and smooth
sumac make up the spotty shrub layer. A few pairs of red-tailed
hawks nest along the edge of the field and glide over its flat expanse
searching for mice, rodents, and snakes (see **#98** for more on snakes).
Kestrels, marsh hawks, and great horned owls also hunt here. Bobwhite quail and ring-necked pheasant nest among the grasses and
shrubs.

To keep the fields from evolving into forests, the preserve staff
plans to set controlled fires. A scientist with expertise in fire ecology
is being consulted about proper techniques, timing, and the ramifi-
cations of such management methods. The field was last burned
about 15 years ago, which explains the lack of good-sized trees.

White, black, and chestnut oaks predominate on the hilly terrain
(**E**), where red-bellied woodpeckers have been seen in increasing
numbers. This 9- to 10-inch zebra-backed woodpecker with a red
cap (females are tan on top) has been extending its range northward.
It is not known, however, if the bird is definitely nesting on the
property.

A botanical community that has caught the eye of regional ecologists for many reasons is the unusual pine swamp at (**F**). White
pine, a northern species, is exceedingly rare as a native tree on Long
Island and is especially rare in a wetland habitat (see **#60**). Two
other noteworthy northern plants, mountain holly and a sedge (*Carex
trisperma*), also grow here, along with two members of the orchid
family, whorled pogonia and moccasin-flower, which are uncommon in such a setting. The entire assemblage is growing on a thick
mat of sphagnum moss. The flora of Pine Swamp is a relic of very
ancient conditions. Over 3000 years ago, the swamp formed in this

isolated pocket, and a vegetative community became established. The various species became stable over the centuries, adapting to changing conditions and surviving to this day.

Remarks: *No collecting of any kind is allowed. Visitors are asked to wear smooth-soled shoes so as not to tear up the trails. Pets are not allowed. Caution is advised during tick season (late March to November). A brochure on ticks and tick-borne diseases is available at the nature hut. Call the preserve office before visiting Mashomack because parking space is limited. The phone number is (516) 749-1001. Camping is available at private campgrounds in the town of Greenport on Long Island's North Fork. On the South Fork, Hither Hills State Park in the town of Montauk allows camping from April through November. For information contact Hither Hills State Park, Montauk, N.Y. 11954; (516) 668-2554.*

13.

Sagg Swamp

Directions: **Bridgehampton, N.Y. From New York City, take the Belt (Cross Island) Parkway to Exit 25A. From there go east about 83 miles, first on the Southern State Parkway to Exit 44, then on Route 27 (which starts as Sunrise Highway, but changes name). At the traffic light in Bridgehampton, turn south (right) onto Ocean Rd. and go 0.3 mile. Turn left onto Sagaponack Rd.; go 0.7 mile to a Nature Conservancy sign on the left. Park on the grass in front of the preserve, but not on the south side of the road.**

Ownership: **The Nature Conservancy.**

Sagg Swamp is the largest remaining red-maple swamp on Long Island, east of Riverhead. Twelve varieties of ferns, three stands of Atlantic white-cedars, and a wide diversity of shrubs, sedges, rushes, vines, and wildflowers make this 84-acre wetland a botanical haven. A small kettle pond supports muskrats, turtles, several species of duck, and other wild creatures. The swamp is believed to have been relatively free of human disturbance for a considerable period of time, perhaps since the late nineteenth century. In contrast, most other such wetlands in the area have been drained and developed.

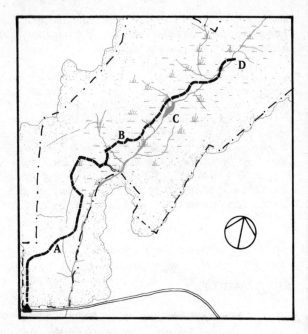

The trail begins at the southwestern portion of the property. The visitor may immediately encounter some isolated wet spots, a mere warning of what is to follow 5 minutes down the path. High waterproof boots are strongly recommended; even so, *much of the swamp may be impassable* when the water table is high.

Open the steel fence gates and proceed. The elevation here in the oak (black, white, scarlet) upland is about 12 to 20 feet above sea level (**A**). Look for sweet pepperbush and highbush blueberry in the shrub layer, wood anemone and Canada mayflower among the wildflowers, and cinnamon and spinulose wood fern. All of these plants prefer moist—but not marshy—soils.

Bear right at a fork, go about 50 yards further, then left and over a plank bridge. A mucky, marshy area can be traversed over rude log boardwalks (**B**). Look for round-stemmed rushes and sphagnum moss. Red maples begin to be the dominant tree. Note the varying bark patterns. The obvious differences between these patterns on different red maples are really an indication of the age of the bark itself, rather than the age of the tree. The bark around the lower parts of an old tree is generally dark gray, furrowed, and somewhat shaggy, while the bark on new limbs, higher up, is smooth and lighter in color. The furrowed appearance develops because this older bark is pushed apart when succeeding layers of new wood are added beneath it. As the tree grows, the bark is usually incapable of expanding and stretching, so it assumes a new configuration. The young saplings, however, have not added a large amount of wood onto their trunks, so their bark is fairly smooth.

The roots of the red maples are not submerged in water, although some may be only inches above it. If the roots are immersed for any length of time, the tree will die from a lack of oxygen. A number of the trees are growing on small mounds, which may be the remains of old stumps. This is one of their ways of adapting to a wetland environment and finding the right niche for germination. Some of the red maples are multitrunked, perhaps as a result of this species' ability to sprout from stumps following a fire or cutting. Thus the four- or six- or eight-trunked red maple you see today may have sprouted from a single predecessor.

Continue cautiously through the swamp until you come to Jeremy's Hole, a small kettle pond to the right (**C**) (see **#99**). A wooden platform here allows you to see the pond clearly. Sagg Stream enters Jeremy's Hole to the north and leaves to the south, heading into Sagaponack Pond and the nearby Atlantic Ocean. Poxabogue Pond, half a mile to the north, is the main source for the swamp, supplemented by rain runoff and a few small feeder streams. Ecologists studying the preserve believe the drainage system and flow have generally remained constant for hundreds of years.

The origin of Sagg Swamp is unclear. One theory holds that the area is a series of partially filled-in kettle ponds. Another suggests that storm runoff and plant growth have partially filled in a natural drainage system to produce a nearly level surface where standing water accumulates. Jeremy's Hole, however, remains classified as a glacially created kettle.

The pond is rich in aquatic vegetation: leafy pondweeds, wild celery, water pepper, watercress, and smartweeds provide a steady food supply for visiting ducks. You may well see 150 black ducks at once, startled into flight by your approach.

A walk through wet terrain continues past the pond along faint trails and over two precarious bridges to a large stand of Atlantic white-cedars on the right (**D**) (see **#30**). These stately trees are part of a group that constitutes the easternmost distribution on the south fork of Long Island. Corings have shown some individuals to be 100 years or older. Note the reddish-brown shredded bark on the younger trees, and a grayer brown, less-shredded bark on the older ones. Royal, cinnamon, and sensitive ferns grow nearby, as do jack-in-the-pulpit and yellow loosestrife, also known as swamp candles. From this point you must return the way you came in.

Remarks: *Walking time is about 1¼ hours. Proper footwear is an absolute must. The swamp may be the most accessible, in terms of land area, during the summer. A fern guide and a wildflower guide will be helpful here. Camping is available at nearby Hither Hills State Park in Montauk. The local Nature Conservancy office in Amagansett would like to be notified beforehand of any visits to Sagg Swamp. Call (516) 267-3748. They also recommend traveling in groups of at least two.*

14.

Merrill Lake Nature Trail

Directions: **The Springs, East Hampton, N.Y. From New York City, take the Belt (Cross Island) Parkway to Exit 25A. From there go east about 90 miles, first on the Southern State Parkway to Exit 44, then on Route 27 (which starts as Sunrise Highway, but changes name). One block beyond the traffic light in East Hampton, turn north (left) onto North Main St. Go 0.6 mile and bear right onto Springs-Fireplace Rd. going northeast (a large green sign says "Springs"). Go about 4 miles northeast; the preserve sign is on the right. Park in the small lot in the field.**

Ownership: **Accabonac Harbor Preserve, The Nature Conservancy.**

The Merrill Lake property is one of an assemblage of twenty parcels constituting the 105-acre Accabonac Harbor Preserve. Most of the holdings are salt marsh, but barrier beach, freshwater wetlands, and upland forest are also included. The main access to the harbor area is through a delightful trail built especially for educational pruposes. A large salt meadow surrounded on three sides by open water makes up much of the walk. Ospreys breed here (see **#22**, **#50**, and **#99**), and many ducks, wading birds, and shorebirds frequent the harbor. Sea lavender, salt-marsh flcabane, and other colorful marsh vegetation may be found alongside several well-known seaside grasses.

From the parking area follow the marked trail through the field. Horses sometimes use this pasture, so exercise caution in walking here. You will soon see the marsh stretching for perhaps one-quarter of a mile off to your left. Continue through a small upland woods where mixed oaks predominate. Cross another equestrian field, go through a gate, and come to the edge of the salt meadow.

The origin of this marsh is typical of those on the glaciated coast of New England. As the level of the seas rose after the glaciers melted (see **Long Island, Cape Cod, and the Islands**), barrier beaches of sand and gravel were slowly created in places along the coast by wave and wind action. Tidal marshes formed only when sea levels had stabilized and protective spits kept out the pounding surf. Salt-marsh cordgrass (*Spartina alterniflora*) could then begin colonizing the area. As time went on, organic matter gradually accumulated around the stems. The dense clumps of grass slowed down the tidal currents that flowed around them, thus intercepting more and more sediments. As the sand, mud, dead vegetation, and other matter built up, the level of the marsh slowly rose to a point where salt-marsh cordgrass was no longer bathed with the twice-daily tides it needed. Another species, salt-meadow cordgrass (*Spartina patens*), took over most of the marsh. It needs the nutrients found in the rich, muddy soil but is a more arid species and thrives without the flooding by ocean tides. You can see it here in the high marsh—an area watered only by the higher tides of the month. The salt-marsh cordgrass now occupies the low marsh, along the very edge of the bay (see **#29** and **#77**).

Early settlers in Accabonac Harbor cut the salt-meadow cordgrass as food for their livestock and as insulation for their houses. The high salt content of the grass helped retard fires. Notice its characteristic tousled or cowlicked appearance, especially by the later part of the summer.

As the trail heads for the water's edge, look for sea lavender and glasswort. Often called the most beautiful of the high-marsh wildflowers, sea lavender is a showy, bouquet-shaped spray of tiny purple flowers blooming in July. Glasswort, a succulent, jointed, cylindrical plant resembling a minute cactus, turns bright red in the fall and is considered by many to be edible.

Here and there are *salt pans*, shallow depressions of various shapes and sizes, some filled with water and others drying down to salt crystals. Plants may be growing in some of them. Pans are formed when pools of ocean water are trapped in slight hollows. As the water evaporates, the salt content increases. The resultant high level of nutrients causes bacterial action to become pronounced, and vegetation within the pans begins to die. The absence of living vegetation in the well-established pans is thus a product of physical and biological factors combined.

The inlet to Gardiner's Bay is to the right: a narrow opening between Cape Gardiner on the left (where the houses are) and Louse Point on the right. To the left of the trail is a small hummock of redcedars and mixed oaks, marsh elder and groundsel-tree. The hummock probably formed from a buildup of sediments carried by water runoff over time, and its elevation, being slightly higher and drier than the marsh, resulted in a change in the vegetational communities. Today cedars and oaks have replaced the saltwater grasses of a thousand years ago.

The trail circles around the hummock and makes its closest contact with open water. Mudflats may be exposed in the bay during low tide. Look for shorebirds such as sandpipers, plovers, and dunlins searching those flats for worms and marine organisms. Larger birds, such as great blue herons, green herons, and snowy egrets, are also commonly seen.

From this point the trail loops back, and the traveler must return the way he or she came in. Notice a series of old mosquito ditches throughout the marsh (see **#46**). The county put them here in order to drain areas of standing water where mosquitoes might breed. The local conservationists, however, would prefer that the fragile preserve be left to natural rhythms.

Remarks: *The walk takes about 45 minutes. Rubber footwear is suggested. Watch out for poison ivy, especially at the hummock (C). Check with the local Nature Conservancy office in Amagansett before visiting, (516) 267-3748. Guided tours can be arranged for large groups. Camping is available at Hither Hills State Park in Montauk.*

15.

Morton
National Wildlife Refuge

Directions: **Sag Harbor, N.Y. From New York City, take the Belt (Cross Island) Parkway to Exit 25A. From there, go east about 73 miles, first on the Southern State Parkway**

to Exit 44, then on Route 27 (which starts as Sunrise Highway, but changes name). In Tuckahoe, turn north (left) on
Route 52 or 38 (they will come together). Go north to North
Sea, then northeast on Noyack Rd. (still Route 38), about
7 miles in all; the refuge driveway is on the left.

Ownership: **U.S. Fish and Wildlife Service.**

The rugged and windswept peninsula that makes up most of the
Morton refuge projects 2 miles into Noyack and Peconic bays. Least
terns and ospreys nest here, and a large population of black ducks
regularly winters in Morton's protected coves and on a brackish
pond. Altogether, 51 species of birds nest on the preserve, and over
225 have been sighted. A variety of vegetation can also be found,
ranging from oak-hickory woods to saltwater grasses and beach
plum.

A walk from the visitor-contact station to the beach passes through
an area of the preserve that has been settled and used by humans
for nearly 300 years. Cattle and sheep have been raised here, as have
apple (see **#74**), pear, and mulberry trees and other crops. Note the
thick stand of redcedar, a pioneer tree often found growing on the
sites of old fields. Poison ivy, an indicator of disturbed land, covers
just about everything along the path. Other conspicuous vegetation
includes black-locust and black-cherry trees, as well as tartarian
honeysuckle. As one gets nearer to the beach, the plantlife thins out
and appears to be stunted, owing to the forces of strong and salt-
laden winds.

A low sandy-and-pebbly beach providing excellent views of the
two bays is open only along the left, or west, side. This section of the
preserve is believed to be a *tombolo*, or sandbar connecting an island
to the mainland (see **#78**). If one looks north up the beach, a series
of high bluffs can be seen. That area is thought to have been one of
the islands that, since the glacial retreat, was connected to the mainland by the long-term deposition of sand and gravel (see **Long
Island, Cape Cod, and the Islands**).

The beach is presently the site of a small colony of least terns, a
diminutive and easily disturbed bird that has been steadily, and in
some cases drastically, disappearing from much of its former range.
Ironically, the least tern staged a strong comeback from the 1920s to
the 1950s after it had been hunted relentlessly for the turn-of-the-
century millinery trade. In the 1951 publication of Richard Pough's
Audubon Water Bird Guide, he called the least tern "the most abundant tern of the region." Now, however, it faces an uncertain future,

chiefly because of its habit of nesting along sandy beaches, which are also popular with real estate developers and sunbathers, and because of increased gull predation.

Here in the East, the least tern can be found breeding in isolated colonies from southern Maine to Texas and along the Mississippi and Missouri river systems. Its nest is merely a small hollow in the sand, well above the high-tide mark, and camouflaged by its proximity to shells and stones. The bird reappeared here in 1982 after a very long absence, but nested without success. Future management plans may call for the restriction of this beach from April to mid-August in an effort to ensure minimal human disturbance (see also **#23**).

Go right at the end of the snow fence onto Jessup's Neck, a high wooded section thought to be one of the peninsula's two former islands now connected by stable sandbars. Red, white, and post oaks and two varieties of hickory (pignut, butternut) predominate. Catbirds are the most successful nesting birds here, thriving in the thickets and dense underbrush. Look for their bulky nests of twigs, leaves, and stems, usually found 4 to 8 feet above the forest floor. The young birds are raised primarily on insects, but the adults seem to prefer small fruits, such as berries and grapes. Listen for their distinct catlike mewing, a call usually given in the presence of predators and during aggressive encounters. They are also excellent mimics of other birds, as is the mockingbird, and are capable of sounding like a cackling hen, a whip-poor-will, or a mellifluous songbird. Catbirds are widespread, breeding throughout a good portion of Canada and the United States and spending the winters south from the Gulf Coast to Panama.

The trail emerges from the woods and proceeds between a brackish pond on the right and the beach on the left. Look for slipper, jingle, and scallop shells at the high-tide mark. Scalloping in these bays between the North and South forks of Long Island is an important business, blessed by unpolluted water, sandy bottoms, and good marine temperatures. The bay scallop (*Argopecten irradians*) ranges from Cape Cod to New Jersey and lives for about 4 years. Its adductor muscle, which keeps the two shells hinged together, is the only part of this tasty mollusk harvested for the table.

Bluffs up to 50 feet high line the beach front from the north side of the brackish pond to near the flattened sandy spit (see **#45**) at the very end of the peninsula. One geological theory proposes that a lobe of the main ice sheet acted as a kind of bulldozer and pushed up this section of the peninsula. It may also be that a second tombolo eventually connected the two wooded "islands."

Prevailing winds from the southwest bringing rain and wind damage have gullied these bluffs considerably. The size of the pebbles here is generally smaller than those on the calmer east side of the peninsula, and this, too, may be the result of fiercer weathering and wave action. Little or no vegetation grows on these bluffs, whereas those on the east side support bayberry, honeysuckle, and other shrubs.

Remarks: *The walk to the end of the peninsula and back is 4¾ miles and takes about 2½ to 3 hours. (The gravel shoreline makes for slow, and somewhat difficult, traveling.) If the beach is closed during least-tern occupation, the peninsula may be off limits. Call the refuge manager at (516) 725-2270 for more information. If the peninsula is closed, there is a ½- to ¾-mile-long self-guiding nature trail on another part of the property. Camping is available about 13 miles away at Hither Hills State Park in Montauk.*

16.

Montauk Point
State Park

Directions: **Montauk, N.Y. From New York City, take the Belt (Cross Island) Parkway to Exit 25A. From there go east about 110 miles, first on the Southern State Parkway to Exit 44, then on Route 27 (which starts as Sunrise Highway, but changes name) to the end. The park is at the tip of Long Island, several miles beyond the village of Montauk.**

Ownership: **Long Island State Park and Recreation Commission.**

Perhaps the most famous landmark on Long Island is Montauk Point, a magnificent beach of high bluffs and awe-inspiring views. At the very tip of the South Fork, 132 miles east of Manhattan, it remains a mecca for those anxious to experience the wide-open space and seasonal moods of the North Atlantic. The park's 724 acres provide excellent tidepooling spots and a variety of pelagic (sea) birds unmatched anywhere else on the island.

The route to the beach begins at the right of the restaurant building. Follow the path down and to the left.

This side of the Montauk peninsula might be called a *cobble* or *boulder beach* (**A**). Notice that the slope is somewhat steep, not as flat as a typical bathing beach along the ocean. Geologists say that slope determines what materials will make up the shoreline. This relatively steep slope is composed primarily of gravels, cobbles, and boulders rather than of sand, because sand is more easily washed away at this angle than is heavier debris.

The granites, gneisses, quartzes, quartzites, and other rocks of cobble size and smaller are generally rounded from the incessant tumbling and turning at the mercy of the water. Also notice the patches of red sand here and the individual rocks that have a reddish or rusty look. The red sand is composed of tiny fragments of garnet, derived from the weathering of schist and other metamorphic rocks. Rusty-colored specimens, on the other hand, are stones whose iron content is oxidizing.

Many varieties of waterfowl can be seen offshore, especially during the fall and winter months, when they have arrived here from their northern breeding grounds. Red-necked and horned grebes,

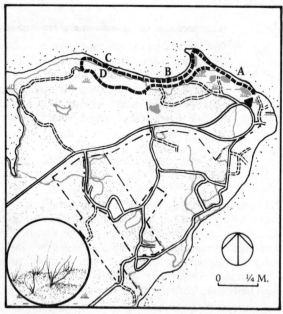

Inset: Beach grass

common and red-throated loons, eiders, scoters (all three kinds), and red-breasted mergansers are just some of the seabirds you may find. Look for the red-breasted merganser diving again and again in search of food. Its bill is long and slender, with toothed edges perfectly suited for catching slippery fish. The winter range of this crested duck extends from northern New England and the Great Lakes all the way down the East Coast to the Gulf of Mexico. It nests on the ground, near water, in the Arctic, Alaska, Canada, and the northern United States (see **#96** for more on migration). Gannets, razorbills, dovekies, and black-legged kittiwakes are some of the pelagic birds, or true seabirds, seen off Montauk.

A series of low bluffs, reaching about 30 feet high, begins on the other side of False Point (**B**). Numerous gullies are worn into the rough faces of these bluffs, evidence of rain and storm erosion. One area of light-tan-colored clay between layers of sand and pebbles is apparent. This is probably an exposure of Montauk till, a subdivision of the larger Manhasset formation, a series of glacially deposited sands and gravels, 150 to 250 feet thick. The finer materials, such as this clay, were most likely brought here by the Wisconsin ice sheet from the nearby deposits of Long Island Sound. Montauk till, in its numerous forms, extends all the way up the northeast coast to Maine. This makes sense when one considers that the terminal moraine along the south fork of Long Island is part of the same glacial terminus forming Martha's Vineyard and Nantucket Island (see **Long Island, Cape Cod, and the Islands**).

During low tide many sea creatures and marine plants can be seen among the large boulders (**C**). Barnacles and mussels have attached themselves to the rocks, along with kelp, Irish moss, and green seaweeds. Notice the distinct line along the rocks where the barnacles stop. This is the demarcation of the lowest high tides of the month. Above this point it is too dry for the barnacles to live; they must be able to open their shells and sweep their feathery cilia through the plankton and nutrient-rich waters, even if only for a short time each day (see **Cape Cod to Portland**).

Go about 25 yards further and cut up above the beach and onto a path left toward the parking lot. The group of shrubs and trees that are hardy enough now to live in this windy and sandy environment were not, interestingly enough, the first kinds of vegetation to colonize the area (**D**). American beach grass (*Ammophila brevigulata*), which can be seen along the entire dune zone, was here long ago, stabilizing the sand with its vigorous roots and rhizomes (see **#79**). Now, white and black oaks, black cherries, shadbush, and American holly are thick and well rooted. Most of the trees are small, less than 30 feet high, due to the strong winds blowing in from the sea.

Blueberry, winterberry, chokeberry, greenbrier, and roses are also here. Notice deer tracks and cottontail-rabbit droppings all along the path. Thick vegetation, such as this secondary dune community, provides good cover for the local mammal population. Even gray fox, an animal quite rare on Long Island, has been reported in the Montauk area.

Continue back along a series of sandy roads. A few freshwater ponds along the way may be good bird-watching territory for resting waterfowl.

Remarks: *Walking time is about 2 hours. The hiker may want to continue down the beach to Oyster Pond, a large body of mostly fresh water, frequented by a good variety of waterfowl. A spotting scope will be useful. Consult birding guidebooks about seasons and exact places. Suffolk County owns a large park to the northwest of this one, Montauk Downs, encompassing Shagwong Point and Big Reed Pond. Also, Hither Hills State Park, which offers camping facilities, is due west 11 miles on Route 27.*

17.

Block Island
National Wildlife Refuge

Directions: **Block Island, R.I. Block Island can be reached by plane and by ferry from New London, Conn., Newport, R.I., and Point Judith, R.I. Point Judith has year-round service; to reach it from Providence, take I-95 and Route 4 south to Route 108. Follow Route 108 for 4 miles to Point Judith and watch for signs for the Block Island ferry on the left. On Block Island, from Old Harbor in New Shoreham center, take Corn Neck Rd. north about 4 miles to the Settler's Rock parking lot at the end of the road. For information on ferry service fares and schedules contact Interstate Navigation Co., Box 482, New London, Conn. 06320; (203) 442-7891. Or, on Block Island, telephone (401) 466-2240.**

Ownership: **U.S. Fish and Wildlife Service.**

The seagull rookery at Block Island National Wildlife Refuge is the largest nesting colony of its kind in Rhode Island. This 29-acre refuge occupies a portion of Sandy Point, a narrow sandspit forming the northern tip of Block Island, and it features a part of the largest relic dune field in the state. These rolling sand dunes serve as nesting habitat for a seagull population that numbers over seven thousand during the breeding season, from June through August.

The major trail at the refuge is a beach road of soft sand that runs north to south along Sandy Point's eastern beach. This road connects two historic points of interest that border the refuge: Settler's Rock, a stone monument marking the first landing site of Block Island's original settlers in 1661, lies south of the refuge at the parking lot adjoining the eastern edge of Sachem Pond; and North Light, a historic granite lighthouse built in 1867, stands at the northern tip of Sandy Point (see **#80** for more on lighthouses).

The seagull rookery lies amidst the sand dunes that are visible to the west of the beach road, though numerous gulls on the fringes of the colony have built nests along the road. The appearance of intruders in the rookery may trigger seagull warning cries (sounding like *ke-ow ke-ow*) and possibly an attack by defensive parent birds, so it is preferable to observe the birds from the road.

Herring and great black-backed gulls are the two species that nest on Block Island; most inhabit the refuge at Sandy Point. According to a 1981 census estimate of the gull nesting population by Richard Bowen, the herring gull is by far the most abundant gull here and also the most numerous nesting bird on the island, with the count numbering about 3,000 pairs. The great black-backed gull totaled about 650 pairs.

Today the herring gull is the most common bird on the northeastern Atlantic Coast, though less than a century ago its small population was threatened by fishermen and egg and plume hunters. Once it was afforded protected status, this species underwent the largest bird population explosion ever witnessed in the United States. Increased availability of food supply was a chief reason. These scavengers will eat from garbage dumps, fish wastes, and other sources of human refuse.

Each year herring gulls return to the same place to breed—the site where they themselves were born. Their nests are no more than shallow depressions in the sand, usually located in beach grass, by a shrub, or near some other type of cover, and may be lined with seaweed, shells, or feathers. The female lays an average clutch of three or sometimes four eggs over a period of roughly 1 week. Thereafter the mating pair never leaves the nest unprotected; one gull always stands guard while the other searches for food. Other gulls are the principal egg predators, though these birds rarely succeed in stealing an egg.

The incubation period lasts about 4 weeks. It may take a chick

1 to 3 days to rupture the egg and emerge. After hatching, the young have a downy gray, speckled plumage, which becomes light and fluffy in a few days. The brownish-gray coloration camouflages the chicks in the beach sand, and only in their second year does the plumage begin to whiten, the tail feathers becoming dark with white rings. As an adult, the herring gull is easy to distinguish from other gulls. It is roughly 5 inches smaller than the black-backed gull, and its "mantle"—the upperparts of the wings and the broad area of the back between the wings—is gray; whereas the great black-backed gull has a characteristically black mantle. Differentiating between the chicks of the two species is more difficult, for the great black-backed chicks are also brownish gray, though the immature gulls have lighter plumage on the head and underparts (see **#77**).

Sandy Point is a sandspit composed of sediments that have been washed by storm waves from the island's cliffs, at Mohegan Bluff and Clay Head (see **#20** and **#19**). The longshore currents that have carried these sediments northward to create Sandy Point continue to do their work, for every year the point lengthens to the north by a few feet as the southern and eastern cliffs are further eroded (see **#45**).

Sandy Point encloses the 80-acre Sachem Pond from the sea, and its brackish waters attract many migratory waterfowl during the fall bird migration. (For migratory species, see **#19**; for more on migration, see **#96**.) The dune field at Sandy Point embraces roughly 118 acres and features typical low beach vegetation, such as bayberry, pepperbush, and wild rose, that covers about 50 to 80 percent of the point.

Remarks: *The hike along the beach road from Settler's Rock parking lot to North Light and back again (approximately 1 mile) takes about 1 hour. The trail is moderately difficult, with shadeless, flat terrain and soft sand over the entire distance. The state of Rhode Island is currently planning to develop several additional foot trails at Sandy Point. These will include a route from North Light south along the western beach of Sandy Point and a trail leading south from Settler's Rock that will connect with the Clay Head Trail along the eastern shore. North Light, which has been replaced as a beacon by a more modern light, is undergoing renovation for use as a maritime museum by the North Light Commission. The Block Island National Wildlife Refuge is open all year.*

18.

Rodman's Hollow

Directions: **Block Island, R.I. To reach Block Island, see #17. From Old Harbor in New Shoreham center, take Old Town Rd. west to Center Rd., and follow Center Rd. south past the state airport to Cooneymus Rd. Turn right onto Cooneymus Rd. and go about 1 mile west to the Rodman Hollow overlook. Park on the right, opposite the refuge sign.**

Ownership: **Town of New Shoreham.**

A plant community of low shrubs and a few small trees dominates Block Island's 11 square miles of rolling hills, sandy valleys, and ocean bluffs. This maritime forest, more like the heathlands or moors of Great Britain than any forest type common to North America, forms one of the most unusual and captivating landscapes on the coast of New England. In this region only Nantucket Island claims equally large expanses of low maritime vegetation. The 37-acre wildlife refuge of Rodman's Hollow features a thick shrub cover of bayberry, blueberry, and other maritime vegetation, which serves as habitat for white-tailed deer, ring-necked pheasants, marsh hawks, and many songbirds. Its several miles of foot trails, which offer a choice of short or lengthy hikes, allow you to enjoy the characteristic plants and wildlife of Block Island's moors.

Block Island was created from glacial till, that is, sediments deposited by the glacier during the last ice age (see **Long Island, Cape Cod, and the Islands**). As the ice sheet retreated northward some 15,000 years ago, its meltwater streams bearing a load of sand and sediments buried a chunk of ice at the present site of Rodman's Hollow. The ice eventually melted, leaving a cavity, or *kettle hole*, which became the hollow you see today (see **#99**). A steep, narrow valley, it runs southward toward the ocean at the southern end of the island. It dips slightly below sea level at its lowest elevation, while the highest point along its upper rim rises about 90 feet above the valley floor near the northern overlook on Cooneymus Rd., offering a sweeping view of the bluffs on the island's southern shore.

Botanists call the type of maritime shrub forest found on Block Island *heathland.* In Great Britain, this term describes areas of uncultivated upland or boggy lowland wastes that are densely overgrown with small shrubs, most notably varieties of heath and heather, as well as small copses of trees. None of the plants growing on Britain's heathlands occurs naturally in North America. The typical shrubs of the coastal moors in New England are largely indigenous species, with perhaps a few species of escaped cultivated plants—such as the varieties of roses at Rodman's Hollow—which have become naturalized in the wild. Both the species common to Block Island and the British heathlands, however, share a tolerance for sterile, acidic soils. At Rodman's Hollow, these plants include bayberry, shadbush, sweet pepperbush, and wild roses, as well as members of the North American heath family (Ericaceae), such as highbush blueberry.

Though the moorland you see today at Rodman's Hollow was sheep pasture roughly a century ago, the origin of the Block Island moors dates back to the deforestation of the land more than 300 years ago. Prior to English settlement in the seventeenth century, the island was forested with oak, elm, pine, cedar, ash, and, in the swamps, scattered stands of alder. The early settlers rapidly cleared this woodland for agriculture and timber, transforming the island into a pastoral landscape of rolling fields, open meadows, and meandering stone walls, which the island's farmers maintained for over two centuries. The decline of agriculture on the island within the last 100 years has triggered the invasion of shrub vegetation on the abandoned pastures and fields. Normally, this maritime shrub vegetation would represent only a temporary stage in the natural succession of the land to a more botanically diverse forest with large trees, perhaps a woodland similar in composition to the precolonial forest. But the Block Island moors are unusual, for the maritime shrub community will remain as the dominant forest type across the island far into the future. This phenomenon, called *arrested secondary succession,* stems from the total destruction of the early forest and the lengthy period of agricultural use that ensued. As a result, the island lacks the stands of mature trees needed as a seed source for forest regeneration. On the New England mainland, cleared lands are naturally reforested from seeds dispersed by the wind or by animals carrying pine cones or acorns. In Great Britain, the ancient heathlands remain open because they are maintained by periodic fires that are set to encourage fresh plants for grazing livestock. On Block Island, it is possible that shearing ocean winds and the high density of the shrub cover across the moors may have discouraged larger trees from becoming established. The character of the Block Island moors will change only if humans reintroduce trees to the island.

The only plant species at Rodman's Hollow that reach anywhere near usual tree size are gray birch and shadbush. The gray birch form a small but conspicuous grove on the northwest side of the valley and can be seen from the overlook on Cooneymus Rd. or from the foot trail. The gray birch is a common invader of old farmland in southern New England, and in the hollow it has perhaps benefited from protection from the ocean wind. The shadbush (*Amelanchier stolonifera*) is easy to identify by its rounded shape, its branches that tend upward, and the one or more slender trunks that grow 15 to 20 feet tall.

By far the most aggressive colonizer of the moorland is bayberry (also called waxmyrtle), which spreads rapidly over open lands in dense, low-growing thickets. The bayberry's leaves are glossy green and aromatic. Its small, waxy berries are used for candlemaking and also provide food for tree swallows, warblers, and even herring gulls during severe winters.

Among the most colorful flowering shrubs at Rodman's Hollow are roses. The rugosa rose is a large, attractive variety that was originally introduced to North America from the Orient, and it has become naturalized in some seashore areas, where it was planted to stabilize beaches and dunes. Its rose-lavender flowers are 2 to 3 inches wide, blooming from June to September. Hybrids of this species and the island's native wild roses are also common here.

The dense vegetation cover at Rodman's Hollow serves as excellent wildlife habitat. The valley and outlying plateaus on this portion of the island are hunting grounds for the marsh hawk (or harrier). This hawk of upland moors, shore meadows, and coastal marshes is one of the most endangered bird species on Block Island, where housing development threatens to diminish the extensive wild habitat required for hunting by this bird of prey. In flight the marsh hawk often glides low over the moors and its ponds and marshes. It is a bird slightly smaller (18 to 24 inches long) than New England's other water-loving hawk, the osprey or fish hawk (see **#22, #50,** and **#99**), which may appear on the island during migratory periods (see **#96** on migration). Both the male marsh hawk (pale gray in color) and the female (brown) display white patches on the rump, but they lack the clear white belly that is so distinctive of the osprey. The marsh hawk's breeding range stretches from the Gulf of Saint Lawrence to the Gulf of Mexico, and it winters as far north as southern New England. In 1981 there were only ten pairs on the island.

White-tailed deer and ring-necked pheasant, both common at Rodman's Hollow, were introduced to the island from the mainland in the last century. The ring-necked pheasant, which in 1981 had an estimated breeding population of fifty pairs on the island, occurs in greater density here than anywhere else in Rhode Island, except during the game-stocking season. Other common birds here include the song sparrow, yellow warbler, common yellow throat, common grackle, gray catbird, robin, American woodcock, brown thrasher, and starling.

Remarks: *Several unmarked but well-defined trails lead through the hollow from the refuge sign at the scenic overlook on Cooneymus Rd. From the road a steep path descends the north slope and then forks into south and west branches. The southward branch extends down the valley floor to the ocean bluffs; the shorter, westward trail ascends the western slope of the hollow and ends at a dirt lane; Black Rock Rd., which runs in a north–south direction from Cooneymus Rd. to Black Rock Point on the shore. Go right to return to the scenic overlook; left to Black Rock Point, a favorite fishing site. Allow at least 1 hour to hike the southern trail (approximately 2 miles) to the shore and back again to the overlook; ½ hour for the shorter, western trail (about 1 mile), returning via Black Point Rd. to the overlook. The trails are moderately difficult, with steep, sandy areas and dense vegetation crowding portions of the routes. Development plans for Rodman's Hollow by the state of Rhode Island's Department of Environmental Management include a formal trail system, a parking lot, and interpretative markers. Rodman's Hollow is open to visitors throughout the year. No overnight camping is permitted on Block Island.*

19.

Clay Head

Directions: **Block Island, R.I. To reach Block Island, see #17. From Old Harbor in New Shoreham center, take Corn Neck Rd. north about 3.3 miles. After passing West Beach Rd. on the left, take the first right east onto an unmarked dirt road and bear left at the first fork to the small parking area and refuge sign.**

Ownership: **Rhode Island Department of Environmental Management.**

Block Island is one of the most spectacular autumn stopovers for migratory birds on the Atlantic Coast. This scenic 11-square-mile island, located 12 miles offshore south of the Rhode Island and

Connecticut border, serves as the outermost resting place on the New England south coast for hundreds of thousands of fall migrants traveling the major flightpath of the Atlantic flyway to their southern wintering grounds. Between 130 and 180 different kinds of birds, representing virtually every species in eastern North America and including many rare birds, may appear simultaneously on Block Island during the height of the fall migration. Casual bird-lovers and professional ornithologists alike come to watch the birds, which are highly visible across the islands low moorland vegetation.

Block Island's fall bird migration is unusually large for the New England region, where the greatest concentrations of migratory birds are generally seen during the spring. The difference here lies in weather fronts and the island's location at sea. The greatest influx of migratory birds occurs during late September and early October, which coincides with the emergence of strong northwesterly winds that accompany cold fronts descending southeastward across the region. Birds flying southward from Canada and northern New England are swept out to sea off their coastal flightpaths by these powerful northwesterly fronts and are unable to fly back to the mainland. At these times, bird enthusiasts gather at the northern end of Block Island, awaiting the arrival of the exhausted birds, which are forced to alight on the nearest land south of the mainland to rest and feed. (See **#96** for more on migration.)

Clay Head is one of the first areas on the northern end of Block Island to receive this teeming array of birds. An imposing ocean bluff composed of colored clay and sand, Clay Head rises some 50 to 110 feet above Block Island's northeastern beaches for a distance of 2 miles. Its blue-, red-, and white-colored clay deposits were laid down by the ice-age glacier that created the island more than 10,000 years ago (see **Long Island, Cape Cod, and the Islands**). These extensive clay cliffs contain an unusual conglomeratelike matrix of unconsolidated glacial till that occurs nowhere else in New England. This matrix of solidified iron oxide goes by the local name "pots and kettles," presumably because parts of it are hollow and make a rattling sound if shaken. The clay deposits here are considered to be of the same high quality as the clay in the Gay Head Cliff at Martha's Vineyard Island (see **#21**).

Clay Head's terrain and vegetation provide cover and food for many migratory species, ranging from deep-woodland birds to those favoring more open or mixed habitats. A rolling expanse of low shrubs, including bayberry and highbush blueberry, stretches along the outer edge of the Clay Head bluffs, allowing an almost unobstructed view of Block Island Sound. Clay Head's vegetation becomes somewhat more diversified a short distance inland from the sea cliff. The shrub forest is interrupted by small grassy clearings, freshwater hollows like the Clay Head Swamp, and belts of red pine that make up one of the island's most extensive stands of tall forest.

Throughout much of this 176-acre tract is a network of largely unmarked, crisscrossing footpaths that have been cut through the moorland shrubbery (see **#18**). This 11-mile trail system, aptly called "The Maze," offers bird-watchers and other hikers access to the more remote and solitary corners of the Clay Head area. The only trail in the maze that is currently marked (blue streamers) leads directly east to the Clay Head Trail, which runs in a north-to-south direction along the upper edge of the bluffs for almost their entire length.

The myrtle (yellow-throated) warbler is one of the most abundant migratory species on the island. It breeds in the northern conifer forests of Canada, wintering as far north as Massachusetts in localities where bayberries are found. Look for its distinctive yellow rump. Only the Cape May and magnolia warblers (reported here in small numbers) have a similar yellow rump patch, but they lack the white underparts of the myrtle warbler. White-throated sparrows flock to the brushy thickets so prevalent at Clay Head and other large areas of Block Island. Listen for their familiar song, which sounds like *Old Sam Peabody, Peabody, Peabody.* You can recognize this bird by its gray breast, white crown, black head stripes, and yellow spot between the eye and bill. Chipping sparrows are also abundant here in fall. This species is distinguished by a reddish cap and a black line through the eye and a white line above it.

The peregrine falcon, or duck hawk, is one of the rarer birds that have appeared at Block Island during the fall migration. This bird of prey, whose skill as an aerial acrobat is legendary, kills small birds with its powerful talons while in flight. The peregrine falcon is a cliff dweller that builds its nests on high ledges. Although this species is found far inland, it prefers coastal areas for its habitat, often migrating along outer beaches and flying long distances across open water. Roughly the size of a crow, it is identified in flight by its long pointed wings and long compact tail. The peregrine falcon, like the osprey and other large birds of prey, became an endangered species after DDT and other insecticides entered the food chain. These toxic chemicals are stored in the birds' fatty tissues and result in a lowered rate of reproduction (see **#22, #50,** and **#99**). In 1981 there were twenty sightings of peregrine falcons at ten different locations along the Rhode Island shore, including Block Island, which was the first definite sign of recovery for this species in the state. The peregrine falcon's breeding range extends to every continent on the globe, but in eastern North America it nests from the Arctic to northern Georgia and northern Louisiana. It winters locally from Massachusetts to northern South America.

Other migratory birds of prey sighted at Block Island include the kestrel, merlin, and sharp-shinned hawk. The marsh hawk, or harrier, is an endangered breeding species on Block Island (see **#18**).

Clay Head and the island's southern sea cliff, Mohegan's Bluffs, are nesting sites for resident barn owls. This rare species, distinguished by its light coloration, long legs, and white, heart-shaped face, nests in holes under the cliffs. The great horned owl and long-eared owl have also been reported here.

Among other upland species that have been sighted in significant numbers during fall migrations are the cedar waxwing, the golden-crowned and ruby-crowned kinglets, and the flicker. Migratory waterfowl are more commonly seen in the ponds, marshes, and harbors across the island. The more numerous waterbirds include the double-crested cormorant, snow goose, common loon, Canada goose, sanderling, white winged scoter, black duck, and greater and lesser yellowlegs. Clay Head is a fine place to watch waterfowl fill the skies with their flight formations.

Remarks: *The only marked trail (blue streamers) at Clay Head leads from the small parking lot at the entrance to the upper edge of the bluffs. The trail is moderately difficult, with rolling terrain and areas of dense thicket. Allow approximately 1 hour to hike to the bluffs and back. Many side trails radiate in all directions off the marked trail leading to the bluff. Hikers using these footpaths through ''The Maze'' should pay careful attention to landmarks, since it is easy to get lost. Future development plans for the Clay Head area by the state of Rhode Island include the establishment of several parking areas, scenic overlooks, reservation and trail signs, and further lengthening of the Clay Head Trail. This route will eventually connect with trails at Block Island National Wildlife Refuge at the northern tip of the island, with access from the Settler's Rock parking area at the northern end of Corn Neck Rd., and will continue southward as far as Ball's Point, located on the shoreline just south of ''The Maze'' and the Clay Head Swamp. Plans for beach-access trails from the top of the bluff are also being considered. Currently, Clay Head lacks trails descending to the beach, and hikers should refrain from scaling its cliffs of soft sand and clay. Block Island National Wildlife Refuge is also an excellent site for bird-watching during the fall migration. Waterfowl may be seen at Sachem Pond at the southern end of the refuge (see* **#17**). *No overnight camping is permitted on Block Island.*

20.

Mohegan's Bluffs

Directions: **Block Island, R.I. To reach Block Island, see #17. From Old Harbor in New Shoreham center, take High St. to Hill Rd. going south, then bear east (left) onto Southeast Rd. Look for the entrance to the scenic overlook on the south (left) side.**

Ownership: **Rhode Island Department of Environmental Management.**

Mohegan's Bluffs are magnificent ocean cliffs towering 75 to 200 feet above pounding Atlantic surf and stretching some 5 miles along the south coast of Block Island. A centuries-old maritime landmark for coastal vessels navigating the treacherous waters of Block Island Sound, this dramatic marine scarp has attracted thousands of sightseers since Block Island's earliest days as an offshore summer resort in the late nineteenth century.

A short trail leading to the edge of Mohegan's Bluffs is located within the 26-acre scenic overlook area off Southeast Rd. The trail begins at a small parking lot, running several hundred feet to an overlook barrier at the cliff edge. From here a steep, strenuous footpath descends to the beach at the base of the cliffs. Hikers should refrain from descending or scaling the bluffs from any other point, since the cliffs are highly fragile and unstable.

Mohegan's Bluffs, like the whole of Block Island, are a mere 11,000 years old. To appreciate how very young this is on the scale of geologic time, you need only consider the birth of the Appalachian Mountains, which arose some 200 million years ago. Block Island is a product of the last ice age, the Wisconsin period, when mile-thick glaciers descended across New England from the north in a time of extreme cold. The glaciers, which had stripped sand, gravel, clay, and assorted small rocks from the mainland as they plowed southward, deposited this glacial till in mounds at their southernmost margin. The southern ice line stretched east to west across New England's ancient coastal plain, which extended far beyond the present-day shoreline. Here the ice unloaded the till in a formation known as a terminal moraine. When the glaciers melted, causing the sea level to rise, the valleys of the ancient plain became submerged beneath huge quantities of water and the higher, moundlike hills of the moraine became islands. Today the terminal moraine forms a snaking ridge that surfaces in the extreme southwest in Long Island and in the far southeast in Nantucket. In between lie other morainal lands, including Block Island and Martha's Vineyard. Block Island belongs to the eastern portion of the terminal moraine, known as the Ronkonkoma Moraine, which rises in Long Island and dips below the sea before reemerging at Block Island.

Mohegan's Bluffs are an impressive illustration of how the ocean has reshaped the glacial islands in southern New England's waters. The stark, bare cliff wall of the bluffs has often been compared to both the clay cliffs of Gay Head at Martha's Vineyard (see **#21**) and the chalk-white cliffs of Dover in England. Like these storm-washed scarps, the bluffs are composed of far softer and therefore less erosion-resistant material than, say, the hard bedrock promontories of Maine. For many centuries storm waves have assaulted the crumbling clays and sands of the cliffs, which geologists estimate are being eroded an average of 5 feet per year. Yet the sediments torn from the bluffs are not entirely lost from the island's land mass. They are carried northward by longshore currents flowing parallel to the eastern coast. Much of this eroded material (as well as sediments washed from the island's eastern cliffs at Clay Head) has been redeposited at the north end of Block Island, forming the sandspit of Sandy Point. This elongated spit is continuously lengthening northward into the waters of Block Island Sound at about the same average rate that Mohegan's Bluffs are being diminished.

Rolling green moorlands stretch away along the top of Mohegan's Bluffs. In agricultural times open fields extended to the edge of the cliffs, but with the abandonment of the farmlands roughly a century ago, a dense cover of maritime shrubs invaded the heights. This broad carpet of bayberry, blueberry, wild rose, sweet pepperbush, and other moorland plants prevents erosion at the top of the bluffs. But on the steep face of the cliffs themselves no plant can long maintain a roothold against the shearing ocean winds and the battering ocean waves of Atlantic gales.

Remarks: *The historic Southeast Light, built in 1874, stands at the scenic overlook off Southeast Road. East of here is a second scenic overlook, also off Southeast Road. Block Island is a popular summer vacation resort. Hotels, cottages, and guest houses provide the majority of the island's lodging accommodations. There are no overnight campgrounds, and camping on beaches and other areas is prohibited by law. Ferry reservations for cars must be made several months in advance for the popular vacation period of mid-June to Labor Day. Those without cars can rent bicycles, mopeds, and cars (in summer) on the island. Block Island State Beach, located on Corn Neck Rd. north of Old Harbor on the east side of the island, offers saltwater swimming.*

21.
Gay Head
Cliffs

Directions: **Martha's Vineyard, Mass. Follow directions for #22 to Vineyard Haven. Take Main St. southwest to West Tisbury, then South Rd. to Chilmark, then State Rd. to the town of Gay Head, about 15 miles in all. The cliffs are 0.7 mile west of town. Parking on the roadside at top of the cliffs.**

Ownership: **Town of Gay Head.**

On the western end of Martha's Vineyard is a mile-long section of multicolored cliffs rising as much as 150 feet above the sea. These cliffs mark the end of the Wisconsin glacier some 12,000 years ago, and are known as the terminal moraine. It was here that the rocks and soils that had been picked up and carried across New England by the ice finally came to rest.

When the ice melted, many different sands, clays, and gravels were deposited here, built up in layers upon one another. This has produced the striking color variations—the white, red, gray, black, and yellow pastel shades—that can be seen on the cliff face. Many of these materials are relics of the Cretaceous period, some 75 million years ago, and are older than any deposits on Cape Cod. They sit on the continental shelf itself, a crystalline basement complex of metamorphic and igneous rock that lies about 770 feet below sea level.

Remarks: *The cliffs are especially beautiful at sunset, when the light plays off the various colors, but in summer the site is usually crowded at this time. Erosion of the cliffs is a problem, so don't walk near the edge.*

22.
Felix Neck
Wildlife Sanctuary

Directions: Vineyard Haven, Mass. Martha's Vineyard can be reached by plane and by ferry from Woods Hole, Hyannis, or Falmouth Heights on Cape Cod, or from New Bedford, Mass. For information and reservations, call Woods Hole or Hyannis, (617) 540-2022; Falmouth Heights, (617) 548-4800; New Bedford, (617) 997-1653. Best service is from Woods Hole; from Boston take I-93 south to Route 3 and cross the Sagamore Bridge onto Cape Cod. Take U.S. 6 southwest about 5 miles; turn south (left) onto Route 28 about 15 miles. At Falmouth, turn right (south) onto Woods Hole Rd. and go about 3 miles to the ferry.

From Main St. in Vineyard Haven center, turn west (right) on South Main St. and take your immediate left onto Edgartown Rd. Go south 4.5 miles to the sanctuary entrance on the left.

Ownership: Massachusetts Audubon Society.

The Felix Neck Wildlife Sanctuary forms a rich tapestry of coastal habitats for a wide variety of wildlife. More than 100 species of native wild birds have been sighted including resident mallard ducks and nesting pairs of the spectacular water hawk, the osprey. This 350-acre sanctuary occupies the "neck" of land jutting into Sengekontacket Pond, which lies on the eastern shore of Martha's Vineyard Island. Sengekontacket, meaning "salty waters," is a great salt pond that is almost entirely enclosed from Nantucket Sound by a narrow strip of beach in the east. Six miles of hiking trails explore portions of Sengekontacket's western beach and salt marshes (see **#29**), as well as the sanctuary's adjoining upland meadows, oak-pine forest, shrub thickets, cattail marsh, and brackish waterfowl ponds.

The self-guiding Jessica Hancock Trail—one of four major hiking trails at Felix Neck—provides the best vantage point from which to see the ospreys that nest at the sanctuary. This short route winds through many different ecological communities found across Martha's Vineyard as a whole. Take the orange trail from the sanctuary's visitor center by following color-coded signposts, and turn right at the first fork in the path at the marker for the Hancock Trail.

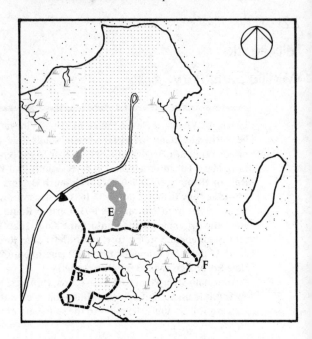

At **A**, the trail wanders through an edge community where plants common to meadow, woodland, and wetland environments are intermingled. Highbush blueberry, bayberry, and wild pasture rose thrive here in the open sunlight, forming a dense shrub thicket. Further ahead, black cherry, sassafras, and old pear and apple trees (see **#74**) grow along an abandoned fencerow, surviving from the time when Felix Neck was a working farm. These species are characteristic of agricultural lands that are reverting to forest along the southern New England seacoast (see **#60**).

Go left at the next trail fork to **B**, where a small glacial pond, or kettle hole (see **#99**), hosts bog plants like sphagnum moss, Virginia chain fern, native cranberry, sedges, and other acid-loving species that favor the nutrient-poor conditions typical of the bog environment. These plants are spearheading the ecological succession of this wet hollow into dry land (see **#56**).

The trail passes through a forest grove of redcedar and pitch pine, and then crosses a wooded red-maple swamp (see **#13**), where members of the heath family, such as swamp azalea and sheep laurel, have established themselves in the understory. At **C**, the trail emerges at the salt-marsh edge. Marsh elder, seaside goldenrod, swamp milkweed, and sea lavender grow in the rich organic marsh soils that are produced by decaying plants and animals.

The trail turns inland from the salt marsh and weaves through a succession of other distinct biological environments, including oak forest, pastureland, and a freshwater cattail marsh. At **D** it arrives in a grassy meadow, which hosts an assortment of flowering plants common to open fields—evening primrose, black-eyed Susan, goldenrod, bramble, and pokeweed. This meadow provides a view of the ospreys, which may be seen in late spring and summer on the manmade nesting platforms that stand on the hilltop to the left of the trail.

These nesting platforms, which imitate the high tree roosts favored by this species, have been placed here to induce these large predatory birds to breed at the sanctuary. The osprey's nest, like that of the bald eagle, is an imposing structure built of sticks. Ospreys usually return to their nesting sites year after year, adding to the nests until they reach astoundingly large proportions. This species always nests along seacoasts, rivers, or inland lakes, for its diet consists almost entirely of fish.

Felix Neck offers a stable breeding ground that is safe from land development and even natural catastrophes like floods. The maintenance of this habitat is an important responsibility of wildlife management groups, since the osprey has been in serious jeopardy in the last several decades. In the 1950s DDT and other pesticides entered the food chain and became stored in the bird's fat deposits, disrupting its calcium metabolism. As a result, the eggs were too soft and broke in the nest. The osprey population suffered a severe decline. It has only begun to recover in recent years after DDT and other toxic chemicals were banned by the federal government.

The osprey resembles the eagle but is smaller, with a wingspread of 5 to 6 feet, as compared with the eagle's wingspan of 6 to 7½ feet. It flies with a distinctive backward crook to its wings, but the most striking feature is the pure white plumage on the underparts. The crown of the head is also white, contrasting with the brown of its upper body. When fishing, it soars high above the air before making a dramatic descent to the water's surface, where it hovers on beating wings until it dives feet first to grasp a fish in its powerful talons. It migrates northward in late spring, nesting and rearing its young throughout the summer. It flies south in October to winter in the Gulf states and points further south (see **#50** and **#99**).

Follow the trail as it returns to the intersection with the orange trail. Go right on the orange trail, which leads to one of the two waterfowl ponds at Felix Neck, then ends a short distance away on the open beach of Sengekontacket. At **E** the waterfowl blind—a small roofed structure—offers a chance to see resident and migratory ducks and geese in the pond. Its brackish waters attract the sanctuary's resident common mallards—large, surface-feeding ducks that inhabit fresh or brackish water. The mallard is one of the most widely distributed ducks in the Northern Hemisphere. It breeds in shallow marshes and beside pools surrounded by tall grasses and herbaceous plants, and generally feeds on water plants like pondweeds and bulrushes. In inland farming regions like the American Midwest, however, mallards often eat agricultural grain corps. They migrate northward quite early in the spring to breed, though at Felix Neck they have become year-round residents.

Continue along the trail to the open beach of Sengekontacket Pond at **F**. Herring and greater black-backed gulls (see **#17** and **#77**) are commonly seen in the sky and water throughout the year, and in winter the pond is frequented by cold-weather ocean ducks and geese.

Southeast of the beach in the middle of the pond is Sarson's Island, which serves as a tern nesting colony at the sanctuary. Terns are ocean birds that resemble gulls, but are much smaller and slighter in build. Most species are white, with black caps. The most common species found on the Massachusetts coast are the least and common terns and, less frequently, the roseate and arctic terns. Occasionally, a pair of terns will stray from the island and nest here on the beach. You may find their nests, which are often no more than scrapes in the sand, roped off by sanctuary personnel to prevent damage to the eggs and nestlings in the early summer (see **#15** and **#23**).

Retrace your steps along the orange trail to the visitor center. Or hike the red trail from its junction with the orange trail at the beach. The red trail follows the edge of the salt marsh and then winds through an oak-pine forest, where it connects with the yellow trail. A right turn on the yellow trail takes you to the tip of the Felix Neck peninsula, where a branch trail on the right leads to a photography blind on the edge of Sengekontacket Pond. A left turn on the yellow trail returns to the visitor center by way of the sanctuary's other waterfowl pond.

Remarks: *The Jessica Hancock Trail is a 30- to 45-minute hike over easy terrain. Numbered trail signs are keyed to an interpretative pamphlet that is available at the visitor center for a small fee. This is an excellent hike for younger children. The hiking circuit that follows the orange, red, and yellow trails is a 90-minute hike over easy terrain. Trail maps for these routes, as well as for four one-way branch trails that radiate off the yellow trail, are available at the visitor center. The center also features wildlife exhibits, including freshwater and saltwater aquariums that display native fish, bivalves, amphibians, and reptiles. A nature library and reference library are located on the second floor. There are several buildings open to the public where injured waterfowl and raptors are housed. Felix Neck, which is open throughout the year, is the most accessible of the wildlife refuges and conservation areas on Martha's Vineyard. If you don't have a car, you can reach the sanctuary by bicycle or moped in less than an hour from any of the island's three major towns: Oak Bluffs, Vineyard Haven, and Edgartown.*

23.

Cape Poge
Wildlife Refuge and
Wasque Reservation

Directions: Edgartown, Mass. To reach Martha's Vineyard, see #22. From Main St. in Vineyard Haven, take South Main St. 0.2 mile to Edgartown Rd. on the left. Go about 7 miles to Main St. in Edgartown, and follow it to North Water St. on the left. At the end of the road is the terminal for the Chappaquiddick ferry. Take the ferry and follow Chappaquiddick Rd. for 2.4 miles to its junction with Dyke Rd. (dirt). Go straight on Dyke Rd. for 0.7 mile to the entrance of the Cape Poge Wildlife Refuge. For Wasque, continue south on Chappaquiddick Rd. for 2.1 miles to the reservation entrance at the end.

Ownership: Trustees of Reservations.

Cape Poge Wildlife Refuge and nearby Wasque Reservation together encompass a vast coastal wilderness area on the eastern coast of Chappaquiddick Island at Martha's Vineyard. The 200-acre Wasque Reservation includes flat moorland and low sand cliffs on the island's southwest point, which borders Katama Bay and Nantucket Sound. From Wasque Point's eastern shore the long, narrow barrier beach of Cape Poge stretches northward for more than 4 miles in the waters off Chappaquiddick. The 484-acre wildlife refuge embraces a huge parcel of the barrier beach, including frontage on Poucha Pond and Cape Poge Bay. Its extensive ocean beach, sand dunes, salt marshes, tidal flats, and cedar thickets provide habitat for thousands of sea and shore birds. The remote peninsula of Little Neck on Cape Poge's northeast shore is nesting territory for snowy egrets, black-crowned night herons, Canada geese, and terns.

Cape Poge and Wasque are both important nesting areas for least and common terns. Terns are small, black-capped birds, with slender wings and forked tails, which look like diminutive versions of their larger relatives the gulls. The four tern species found in Massachusetts are the least and common terns and, less frequently, the roseate and arctic terns. The delicacy and gracefulness of the terns belie their great aerial prowess and, in the arctic tern, a capacity for long-distance flight on transpolar migrations that is unrivaled among birds. The arctic tern winters in Antarctica and flies north 11,000 miles to its primary nesting territory in the Arctic tundra. A few nest as far south as Massachusetts. The other three terns found in the state are less ambitious, wintering only as far south as the eastern coast of South America and flying north in spring to breed along the North Atlantic beaches.

Terns, like gulls, are colonial seabirds. Depending on the species, their nesting colonies may number hundreds or thousands of birds. Nesting within large colonies affords the birds protection through sheer numbers, and makes it easier for them to find food by following the flock. Tern nests are small, open depressions called "scrapes," scratched into the sand or stones of a beach near the high-tide line. The birds usually nest in areas where vegetation is scarce, so they can more easily watch over their young chicks and sight predators. Rats, skunks, seagulls, and large birds like owls or hawks prey upon the eggs and young chicks. The intrusion of outsiders, including humans, into the colony brings shrill cries of alarm from the birds, which often attempt to fend off a predator by striking at it with their pointed bills.

Terns show a high rate of mortality for the young. Studies show that up to 8 percent of the chicks hatched in a colony do not survive the first year. Predation, severe weather, and lack of food are the major causes of death. But terns, like most ocean birds, have long life-spans, averaging 12 years. A mating pair need to raise only two or three offspring to adulthood during their lives to maintain population stability.

Yet the tern colonies along the New England coast have declined to seriously low levels in recent years. The loss of suitable nesting habitat is a major reason for this population threat. Development of New England's beaches for recreation has displaced some tern colonies. Another major factor is the dramatic population explosion of the herring gull within roughly the last 50 years (see **#17**). Herring gulls compete with terns for nesting sites on beaches. At these refuge properties and others in New England, there are efforts currently under way to stop the population decline. Protection of the nesting colony itself is an important part of this work. At Cape Poge and Wasque the nesting areas have been fenced off to prevent unwitting humans walking or driving along the beaches from injuring the sandy-colored tern eggs and chicks.

The two common tern species nesting at Cape Poge and Wasque Point look very much alike, with their white breasts, gray wings, and black caps. The distinguishing features are their size and the color of their bills. The 15-inch-long common tern has an orange-red bill with a black tip; the smaller, 9-inch-long least tern has a yellow bill. The less common roseate tern has a pinkish cast to its white breast in the breeding season, and a mostly black bill. The arctic tern has a deep red bill and legs. Least and common terns fish for mackerel, sand launces, and pipefish along the shallow waters of the beaches.

Remarks: *Terns nest in colonies during late spring and summer. Because human intrusion threatens the young chicks, a colony should be observed only from a discreet distance with the aid of binoculars. Signs and fences mark the location of nests. Bird-watchers should consult the Cape Poge refuge superintendent for the current status of the tern colonies. Hiking is difficult in these vast and sandy reservations. It is preferable to drive an oversand (four-wheel drive) vehicle along the various soft-sand beach roads; obtain a permit to do so from the Cape Poge superintendent.*

Poucha Pond is a waterfowl habitat, which lies close to the entrance of Cape Poge and is accessible by foot. Species include black duck, Canada goose, goldeneye, merganser, bufflehead, and bluebill. Surfcasting for blue-fish and striped bass is permitted at both properties. The reservations are open all year, daily, from sunrise to sunset. For more information contact the Trustees of Reservations, 224 Adam Street, Milton, Mass. 02186; (617) 698-2066.

Nearby Place
of Interest

Long Point Wildlife Refuge, West Tisbury: **Take the West Tis-bury Rd. west from Edgartown center and turn left onto Deep Bottom Rd. past the airport entrance. Drive south** on Deep Bottom Rd. and follow the refuge signs to the parking area.

This 580-acre reservation situated on the south coast of Martha's Vineyard has shore frontage on Tisbury Great Pond, Middle Point Cove, Long Cove, and the Atlantic Ocean. Swimming, surf fishing, and picnicking are allowed. The reservation is open daily in summer, on weekends and holidays only in late spring and early fall. Owned by the Trustees of Reservations.

24.

Coskata-Coatue
Wildlife Refuge

Directions: Nantucket, Mass. Nantucket Island can be reached by plane and by ferry from the same points as for Martha's Vineyard; see #22. From Nantucket center, take Orange St. east to the first traffic circle, where Milestone Rd. leads east for about 0.3 mile to Polpis Rd. Turn northeast (left) and go about 4.5 miles. Turn north (left) onto Wauwinet Rd.; follow it to the refuge entrance at the end.

Ownership: Trustees of Reservations.

The long and curving sands of Coskata-Coatue rise from North Atlantic waters to form the northeastern "hook" of historic Nantucket Island. This remote barrier-beach complex, which lies some 35 miles to sea south of Cape Cod, is one of the most isolated coastal wilderness areas in southern New England waters. The wildlife refuge encompasses 963 acres of sandy beaches, dunes, salt marsh, oak forest, and shrubby, windblown moors, stretching across the two interlocked barrier beaches of Coskata and Coatue, which together comprise an area of more than 1,200 acres.

Nantucket was created more than 11,000 years ago from sediments stripped from the New England mainland by ice-age glaciers descending from the far north. Since that time the sea has continued to shape this beautiful island, which the Indians named Nantucket, or "Land Far Out to Sea." Coskata and Coatue are two long fingers of sand that have been formed within the last several thousand years. Their sands were once part of Nantucket's eastern headlands, which over many centuries were worn away by the repeated assaults of storm waves. Carried northward by longshore currents in the waters off the eastern shore, these eroded sands came to rest on the bottom of the sea off the northeastern coast at Wauwinet. Eventually enough sand was deposited by the currents for a newly created sandbar to rise above sea level: the beach of Coskata. Today Coskata extends from Wauwinet north for roughly 5 miles to its outermost tip at Great Point, a virtually waterlocked landmark between the open Atlantic and Nantucket Sound.

The hook of Great Point looks northward over dangerous waters concealing the treacherous Nantucket Shoals—the drowned remnants of lost islands and new lands in the making that have yet to surface above the sea. The southern portion of these shoals, which stretch between Monomoy Island off Cape Cod's southeastern coast and Great Point, is called Point Rip. This is the underwater continuation of Coskata, over which the Great Point Lighthouse has flashed its beacon as a warning to mariners for more than a century.

The sands that made Great Point and Point Rip also created Coatue. The formation of Great Point changed the direction of the longshore currents, which follow the shore; where they once flowed northward, they shifted to the southwest. The sands carried by the currents began to accumulate along Coskata's western shoreline, which eventually grew into the baymouth bar we call Coatue. This shifting bar runs roughly parallel to Nantucket's northern coast, enclosing its large harbor from the waters of Nantucket Sound. Graceful, archlike coves indent its entire southern beach; these were produced by the ceaseless activity of tidal currents moving beach sands in opposing directions.

Though the soils of Coskata-Coatue are poor and sandy, some hardy plants thrive here. You will find American beach grass, poverty grass, and the prickly-pear cactus (*Opuntia humifusa*), normally found in the southeastern United States. The only cactus growing in the eastern United States, the prickly pear is recorded at only a few other isolated sites within New England, chiefly at Cape Cod. Like the deserts of the American West where many types of cacti grow, the porous beach sands here lack the tills and clays necessary for the retention of water at the root zone. However, this is ideal habitat for the prickly-pear cactus. It can survive exceptionally dry conditions because of a unique evolutionary adaptation that allows it to store water over long periods of drought. Whereas most plants lose moisture by evaporation through their foliage, cacti have leafless green stems that perform the function of photosynthesis normally carried out by leaves. The fleshy stems are ribbed, allowing the plant to swell like a sponge when water is available. The prickly spines evolved to protect the succulent plant from animal predators seeking water in arid environments. The spines also shade the stems and absorb some moisture from morning dew. At Coatue, the prickly-pear cacti form green clumps that hug the sands of low dunes. Tiny yellow flowers bloom in late June and early July.

Many of the northern plant species growing on Nantucket appear in the somewhat moister shrub forests of the moors. The history of Nantucket's moors is one of the more revealing segments in the story of the island's natural development. Prior to English settlement of Nantucket during the seventeenth century, the island was forested with large oaks and pine. This original woodland was swiftly cut to obtain timber and to clear land for pasture; and for several hundred years sheep were grazed across Nantucket's treeless "Commons," as the moors are known locally. Agricultural decline later triggered the reforestation of the abandoned pastures, which has produced the shrubby moorland of low vegetation—including bayberry and blueberry—that persists today. Strong ocean winds, sterile soils, and perhaps a lack of sufficient mature trees for seed distribution have prevented the growth of large trees across the moors. Nantucket's Commons, which resemble the ancient heathlands of Great Britain far more than any plant community found in North America, represent the only extensive region of moorland in New England, with the exception of Rhode Island's Block Island (see #18).

Fittingly, the island is the only place in New England where Scotch heather (*Calluna vulgaris*), the common shrub of Britain's moors, has become completely naturalized in the wild. Introduced by humans to Nantucket in the last century, this lovely, ground-hugging plant carpets the moors at Coskata with tiny, pinkish-purple flowers in late summer. The flowers form spikes at the end of the stems, which grow as a low, bushy mound of yellowish-green foliage.

A very small colony of gray seals inhabits Nantucket Harbor and the beaches of Coskata-Coatue. This species occurs in far greater numbers in the Gulf of St. Lawrence and north to Labrador. Gray seals are believed to have been more abundant along the southern New England coast in the past, and this colony may be a remnant herd. The gray seal is large, the male measuring as long as 10 feet and the female 7½ feet. Its coat is dark gray above and somewhat lighter below, and dark spotting and other color variations are common. A social animal, the gray seal appears in groups, and its breeding colonies in the far north can number as many as nine hundred individuals. It can dive to depths up to almost 500 feet, remaining submerged for as much as 20 minutes in search of fish. It eats cod, flounder, pollock and cuttlefish as well as crustaceans, squid, and mollusks. Often the seals climb out of the water to bask on sandy beaches and on ledges in rocky coastal areas.

The western black-tailed jackrabbit is the most unexpected of Nantucket's wildlife, for this is an animal of the American West. The Nantucket Sportsmen Club imported the jackrabbit from Kansas in 1925 to run to the hounds in the style of an English fox hunt, for no foxes were to be found here. The black-tailed jackrabbit is the most common and abundant rabbit of the Great Plains, where its natural habitat consists of prairie, meadows, and barren lands where the vegetation cover is low. It has adapted well to Nantucket's dunes and moors, though little is known about its biology on the island. The black-tailed jackrabbit is impossible to mistake because of its large size—up to 22¾ inches long as compared with the 14 to 18 inches of the eastern and the New England cottontails. This jackrabbit's huge, black-tipped ears, as well as its powerful hind legs and large feet, are also distinctive. It can hop 5 to 10 feet in a single leap, and when frightened, as much as 20 feet, and it can run at speeds as high as 35 miles per hour over short distances.

Coskata-Coatue is an excellent bird-watching area. Black ducks, mallards, and Canada geese feed in the shallows along the refuge's beaches, while diving ducks such as scoter, goldeneye, eider, canvasback, scaup, bufflehead, and ringneck flock offshore. Shore birds include the curlew, oystercatcher, and great blue heron. Common and least terns nest on the beach. Great Point serves as a pelagic lookout, and it is also a popular fishing spot for bluefish and striped bass.

Coskata Pond, a tidal estuary, serves as a habitat for cunner, white flounder and white hake, as well as bay scallops, quahogs, and softshell clams. One of Nantucket's scattered stands of oak forest grows on the uplands around Coskata Pond, which in the north borders salt marshes. White-tailed deer may be seen here.

Remarks: *The refuge has no hiking trails, and walking is difficult because of soft sands and lack of shade. Access to both Coskata and Coatue is by sandy beach roads that are suitable for oversand (four-wheel drive) vehicles only. These roads allow visitors to drive to various points throughout the refuge, which can then be more enjoyably explored on foot. The distance from the refuge entrance to Great Point is approximately 5 miles. The refuge is open all year. To drive on the roads, you must obtain a permit from the refuge manager on the property. For more information contact the Trustees of Reservations, 224 Adam Street, Milton, Mass. 02186; (617) 698-2066. Coskata-Coatue Wildlife Refuge borders two adjoining parcels that are open to the public: Coatue Wildlife Refuge, a 348-acre tract occupies the south-*

western half of Coatue beach and is owned by the Nantucket Conservation Foundation (see Nearby Places of Interest, below), and a 40-acre property at the tip of Great Point owned by the U.S. Fish and Wildlife Service.

Nearby Places of Interest

Nantucket Island: Once a legendary nineteenth-century whaling port immortalized in the pages of Herman Melville's *Moby Dick*, the island of Nantucket is today an exclusive summer vacation resort catering to tourists. To some extent, its historic sites and saltwater recreational activities have overshadowed its exceptional opportunities for nature exploration. With as much as one-quarter of the total island protected from commercial and housing development, Nantucket has an abundance of conservation areas, wildlife refuges, state forest lands, and other protected natural areas.

The Nantucket Conservation Foundation is the largest property holder of these protected lands. As of 1982, it had acquired more than 5,728 acres, or 18 percent of all land on the island. Many of these areas are open to the public for nature study, picnicking, hiking, and sightseeing, though no overnight camping is permitted. Some foundation properties are currently under planning for trail development and other uses compatible with nature study. A few of the properties owned by the foundation are described below.

The 109-acre Eel Point Reservation is a hook of land overlooking Madaket Harbor on the northwest end of Nantucket. It has extensive dunes and marshlands, where fish, shellfish, and crustaceans are found in abundance. From Nantucket center, take Madaket Rd. west to Eel Point Rd. on the right.

The 737-acre Cranberry Bog is one of the largest bogs of its kind in New England. To reach it, take Milestone Rd. east from the first traffic rotary off Orange St., east of Nantucket center. The 513-acre Larsen Acres, located on the south side of Milestone Rd., is a remote tract of moorland bordering the south coast of the island. The 189-acre Pocomo Meadows and Medouie Marsh include two parcels with waterfront on Polpis and Nantucket harbors. They are located east of Nantucket center off Wauwinet Rd. For more information on these properties, call, write, or visit Nantucket Conservation Foundation, Inc., 118 Cliff Rd., Nantucket, Mass. 02554; (617) 228-2884.

Overnight accommodations on Nantucket include hotels and guest houses; there are no campgrounds. Lodgings must be reserved far in advance for the peak vacation season of July and August. Off-season rates for lodging are generally lower. For information on lodgings and transportation, contact the Nantucket Chamber of Commerce, (617) 228-1700.

25.

Lowell Holly
Reservation

Directions: Mashpee, Mass. From Boston, take I-93 and Route 3 to the Sagamore Bridge onto Cape Cod, about 50 miles. From there go 4 miles east on U.S. 6 to Exit 2. Turn south onto Route 130; go 7.3 miles to South Sandwich Rd. Turn left and go 0.7 mile to the entrance on the left. Follow the dirt road to the parking lot.

Ownership: Trustees of Reservations.

Lowell Holly Reservation is on a wooded peninsula between two of the largest freshwater ponds on Cape Cod. Several scenic trails pass through different woodland habitats, including outstanding examples of native rhododendron and American holly trees.

Beginning at **A** the trail, which is marked with white circles on trees, follows an old road past the largest of the holly trees on the reservation. The American holly is closely associated with the somewhat more southerly sand-plain community and is here very close to the northern limit of its range. A Coastal Plain species that in this region occupies sandy habitats similar to those found farther south, the American holly requires moist soil conditions combined with the warmer temperatures found near the ocean. It is recognized by its leathery, spiny evergreen leaves and the distinctive red berries of the

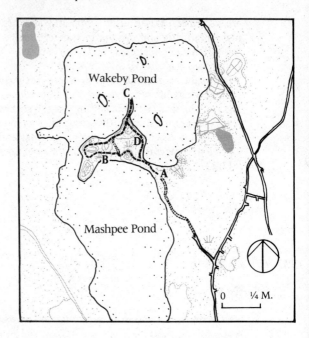

female. Although it is usually an understory tree, these examples are about 40 feet tall, the upper limit of its size.

The trail continues into the woods, which are dominated by beech, pitch pine, red maple, and white oak, all of which do well in the sandy but moist soil, then rises to the ridge of the hummock that forms the peninsula. Notice (**B**) the proliferation of lichens (see **#88**) and mosses, particularly pincushion moss, on the rocks here. The shade provided by the thick canopy of trees, as well as the omnipresent moisture, comprise an ideal habitat for these species. The Wheeler Loop Trail, which is marked with triangles painted on trees, leads through a large stand of pitch pines. The ample water supply has enabled these trees to reach particularly great heights.

Continuing around the peninsula, you will come to a trail marked with squares leading out to a sandy spit of land (**C**). Blueberry, huckleberry, and ferns grow well close to the water's edge. Passing through a grove of large beech trees, you will reach the tip of this small peninsula, most likely built up by deposits from the Wisconsin glacier as it receded about 10–15,000 years ago (see **Long Island, Cape Cod, and the Islands**).

Returning to the main trail, follow it downhill as it passes through large and dense clusters of rhododendron (**D**). Some of these plants grow as high as 15 feet due to the ideal moisture and sandy soil conditions; they blossom between mid-May and early June. The trail continues along the edge of the pond, through fern glens and more beech groves. Holly trees, younger and smaller than those found at the beginning, are scattered throughout, accompanied by more rhododendrons. Rejoin the main entry trail here, which returns to the parking area.

Remarks: *The walk is approximately 1 hour over easy terrain. Camping, fishing, hiking, and other activities are available at Cape Cod National Seashore (see* **Cape Cod National Seashore**).

26.
Stony Brook
Herring Run

Directions: **Brewster, Mass. From Boston, take I-93 and Route 3 to the Sagamore Bridge onto Cape Cod, about 50 miles. From there go 21 miles east on U.S. 6 to Exit 9, then 4 miles north on Route 134. Turn east (right) on Route 6A; after about 0.8 mile branch right onto Stony Brook Rd. Follow it about 2 miles to a small roadside parking lot across from the Stony Brook Grist Mill.**

Ownership: **Town of Brewster.**

For thousands of years the Atlantic herring, known to science as *Clupea harengus* and to local people as the alewife, has enacted a yearly spectacle in which instinct, physical struggle, and predatory violence are joined within a natural ritual of death and regeneration. Each spring thousands upon thousands of these fish migrate inland from the Atlantic up streams and tidal creeks along the eastern seaboard. Driven by a homing instinct to return to their birthplaces in interior freshwater ponds, the alewives embark upon a fierce struggle against powerful currents and predators to spawn a new generation of young in these ancestral inland waters. This upstream migration, and the subsequent downstream journey of parent and young back to the sea, embodies the universal urge of all species to survive.

Stony Brook Herring Run is one of Cape Cod's best-known and most accessible herring runs. The small reservation (also known as Stony Brook Mill Site) includes a number of ponds and portions of Stony Brook, with its lovely fishways, seining pool, waterfall, and tree-lined hiking paths. Stony Brook is also the site of a historic 1877 grist mill, the last survivor in a succession of early water-powered mills dating back to 1633 that stood in this area.

The alewife is known as a herring on Cape Cod, though it goes by a variety of local names throughout its range from Newfoundland to the Carolina coasts. Although the alewife is a member of the herring family, it should not be confused with the sea herring. The alewife species is known as an anadromous fish, like shad (see **#43**) and salmon, which means that it migrates inland to breed in fresh water but spends the rest of its life in the ocean. The sea herring, on the other hand, is a completely saltwater fish. Unlike the sea herring, the alewife is not especially prized as a source of food; in past centuries it was more commonly used as a source of fertilizer for raising crops.

The alewife is largely a plankton eater. It is a swift swimmer and measures 10 to 13 inches as an adult, the female being slightly larger than the male. The fish begin to breed at the age of 3 or 4; and generally spawn a maximum of three times. By analyzing an alewife's silver-gray scales, naturalists can tell how many times it has spawned.

The annual spring migration of the alewives begins roughly at the vernal equinox, when the sun crosses the equator and day and night are of equal duration. The adult fish initially congregate in schools in the brackish water at the confluence of freshwater streams and saltwater inlets or bays, awaiting the moment when the temperature of the fresh water exceeds that of the ocean. This warming of the inland waters, which on Cape Cod occurs sometime between mid-April and late May, depending upon the severity of the winter, is essential to the incubation of the alewives' eggs and thus triggers the commencement of their upstream navigation. At first only a few fish venture up the streams and tidal creeks. Gradually, increasingly larger schools appear, until the peak migration period sees the freshwater channels flooded with wave upon wave of shimmering alewives.

At Stony Brook the alewives arrive from Cape Cod Bay and enter Paine's Creek, a tidal stream that weaves through salt marshes and forms the lower reaches of Stony Brook. The appearance of the fish attracts a multitude of predators, including gulls, herons, and eels. Herring gulls (see **#17** and **#77**) are the most numerous and voracious. They flock upon the creek banks and circle in the air above the water's surface, following the alewives for the entire length of

Stony Brook's course from the bay to its headwaters at the inland ponds by Stony Brook Grist Mill.

Other hazards also take their toll on the alewives. Some fish stray into secondary channels, from which they are unable to escape. Some die from exhaustion or from physical injuries resulting from obstacles in their paths in the streambed. Still others become hopelessly trapped in crevices between rocks or other debris.

Moving upstream from the sea, the alewives face an increasingly stiffer current of foaming white water as they near the fishways in the old mill-site area of the reservation. The fishways are designed to facilitate the swift movement of the alewives from one pool to the next one higher up the fish ladder, which, in effect, graduates the natural uphill slope of the brook. The water plunging down the fishways is controlled from a sluice gate in a dam located upstream at the outlet of Stony Brook's headwaters. This gate regulates the volume of water: if the flow of water is set either too high or too low, it can impede the upstream progress of the fish as they ascend the fishway. Alewives do not leap from pool to pool up the fish ladder like salmon, but rather swim vigorously through the rushing water.

The first series of fish ladders at Stony Brook is located on the downstream (north) side of Stony Brook Rd., opposite the grist mill. This portion of the brook briefly forks into two channels, which include the fish ladder and a waste stream. The fishways here vary in size, but on average are about 2 feet deep. Pathways hug the edges of the fish ladder, and several footbridges span the waste stream, providing an opportunity to watch the alewives either climb the ladders or return to the sea down the waste stream.

The upstream (south) side of the herring run lies to the east of Stony Brook Grist Mill. Behind the mill are the ponds that form the headwaters of the brook and the destination of the spawning fish. The largest of these interconnected bodies of water—Lower Mill Pond, Upper Mill Pond, and Walker Pond—are located successively southward from the mill. Before the alewives can reach these ponds as they migrate upstream, however, they must mount a short fish ladder after emerging from the brook as it passes beneath the road. The fish ladder leads to the seining pool, from which the alewives were once harvested with nets before they reached the ponds. Beyond the seining pool, the fishway extends for the final stretch of the run to the outlet of Lower Mill Pond. This straight ladder is 20 feet long, with pools measuring about 4½ feet in diameter and 28 inches deep. This ladder is the last hurdle for the spawning alewives before they enter the ponds to deposit their eggs.

The placid freshwater ponds serve as incubators and nurseries for the young alewives. The adult female deposits between 60,000 and 100,000 eggs in the ponds, which the male quickly covers with milt (the secretion from its reproductive glands). Many of these billions of eggs are rapidly devoured by suckerfish. Yet millions of eggs survive, and within 3 to 6 days after they have been deposited, small alewives are hatched in the warm, fresh waters. Tiny schools of fish flit shadowlike through the dappling pond waters. Many are eaten by larger, freshwater fish, as well as frogs, herons, kingfishers, and other predators. But many others live to journey to the sea.

By the time the inland migration of the adult alewives has begun to wane in late May, the earliest spawners have begun the return passage to the ocean. The first week of June usually sees more alewives going downstream than swimming inland, and this mass exodus to Cape Cod Bay will increase as the month goes on.

By midsummer, the adult alewives have left the ponds at Stony Brook, and the odyssey of millions of young alewives is fully under way. Their migration to the bay will stretch throughout the summer and fall, as late as November. During this period the young alewives heading seaward become larger, growing to a length of about 5 inches. These late migrants are better suited for surviving the rigors of the sea than the earlier small fry. Now they must face new dangers, including predatory saltwater fish. Those alewives that survive for the next 3 or 4 years will then have to navigate again the currents of Stony Brook to fulfill the ancient cycle of spawning and sacrifice.

Remarks: *Alewives can be seen in varying numbers at Stony Brook for about 7 months of the year, from mid-April to November. There is no formal trail system, but you can roam the paths and bridges of the mill site and the herring run. Both the downstream (north) area of the fishway and, across Stony Brook, the upstream (south) portion that includes the seining pool, fish ladder, Lower Mill Pond, and the grist mill, are open to the public. A fuller account of Stony Brook's alewife migration may be found in* The Run *(1959), an outstanding book by John Hay. Stony Brook Grist Mill operates in the summer months as a working museum, complete with churning waterwheel fed by a wooden sluice.*

Nearby Place of Interest

Wing Island and the Cape Cod Museum of Natural History: **Wing Island is located on Route 6A in Brewster, about 1½ miles west of the junction of Routes 6A and 137. The**

Cape Cod Museum of Natural History is located a short distance east of Wing Island.

If you want to view the alewife migrations downstream of Stony Brook Herring Run near the watercourse's mouth at Cape Cod Bay, Wing Island and the Cape Cod Museum of Natural History offer several nature trails. The John Wing Trail on Wing Island is a 1⅓-mile, or 60- to 90-minute, hike through salt marsh, bay beach, and upland forest, bordering on the mouth of Paine's Creek (the lower reaches of Stony Brook). The trail originates at a small roadside parking lot and branches off in two directions a short distance beyond its starting point. The branch on the right leads to the mouth of the brook on the bay. A map of Wing Island is posted on a display board at the head of the trail. Visitors are permitted to park at the nearby parking lot of the Cape Cod Museum if the town lot is filled to capacity.

The Cape Cod Museum of Natural History has two nature walks through marshes and upland forest. The South Trail begins opposite the main museum grounds on the south side of Route 6A. It winds through marshland, abandoned cranberry bogs (see #31), and a hardwood forest of tupelo and beech. The North Trail is a short loop on the bay side of the museum grounds. It skirts salt marsh and creek, wandering through stands of tupelo and sassafras trees. The museum also has a wide array of natural-history displays and live-animal exhibits, scheduled lectures, and special nature programs.

27.

Wellfleet Bay
Wildlife Sanctuary

Directions: South Wellfleet, Mass. From Boston, take I-93 and Route 3 to the Sagamore Bridge onto Cape Cod, about 50 miles. Follow U.S. 6 east and north for 38 miles to North Eastham. The entrance to the sanctuary is 3.8 miles farther along U.S. 6, on the left.

Ownership: Massachusetts Audubon Society.

Wellfleet Bay Wildlife Sanctuary features an outstanding array of bird, animal, and plant life in a diverse coastal environment. This popular 720-acre preserve encompasses upland forest, moorland, a freshwater pond, and bay beach. The chief attraction, however, is Wellfleet Bay itself, a broad estuary (see **#59** and **#72**) sheltered from Cape Cod Bay by a barrier of islands and bars. The salt marsh and tidal flats of the estuary offer an abundant source of food for marine life, birds, and animals, since they serve as a nursery for fish and such invertebrates as mollusks and crustaceans (see **#29** for marsh formation). The rich supplies of vegetation and marine animals attract migrating shorebirds and waterfowl following the Atlantic flyway down the East Coast (see **#96** on migration). Over 250 birds, including many shore and sea species, have been recorded at Wellfleet Bay.

The Goose Pond Nature Trail, a self-guiding circuit through the sanctuary's varied habitats, provides an excellent opportunity to appreciate both wildlife and a wide sampling of Cape Cod's common flora. It begins at the parking lot on the bay side of the sanctuary office. At **A** it crosses a dike separating Silver Spring Brook (on the left) from the salt marsh (on the right). Here the dike has widened

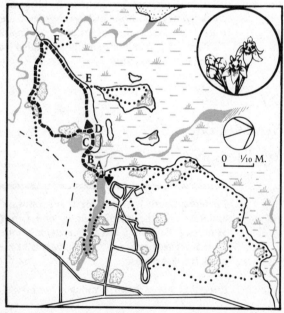

Inset: Swamp milkweed

the brook into a pond. Numerous wetland plants grow along the pond's banks, including swamp milkweed, marsh fern, purple loosestrife, and slender white-poplar trees. White water lilies carpet the pond's surface, and from mid-July to mid-August they are adorned with white blossoms. On the left a path leads from the main trail through a shrub thicket and skirts the edge of the brook, a good spot from which to enjoy the wildlife of the pond.

The snapping turtle is the largest, most formidable predator of the pond, feeding on water plants, carrion fish, and occasionally young waterfowl. Its long tail, large head, and rough, dark-green shell (8 to 18 inches long) distinguish this largest of the region's turtles. The painted turtle is much smaller (4½- to 6-inch shell length) than the "snapper," but more colorful. Its smooth black shell has red and yellow markings, and its black head is yellow-spotted. Look for this wary turtle sunning itself on rocks or brush along the banks.

The pond and adjoining salt marsh attract flocks of redwing blackbirds from March to October. The male is black with distinctive red shoulder patches trimmed in buff-brown; the female and young are brown with many lighter stripes below. Redwings nest in reeds or thickets around marshes and other wetlands from eastern Canada south to Florida and Texas, wintering across the southern United States. Their nests usually consist of grasses and weeds, resting less than 15 feet above the ground in low bushes. Their diet includes salt-marsh plants and weeds, as well as insects during the warmer months.

Return to the main trail at the dike and watch for secretive marsh birds that may emerge from hiding places in the thick cattails. Rails are stout wading birds of coastal marshes and are usually sighted only if they have been alarmed. Disturbed from the marsh reeds, they will fly for a short distance before dropping out of sight again. Rails have weak wings, but strong legs and spreading toes that are developed for running through the reeds to escape danger or to stalk their prey. Of the three species reported at Wellfleet, only the clapper rail nests here and can be seen with any regularity throughout the year. (The smaller Virginia and sora rails are very occasional and limited in number during the summer.) The clapper is one of New England's largest rails, measuring 13½ to 16 inches long. It is grayish-tan on the upper parts, white on the upper throat and on the underside of the short, upturned tail, and has brown wings. Because of its chickenlike appearance as well as its rarity on inland waters, it has been dubbed the mud-hen or salt-marsh hen. It eats small fish and crustaceans, other small marine animals, and parts of water plants. Its range extends north from the Gulf Coast into southern New England.

At **B** the trail winds through an area of upland forest bounding the salt marsh. Norway spruce and red pine were planted here about 50 years ago to stop erosion after the land had been cut clear for farming and then abandoned. Woodland birds seek shelter in the evergreen foliage, while species such as chickadees and nuthatches extract seeds from the cones of Norway spruce for winter food. Another common bird in this woodland is the rufous-sided towhee, which from May to October is one of the most abundant landbirds across the cape. This local nesting species breeds in brushy woodlands, edges of swamps, and old pastures. The towhee is largely a ground bird that scratches in dead leaves for insects, spiders, and worms, as well as consuming wild fruits and various seeds. It is easily recognized by its orange sides and white breast, contrasting sharply with black wings and back on the male, brown on the female. Listen for the song (*Drink your tea-e-e*), which may alert you to the presence of this shy bird.

At **C** the trail emerges at the edge of the marsh and crosses a causeway between Goose Pond and mudflats. Goose Pond is gradually evolving into dry land, a natural process of wetland succession that has been accelerated by storm tides washing sand from the causeway into the pond.

Greater yellowlegs is a common wading bird here during the spring and fall, dabbling with its bill for small fish or probing in the mud for small worms and crustaceans. This large species of sandpiper is the most conspicuous shorebird in the eastern United States. It shows a wingspread of 2 feet as it glides to a landing in the marsh, its distinctive yellow legs extended behind it. It is distinguished from the lesser yellowlegs by both its larger size and voice; its three- or four-syllable *whew-whew-whew* is quite different from the one- or two-note *cu* or *cu-cu* of the lesser. The northern breeding grounds of the yellowlegs extend from Labrador and Hudson Bay south to southern Manitoba and Newfoundland. The birds migrate throughout the United States, wintering from the Carolinas south to the Gulf of Mexico and the Caribbean.

Other common waders here include herons. The great blue heron is common along the coast as well as at inland ponds and rivers, and its long neck, legs, and tapering bill have come to embody our popular conception of herons. The tall, angular great blue (42 to 52 inches long) contrasts with the much smaller green heron (15½ to 22½ inches long). The latter (both male and female) has short yellow legs and a short rusty-brown neck. Its crest, tail, and wings are glossy green, and its back a darker green. This solitary bird is the only heron known to breed at Wellfleet Bay. Its twig nests are commonly built in trees near the water, where it can fish or gather aquatic insects and crustaceans. The green heron winters in southern waters. Other long-billed shorebirds you are likely to see foraging for food in the mud or sands of the tidal flats are short-billed dowitchers (May to October) and semipalmated and least sandpipers (May to September).

The trail leaves the causeway and winds briefly through a shrub thicket of beach plum, highbush blueberry, and shadbush. A short path branches to the right of the trail and takes you to an overlook (**D**) at the edge of the salt marsh. This is a fine vantage point from which to scan the water and sky for waterfowl, especially during migratory seasons in spring and fall. The Canada goose is a familiar Cape Cod migrant, whose numbers peak at several thousand in the spring from about March 15 to April 15 and in the fall from October 10 to November 20. It frequents sand and mudflats, shallow marshes, wet meadows, and spacious freshwater ponds, where it feeds on grasses and marsh plants.

The brant, also seen here, looks somewhat similar to the Canada goose but is much smaller (23 to 30 inches long). Flocks of brants fly in an irregular line rather than in the V-formation of Canada geese. They are generally found in the shallow waters of bays and estuaries, preferring eelgrass as a food. Their spring migration (peaking March 25 to April 30) takes them to the coastal tundra in the lowlands of far northern Canada. They migrate south along the Massachusetts coast and sometimes winter in its ice-free bays. In the fall, brants usually appear in October and peak in November.

The path quickly returns to the main trail, which forks at this point in two directions. Take the trail on the right, which goes straight ahead through a flat stretch of heathlands. Chinkapin oaks, dwarf sumac, and sassafras form low-growing thickets. On the sandy slope of a dune to the trail's left grows a sprawling mat of bearberry, a common Cape Cod heath plant.

At **E** the trail reemerges at the edge of the salt marsh near a cabin. From this point, it skirts the edge of the upper marsh meadow. At high tide the water rises along this stretch of the trail, and foot travel can be difficult. Many saltwater plants of the upper marsh grow here, including beach grass, sea lavender, dwarf wild rose, and salt-meadow cordgrass or high-tide grass (*Spartina patens*). Salt-marsh cordgrass (*Spartina alterniflora*) reaches as high as 4 to 6 feet in the wettest reaches of the marsh to your right (see **#14** and **#77**).

A right turn along this portion of the trail will take you to Try Island during low tide. This small forested island was named for a "try works," which produced oil from whale blubber when Wellfleet was a major whaling center in the nineteenth century. The island is a fine bird-watching site, since it lies further out in the marsh; but hikers who take the trail loop around the island should be alert for rising tides that may strand them by separating them from the mainland.

Further up the main trail is another secondary trail that crosses a footbridge over Hatches Creek to Bay Beach. The approach to the footbridge may become submerged at high tide. (The tide is rising if the stream flows from right to left.)

Around the approach to the footbridge rustling cordgrass at low tide betrays the presence of thousands of fiddler crabs in the tidal flats (**F**). Fiddler crabs are adapted to the environmental stress of salt marshes. Primitive lungs enable fiddlers to submerge without oxygen for long periods, while an ability to control their internal salt balance lets them withstand both high and low salinity levels in different areas of the marsh. There are two species: the sand fiddler digs burrows in the banks of the higher marsh, whereas the mud fiddler burrows in the mudflats. Male fiddlers of both these species have a single large claw, which they wave in the air while standing near the entrances of their burrows at low tide in a mating ritual to attract females during the summer breeding season (see **#46**).

A footpath on the edge of the marsh appears on the left, running parallel to an old roadway that heads inland. Marsh elder, black and salt-marsh grasses occupy this drier upland ground as the footpath begins to lead away from the marsh. Cross the roadway and follow the trail as it wanders through a grove of black-locust trees. Soon it emerges in a sunny, open area where many plants typical of Cape Cod's heathlands can be seen, including broom crowberry, sickle-leaved golden aster, and man's beard grass. Follow the trail as it weaves over the heath and runs for a final stretch through a stand of scrub and black oaks before ending at the fork passed earlier. Go right at the fork, retracing your steps across the Goose Pond causeway and the dike at Silver Spring Brook.

Remarks: *Goose Pond Trail (1½ miles) is a 60-minute hike for the main portion; 90 minutes including the secondary trails to Try Island and Bay Beach. A comprehensive trail booklet is available for a small fee at the sanctuary office. It describes 71 plants, identified by numbered reference markers posted along the route; discusses plants and animal communities; and includes a checklist of over 250 birds. The terrain is easy, but waterproof boots are recommended for the wet-marsh edges and soft-sand areas. Binoculars will aid in the identification and enjoyment of birdlife. Bay View Trail is about a 60-minute loop over easy terrain. This trail ranges eastward from the parking lot along the edge of the salt marsh and then curves inland through pitch-pine woods. Inquire at the sanctuary office for information on guided nature walks in summer and other special programs. Camping (in summer) is restricted to members of the Massachusetts Audubon Society. For information, write: Wellfleet Bay Wildlife Sanctuary, P.O. Box 236, South Wellfleet, Mass. 02663.*

Cape Cod
National Seashore

Directions: **The Cape Cod National Seashore lies along the "forearm" of Cape Cod, and directions to the individual sites that follow are given from Exit 13 on U.S. 6, where Route 28 goes south and U.S. 6 continues north. To reach that point from Boston, take I-95 and Route 3 to the Sagamore Bridge onto Cape Cod, about 50 miles. Follow U.S. 6 east and north about 36 miles to Eastham. Salt Pond Visitor Center, at the National Seashore's southern end, is just north of Eastham on U.S. 6 at Nauset Rd. For the Province Lands Visitor Center at the north end, continue on U.S. 6 another 22 miles past Eastham. At the traffic light in Provincetown (about 2 miles past the sign at the Truro-Provincetown line), turn right onto Race Point Rd. and follow it to the center.**

Ownership: **National Park Service.**

Cape Cod's unique ocean and land geology, plant communities, and wildlife have attracted American naturalists from Henry David Thoreau to Henry Beston, for over two centuries. Today thousands of visitors are drawn to the Cape's shores each year to enjoy its natural features, as well as its rich maritime tradition, classic architecture, and the colorful folklore of its past.

Cape Cod National Seashore was established in 1961 to preserve the natural heritage of Outer Cape Cod. Today the National Seashore embraces most of the 27,000 acres it will finally encompass when completed. The majority of the park spans the eastern side of the Cape's "forearm," extending 40 miles from Provincetown in the north to Chatham in the south. In the west it includes the Great Island and Bound Brook sections of Wellfleet on Cape Cod Bay. Although a number of small parcels within the seashore's authorized boundaries remain in private ownership, the preponderance of the park's area is public land, with considerable areas set aside for recreation.

At the time the National Seashore was founded, it represented an innovative conservation effort on the part of the federal government and the Commonwealth of Massachusetts to protect a largely unspoiled seacoast from a threatening tide of private and commercial development. Similar preservation efforts have now established national parks and wildlife refuges along other unique American seacoasts, including Acadia National Park at Maine's Bar Harbor (see **#96**). This rugged granite headland stands in marked contrast to the smooth beaches and shifting dunes of the Cape Cod sand plain.

Cape Cod National Seashore includes a wide array of natural environments. There are ocean and bay beaches, salt and freshwater marshes, grassy moorland and scrubby heath, as well as oak, pitch-pine, and redcedar forests. Freshwater ponds, streams, and red-maple swamps lie inland from the coast. Rare stands of Atlantic white-cedar and American beech trees represent the forests of Cape Cod's past. The geological ice-age origins of the peninsula are also apparent, from the kettle holes indenting Eastham's, Wellfleet's, and Truro's glacial outwash plains to the knobby, picturesque kame hills of Nauset. Perhaps the most dramatic scenery in the park are the postglacial land forms sculpted by water and wind, such as the majestic sea cliff overlooking the 40-mile beach along the Atlantic shore, the famous sand dunes of Provincetown, and the long sandspit of Nauset Beach (see **Long Island, Cape Cod, and the Islands**).

The National Seashore contains four major visitor areas—Nauset (Eastham), Marconi Station Site (Wellfleet), Pilgrim Heights (Truro), and the Provincelands (Provincetown)—all of which contain unique natural features and various hiking, swimming, and other recreational facilities (summarized in the following). The geographical distribution of these four major visitor areas generally corresponds to the four major geological regions of outer Cape Cod. Beginning in the south, Nauset Area is situated within the juncture of the kame hills of Eastham and the flat tablelands of the Nauset Plains; Marconi Station Site in the rolling highlands of the Plains of Wellfleet-Truro; Pilgrim Heights in the moorlands of the plains of North Truro; and the Provincelands in the dune country of Provincetown.

Because Cape Cod is an immensely popular summer resort area, those wishing to visit the National Seashore are urged to plan summer trips well ahead of time. Reservations for lodgings during peak season should be made at least several months in advance. Many regular Cape Cod vacationers prefer to visit the region during the quieter, less crowded months of April, May, September, and October, which are also the months of bird migrations.

Salt Pond Visitor Center in Eastham and Provincelands Visitor Center in Provincetown are located at the southern and northern ends of the National Seashore, respectively. Facilities and services include natural- and human-history exhibits, orientation films, information desks, bookstores (maps, pamphlets, and books on Cape Cod), rest rooms, and handicap access. During summer months, park rangers conduct guided tours, evening lecture programs, on-site historical tours, and various special programs. Cape Cod National Seashore is open year-round. Salt Pond Visitor Center is open year-round, but hours vary seasonally; call (617) 255-3421. Provincelands Visitor Center is subject to winter closing; call (617) 487-1256 for information.

There are nine self-guiding nature trails in the seashore, including one or more trails in each of the four major visitor areas, and two located elsewhere. Six trails are described in this volume; summaries of three others are mentioned in Remarks sections as nearby trails. Pets are prohibited from nature trails. Trail pamphlets are available from dispenser boxes at the head of each trail, or they can be purchased together in a kit from the visitor centers' bookstores. Plant identification markers posted along the trails highlight common and unusual specimens of Cape Cod flora. The majority of trails are, at worst, of moderate hiking difficulty, and average hiking time rarely exceeds 1 hour.

Bicycle trails, bridle paths, and oversand vehicle routes are designated at certain areas of the National Seashore. Folders and maps are available at visitor centers. Use of oversand vehicles is by permit only. Bicycle trails (paved surfaces) may be used by hikers, but bicycles retain the right-of-way. Trails include Nauset Trail (1.6 miles), Eastham; Head of the Meadow Trail (2 miles), Truro; Provincelands Trail (7.5 miles), Provincetown.

Picnic areas are located at Doane Rock, Eastham; Pilgrim Heights, Truro; Provincelands Beech Forest, Provincetown; Great Island, Wellfleet. Open fires are prohibited. Regulations are posted.

There is swimming, with lifeguard services, at the following public beaches: Coast Guard Beach and Nauset Light Beach, Eastham; Marconi Beach, South Wellfleet; Head-of-the-Meadow Beach, Truro; Race Point Beach and Herring Cove Beach, Provincetown. Surfing is allowed in designated areas at beaches run by the National Seashore.

Surf fishing is permitted along seashore beaches away from swimmers. Saltwater fishing requires no license. Freshwater fishing requires a Massachusetts fishing license. Town licenses must be obtained for shell fishing.

Upland game and migratory wildfowl may be hunted in designated areas in specific seasons. Federal, state, and local laws apply. A folder is available at the visitor centers.

Camping is prohibited everywhere in the National Seashore. Information on private campgrounds, other lodgings, accommodations, and restaurants can be requested from Cape Cod Chamber of Commerce, Hyannis, Mass. 02601. (See Remarks, below, for public campsites.)

Remarks: *Roland C. Nickerson State Park, located on Route 6A in Brewster, approximately 1½ miles east from the junction of Routes 6 and 6A in Orleans, features the only state campground on Cape Cod. This 1,779-acre inland park (no ocean frontage) contains nine freshwater ponds surrounded by hardwood and pitch-pine forest, as well as a stand of second-growth white pine (an unusual species on Cape Cod). The park is also the habitat of the rare saw-whet owl. Cliff Lake Nature Trail is approximately a 3-mile hike through upland forest and around the lake shore. Cliff Lake, a glacial kettle, is the largest pond in the park. There are recreational facilities for hiking, swimming, fishing, boating, and bicycling. The 420 campsites for tents and trailers are available on a first-come/first-served basis (no reservations). The popular campgrounds are usually full continuously in summer vacation months. The park is open from April to November. Call (617) 896-3491.*

28.
Fort Hill

Directions: **Eastham, Mass. See directions for Cape Cod National Seashore. From Exit 13, continue north on U.S. 6 about 2 miles; turn right on Governor Prence Rd. For the Fort Hill Trail, turn left at the first parking lot. For the Fort Hill Overlook, drive to the second parking lot at the end of the road.**

Ownership: **Cape Cod National Seashore, National Park Service.**

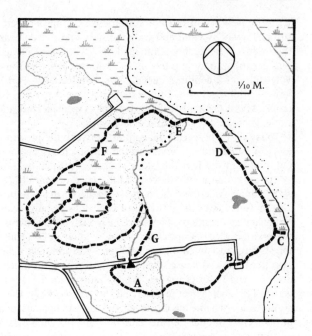

The natural abundance of the ocean and the land sustained Cape Cod's Indians, colonists, and their descendants, beginning as early as 4,000 years ago. For centuries the harvest of the shorelands was as essential for human existence as the harvest of the sea itself. And nowhere on Cape Cod was the earth more fertile and more bountiful than in the verdant fields spreading from shore to shore across the Plains of Eastham.

The Nauset Indians were the first people to farm at Nauset or Eastham. When the French explorer Samuel de Champlain charted Nauset Bay in 1605, he discovered Indian villages and fields on the upland shores. In 1646 Plymouth colonists founded the town of Eastham, which became the first English settlement on the lower Cape and one of the four original Cape Cod towns. At that time the Nauset region was still heavily forested, but the arrival of English planters brought rapid change. Timber was cut for building houses and ships and was used as fuel for the hearth and later for boiling seawater to extract salt. Fields were cleared for crops and grazing. It had taken centuries for Cape Cod's organic, but thin layer of topsoil to build up upon the underlying gravel, sand, and clay of the glacial sand plain (see **Long Island, Cape Cod, and the Islands**). But with the destruction of the forest, these rich topsoils were rapidly stripped away by wind and water erosion, and overcultivation further reduced the fertility of the land. By 1850 Cape Cod agriculture was declining; only in a few areas of unusually fertile soil, such as Fort Hill, did it continue into the twentieth century. Fort Hill was farmed until the 1940s. During its heyday rye, corn, and hay were cropped here. Orchards and vegetable plots were planted, and sheep, cattle, goats, and cows grazed in its pastures.

Today Fort Hill reveals the contrast between the present-day forests of postagricultural lands and the farming landscape of the past. On the heights of Fort Hill, stone walls border open fields of windswept grass that gently descend to the edge of Nauset Marsh (see **#29**). Such wide-open fields persisted in Eastham until the late 1800s. Today seasonal mowing of Fort Hill's sloping fields by the National Park Service has prevented the growth of new forests, thereby preserving a slice of Cape Cod's past. Elsewhere at Fort Hill, though, forests have reclaimed former fields and pastures. Old-field succession has produced dense stands of eastern redcedar on fields abandoned in the 1940s (see **#60**). Wetland succession has seen a resurgence of red-maple trees in a lowland swamp (see **#13**). This selective conservation scheme has created diverse upland habitats for an array of plants and animals, further enriching an area already famous for its abundant salt-marsh life.

Fort Hill Trail originates on the west side of the historic Penniman House, built in 1867 by a wealthy whaling captain, Edward Penniman, after his return from years at sea. The grand Victorian house stands opposite the first of Fort Hill's two parking lots on Governor Prence Rd., and the trail begins to the right of it. Walk behind the house and its adjacent barn and follow the trail as it descends into a low-lying grove of black-locust trees and shrub thicket (**A**) that have overgrown a former orchard. The spreading apple tree on the side of the trail indicates that this area was once sunlit and spacious (see **#74**). Black locust is a southern species that has become naturalized in areas of Cape Cod. It was introduced probably as a source of timber for fenceposts because of its resistance to decay and possibly as a natural means for replenishing soils that had become sterile after years of continuous cultivation. Locust leaves decay into humus that is rich in magnesium, calcium, and potassium. Their ability to increase nitrogen in the soil promotes the growth of grass on the ground beneath them. Although this species is short-lived, it grows quickly and spreads rapidly by sprouts to form extensive groves on the edges of fields and other open lands.

Soon the trail emerges at the base of Fort Hill itself and climbs its open slopes to an overlook at **B**, which is located at a parking lot on the summit. Below the overlook to the east lies one of the most enchanting vistas in the Cape Cod National Seashore. Fields laced with stone walls and fringed with redcedar trees sweep down to the edge of Nauset Marsh. The salt marsh forms an alluvial expanse of green marsh meadow dissected by winding tidal streams, muddy tidal flats, and blue open-water bays. Further east a thin, elongated finger of barren sand encloses the marsh from the wide Atlantic. This narrow sandspit is Nauset Beach, a low baymouth bar running north to south across the mouth of the marsh. To the east is Nauset Inlet, a narrow gap in the bar that serves as the only entrance to the marsh from the sea.

The trail descends the east slope of Fort Hill to the edge of Nauset Marsh. A large glacial boulder (or *erratic*) at **C** was transported here by the glaciers from an area of hard bedrock in the north. Once buried beneath glacial debris, the erratic was finally exposed above ground by wind and wave erosion (see **#85**). Glacial erratics on Cape Cod are particularly numerous in moraines and in areas that geologists refer to as *ice-contact deposits.* In simple terms, ice-contact deposits are areas that were located close to the edge of the glaciers. These deposits usually include rock debris (called *drift*) of varied types, boulders, silt, clay, sand, and gravel that have been well sorted and stratified by water, as well as unstratified till.

The Fort Hill area in the southern part of Eastham is a type of ice-contact deposit known as a *kame belt.* Kames are knobby hills of rock debris that once occupied holes in the ice sheet. This debris was transported across the top of the ice sheet by meltwater streams and deposited over the edge of the glacier in conical-shaped heaps. The picturesque, irregular terrain of the Fort Hill area originated in this way. Its rolling shoreline of pear-shaped hills and uneven knolls contrasts sharply with the exceptionally flat, smooth tableland lying north of Fort Hill in Eastham. This northern area, called the Eastham Plain, is one of three outwash plains that together make up the vast bulk of the lower Cape from North Eastham to North Truro.

The kame belt, on the other hand, is a relatively small geological zone. It extends across the width of Eastham from the Atlantic to Cape Cod Bay. Its northern boundary runs from about Nauset Light in the east to First Encounter Beach in the west. In the southwest the kame belt ends at Rock Harbor, whereas in the southeast it terminates around the Fort Hill area.

On the trail's right, stairs lead down the steep bank of the marsh to the water's edge. Several smaller erratics are visible along the tidal flats here. Sandpipers and other shorebirds might be glimpsed along the flats as they forage for small crustaceans in the mud or fish for minnows in the shallows. Long-legged wading birds, such as herons and yellowlegs, frequently inhabit the remoter reaches of the marsh during the warm-weather months. Salt marshes are the most productive ecosystems in the world, serving as incubators and nurseries for marine life, which in turn attracts numerous species of birds. Among the waterfowl that visit Nauset Marsh during their spring and fall migrations are the pintail, oldsquaw, and green- and blue-winged teal. Cold-weather months (late fall to early spring) may bring the canvasback, common goldeneye, bufflehead, common eider, greater and lesser scaup, common and red-breasted merganser, white-winged scoter, and brant goose. Black duck, mallard, and Canada goose can be seen in varying numbers throughout the whole year.

Retrace your steps back to the main trail, which continues northward along the base of Fort Hill. Cherry, southern arrowhead, and shrub vegetation screen the marsh (on the right) from sight for portions of the route. In the field, scrub thickets hug the edges of the stone walls, which are laid out in parallel lines rising up the slope. The horned lark, brownish in color with a white breast, is a ground bird that feeds on insects and seeds in the grasses of open fields along the Cape Cod coast. Small feathers resembling "horns" on the crest are visible close up.

The third stone wall that appears along this section of the trail marks the boundary between open field and dense redcedar forest (**D**). This forest represents a half-century of old-field successional growth. If the adjoining field were left unmowed and undisturbed for about the same length of time, it would probably evolve into a similar stand. Eastern redcedar is a prominent pioneer species on postagricultural lands throughout Cape Cod. This sun-loving species invades abandoned fields and pastures prior to most other species, for its seeds germinate well in turf. Usually it will precede the growth of pitch pine (the other common Cape Cod pioneer species) by a few years on a given site. The course of old-field succession may vary greatly, however, from one place to another (see **#38**). Local climate, soil type, availability of water, the composition of nearby trees for seed dispersal over open land, as well as a history of disturbances such as fires or storms, are all determining factors.

This border area where field meets forest offers a varied habitat, with many sources of food and shelter for mammals. On the edge of field and forest, woodchuck burrows may be found, marked by dirt piles at their entrance holes. The nocturnal red fox may be glimpsed in fields hunting mice, such as the meadow jumping mouse, which lives in grassy hummocks or hollow logs. In the early-morning hours, white-tailed deer may gather at the field's edge, graceful silhouettes shrouded in misty ocean light.

The trail continues through the redcedar forest and soon emerges at the Skiff Hill interpretive shelter (**E**), a display pavilion that overlooks Nauset Marsh. Indian Rock, another large glacial erratic, has been moved to this location from the water's edge. The narrow grooves and concave surface of the rock were used by the Nauset Indians to shape and sharpen implements such as stone axes, adz blades, fishhooks, and bone points. Four of these large grinding rocks have been discovered near the sea at Nauset Bay.

At the Skiff Hill shelter the trail branches into two directions. Fort Hill Trail, on the extreme left, turns inland here and leads back through redcedar forest. The trail that continues straight ahead (paved surface) descends past a rest-room building on the right and connects with the Red Maple Swamp Trail (**F**) on the left. This boardwalk trail winds through a mature red-maple swamp. Notice that the great majority of the red maples are coppice trees, which means that more than one trunk grows from the same root system or stem. Coppice trees are signs of second-growth forest, where new trees sprouted from the same stumps. Red-maple swamps on Cape Cod were widely logged by early settlers. When wood eventually became scarce throughout the region, the peat in the swamp bottom was burned as fuel. A wide array of woodland swamp vegetation is visible along the trail, including common elder, highbush blueberry, sweet pepperbush, swamp azalea, catbrier, fox grape, and water willow. A grove of tupelo (blackgum) grows around the trail's halfway point.

The trail finally leaves the wet lowland of the swamp and ascends a slope to an abandoned field that is being colonized by redcedar. Here the Red Maple Swamp Trail ends and intersects with the Fort Hill Trail. Turn right at the trail sign and walk through the field (**G**); the trail will soon lead you back to the parking lot opposite the Penniman House on Governor Prence Rd.

Remarks: *Fort Hill Trail (including Red Maple Swamp Trail) is a 1½-mile, 60-minute hike over relatively easy terrain. There are some steps and high hillsides. Portions of the Red Maple Swamp along the boardwalk may be wet after rainy periods and have tree roots exposed aboveground. Trail leaflets can be obtained from the dispenser box at the parking lot. Plant identification markers are posted along the route. This is an excellent scenic hike for older children. Inquire at nearby Salt Pond Visitor Center (see* **Cape Cod National Seashore***) for information on guided tours of the Penniman House.*

29.

Nauset Marsh

Trail

Directions: Eastham, Mass. See directions for Cape Cod National Seashore. From Exit 13, continue north on U.S. 6 about 3 miles. Just beyond Eastham center, at the corner of Nauset Rd., is the Salt Pond Visitor Center. Park there.

Ownership: Cape Cod National Seashore, National Park Service.

Nauset Marsh lies in a sheltered bay behind the long, narrow sandspit of Nauset Beach on Cape Cod's Atlantic shoreline. This large salt marsh and the beach, bays, and tidal flat surrounding it are an important ecological environment as well as a site of great beauty. A nursery for many forms of marine life in a highly productive food chain, Nauset Marsh attracts thousands of shore and sea birds in flight along the Atlantic flyway, a major East Coast migratory route. From overlooks on the Nauset Marsh Trail one can see green marsh meadows threaded with meandering tidal creeks. Upland hills mantled in dusky-green summer foliage or vivid tongues of autumn colors surrounding the marshlands on all sides but the east, where, beyond the sandy finger of Nauset Beach, the broad sky overspreads the sea.

In 1605 the French explorer Samuel de Champlain charted Nauset Bay and found it navigable. Yet in the centuries since his explorations, a salt marsh has grown up behind Nauset Beach. Salt marshes can only exist where a barrier beach (also called a *baymouth bar*) shields a bay from the turbulence of the open sea. Nauset Beach is such a baymouth bar, a type of sandspit that almost completely closes off the bay from the ocean. Only a narrow inlet allows ocean tidal waters to flow in and out of the bay and its extensive marshes. Nauset Beach, like all sandspits, is the product of a process called *shore-drifting.* In simple terms, shore-drifting occurs when sand, gravel, and other sediments are washed from sea cliffs and beaches by storms into the ocean. Longshore currents carry these sediments along the straight coastline until a bay or inlet interrupts them. A bay, like Nauset, represents an abrupt landward curve in the shoreline where deeper waters occur. Longshore currents do not follow the landward curves of the bay, but instead continue to travel in a straight line. As the currents move across the deep waters at the mouth of the bay, the suspended sediments sink to the bottom and gradually accumulate to form an underwater sandbar. At Nauset Beach, sediments from further north were carried southward by the longshore currents, and gradually the sandbar lengthened and rose above sea level to create a sandspit over 2 miles long across the mouth of the bay. Thus the stage was set for the development of a salt marsh in the quiet waters behind Nauset Beach.

Salt marshes gradually evolve from the buildup of sediments that are deposited by tidal currents in an undisturbed bay, called a *lagoon*. Sediments of clay and silt slowly raise the floor of a bay until mudflats are exposed above the water surface at low tide. Once exposed, the mudflats are colonized by spartina grasses, which then trap additional sediments between their stems and raise the mudflats to the high-water level. This becomes the flat surface of the salt marsh, which is broken throughout by winding tidal creeks that channel the tidal flood and ebb waters through the marsh. Thick layers of peat produced by decaying vegetation and other organic matter also develop on the surface of the salt marsh. Because the dense, muddy sediment in which salt-marsh plants grow is rich in bacteria but poor in oxygen, the decomposition of organic matter is slow, and the peat builds up rapidly. In the oldest salt marshes, such as the Great Marshes behind Sandy Neck spit in Barnstable, the study of the age of peat layers has determined the rate of rising sea level over a 3,000-year period.

A mature salt marsh may have taken 500 to 600 years to develop. The older, higher ground in a mature salt marsh is called the marsh meadow, where high-tide grass or salt-meadow cordgrass (*Spartina patens*) is the dominant plant. Although the upper marsh meadows are dry for long periods during the year, salt-meadow cordgrass nonetheless must be immersed by the high springtime tides in order to survive. At other times of the year the narrow tidal creeks contain the ocean tidal waters within their banks and the lowest reaches of the marsh. These low- or mid-tide areas are flooded twice daily at high tide. Here the dominant plant is salt-marsh cordgrass (*Spartina alterniflora*), which grows thickly in the wettest regions of the marsh. It is a stiff, tall grass (4 to 6 feet), and early settlers once used it to thatch the roofs of buildings. It is one of the first plants to colonize a young salt marsh (see **#14** and **#77**).

These spartina grasses and other salt-marsh vegetation are uniquely adapted to the severe environmental stresses that are characteristic of salt-marsh estuaries. An *estuary* is an area where tidal salt water and fresh water are continuously intermixed, such as the mouth of a bay or river emptying into the sea (see **#59** and **#72**). Salt marshes can only occur in this estuarine environment. Stresses produced by regular fluctuations of salinity, temperature, and moisture are inhospitable to strictly freshwater or strictly marine vegetation. Yet for the few plants and marine life that have adapted to salt marshes, this ecosystem is exceptionally productive. Nutrients from both fresh and salt water enrich the marsh, which, in turn, enriches the larger estuary when, twice daily, ebb tides flush the nutrients of decomposing plants into the estuary. This nutrient-rich habitat supports a vital food chain of life, ranging from microscopic plankton to shellfish, fish, birds, and mammals. The most fertile fields of the grain belt in the American West do not produce as much food per acre as a salt marsh.

Nauset Marsh Trail begins at the outdoor amphitheater located behind the Salt Pond Visitor Center. A staircase descends to an area of salt flats around the eastern (left) side of the Salt Pond (**A**). The pond lies in a depression of the land surface called a kettle, a common geological feature throughout Cape Cod (see **#32** and **#99**). Salt Pond originally held fresh water, since it was the freshwater

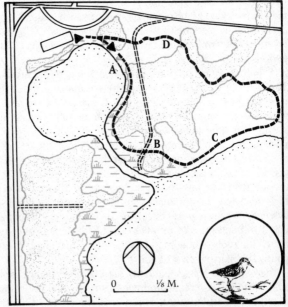

Inset: Semipalmated sandpiper

table that had risen and filled the glacial hole. But then the ocean carved a tidal channel connecting the pond to Nauset Marsh. Today salt water is carried into the pond twice daily by flood tides that support marine life including oysters, mussels, quahogs, and fish. They, in turn, provide food for many shorebirds that frequent muddy or grassy flats.

Sandpipers are small shorebirds that are commonly found at Salt Pond and the tidal area adjacent to the dike (located a little further ahead on the trail). The semipalmated sandpiper is common on Cape Cod and on the Atlantic Coast generally. It has a gray-brown back, white belly, and black legs, and measures 5½ to 6½ inches long. The slightly smaller least sandpiper is often seen with it, since both species feed on worms, small crustaceans, and aquatic insects.

At **B** the trail leads along the top of the earthen dike that extends across the tidal flats to the upland hills beyond. The dike (no longer functional) was constructed to prevent the inflow of brackish waters into the lowland on its eastern side. The hills around this lowland area create a natural basin where fresh water can run off the slopes into the impoundment behind the dike. A change from salt to fresh water favored the invasion of freshwater marsh plants as long as the dike remained functional. The construction of such earthen dikes in salt marshes was once fairly common throughout Cape Cod. Once an impounded marsh was drained of salt water and infiltrated with fresh, a hay meadow could be developed and easily harvested. Here the purpose of the dike was to attract waterfowl for hunting by providing a more diversified diet of freshwater vegetation.

After crossing the dike, the trail climbs steps through a hillside forest of eastern redcedar, pitch pine, and oaks. At the top of the hill an overlook (**C**) on the northern edge of Nauset Marsh offers an opportunity to study the topography and enjoy the view. An open stretch of water just below the overlook is Salt Pond Bay. Nauset Beach lies to the east, separating the marsh from the open Atlantic beyond it. Looking east-southeast across the extensive marsh flats lies Nauset Harbor near the narrow inlet that opens into the sea.

Thousands of birds gather in Nauset Marsh in the summer months. Long-legged wading birds such as the snowy egret or great blue heron float gracefully on outspread wings. The marsh hawk patrols the grassy areas around the marsh in search of small mammals (see **#18**). Many waterfowl arrive during migratory season, and some winter here or at other areas of the Cape if the winter cold is not severe and the bays remain unfrozen (see **#96** for more on migration). Cold-weather ducks include the red-breasted mer-ganser, bufflehead, common eider, canvasback, and common goldeneye, among many others. Black ducks, mallards, and Canada geese are common residents throughout the year.

The trail skirts the upland edge of the marsh for a short distance and then turns inland, winding through groves of eastern redcedar. This area was used as a golf course until the early 1930s. The abandoned fields quickly filled in with redcedar, which, like pitch pine, is a pioneer species that invades open areas ahead of other species (see **#60**). Redcedar usually cannot reproduce in great numbers after a stand has fully matured, since the canopy blocks the sunlight required by the young seedlings to grow.

Follow the trail downhill as the stand of redcedar thickens and intermingles with oak and pitch pine. Soon the trail passes a wet swale of tangled understory growth and then emerges into an open area, where it crosses a paved bicycle path. Here it leads through a grove of black-locust trees growing on the site of a former farmstead (**D**). This southern species was introduced here to enrich the soil with nitrogen after the land had become sterile from years of continuous use.

Beyond the locust grove Nauset Marsh Trail joins the Buttonbush Trail at the edge of Nauset Rd. The Buttonbush forks in two directions at this point; go left, following it to the parking lot at the Salt Pond Visitor Center.

Remarks: *Buttonbush Trail (½ mile) is a short, self-guiding nature walk for the handicapped and visually impaired. Common Cape Cod plants and freshwater-pond life are described in interpretative trail markers, with texts in braille and large print. A guide rope leads hikers around this easy loop, which originates at the parking lot.*

*Doane Rock (formerly called Enos Rock) is located off Doane Rd. Drive east on Nauset Rd. from Salt Pond Visitor Center to the Doane Rock picnic area sign. A marker at the picnic area identifies the 1644 house site of Deacon John Doane, one of Cape Cod's first settlers. This metamorphic rock of crystallized volcanic lava is the largest glacial erratic (see **#85**) on Cape Cod, measuring about 45 feet long, 25 feet wide, and 18 feet high.*

Also located within a few miles of the Salt Pond Visitor Center are two Atlantic beaches. Nauset Light Beach stretches away from the base of a high sea cliff, or marine scarp, *which extends many miles northward along the outer Cape's Atlantic shoreline to the highlands of Truro. The scarp, which at this point is about 75 feet high, is the product of erosion by storm waves. It is the source of the sand-and-gravel sediments transported by longshore currents to form sandspits such as Nauset Beach or, in the north, the sand dunes of Provincetown (where the longshore currents flow north rather than south).*

Coast Guard Beach provides access to Nauset Beach. A Jeep trail (about

1½ miles one-way) follows the western edge of this narrow spit. Thousands of shorebirds can be observed in the extensive marshlands, which protrude into Nauset Bay from the spit's landward side. Naturalist Henry Beston's "Outermost House" stood on Nauset Beach until destroyed in the great winter blizzard of 1978. The waves from this storm also destroyed the beach parking lot and ripped open an inlet at the beach's northern end.

Nauset Marsh Trail (1 mile) is a 45- to 50-minute hike over moderately difficult terrain, with some steps and sandy stretches. Plant identification markers are posted along the route. A trail leaflet can be obtained in a dispenser box at the head of the trail. Binoculars will heighten enjoyment of the birdlife and seascape. Nauset Bicycle Trail (about 1½ miles, paved surface) runs from the Salt Pond Visitor Center to Coast Guard Beach. Hikers may use the trail, but bicycles retain the right-of-way. Nauset Light Beach (Eastham) offers swimming and lifeguard supervision. Nauset Light (not open to the public) was moved to its present site from Chatham in 1923 and can be seen from the beach parking lot. Take Nauset Rd. east to Doane Rd., turn left onto Ocean View Dr. and follow the signs. Coast Guard Beach (Eastham) has swimming and lifeguard supervision and access for the handicapped. Inquire at the Salt Pond Visitor Center (see **Cape Cod National Seashore**) for hiking assistance, guided tours, and parking for Nauset Beach.

30.

Atlantic White-Cedar Swamp

Directions: **Wellfleet, Mass. See directions for Cape Cod National Seashore. From Exit 13, continue north on U.S. 6 about 8 miles to the entrance of Marconi Station Area on the right. Follow the signs on the entrance road for Marconi Station Site to the parking lot.**

Ownership: **Cape Cod National Seashore, National Park Service.**

The Atlantic White-Cedar Swamp at Cape Cod National Seashore represents a rare plant community in coastal New England. A largely southern, sun-loving conifer, the Atlantic white-cedar is a pioneer tree species, invading swamps or bogs along the Atlantic Coastal

Plain in the wake of forest disturbances. Often forming pure stands in acid, peaty soils, the tree is known for a dense growing habit, which may be unrivaled by any North American tree. Under favorable conditions, a stand of Atlantic white-cedar can become virtually impenetrable, so closely spaced that a solid evergreen canopy casts the forest understory in deep and continuous shade.

The Atlantic White-Cedar Swamp is the natural highlight of the Marconi Station Area in the town of Wellfleet. A virtually unspoiled tract of beach, sea cliff, dunes, and woodlands, Marconi Station Area lies at the narrowest point of the outer Cape between the Atlantic Ocean and Cape Cod Bay. Few other sites on Cape Cod offer such a superb panorama of land and sea. From an observation platform (**A**) at the Marconi Station Site parking area, which overlooks the Atlantic from the top of a high sea cliff, there are excellent views of Marconi Beach immediately below, stretching northward past the coastal community of Wellfleet-by-the-Sea and southward toward Nauset Light. In the west, glimpses of Cape Cod Bay are visible across the low scrub forest of South Wellfleet.

Marconi Station Area illustrates natural diversity within the coastal environment. The Atlantic White-Cedar Swamp Trail includes not

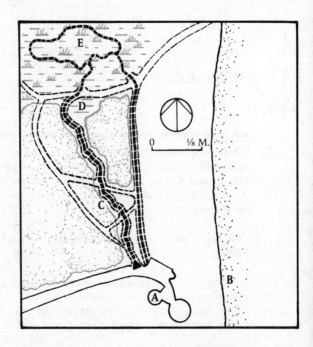

only the unique cedar swamp but also several other typical plant communities of outer Cape Cod. Critical, if sometimes subtle, ecological variations are evident within this relatively small area. Proximity to the ocean and the availability of fresh water determine the conditions peculiar to each plant community, all of which are adapted to the porous, sterile soils (called *podzols*) that are characteristic of the Cape Cod sand plain.

The least hospitable habitat for life is found at the very edge of the sea. Dry, drifting sand offers few rootholds and little moisture to sustain life. Salt spray and ocean winds can kill or stunt the growth of even the hardiest vegetation. Where the erosional forces of water and wind have been joined (see **#74**), such as on the steep sea cliff at Marconi Station Area (**B**), even the resilient American beach grass—the stabilizer of sand dunes—finds life difficult (see **#79**). Walk from the observation platform to the top of the high sea cliff— or marine scarp—located below the Marconi Shelter, the open-air exhibit pavilion. This smooth scarp has been eroded 170 feet since 1902, a dramatic illustration of the ocean's assault on the land. The scarp represents the harshest habitat for life within the coastal region. Further inland, conditions are milder and more life-sustaining.

The first portion of the Atlantic White-Cedar Swamp Trail weaves through a woodland dominated by stunted pitch pine and bear oak (**C**). These low-growing trees form a dense thicket behind the scarp and its adjacent sand dunes. Both tree species commonly occupy such exposed sites, where ocean winds often reach gale force and prevent larger trees from becoming established. Bear oak is probably the most common oak species on Cape Cod, thriving on the driest and most sterile soils. Rarely exceeding 10 feet, and often little bigger than a shrub, the tree is a rapid sprouter in areas disturbed by fire or logging. Also known as scrub oak, it was an early pioneer on this site, which had been stripped bare of forest by the 1850s. The stunted size is not a good indicator of the age of the bear oak, nor the pitch pine, since pruning ocean winds keep these species low to the ground. In fact, some of the bear oaks here have been determined to be 100 years old; and the pitch pine—including both these stunted trees and some larger specimens that appear further down the trail—are about 75 years old. Bear oak may eventually prevail over the sun-loving pitch pine, whose small seedlings fare poorly in the shade. In turn, the bear oak may gradually be succeeded by larger white and black oaks, or perhaps the American beech, the climax tree of Cape Cod's forest. The woodland succession will take centuries to occur, however, and unexpected disturbances could retard or modify it.

As the trail descends the gently sloping terrain and heads inland, pitch pines reach greater heights, and bear oak is replaced by larger white and black oaks. Greater protection from the ocean winds, coupled with an increase in soil moisture as the freshwater table begins to intersect with the surface of the land, provides more abundant nourishment for increasingly varied groups of plants. The greatest proliferation of species occurs on the upland soils around a red-maple swamp forest (**D**) (see **#13**). Here the soil is moist yet well drained, and the podzols have been enriched with organic matter produced by decaying vegetation. A groundcover of checkerberry, wild sarsaparilla, and mayflower flourish in the leafy humus beneath large oak trees. The red-maple tree dominates the soggiest soils closer to the water, where such plants as sheep laurel, highbush blueberry, sweet pepperbush, and inkberry enjoy the constant dampness.

Follow the signs directing you to the right at an abandoned dirt road after you leave the red-maple swamp. The entrance to the boardwalk trail in the Atlantic White-Cedar Swamp appears on the left. The boardwalk quickly ushers you into the cedar swamp (**E**), where you should bear to the left at the first fork.

Atlantic white-cedar trees of varying ages grow very densely in the swamp. The understory of the swamp supports few flowering plants, since the water and soil are intensely acidic. (Among the handful of such flowering species, watch for the swamp azalea, its white flowers providing rare color to the shady swamp in early summer.) A number of nonflowering plants manage to live here, however, the most conspicuous being the small, shrubby beard lichen (see **#88**). This branched light-green lichen grows on the trunks of the cedars.

The low depression in the terrain occupied by the swamp is a *kettle hole*. A product of the Wisconsin glacier's Ice Age, the depression was formed when a block of glacial ice was buried by sand and gravel as the ice sheet retreated. A warming climate melted the ice block, leaving a depression that would later become filled with fresh water as the underlying water table rose (see **#99**). Subsequently, climatic fluctuations brought dry conditions to this region, so that both swamp and land vegetation invaded the kettle hole at different times. The 7-foot layer of peat that composes the swamp bottom is the legacy of these plants.

Climatic fluctuations also explain the presence of the Atlantic white-cedar in the Northeast. This typically southern species (also called southern white-cedar in some regions) spread up the Coastal Plain during a warmer epoch, invading swamps and wetlands as far north as central Maine. Relic colonies of white-cedar today remain scattered throughout coastal New England, though these isolated stands are by no means virgin swamp forests. The cedar is a highly desirable wood, and cedar swamps were heavily logged by early New Englanders. The present-day forests are therefore remnant-successional stands where this pioneer species has invaded cut-over or burned wetlands. Only a handful of Atlantic white-cedar was growing a century ago at this site. But these few trees produced a new generation between 1900 and 1920, which are now the largest individuals in the swamp.

Prized for its durability, lightness, and the ease with which it could be crafted, the Atlantic white-cedar was used for doors, rafters, shingles, planking, and many other components of New England buildings. Resistance to decay made white-cedar the choice wood for fence posts; water and organ pipes were more specialized products. During the Revolutionary War, the tree produced charcoal for the manufacture of gunpowder for the colonial forces. So desirable was the wood, in fact, that when the supply of living trees had been exhausted in the early 1800s, ancient logs were recovered from the swamp bottoms and found fit for use.

In the distant future Atlantic white-cedar may be succeeded in the swamp by tupelo and red maple, two other wetland species that can already be seen invading areas of the swamp. Because Atlantic white-cedar, like most conifers, requires plentiful sunlight to mature, small saplings cannot prosper in the deep shade of the swamp understory. The Atlantic white-cedar will have to rely on forest disturbances—windstorms, fire, or disease—to open the forest canopy, thereby slowing the succession to other species. The strong likelihood of such disturbances occurring in the several centuries necessary for the next stage of succession to become complete suggests that the Atlantic white-cedar swamp will continue to exist here for many centuries to come.

Follow the boardwalk as the trail completes its circuit through the swamp and finally reemerges at the road. Trail signs lead you back to the parking area via a return route that skirts a field that is reverting to pitch pine.

Remarks: *The Atlantic White-Cedar Swamp Trail (1¼ miles) is a 45- to 60-minute walk of only moderate difficulty. It includes some steps and a few stretches of soft sand. A trail guide including map is available at a dispenser box at the start of the trail. Signs posted along the route show trail direction and identify common plants. Marconi Station Area is a significant historical site. The first U.S. transatlantic wireless telegraph station was built here in 1901–1902, by Italian physicist Guglielmo Marconi. Marconi's Wellfleet Station stood on a spot near the present-day Marconi Shelter, which features several exhibits highlighting Marconi's milestone scientific achievements. In 1903 the age of modern communica-*

tions began at Wellfleet Station with the transmission of the first transatlantic wireless broadcast, an exchange of messages between President Theodore Roosevelt and King Edward VII of Great Britain. Turn right off the entrance road to Marconi Station Area to visit nearby Marconi Beach.

Nearby Place
of Interest

Great Island Nature Trail, Wellfleet: **From Wellfleet Center, turn right at the town pier on Kendrick Rd., then turn left on Chequesset Neck Rd. and proceed to the parking lot.**

This is the longest, most difficult hike in the National Seashore. The only trail located on the Cape Cod Bay side of the park, this route explores the site of an early whaling center (see #64 for more on whales). Once surrounded by water, Great Island was connected to the mainland by a sandspit around 1830. Currently, it forms the northernmost portion of an island chain that shelters Wellfleet Harbor from the open bay. From the island's southern extremity, the submerged remnant of historic Billingsgate Island is often visible at low tide. Once the site of an early colonial village, it was fully claimed by the sea in 1935. Great Island itself was a busy coastal outpost for shore whalers and oyster fishing prior to the mid-1700s. Today a wayside exhibit on the trail marks the site of a tavern built here in 1690, which served the crews of coastal vessels. The exhibits interpret the findings of an archaeological dig at the tavern site. The island's original hardwood forests were completely logged by 1800, but pitch pine was planted here in the 1830s. Pine, scrub oak, shrub vegetation, and salt marsh now compose the terrain.

The trail begins at the Great Island parking lot and picnic area. Hikers can choose to take only a portion of this 8-mile trail (maps are available at the head of the trail). The final stretch of the trail down Jeremy Point becomes submerged at high tide. Hikers are advised to wear protective footgear for walking in the soft sand and to bring a hat and drinking water, as the sun can be intense.

31.
Pamet
Cranberry Bog.

Directions: **Truro, Mass. See directions for Cape Cod National Seashore. From Exit 13, continue north on U.S. 6 about 18 miles to North Pamet Rd. in Truro. Park at the Environmental Education Center on the right.**

Ownership: **Cape Cod National Seashore, National Park Service.**

In the centuries since the Pilgrims first set anchor off Cape Cod, many images from nature have come to symbolize life on this small seaward hook of land along the Atlantic Coast: the whale and the cod, sand dunes and salt marsh, pine forests and white beaches. But few Cape Cod symbols have reigned so large over the public imagination—and palate—as the Cape Cod cranberry.

Wild and cultivated cranberry bogs represent a unique natural feature and a historically significant agricultural industry. Only a few other regions in the United States possess the cool, moist climate and boggy environment required for cranberry growing. In the wild, cranberries grow in low, sandy swales, such as the sheltered valleys between the sand dunes at Provincetown, in places where acid, peaty soils and fresh water are ample. Cultivated bogs require similar growing conditions, but on a more extensive and artificially controlled scale. Whereas wild cranberries grow in damp lowlands that turn dry in the summer growing season, the cultivated bog must regulate its water level with a system of drainage ditches.

Cultivated bogs were once more numerous across the Cape than they are today. In the late nineteenth century the cranberry became an important export crop for a region facing the decline of its major fishing and shipping industries. Tourism has now replaced the cranberry industry at the center of the Cape Cod economy, though the area today still produces about 10 percent of the Massachusetts crop.

Pamet Cranberry Bog is a fine example of the cultivated bogs once so prevalent on Cape Cod. A short trail begins at the parking lot adjacent to the Environment Education Center, crosses North Pamet Rd., and then leads down a hillside through a pitch-pine forest. At the bottom of the hill, it circles the edge of a pond—a reservoir for the cranberry bog—before finally emerging on the flat, open spaces of the bog itself. Signs direct you along the route, and a trail leaflet is available at the dispenser box at the head of the trail.

Take the trail down the hill and around the edge of the pond. A plank walkway stretches across the cranberry bog, to the right of the pond. Exercise caution when using the walkway at times when the bog is flooded; the unsupported planking may float on the surface of the water as much as 6 to 10 inches above the submerged ground. The surface of the bog looks like a deep-green mat and is composed of a multitude of the vinelike evergreen plants. A member of the heath family, the cranberry displays white flowers from June to early July, and ripening red fruit from September to October. Ditches ring the bog's perimeter and crisscross its full expanse, allowing for swift flooding or draining. Flooding in winter protects the cranberry plants from frost and cold, dehydrating winds. In spring the flooding shelters flower buds and in autumn the flavorful berries. (Most modern cranberry bogs use sprinkler systems rather than flooding.) At all other times the water level in the bog is usually 10 to 12 inches below the bog's surface.

The origin of the Pamet Cranberry Bog is typical of cultivated bogs. Cranberry bogs were usually created in cleared swamps because of the deep layers of rich peat that had accumulated over the centuries in the swamp bottoms. The Pamet Bog, which was begun in the 1880s, lies in a former red-maple swamp (see **#13**); other Cape Cod bogs were often developed in Atlantic white-cedar swamp forests (see **#29**). These swamplands were cut clear, and stumps and roots were removed from the peaty soil layers. After a system of ditches was dug, the bed of the cranberry bog was covered with a thin layer of sand. Sanding the meadows, as the operation was known, became a regular practice in the early 1800s, after it was discovered that sand blown over cranberries—which occurs naturally in the wild-cranberry patches in the dune country—produces a better crop. Harvesting procedures have changed over the years with various innovations. Originally, the cranberries were harvested by hand, usually by women, who picked the fruit as they crawled down the rows of plants on their knees. Later, cranberry scoops were used; today cranberries are harvested by mechanical pickers. Retrace your steps across the plank walkway and back along the trail to the parking area.

Remarks: Pamet Cranberry Bog Trail (half a mile) is a short 20- to 30-minute walk over moderately difficult terrain. The bog is periodically flooded to a shallow depth during the year, so it is advisable to wear waterproof boots. Wild cranberries can be seen in the dune country at the Provincelands Area in the Cape Cod National Seashore. Be prepared for lots of mosquitoes during the summer months.

32.

Pilgrim Heights

Directions: North Truro, Mass. See directions for **Cape Cod National Seashore.** To reach that point from Boston, take I-93 and Route 3 to the Sagamore Bridge onto Cape Cod, about 50 miles, then follow U.S. 6 east and north about 33 miles to Exit 13. Continue north about 21 miles to the junction of U.S. 6 and Route 6A in North Truro; 2.1 miles further north on U.S. 6, the entrance is on the right, marked by a sign.

Ownership: **Cape Cod National Seashore, National Park Service.**

Lying within sight of the sea, the pitch-pine and oak forests, heathlands, and salt-marsh dunes of Pilgrim Heights offer glimpses into the geological and human history of this area. The Pilgrim Spring Trail, one of two hikes here, leads to the site of a freshwater spring, where the Mayflower Pilgrims are believed to have drunk their first New England water after landing on Cape Cod in November 1620. The Small Swamp Trail features an ancient marine scarp landlocked from the ocean, a legacy of Cape Cod's changing shoreline. It overlooks Salt Meadow, a broad freshwater marsh bounded by sand dunes, which once formed part of a vanished harbor.

Small Swamp lies in a glacial kettle and supports a wetland plant community. The Small family farm stood in the swamp in the nineteenth century, built on lands originally inhabited by Indians as early as 4,000 years ago. The interpretative exhibit shelter on the edge of the parking lot offers an informative display illustrating the geological history of *glacial kettles.* Kettles were created near the end of the Pleistocene epoch (or late Ice Age) some 15,000 years ago. Large blocks of glacial ice were buried beneath layers of gravelly outwash debris carried across the land surface by meltwater streams. They remained scattered across Cape Cod as the glaciers retreated in the wake of the warming climate. When they finally melted themselves, they left dry cavities in the terrain. Many of these depressions, or kettles, were later transformed into ponds or swamps as the water table rose above the floor of these low-lying hollows (see **#99**).

A sign for Small Swamp Trail appears to the right of the shelter. The trail descends a series of steps through a pitch-pine forest, following a rail fence to a fork. A right turn at the fork leads along a relatively level stretch of the trail, as it cuts across the prevailing

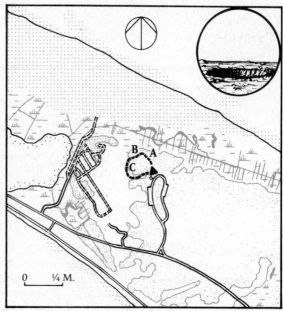

Inset: Kettle hole

northwestward decline of the land. Black oak mingles with pitch pine here. Although it seldom reaches its maximum-height range of 40 to 80 feet under these dry, windswept conditions, black oak is one of the larger species of oak across Cape Cod. (Scarlet and red oak are the other large species; bear oak rarely exceeds 8 feet.) Like scarlet oak, it typically grows on hilltops and midslope habitats. The thick, scaly bark of mature trees is deeply furrowed, the yellow inner bark was once used by Native Americans and settlers as a source of tannin and yellow dye.

A flight of steps again leads downhill and emerges from the oak and pine forest into a more open landscape of sand dunes and heath. At **A** the trail joins a sandy ridge, where a scenic overlook faces north across Salt Meadow, a freshwater marsh dissected by meandering creek, and beyond to the Atlantic. Between the grassy marsh and ocean a ridge of sand dunes forms the upper shoreline, enclosing Salt Meadow from the sea.

This attractive vista of green marsh meadow and dunes against the background of the ocean represents a very young landscape on the scale of geologic time (see **Long Island, Cape Cod, and the Islands**). The sandy ridge of dunes on which you now stand is a former marine scarp (or sea cliff), which roughly 3,000 years ago was the original shoreline of Pilgrim Heights. Salt Meadow only came into existence much later, after the present-day shoreline evolved from a sandspit that eventually separated the area that became the marsh from the sea. This sandspit was the product of the shore-drifting of sand carried northward from the southern sea cliffs of Truro and Wellfleet and deposited here by longshore currents. Over the centuries this sandspit was built up by ocean waves, as breakers swept sand and gravel up the beach slope of the spit. Gradually it lengthened into the northwest, extending beyond the end of Cape Cod's original glacial landmass, which today exists as the landlocked headland we know as High Head (visible just a short distance from this spot off Route 6 south of Pilgrim Lake). The sandspit also broadened as it grew longer, the accumulating sands fanning out into a hook that became the distinctive "fist-shaped" extension of the lower Cape we now call the Provincelands. At the same time, ocean waves on the western side of the spit were eroding the scarp of High Head and depositing its soil in a succession of small sandspits, one in front of the other. Over time they were joined to each other and to the larger sandspit originating at Pilgrim Heights. Subsequently, these joined spits were transformed by wind erosion into sand dunes (see **#34**). Meanwhile, at Pilgrim Heights a saltwater lagoon was created on the landward side of the sandspit. This lagoon lying between the spit and the ancient scarp was the early ancestor of Salt Meadow.

Continue along the trail, which curves northwesterly along the ridge to a second overlook (**B**) on the right. Here again you can look across Salt Meadow and beyond the shoreline of dunes to the Atlantic. In the years after the formation of the Provincelands, Salt Meadow long remained an open-water extension of a former bay. At that time Salt Meadow, then known as East Harbor Creek, was a tidal estuary (see **#59** and **#72**) of the former East Harbor, which opened onto Cape Cod Bay. Today Pilgrim Lake, which lies over the high hill to your left, is the surviving vestige of East Harbor. In 1869 a sandspit (Pilgrim Beach) closed off the mouth of East Harbor from Cape Cod Bay, transforming in into a lake. East Harbor Creek—or Salt Meadow—was, in turn, severed from Pilgrim Lake by the construction of a man-made dike. Over the years windblown dune-sand and tidal sediments had been accumulating in the bottom of East Harbor Creek, resulting in the development of a salt marsh—or "salt meadow" (see **#29**). The dike, located only about ½ mile northwest from this point, changed the saltwater marsh to a freshwater environment.

In 1620, when East Harbor was still open to Cape Cod Bay, the

Pilgrims anchored the *Mayflower* in Provincetown Harbor. On November 15, soon after landing, a small band of Pilgrims followed East Harbor Creek in pursuit of Indians they had sighted. The Indians vanished, and the Pilgrims, then lost, quenched their thirst at nearby Pilgrim Spring. The landscape you see before you, though much altered in more than three and a half centuries, is nonetheless the same ground over which the Pilgrims trod in search of fresh water in a strange land.

Peaked Hills Bars lie offshore along this stretch of the coast between Race Point in Provincetown and Highland Light in Truro. More ships have been wrecked on those dangerous shifting underwater sandbars than at any other point along the entire Atlantic Coast. When the British man-of-war *Somerset* was wrecked on the bars in 1778, the colonists marched the surviving crew members all the way up the Cape to Boston.

The trail moves down a series of steps through the dunes. Bearberry thickets carpet a dune on the trail's edge. This low-growing, vinelike ground cover thrives in sunny sites in the open dunes and heathlands, spreading in a dense mat to bind the loose sand. Small, glossy leaves are joined by pinkish-white flowers in late May and early June. Bearberry's famous scarlet fruit, called hog cranberries, ripen in September.

The trail swings left at the bottom of the steps and then levels out in the kettle (**C**) below the dunes. A grove of quaking-aspen trees marks the transition from the dry, hot sands of the upper dunes to the moist soils of Small Swamp. As the trail leads around the edge of the swamp, wetland plants, such as swamp azalea, highbush blueberry, and black cherry, appear on the left. These species invaded this kettle after the water table rose to the surface some 2,000 years ago. Dry conditions that in the future may be caused either by a drop in the water table or the buildup of peat and windblown sands in the swamp bottom would favor a wetland succession to red maple and tupelo. The final stage of the successional process would be the takeover of the kettle by American beech, the climax-tree species of Cape Cod.

Prior to European colonization, Indians cultivated the land at Pilgrim Heights. By about A.D. 500 Native Americans were raising corn, beans, squash, and other crops. They cleared the land through controlled burning, then grew crops for several seasons, before migrating on to other lands. Periodic Indian migrations from one place to another allowed cultivated ground to replenish its nutrients before the Indians returned. The seven and a half layers of peat in the swamp reveal this pattern of Indian farming: layers in which corn pollen has been detected are separated by intervening layers where there is no trace of agricultural crops.

European colonists also cultivated Cape Cod lands, but their custody of the earth had far less desirable ecological consequences. By 1850 the Truro plain—and Cape Cod as a whole—had been severely depleted from logging, overgrazing, and continuous cultivation. Yet agriculture remained essential to this geographically isolated region, and subsistence farming continued throughout the nineteenth century. In the 1860s, for instance, Thomas Small settled a 200-acre farm at Pilgrim Heights. This sheltered swamp was the site of his house and farm buildings. The farm was active until 1922, raising cows and harvesting corn and asparagus. Today the wetland vegetation has reclaimed the land, though some plant varieties cultivated in the old farmyard can still be seen here: apple, grape, lilac, and plum, among others.

The trail leaves Small Swamp, climbing steps up a hill forested in black oak. It emerges at a fork in the trail; a right turn leads up the steps that return you to the interpretative shelter at the parking lot.

Remarks: *Small Swamp Trail (¾ mile) is a 30-minute loop over moderately difficult terrain, with many steps and sandy stretches. Pilgrim Spring Trail (¾ mile) is a 30-minute loop over more moderate terrain. It leads through a pitch-pine forest to an overlook of a cattail marsh and then dips into a scrub lowland to Pilgrim Spring. Trails include plant identification markers along the routes. Trail leaflets (no map) are available from the dispenser boxes at their heads. The interpretative-exhibit shelter includes a relief map of the area and a display tracing the routes taken by the Pilgrims as they explored Lower Cape Cod in 1620. A picnic area is adjacent to the parking lot.*

Nearby Place of Interest

Head-of-the-Meadow Beaches, Truro: **Take Route 6 south from Pilgrim Heights to Head-of-the-Meadow Rd. on the left.**

Swimming with lifeguard supervision is available. Head-of-the-Meadow Bicycle Trail, (2 miles, paved surface) runs from Head-of-the-Meadow Beaches along Salt Meadow north to High Head Rd. (south of Pilgrim Lake off Route 6). Hiking is permitted, but bicyclists retain the right-of-way. Some of the finest parabolic dunes on the lower Cape are visible from this trail. *Parabolic* **or** *blow-out dunes* **are shaped like horseshoes. The windward side is the open end of the horseshoe, where sand has been scooped out by**

the wind to form a low-lying basin. The higher curve of the horseshoe is built up from these windblown sands (see #34).

Provincelands Visitor Center, Provincetown, has information for hikers and other services (see **Cape Cod National Seashore.**)

33.
Provincelands
Beech Forest

Directions: **Provincetown, Mass. See directions for Cape Cod National Seashore. From Exit 13, continue north on U.S. 6 about 28 miles to Provincetown. Turn right at the traffic light onto Race Point Rd., then turn left at the sign for the Beech Forest Trail, and park.**

Ownership: **Cape Cod National Seashore, National Park Service.**

The American beech tree represents the climax species of the Cape Cod forest. In the long centuries of the land's natural development, the beech climax forest is the ultimate stage of forest succession. Once mature, the beech forest will reproduce itself indefinitely. Only such forest disturbances as fire, storms, or logging can alter the character of this climax, or "steady-state," forest community.

The Provincelands Beech Forest is one of the few surviving examples of the Cape Cod climax forest. During the seventeenth and eighteenth centuries, such beech forests were largely depleted by European colonists, who logged and overgrazed the Provincelands. Earlier, in precolonial times, frequent forest fires swept across Cape Cod, which may also have diminished the fire-sensitive beech, a species incapable of sprouting from burned stumps.

The Beech Forest Trail offers a short enjoyable hike with great variety. Two interconnecting circuits—the Pond Loop and the Beech Forest Loop—together feature two freshwater dune ponds, sand dunes, and the beech forest itself, each of which represents a particular phase in the natural history of the Provincelands.

The trail begins at the parking area, where a trail leaflet (including

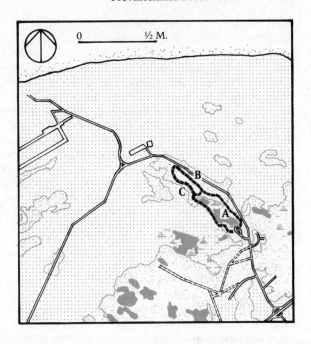

map) can be obtained at a dispenser box. The first half of the Pond
Loop skirts the edges of two dune ponds before meeting the Beech
Forest Loop. This portion of the Pond Loop (**A**) reveals a diverse
array of plantlife clustered around the ponds. The dune ponds themselves are shallow depressions that extend below the freshwater
table. Unlike many Cape Cod ponds, which occupy kettle holes
(depressions formed by melting blocks of glacial ice—see **#32** and
#99), the dune ponds are of more recent, postglacial origin. Some
dune ponds occur where the wind has scooped shallow depressions
in sandy lowlands. Others originated in swales that developed between former spits, which were landlocked as Provincetown's landmass expanded westward, the product of a complex process of erosion on the eastern shoreline and sediment buildup in the west (see
#34).

The abundant vegetation growing in and around the ponds is
distributed according to each individual plant's need for water. The
water lilies in the pond and pitch pine on the high, driest grounds
farthest away from the ponds represent two extremes of natural
adaptation. White water lilies thrive in deep water, because they
require constant submersion of their roots in order to survive; whereas

the deep-rooted pitch pine excel where the water table lies far beneath the land surface. Between these two extremes grow trees such as the red maple, tupelo, and oak, as well as understory vegetation such as inkberry, sheep laurel, Virginia rose, and beach plum.

Soon after passing the second dune pond, the trail comes to a fork—proceed straight ahead along the Beech Forest Loop. The trail follows the low-lying floor of a narrow valley (**B**) between two sand dunes, where beeches and occasional large pitch pines grow on the slopes. The American beech is readily identified by its uncommonly smooth, light-gray bark and saw-toothed leaves, which turn a soft yellow or brown in the fall. Although the beech is usually associated with the northern forest, where it proliferates on moist, shady slopes, the maritime habitat of Cape Cod also possesses the cool, moist conditions, as well as the acid soils, required for the development of beech forests. Visible along the trail are many of the understory plants identified with the beech forest, all of which thrive in acid soils: starflower, spotted wintergreen, mayflower, as well as the occasional red-maple tree.

The trail soon swings to the left, ascending steep steps to the top of a wooded dune. As the trail sharply descends the dune, it enters an area of the beech forest (**C**) where an encroaching, barren sand dune looms above the trees. The path wanders through a stand of large spreading beeches growing in the shadow of the intruding dune. The trunks of several trees nearest the dune have become engulfed by sand—a scene that has been reenacted many times in the Provincelands in the wake of its deforestation. The dune country, which surrounds the beech forest and threatens its very existence, offers a study in ecological contrast. Less than a century after the Pilgrims first landed at this outermost point of Cape Cod, logging and uncontrolled grazing brought about the soil erosion of the sand dunes on a massive scale. In the absence of stabilizing vegetation, the rich organic topsoils of the beech forest—the product of centuries of natural development—were swept away by the ocean winds, while the verdant plantlife of the once-shady forest understory perished in the hot sun and the dry, windblown sands. By 1714 the village of Provincetown itself and its harbor were threatened with inundation from the creeping dunes—a prospect that finally forced the planting of beach grass (see **#79**) in the early 1880s and, at the turn of the century, pitch pine and other vegetation, which surround Provincetown today.

Yet even now tracts of the Provincelands still resemble the barren landscape that Henry David Thoreau, in his classic account of his travels across Cape Cod in 1849, called a desert. Realizing the dire ecological legacy of the early colonists, Thoreau observed a barren wasteland where a wood-starved populace scavenged beaches for rotting driftwood and hunted sand dunes for reemergent forests long buried by the sands. Crossing the dunes, Thoreau described such a dead forest: "In one place we saw numerous dead tops of trees projecting through the uninterrupted desert . . . where thirty or forty years before a flourishing forest had stood, and now, as the trees were laid bare from year to year, the inhabitants cut off their tops for fuel."

Today pitch pine, beach grass, and other vegetation have been planted to halt the progression of the dunes. Such erosion-control measures should prevent a recurrence of the haunting scene sketched by Thoreau. By stabilizing the sand dunes, plants such as those now established can constitute the first phase in the reforestation of the land, eventually restoring the Provincelands to something akin to their precolonial condition.

Follow the Beech Loop until it reconnects with the Pond Loop past a short flight of stairs. Go right at the fork, continuing along the trail as it tracks through soft sands. This stretch of the Pond Loop, hugging the slope of the encroaching sand dune, overlooks the dune ponds on your left as it returns to the parking lot.

Remarks: *The Beech Forest Trail (1 mile) is a 45- to 60-minute hike. The trail is over moderately difficult terrain, with some steep steps and stretches of soft sand. Signs posted at intervals indicate trail direction and identify common plants. This is the sole trail in the Provincelands Area of the Cape Cod National Seashore reserved exclusively for hikers. A network of bicycle trails, however, is open to hikers in the dune country, though right-of-way is given to bicyclists. Inquire at the nearby Provincelands Visitor Center for information about guided nature tours via oversand vehicles through the dunes. The Provincelands Area Visitor Center and Race Point Beach are located just north of the Beech Forest parking area, off Race Point Rd.*

34.

Provincelands

Directions: **Provincetown, Mass. See directions for Cape Cod National Seashore. From Exit 13, continue north on U.S. 6 about 26 miles to the Truro-Provincetown line. For Mount Ararat Sand Bowl, continue just beyond the** line to a parking area on the north (right) side of the road, posted "Dune Parking." For Race Point Beach, continue another 2 miles to the traffic light at Provincetown; turn right onto Race Point Rd. and follow signs to the beach parking lot.

Ownership: **Cape Code National Seashore, National Park Service.**

Great sand dunes and sweeping ocean beaches highlight Cape Cod's most stunning and unusual natural landscape—the Provincelands. Set on the northernmost tip of outer Cape Cod in historic Province-town, this is geologically the youngest region of the Cape. Yet its shifting sands, already eroded by wind and water, foretell the fate of all Cape Cod.

Mount Ararat Sand Bowl and Race Point Beach are two especially fine sites for exploring the sand dunes and ocean beaches of the Provincelands, as well as for appreciating its geological history. Mount Ararat Sand Bowl has a dune walk to the summit of one of the highest and best-known sand dunes in the area. Located just north of Pilgrim Lake in one of the region's oldest dune belts (the so-called Biblical Dunes), Mount Ararat offers panoramic views across the low-dune country to the Atlantic shore. The short trail originates at the small parking lot on Route 6 and follows a fence up the slope of a dune to Mount Ararat on your left. Soft sand makes walking difficult and slow. On windy days the sting of airborne sand may make hiking unpleasant or even impossible. Avoid veering off the trail into areas where grass and other vegetation are growing. These plants represent an important human conservation measure, for they bind the sands of the dunes and thus prevent the inundation of the highway in back of you. The plants can be damaged if disturbed in any way, since the loose sands make for a very fragile ecosystem.

Climb the trail to the top of Mount Ararat, which rises to a height of about 100 feet. Look southeast beyond Pilgrim Lake on your right to the brown, sandy cliff rising some 50 feet above the surface of the lake. This ancient, landlocked marine scarp is High Head, formerly the northern headland of Cape Cod's original glacial landmass (see **Long Island, Cape Cod, and the Islands**). Some 6,000 years ago this cliff gazed upon open ocean in the area where the Province-lands now lies. The Provincelands is composed of sandspits built up from eroded sand and gravel that was torn away by storm waves from the eastern sea cliffs of Wellfleet and Truro to the south, as well as from High Head itself. Longshore currents following the coastline carried this eroded debris northward and then deposited it off High Head. Once the spits had formed, waves swept sand up the beaches, and slowly the spits were raised above the high-water level (see **#29**).

The first and largest of these sandspits originally developed off the beaches of North Truro (see **#32**). Over time, it lengthened to the northwest beyond High Head and gradually assumed the shape of a narrow sickle, whose point curved increasingly westward in the direction of the Massachusetts mainland. This sandspit was to form the basis of the "fist" or "fishhook" of Provincetown as we know it today. But in its infancy it was much narrower than it is presently. Although it now lies buried beneath the sand dunes, geologists believe that this original spit ran along the northern shore of Pilgrim Lake, through the old dune belt at Mount Ararat, to the vicinity of Herring Cove Beach. Over the centuries it was continuously widened as the longshore currents deposited more and more sand from the southern sea cliffs along the spit edge. Meanwhile, other loose sand was eroded from High Head and grew into a succession of new, smaller spits, arising parallel to one another in the waters off High Head. This series of spits thus landlocked High Head from the open ocean. As they pushed further and further into the water, lagoons that had become trapped between the spits eventually evaporated to form a single, large area of dry land. With time, this area merged with the original, sickle-shaped sandspit.

A much more recent sandspit on the western side of the Provincelands is Pilgrim Beach, over which the highway now runs. This thin finger of sand divides Pilgrim Lake from Cape Cod Bay. But in the not-too-distant past Pilgrim Lake was a saltwater inlet, known as East Harbor, until Pilgrim Beach completely sealed it off from Cape Cod Bay in 1869.

The Provinceland's sand dunes—a type known as *coastal dunes*—were created over a period of centuries as the shoreline continually pushed north into the ocean. Coastal dunes form above the high terraces of the upper beach as the prevailing ocean winds blow loose sand from the beach in a landward direction. Here the prevailing wind is from the northwest.

There are three major zones comprising a beach (which you can later identify at Race Point Beach) that to varying degrees are subject to the effects of waves and wind. Closest to the water is the *foreshore*, which is constantly buffeted by waves. The *summer berm* is a flat or sloping terrace above the foreshore and represents the high-water mark where sand is stranded by the small summer ocean waves. The flat *winter berm* is the highest, most landward zone, which is built up by the highest waves of winter storms. Loose sand blown off the winter berm nourishes the coastal dunes, which lie behind the winter berm in formations called *dune belts*.

In a well-developed dune region, such as Provincetown, there are usually a series of dune belts extending in generally parallel lines from the beach. The foredune, lying nearest the beach, is the most exposed dune belt. Salt spray, drying winds, and erosion from large winter-storm waves make this region almost uninhabitable for most vegetation. The interdune and backdune belts are located successively inland from the foredune, and these environments are respectively more stable and life-sustaining because they are more sheltered. Each of these two inland dune belts was itself the foredune at earlier times. Mount Ararat, for instance, which is now part of the Provincelands' older backdune region, originally stood exposed to the sea. But as the land expanded on the north, it was landlocked by the seaward growth of the beach and was succeeded by a new foredune.

The wind is the prime shaper of the Provincelands. It animates the ocean, blowing over the water's surface to produce waves that create and destroy ocean beaches. More apparent here are the direct effects of the wind's energy on the dunes. Sand dunes are in constant motion. To the human eye this movement of countless loose sand grains may be invisible except on the windiest days. The winds force grains of sand to leap into the air and bounce upon the ground. As one grain bounces upon another grain, it forces the other to move as well, triggering a seemingly endless chain of motion. Together this dancing of the sand grains produces a phenomenon called *surface creep*, which is the widespread movement of the sands across the surface of the dunes.

Without vegetation to anchor the loose sands, the town of Provincetown would soon become engulfed by drifting sand blowing to the west. This almost occurred in the nineteenth century, after Provincetown's early European settlers cut down the forests that once grew upon the dunes and permitted cattle to graze uncontrolled. (See **#33**.) Beach grass and pitch pines had to be planted to stabilize the shifting sands in both the early and the late 1800s.

Beach grass grows in the foredune region, one of the few plants capable of surviving so close to the ocean. This is a coarse, tall (1½ to 2 feet) grass, topped with a narrow spike of white flowers in the spring. Its creeping underground stems trap loose sand and, like trees on a windy plain, the grasses act as a kind of miniature windbreak at the ground's surface. Beach grass in the foredune not only helps prevent erosion from surface creep, it can also allow the dunes to rise to heights not otherwise possible (see **#79**). The foredune can therefore serve as a more effective buffer against large winter-storm waves.

In the backdune a greater variety of vegetation has been planted in a belt around Provincetown's residential and commercial center for erosion control. These plants range from woolly beach heather, also known as poverty grass, to the comparatively large pitch pine. Woolly beach heather has small, gray-green leaves growing close to the stem, and in late spring bears yellow flowers. Pitch pine is the common pine of the Cape Cod sand-plains region. In sheltered areas this deep-rooted conifer can reach heights of about 40 feet. But such large specimens are seldom seen in the Provincelands, where the flat terrain provides few obstructions against shearing ocean winds.

Race Point is Cape Cod's northernmost beach. From the parking lot at the end of Race Point Rd., you can take paths down to the foreshore from the foredune. Here you can easily identify the various beach zones just described and can also observe the action of the breakers as they roll toward land. The accumulation of sand on a beach is caused by the continuous inward and outward flow of waves. The water running up the foreshore is called the *swash,* and it sweeps sand and gravel before it. Much of this swash sinks into the beach sands, but the remainder—called the *backwash*—runs back down the slope of the beach, taking some of the sand and gravel with it. As long as the source of these sands continues to feed the longshore currents that transport this debris to the Provincelands, the buildup of Race Point Beach into the north will go on.

Race Point is the last and outermost of the sandspits that form the Provincelands as we know it today. Currently, the Provincelands is still growing into the open water as the currents continue to carry sand and gravel up the coast. (Some of these sands have also been carried around the western shore of the Provincelands to form Long Point, the trailing sandspit that shelters Provincetown Harbor.) But in the distant future, the Wellfleet and Truro sea cliffs that supply these sands to the Provincelands will finally disappear. Over many centuries the original glacial landmass of the outer Cape has lost about 2 miles from its Atlantic side from storm-wave erosion. Geologists believe that many centuries hence, the most narrow portion of the peninsula in Wellfleet (near the National Seashore's present-day Marconi Station Site) will be cut through by the ocean, dividing the outer Cape into two halves. The northern lands extending from Wellfleet to Provincetown will become an island. This change will constitute only the first step in the complete leveling of Cape Cod by ocean and wind erosion. It will more immediately expose the low-lying Provincelands to the gradual loss of its lands, for no longer will the southern sea cliffs exist as a source of building material for this outermost Cape Cod sandspit. Instead, the ocean will begin to erode the Provincelands, scattering its sands into shifting islands and submerged shoals. The glacial landmass of the Cape will probably take longer to erode away, with portions assuming the character of the present-day Provincelands before being reclaimed by the sea.

Remarks: *Mount Ararat Dune Walk is a 30-minute loop through soft sand. Wear sturdy footgear for this short, but difficult hike. Binoculars can enhance appreciation of the scenery. Race Point Beach has no defined trails, but hikers can wander the beach as they desire. Old Harbor Lifesaving Station, originally on Nauset Beach in Eastham, was moved to Race Point Beach in 1978, and now serves as a small museum with historical exhibits. There is swimming with lifeguard supervision in summer. Rest rooms and bathhouses are available at the parking area. Provincelands Visitor Center, Race Point Rd., is nearby (see* **Cape Cod National Seashore***). There are fine views of the dune country from the observation deck. Provincelands Bicycle Trail (7.5 miles, paved surface) is open to hikers, but bicycles retain the right-of-way. A folder and map are available at the visitor center.*

Oversand recreational vehicle trails in the Provincelands can be used by hikers. Use of oversand vehicles is by permit only. Park rangers may conduct guided nature tours via oversand vehicles in summer. Inquire at the visitor center for a trail folder and information on guided tours. Herring Cove Beach, Provincetown, is located at the western end of Route 6. Swimming with lifeguard supervision, rest rooms, and a bathhouse are available. Pilgrim Monument, Provincetown Center, offers panoramic views across the Provincelands.

Long Island Sound's North Shore and the Rhode Island Coast: Sound and Bay

Like the moraine-crowned landscapes of the Cape and islands, the topography of the mainland coast behind them bears the imprint of the Pleistocene glaciers and their aftermath. Scattered along the coast between the mouth of the Hudson River and Buzzard's Bay lie errant boulders, traces of moraines, which are mounds of rubble and sand left by the ice sheets, and other relics of glacial advance and retreat. Wrinkled into myriad bays and estuaries, the ragged face of the shoreline was delineated by the rise of the sea after the last ice sheet melted. Even so, the results of glaciation are not conspicuous enough to obscure the geologic handiwork of earlier ages.

The low hills that roll to the sea along most of the coast belong to the New England Upland, which stretches north through Maine and west into New York, part of the much wider Appalachian Highlands. As inland, the coastal countryside is studded with outcroppings of granite and gneiss bedrock, like those at the Westwoods in Guilford, Connecticut, and Bluff Point State Park in Groton, Connecticut.

Before and during glacial times the hills now abutting the water's edge stood far inland behind a low coastal plain, like those of the Piedmont that now overlook the Coastal Plain of the Mid-Atlantic states. Immediately south of the hills in what today are Connecticut and Westchester County, New York, a river—or river system—carved a valley about 100 miles long, roughly on an east–west axis. The exact course of the river is uncertain but the valley it excavated became the basin of Long Island Sound.

After the last ice sheet put the finishing touches on Long Island and melted back across the sound, it stopped momentarily along the shore of Connecticut and Westchester, just long enough to leave a few traces of moraines. One is in the Norwalk, Connecticut, area, the other about 60 miles east, between Madison and Old Saybrook, ending near the mouth of the Connecticut River. Glacial sand is spread more thickly in these areas than in other parts of the Connecticut coast, covering much of the bedrock.

Close to the Connecticut coast lie several bundles of small islands. The Captain Islands near Greenwich, the Norwalk Islands, and Falkner Island off Guilford are dabs of moraine. The Thimble Islands off Branford, colonized during the summer by the wealthy and said to be the site of Captain's Kidd's buried treasure, are bedrock topped by touches of glacial sand and gravel like that on the floor of the sound.

Meltwater from the ice sheets left sand and gravel called outwash in a few places along the shore, notably off Bridgeport and New Haven, in the form of sandy deltas. As the glacier melted, water sloshing from the dripping ice into the basin of the sound pooled, forming a freshwater lake. Low ridges, now submerged, kept the

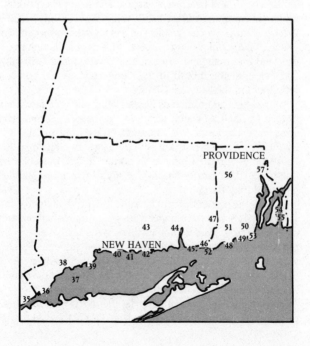

ocean from pouring into either end of the basin until about 8,000 years ago, when the sea rose high enough to cover the old river valley.

As the sea rose toward the interior hills, it flooded valleys between them. Many of the narrow, deep harbors in Westchester and Connecticut, as well as that at New Bedford, Massachusetts, the lower Hudson, and Narragansett Bay, are drowned valleys. Some of the hills on the new shoreline became headlands, which if covered with glacial debris supplied sediments carried by waves to form beaches elsewhere. The headland at Bluff Point, for instance, provides the stuff of which nearby Bushy Point Beach is made.

Most beaches on the northern shore of Long Island Sound are narrow, generally rocky, and often floored with cobble, stones smoothed by wave action and tightly packed near the water line. The same is true of the southeastern corner of Massachusetts. In between lie the sandy beaches of Rhode Island, where the recessional moraine that stretches northeastward from the northern shore of Long Island curves and skims the mainland, showing the position of the ice. Unlike the rest of the coastal region discussed here, that of Rhode Island somewhat resembles the environment of the Cape and islands.

Elsewhere sand beaches are sparse and scant, except those accumulated behind man-made breakwaters. Some sandy beaches have special features, such as spits, fingers of sand projecting into the water, and tombolos, long, narrow strips of sand linking two islands or island and mainland. An example of a spit is at Griswold Point, Old Lyme, at the mouth of the Connecticut River. Tombolos are prominent in the Norwalk Islands.

Where spits and tombolos lie parallel to the mainland, separated from it by shallow water, they serve as barrier beaches. The most spectacular barrier beaches along the coast front the sea in Rhode Island, in places such as the Ninigret Conservation Area. Between Point Judith and the Connecticut border, in fact, most of the shoreline is edged by barrier beaches, many of which are jammed with bathers during the summer.

Behind the barrier beaches lie salt ponds, and often tidal marshes. Tidal marshes also form a green fringe on many harbors and estuaries along the coast, although these wetlands have been severely reduced by dredging and filling. Many surviving marshes are small, such as those of the Marshlands Conservancy in Rye, New York. Some large marshes do remain, however, including those at the mouths of the Connecticut and Housatonic rivers.

West of the Connecticut River lie the oldest tidal marshes. Their peat may reach more than 15 feet deep. East of the river, particularly in Rhode Island, the marshes are younger—some only a few thousand years old—and shallow. The peat in some of them is only about a yard deep.

Where the environment has not been substantially degraded, the salt marshes are backed on the upland side by bayberry, huckleberry, switch grass and a variety of shrubs that inland merge with forest. The typical forest of the coastal area is hardwood, including white oak, black oak, pignut hickory, and mockernut hickory. Blackgum, black cherry, and sassafras also are common.

A few species of trees whose range is centered far to the north also reach into the coastal region of the southern New England mainland. Sweetgum has its northernmost limit in southwestern Connecticut. A large stand of this tree can be seen at the Marshlands Conservancy. Other southern trees found at scattered locations along the coastal strip are post oak and persimmon. Survival of these species along the coast, but not inland, is due to the moderating influence of the sea upon winters, which makes the coast several degrees warmer than inland areas.

In extreme eastern Connecticut—Pachaug State Forest, for instance—pitch pines and some white pines begin to mix with the hardwoods. Some areas of Rhode Island are heavily coniferous with a scattering of oaks, much like the forests of the Cape and islands.

As elsewhere in southern New England, the forest is largely growth that has started to mature on abandoned farmlands. Throughout the area, woodland is replacing open space that in turn was carved out of the primeval wilderness in colonial times.

From an airplane during the spring and summer, the coastal region looks like a sea of greenery, with urban areas scattered along the shoreline and at a few inland sites, such as Middletown, Connecticut. The look stems from the fact that even in the heavily settled suburbs of New York City and Providence, Rhode Island, for instance, trees abound, masking development.

Actually, however, except for modest islands of rural countryside in places such as the lower Connecticut River valley and around Little Compton, Rhode Island, the coastal strip is heavily populated and in many spots highly industralized. Yet even so, the variety and abundance of wildlife is astonishing. Almost all the different groups of wildlife found in less-settled sections of southern New England are represented in the coastal region, even on the fringes of New York City, and to a surprising degree within it and other urban areas. White-tailed deer browse within sight of Manhattan's skyscrapers, and Canada geese throng on Fairfield County, Connecticut, golf courses. Raccoons profit by scavenging road kills and the contents of trash cans, even in parts of mid-Manhattan. Many of the same shorebirds that migrate along the outer beaches of Long Island can be seen on the northern rim of the sound. As a measure of the region's ability to support wildlife, coyotes have been expanding into many neighborhoods, including some within commuting distance of New York City and Providence. Bald eagles winter within sight of the fashionable shops that line the main street of Essex, Connecticut, a few miles up the Connecticut River from salt water. That most woodsy of birds, the wild turkey, has been reintroduced by wildlife agencies in eastern Connecticut and southern Rhode Island and is thriving, just as it has in the wilder sections of the interior.

The animal life that has suffered most because of human activities is that of the immediate seashore. Heavy development and industrialization, together with pollution of inshore waters, has destroyed vast stretches of habitat for fish, invertebrates, aquatic birds, and similar creatures. With increased environmental awareness and subsequent improved management of the coast's natural resources, however, the situation has taken a turn for the better. People can harvest shellfish, for instance, on mudflats and in shallows contaminated a decade ago. Terns are breeding on beaches from which they had vanished for years. The salvation of the region has been the maintenance of myriad state forests, wildlife management areas, bird sanctuaries, and similar natural sites. They retain a refreshing sense of the natural world at the doorstep of megalopolis.

—Edward Ricciuti

35.
Marshlands
Conservancy

Directions: Rye, N.Y. From New York City, take I-95 north to Exit 11, about 15 miles north of the interchange with I-295 for the Throg's Neck Bridge. Go east on Playland Parkway 0.4 mile, then south on U.S. 1 for 1.5 miles. Turn east (left) onto the Marshlands driveway, marked by a small sign.

Ownership: County of Westchester.

In the midst of suburbia, this is a wonderful salt marsh that has not succumbed to developers and that gives the visitor a sense of what the coastline looked like before much of it was drained and filled. The Marshlands Conservancy property can be explored by walking a 1½-mile trail that passes through a woodland down to the salt marshes and shoreline of Long Island Sound (see **Long Island Sound's North Shore and the Rhode Island Coast**). It is one of the few remaining salt marshes (see **#29**) close to the New York City limits, and a good place to see shore and wading birds.

Before approaching the water, the trail winds through a fine stand of sweetgum trees (**A**), a southern species that reaches its northern limit in nearby southwestern Connecticut. Look on the ground for the round seedballs covered with numerous spiny projections. The present grove apparently traces its origins to a few shade trees left for domestic animals when this area was a pasture. The name *sweet-gum* derives from a gummy compound or sap the tree produces. Called *storax,* it is used in making perfume, adhesives, and salves.

The habitat changes dramatically as the trail leaves the forest and passes alongside a huge open field with abundant wildflowers (**B**). Among them is butterfly weed (*Asclepias tuberosa*), a protected species in New York State. This colorful member of the milkweed family has been losing the open and sunny habitat it needs as farms and fields throughout the region have reverted to woodland. There were also, more fires in days past, set primarily by Indians and farmers, and these helped create conditions in which the butterfly weed could flourish. Today the field is mowed every year in late fall after the butterfly weed has completed its annual seed dispersal. Look for its

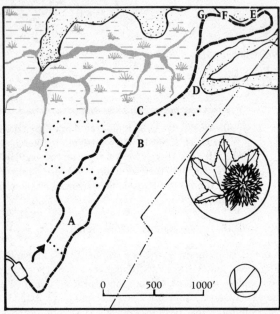

Inset: Sweetgum

bright-orange flowers from June onward. Other members of this botanical community are more familiar, and equally pleasing. Look for wild strawberries blossoming in April, and asters and goldenrods that begin to bloom in June but really take off in August and September.

An overlook (**C**) to the left of the trail provides a panoramic view of the marsh and Milton Harbor, a narrow arm of Long Island Sound. The harbor sits between two small ridges, the one you're standing on and the one making up the strip of land directly across the channel. The topography has been created by a process called differential erosion: the ridges have remained higher than the harbor area because they are made of a more resistant rock and consequently have not weathered nearly as much. Although the entire area is metamorphic, the composition of this ridge (amphibolite, hornblende, quartz, and epidote) is tougher than the schists below.

A pair of binoculars is handy here for a sweep of the marsh. Look for a variety of birds associated with the mudflat and salt-marsh environment. Snowy egrets and other members of the heron family are usually present during the warmer months. Their long legs and daggerlike beaks help them catch small fish, crabs, and other crustaceans. Also be on the lookout for sandpipers and plovers, whose probing bills search the mud for worms and a variety of invertebrates.

Two major types of saltwater grasses are visible from this point (**D**). On the right, with its typical "cowlick" appearance is salt-meadow cordgrass (*Spartina patens*). On the left is the tall, straight-standing salt-marsh cordgrass (*Spartina alterniflora*); it receives a bathing of salt water twice daily during the high tides and is situated in what is thus known as the intertidal zone. The salt-meadow cordgrass is in an area of the intertidal zone known as the high marsh and is washed with seawater only at the highest tides (see **#14** and **#77**). (Spike-grass is also found here.) These grasses are extremely productive and play a crucial role in the complex salt-marsh food web. Their seeds are eaten by black ducks, their decaying stems and parts feed many of the small wetland animals, and the rootstocks of salt-marsh cordgrass contribute a large part to the diet of wintering Canada geese.

Step off the main trail and walk along the beach if the tide permits (**E**). A few chunks of weathered granulite bedrock stick their noses out of the sand here. Notice the pinkish-brown color, which is due to the oxidation, or rusting, of small amounts of iron contained in two of the constituent minerals, mica and feldspar.

The bedrock is an assemblage of three types of metamorphic rocks: gneisses, schists, and granulites. They are the products of older rocks that were changed by the great heat and pressure of colliding continental plates, approximately 450 to 550 million years ago. When the African and North American plates hit, they welded together the sedimentary and volcanic rocks that made up the old coastline and changed not only their form but also their chemical composition. After the plates separated, the East Coast of the United States took a new shape with different rock types such as you see here.

The rocks along the beach are composed primarily of quartz, feldspar, muscovite and biotite mica, garnet, and sillimanite. These minerals, in their present configurations, were formed during the metamorphism. An excellent example of a metamorphic rock is a large piece of biotite schist that sits back a bit from the shoreline (**F**). A profusion of black or biotite mica and many small garnet crystals is immediately evident to the naked eye. The dark color of the mica is due to a high iron content, while the garnet's color is from magnesium and aluminum.

Look over the wrack line on the small sandy beach (**G**). A *wrack line* is the narrow strip of stranded vegetation and other materials that are deposited by the last high tide washing up on the beach. Dead seaweeds, such as knotted wrack and sea lettuce, along with beach grass and driftwood are typical components of wrack. But if you look closely, you'll also find crab shells, remains of skate egg cases, various shells, and anything else caught by the incessant tide. As Rachel Carson wrote in *The Edge of the Sea,* "In the litter and debris of the beach there may be few living creatures, but there is the suggestion, the intimation, of a million, million lives, lived in the sands nearby or brought to this place from far sea distances."

Follow the trail back over the causeway, up the hill, and along the field to the parking lot and museum building.

Remarks: *The walk takes about 2 hours. Rubber-bottomed shoes or boots are useful here, especially for walking along the beach. The small museum houses several saltwater tanks, a display of mounted shorebirds, and a literature table. A detailed trail guide is available free of charge. Picnic tables, bathrooms, and a water fountain are also found here. The building is open from 10:00 a.m. to 5:00 p.m. Wednesdays through Sundays; the trails are open daily from dawn to dusk. Bring a wildflower field guide if you visit during the warmer months.*

36.

Audubon Fairchild

Garden

Directions: **Greenwich, Conn. From New York City, take the Hutchinson River Parkway north about 17 miles from the Cross Bronx Expressway. Take I-684 north about 9 miles to Exit 3. Go east on Route 22 (northbound, away from Armonk) 0.4 mile, then turn south (right) onto Route 433. Go 2.5 miles; turn east (left) on North Porchuck Rd. After about 0.6 mile, the sanctuary entrance is on the right.**

Ownership: **National Audubon Society.**

Once the vision of a nineteenth-century conservationist and now a 135-acre preserve open to the public, Audubon Fairchild Garden is known far and wide for its wealth of wildflowers spread among the woods and meadows of lovely southwestern Connecticut. More than five hundred species of plants grow here; most are native to the

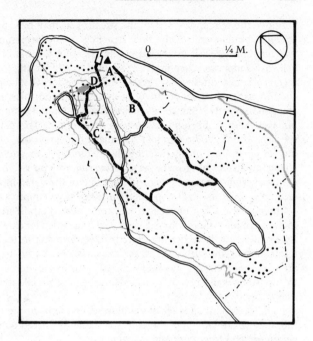

region, but some were introduced by Benjamin Fairchild from other parts of the Northeast, and from Asia and Europe. The garden is a good birding area, especially during the spring migration, when one will most likely see a wide variety of warblers and other songbirds (see **#96** for more on migration).

Enter deep woods from the northeast corner of the parking lot onto the dirt Gray Glen Rd. (**A**). The forest is a moist low- to mid-slope community dominated by black birch, red oaks, and other mixed hardwoods, with witch-hazel, maple-leaved viburnum, and sweet pepperbush in the shrub layer, and cinnamon fern, Canada mayflower, and others among the herbaceous plants. During the warmer months you'll hear the wood thrush, ovenbird, scarlet tanager, red-eyed vireo, veery, worm-eating warbler, and pileated woodpecker. The first real congregation of wildflowers comes just a short distance down the trail along the edges of Sing-A-Long Brook. Here are several varieties that prefer wet habitats; the delicate marsh blue violets (*Viola cucullata*), the simple white- or pink-flowered cuckoo flower (*Cardamine pratensis*), and the familiar bright-yellow marsh marigolds. Two more common wetland plants, skunk cabbage and false hellebore, are also present.

Above the gurgling waters of the stream you may hear the surprisingly birdlike trill of the gray tree frog. Many beginning bird watchers mistake this unusual amphibian's voice for that of a red-bellied woodpecker. Tree frogs are adapted to a life in the forest by means of small adhesive discs at the ends of their toes that help them cling to bark. They eat a variety of live insects, and their hunting ability is indirectly enhanced by their variable coloration which camouflages them at different seasons and times of day. This particular species is usually colored to match its name (i.e., gray) but, depending on conditions of temperature, light, moisture, or stress, may change to shades of brown, green, or pearl-gray. You will have an extremely difficult time trying to locate one of these 1½-inch-long creatures, because it will stop singing as soon as you approach.

Three-quarters of Connecticut was once cleared, and early photographs of the preserve show a great deal more open land and fields than now exist. Note the tall redcedar trees growing in the shady forest to the right of the trail; these are survivors of a life begun in an abandoned clearing decades ago (**B**). (Further along on Forest Rd. are stone walls, probably erected long before Fairchild took over the property in the 1890s.)

Look for several varieties of wildflowers and ferns in the mature forest. Here are false and also true Solomon's seal, wild oats, wild geranium, and New York and marsh fern.

A sprinkling of beautiful large-flowered or white trillium (*Trillium grandiflorum*) dots the woods with color. Fairchild may have planted these many years ago. However, the species is native to the area, and the plants may be indigenous. The name *trillium* is derived from the Latin word for "three," for the plant has three leaves, three sepals, and three petals. These early-spring members of the lily family are perennials, preferring moist, rich woods, and grow from a rhizome or underground stem. Look for the 8- to 16-inch-high plant with white petals about 2 inches in length during late April and early May.

The Meadow Rd. leads past may apples, jewelweed, and wild leeks to the more gardenlike portion of the property, essentially a series of mowed paths through a large wildflower-, shrub-, and fern-filled wet meadows (**C**). The openness of this area is a refreshing contrast to the deep woods, and different birds can be found here nesting in the kind of niche or habitat they favor. Yellow warblers sing *sweet-sweet-sweeter-than-sweet* and common yellowthroats call *witchity-witchity-witchity.* Catbirds mew their unique call, and song sparrows repeat their frequently musical though monotonous tones. Rose-breasted grosbeaks are also here.

The trails or garden paths in this part of the preserve lead toward Shadow Pond, but take your time getting there, as the flowers here are delightful. Look for early azalea, multiflora roses, iris, cow parsnip, and dwarf ginseng, just to name a few.

Shadow Pond is a shallow, man-made body of water that attracts mallards, wood ducks, and solitary sandpipers (**D**). Naturalist Ted Gilman notes that he frequently sees these migrating shorebirds on the little mudbar in the pond during May. The sandpiper may have another 500 to 1,000 miles to fly before it reaches its Canadian breeding grounds.

It was Fairchild's philosophy to make use of naturalistic plantings, matching those introduced varieties to their original environments. Sitting on the bench at Shadow Pond or strolling along the many trails, one cannot but appreciate the love and dedication that helped create a place of such beauty. After Benjamin Fairchild's death in 1939 at the age of 88, the garden was supervised and maintained for some years by Fairchild's friends and his nephew, B. Tappen Fairchild. It was given to the National Audubon Society in 1945.

Remarks: *Walking time is about an hour. There are many other trails to explore that lead to an interesting variety of habitat, including the banks of the Byram River, the ledge trail where bleeding heart grows, and the laurels and rhododendrons of the northern end. The garden is a beautiful spot to visit in any season. Two books written about the plants of the preserve are available at the environmental bookstore of the Audubon Center in Greenwich, just a mile to the north, off Riversville Rd. The center is located on 285 acres of property, highlighted by miles of trails along ridgetops, stream bottoms, and pondsides. The center's naturalists often conduct walks and natural-history events. The garden is open 7 days a week, from dawn to dusk. The center is open from Tuesday through Sunday, from 9:00 a.m. to 5:00 p.m. Call (203) 869-5272 or write to 613 Riversville Rd., Greenwich, Conn. 06830, for more information.*

37.
Norwalk Islands

Directions: **Norwalk, Conn. The islands can be visited only on the tour sponsored by the Saugatuck Valley Audubon Society of Norwalk. For schedules, reservations, and direc-**

tions to the boat landing, call Mrs. Russell Quick at (203) 866-7830.

Ownership: **City of Norwalk; National Audubon Society; private.**

Within sight of Manhattan's skyline lies a group of small islands that are prime birding areas. The Norwalk Islands just off the southwest coast of Connecticut form the largest heron colony on the North Atlantic coast, with eight species of these exotic long-legged birds present in large numbers.

Access to the five islands in the chain is restricted so that the nesting birds will not be disturbed. The local Audubon Society operates a day-long tour on weekends from April to October. You will probably visit two or three of the islands (the itinerary varies depending on bird activity), accompanied by a naturalist who discusses the islands' birds and natural features.

As the boat leaves Norwalk Harbor, several types of sea and shore birds can be seen on the rocks and buoys that dot the bay. Double-crested cormorants, large black birds often confused with geese and loons, fly in wedge-shaped formations low over the water. They are very common during the summer along the New England coast and are sometimes seen inland on lakes and rivers. They winter along the Gulf and South Atlantic coasts.

Scan the rocks for an American oystercatcher, a large black-and-white shorebird easily identified by its large bright-red bill. This bird is a recent *émigré* to this region, being more common further south along the Virginia and Carolina shores. Like some of the herons and egrets nesting on the islands, it has expanded its range northward in search of new feeding grounds. The year 1983 was the second year that oystercatchers have nested on these rocks, and they have raised three young.

The boat comes to rest on the shore of Shea Island, one of the largest islands, a 50-acre habitat of salt marsh, sandy beach, and mature woodland (see **Long Island Sound's North Shore and the Rhode Island Coast**) that is home to several thousand gulls and hundreds of nesting pairs of black-crowned and yellow-crowned night herons; snowy, great, and cattle egrets; glossy ibis; green herons; and little blue herons. Occasionally a Louisiana heron is seen here, having wandered north from its usual southern territory. Herons, and the closely related egrets, are long-legged wading birds that feed in the shallow mudflats here and on the mainland. They have moved their range north as populations have increased and new feeding areas have had to be found. The Norwalk Islands provide a secure nesting area where they can breed relatively undisturbed by humans. These islands are also used for study of the herons' feeding and migratory patterns. Ornithologists band and color the wings of some birds in order to track them. The herons have been found feeding over a large area stretching from Long Island to Milford Point, Conn., and some that were banded here have been found wintering along the Gulf Coast and in Puerto Rico.

Walking along the shoreline toward the feeding areas, you can see that the plant community falls roughly into zones, depending on a species' ability to adapt to the high salt concentrations and the aridness of the sandy, rocky soil. Closest to the water is the *alterniflora* zone, made up of small plants with tough, fleshy skin that holds moisture within the plant and helps it withstand alternate flooding by tides and exposure to air and wind. A few feet up the shore is the second zone, which is dominated by beach grass, *Spartina patens* (see **#14** and **#77**). A third zone is known as the *Salicornia* and is dominated by the hardy goosefoot plant, so named because of its resemblance to a goose's foot. It has a very tough covering that can withstand the harsh winds and salt spray off the water. Beyond this is a large open area of salt marsh, a type of habitat that is one of the richest ecosystems in the world (see **#29**). Note the very tall beach grass here. Nutrients from marsh plants and organisms produce about eight tons of biomass per acre annually, about double what can be produced in cultivated fields. The salt marsh is very important in providing nutrients for shellfish, bluefish, bass, and other marine life in the surrounding ocean waters. The marsh also acts as a filter to trap and neutralize pollutants, thereby keeping them out of the food chain.

In the mudflats beyond the salt marsh you may see a glossy ibis, a large brown bird with long legs and a downward-curved bill. It pecks around in the shallow water looking for hermit crabs and other small crustaceans. Ibises are closely related to herons but can be differentiated in flight because, unlike herons, they fly with their necks outstretched.

Flying overhead between the shore and the dense oak woodlands of the interior are many black-crowned night herons. There are about 500 pairs nesting on this island alone. They are distinguished by a black-gray body and a white underbelly. On a midsummer visit, you are likely to see young birds, more brownish in color than the adults, practicing their flying techniques by soaring high in the air and suddenly dropping.

Circling around the island, the trail leads through a particularly arid area where many prickly-pear cacti grow low to the ground (see **#24**). They blossom in late June with beautiful yellow flowers, and their ripe fruit in late summer is said to be delicious. Cacti, of which this is a major New England colony, are remnants of a time when this region was warmer than it is now. They have survived here where the moderating effect of the ocean has created a microclimate in which the cacti thrive.

The trail now opens up onto a beach composed of coarse sand and small stones, which give a clue to the geological origins of the islands. Like Long Island directly across the sound, the Norwalk Islands are part of the terminal moraine of the Wisconsin glacier. Here is where the glacier stopped its advance and, as it began to recede, deposited loose stones and sand that it had carried for hundreds of miles. These deposits became many of the islands that dot the southern New England coastline (see **Long Island, Cape Cod, and the Islands**).

Just before returning to the boat landing, the trail passes through a low grassy and shrubby area that serves as a rookery for hundreds of gulls. In this hollow, herring gulls have several hundred nests under bushes. Even when there are no eggs or young birds in the nests, the adult birds do not appreciate human intrusion into their territory. They circle overhead, squawking loudly and dive-bombing—they are often bold enough to knock off a person's hat (see **#17** and **#77**).

After a 3-hour visit to Shea Island, the tour may go to Chimon Island, another large island. Here you can explore on your own for about 2 hours the bird, shore, and plant communities, which are very similar to those of Shea Island.

Remarks: *A birding book, binoculars, and a camera are useful on this trip. Also bring food for lunch. There is plenty of room aboard the boat for coolers and other gear. Swimming is permitted on the island's beaches. Reservations are necessary (see Directions), preferably several weeks in advance.*

38.

Devil's Den
Preserve

Directions: Weston, Conn. From New Haven, take I-95 west to Milford and the Merritt Parkway (Route 15) west to Exit 42, about 30 miles in all. Go north on Route 57 about

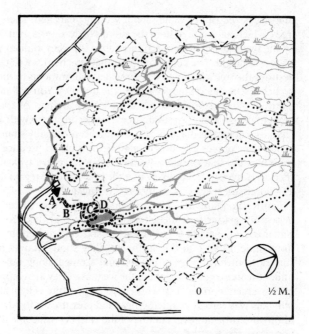

3 miles to Weston center. Travel north about 1.8 miles on Route 53; turn west (left) on Godfrey Rd. Go 0.5 mile and turn left on Pent Rd. The preserve's parking area is on the right.

Ownership: **The Nature Conservancy.**

The largest undeveloped area in southwestern Connecticut, Devil's Den consists of over 1,500 acres of primarily deciduous woodland, as well as low-lying swamps, high ledges with rock outcrops affording fine views, and steep slopes that offer a challenge to the hiker. At least 450 plant species have been identified here, and detailed guidebooks to trees, flowers, ferns, and geological findings are available at the preserve headquarters. Over 20 miles of trails wind through the preserve. The 1½-mile Laurel Trail, one of the easiest and most accessible, begins at the parking area and leads through areas representative of the whole preserve, and of the surrounding region as well.

As the trail leaves the parking area, it passes through stands of young American chestnut trees (**A**). Chestnuts, once the dominant species in this region, were virtually eliminated by the chestnut blight that struck the United States about seventy years ago. These young trees, which have grown from the stumps of dead trees, will be killed by the blight before they reach more than 2 inches in diameter and 15 feet in height. The blight, a fungus that attaches itself to the bark, destroys the tree's ability to deliver water and nutrients to the upper branches. Unable to produce leaves, the tree dies. You will note that many of the chestnuts here are tagged; they are part of an experiment to develop blight-resistant trees by injecting them with a harmless strain of fungus that seems to counteract the deadly strain. If this experiment proves effective, it may be possible to produce blight-resistant trees that can grow to the former large size typical of this species. However, it is unlikely that the tree will ever regain its status as a dominant species in southern New England.

Farther along the trail are two boulders (**B**) deposited here by the Wisconsin glacier as it melted about 10,000 years ago. Known as *glacial erratics,* having been picked up and carried here by the ice from some distance to the northwest, they show grooves on their surface from having been dragged and scraped along other rocks under the tremendous weight of the ice mass. They are composed of gneiss, a metamorphic rock whose layered structure of light and dark minerals was caused by intense heat and pressure during the period of upward thrusting and faulting of the earth's crust some 250 million years ago.

As the trail winds through a small hollow, it passes through the re-creation of a charcoal-manufacturing site (**C**). This was a major rural industry here 150 to 200 years ago. Most of the surrounding land was clear-cut for charcoal production, and later was used for agriculture. Originally an oak-hickory forest, the woodlands are in a well-developed stage of succession, having returned to a mature forest such as existed two or three centuries ago. The trees that began to reclaim the open pasture about 100 years ago were mostly gray birch and redcedar. Known as pioneer species, these are often the first trees to reclaim open land that is not maintained. They thrive in direct sunlight and are fast-growing, reaching maturity in 20 to 30 years—a relatively short time. However, their seeds cannot take hold in the shaded ground beneath them. Other species—here, primarily oaks, hickories, and red maples—which require shaded conditions, became established in the understory. About 30 to 40 years after the start of the successional process, the oaks, hickories, and maples overtook the cedar and birch to become the dominant species. These hardwoods are slower-growing than the softer pioneer species and more tolerant of competition for light and water. They will live on in an area for many decades because their mature trees block sunlight from the forest floor, inhibiting the growth of any competing understory species. If the forest as a whole remains essentially undisturbed either by cutting or disease, then these shade-loving species will continue to dominate here, new seedlings of the same species continually growing up to replace the older trees.

The soil and moisture conditions in different regions of New England dictate that different species will be involved in the successional process. For example, in the sandy soil of Cape Cod redcedar is the pioneer species, but it later gives way to pitch pine rather than maple since pitch pine is more tolerant of the arid conditions. Finally, the pines will give way to varieties of oak—bear and scrub—which have adapted to dry conditions and can become established in the shade of the pitch pines. In central New England, white pine is a pioneer species, along with gray birch, and often becomes the dominant species as well. In northern New England, conifers such as spruce and balsam are frequent pioneers on open areas, eventually shifting to a mature northern hardwood forest.

The trail rises beyond the charcoal site to a rock ledge that was exposed by the glacier, which pulled the topsoil away from the high places and deposited it in the lower areas. The topography here is relatively rugged, owing to this plucking and quarrying action of the glacial ice. Some deep grooving can be seen here, as well as smoothing or polishing of the rock from the movement over it of fine-grained sands. The trail descends through some eastern redcedars on the right and circles past an exposed ledge of granite. Archaeological diggings have shown that the space under the rock overhang (**D**) was used by local indians as a hunting shelter as long ago as 1,000 years. As the trail proceeds to the shore of Godfrey Pond, the trees become mostly beech and birch, in contrast to the red and white oak found on the upper slope. This indicates that the area was more recently cleared and that the successional process is at an earlier stage.

Godfrey Pond is a man-made lake, created by a dam to produce power for a mill that stood here from the early 1800s to about 1900. A large glacial deposit of rock at the north end marks the point where a brook flows into the pond from the uplands. The trail continues around the pond and over a dike at the south end where the mill used to stand. The trail then leads away from the pond through an area where pink lady's slippers proliferate in late May and early June. The cool, moist, shaded microclimate in this area is also an ideal habitat for ground pine, shining club moss, and a wide variety of lichens and ferns. The tallest fern here is the New York fern, which reaches over 2 feet in height. It has a distinctive dark green color and grows in extensive masses.

The Laurel Trail continues uphill, where more glacial evidence can be found in the rocks and boulders scattered about, and rejoins the main trail returning to the parking area.

Remarks: *This is an easy walk, taking about 1 hour. There are many other trails that can be explored, some of them all-day hikes. Consult the trail map available at the preserve headquarters. A warden/naturalist is sometimes also available to answer questions. Cross-country skiing is permitted in the winter. For information about the preserve's scheduled activities contact the headquarters at Box 1162, Weston, Conn. 06883, (203) 220-4991.*

39.
Milford Point
Sanctuary

Directions: **Milford Conn. From New Haven, take I-95 about 9 miles west to Exit 34. From the exit, turn east (left) onto U.S. 1 and go 0.2 mile to a light at Lansdale Ave. Go right here, and in 0.4 mile continue to bear right as Lansdale Ave. joins Milford Point Rd. In another 0.3 mile you come to an intersection at Naugatuck Ave.; continue straight past the tennis courts and Court St. after another 1.1 miles. Shortly, the road bears right, and in another 0.8 mile, after a sharp left in the road, you come to a stop at the junction of Seaview Ave. Turn right and proceed 0.3 mile to the New Haven Bird Club Sanctuary. A large sign marks the entrance—take the right fork into the sanctuary parking lot.** *Do not take the private road on your left.*

Ownership: **State of Connecticut; leased by the New Haven Bird Club.**

A special 12-acre parcel of beach has been preserved on this heavily populated section of southwestern Connecticut coastline. Just offshore, two small barrier beaches rise above the highest reach of the water and serve as nesting grounds for up to two hundred least terns. At low tide, extensive mudflats stretch to these grounds, affording a rich feeding area for shorebirds and herons. Above the high-tide line, low-dune areas support nesting shorebirds such as killdeer and piping plover. A short, intertidal walk out to Milford Point allows for a wide-open view of Long Island Sound to the south and an additional 890 acres of mudflats to the west (see **Long Island Sound's North Shore and the Rhode Island Coast**).

Pass under the trees and check in at the shelter. There is a list of recent wildlife sightings here that you can scan for anything of particular interest. Continue across the private road (please do not use this at any time) and out onto the beach. This first section up to the wooden fence along the southern boundary is owned by the sanctuary.

The upper beach is dominated by beach grass, which stabilizes a shallow dune system (**A**) (see **#79**). The scientific name for this plant is *Ammophila*, or "sand lover," and is a highly appropriate description of its life-style. As it grows, beach grass sends out branching, horizontal stems whose tips emit new leaves and long, fibrous roots. If sand continues to bury the plant, it grows fast enough to keep new leaves uncovered. This network of vegetation can securely anchor a sand dune, and only severe attacks by wind or water can eat into this firm holdfast of roots and rhizomes. Consequently, damage to this stabilizing vegetation can cause great devastation along dune systems. Among the clumps of beach grass, beach pea and seaside goldenrod also grow, adding much color as they bloom.

These dunes (**B**) provide cover for the nesting piping plover, a shy, solitary species whose numbers have been decreasing in recent years due to human disturbance. It is identified by its pale, sand-

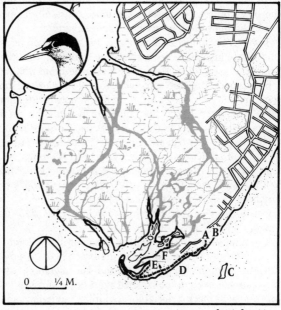

Inset: Least tern

colored upper parts, orange legs, and a yellow-tipped black bill. This coloring provides excellent camouflage on the dry sand of the beach, and piping plovers can often avoid danger simply by running or crouching motionless.

Piping plovers are early migrants, and by April and early May they will arrive at nesting grounds all along the Atlantic Coast, having left behind their wintering grounds in southeastern North America (see **#96** for more on migration). The female lays four speckled, buff-colored eggs in a slight hollow lined with stones or shell fragments and situated along the dunes and upper beach. Both sexes incubate the eggs; watch for the off-duty mate feeding along the waterline or on the exposed mudflats. Listen for its haunting, rich, whistled call of *peep-lo* as it flits across the sand. Piping plovers are very deliberate in their feeding—they run a short distance, pause, cock head to the side, and make a stab at a food item. They eat marine worms, larvae, crustaceans, and mollusks. Later they will bring the chicks across the sound to feed at the waterline. These movements across the beach-face make the chicks particularly vulnerable to heavy beach traffic, especially that of off-road vehicles. Sanctuary protection allows them to continue to nest in this populated section of Connecticut.

The two small barrier beaches (**C**) lying offshore are a nesting place for least terns and serve as a stopover for many other migrating birds, such as laughing gulls and common and roseate terns. During the breeding season these sandy areas, constantly lapped with an everchanging waterline, are home to least terns.

Least terns are the smallest of the North American terns and have undergone increasing decimation due to human disturbance in recent years (see **#15**). Here, with the same protection afforded the piping plover, they are somewhat free of human pressures. Watch them as they feed along the shoreline waters. With light, buoyant flight they often hover, then dive down and skim small fish and crustaceans off the surface of the water, earning them the name "little striker." The fish are consumed immediately or brought back to the nest to help satiate a hungry chick. Although small in size, least terns are extremely aggressive and protective while nesting. With a shrill *kip-kip-kip* call, they dive and swoop incessantly at anything perceived as a threat. Sharp, needlelike bills serve as a lesson to anyone who wanders too close. (See **#23** for more on terns.)

Continue along in the intertidal zone to Milford Point (**D**). Please be sure to stay well down along the beach here, as private houses line this portion. During spring and fall migrations, the exposed mudflats are likely to be covered with numerous species of shorebirds, such as black-bellied plover, dunlin, sanderling, and the petite semipalmated sandpiper. At the same time, the open water beyond may attract good numbers of waterfowl, including bufflehead, scoter, goldeneye, and red-breasted merganser. During the winter months impressive rafts of scaup may also congregate (see **#45**).

Once out on the point, the sandy beach opens up once again, supporting vegetation that includes tall wormwood, scattered clumps of bayberry, salt-spray rose, and a small stand of tree-of-heaven (*Ailanthus*) (**E**). The presence of tree-of-heaven here is testimony to previous use of the land as a parking lot. This introduced species is remarkable for its hardiness and rapid growth, allowing it to withstand the rigors of poor, sunbaked earth and still flourish. Thus it is able to thrive in the cracks and crannies of pavement in many cities along the East Coast. Tree-of-heaven is distinguished by its gray bark with pale-buff fissures running perpendicular to each other along the trunk; stout, ocher yellow twigs covered with a fine down; and a strongly unpleasant odor emitted from its flowers as they bloom in June. These trees, along with the vegetation just mentioned, allow migrating species such as Savannah and song sparrows, yellow-rumped warblers, and chickadees adequate cover.

The 890 acres of marsh along the west side of the beach are part of the Charles E. Wheeler Preserve (**F**). This area can be a mecca for shorebirds and a feeding place for numerous heron species and waterfowl in the off-hunting season. Look especially for mallards and black ducks, both of which build their nests along the marsh edge in spring.

Remarks: *A spotting scope is useful, though not necessary, for birding in this area. More species of shorebirds and herons are present at low tide than at high tide, so plan accordingly. Hunting is allowed on the Charles E. Wheeler Preserve during season. Kevin Gunther is the caretaker of this property and can be very helpful with any questions you may have. A thorough description of the birds to be seen at Milford can be found in* Twenty-five Birding Areas of Connecticut *by Noble S. Proctor. Please respect all private property. Camping is available from April through September at Sleeping Giant State Park, about 15 miles away between Hamden and Wallingford. For information contact Sleeping Giant State Park, 200 Mount Carmel Ave., Hamden, Conn. 06351.*

40.

Westwoods

Directions: Guilford, Conn. From New Haven go east on I-95 about 12 miles to Exit 57. Turn southeast onto U.S. 1 toward Guilford. Turn right on Peddlers Rd., just before Bishop's Orchards. Go 1 mile on this road to a small parking area on the left, just past Denison Rd.

Ownership: Four cooperating state and private agencies and several private ownerships; inquiries handled by Westwoods Trail Committee of the Guilford Land Conservation Trust.

Less than 1 mile from the center of Guilford lies the enchanting 2,000-acre Westwoods preserve. Rocky dens and caves, created by the fracturing of huge granite outcrops, are set in the midst of a mature hemlock forest. A series of wooded swamps, small streams, and a large lake emptying into Long Island Sound (see **Long Island Sound's North Shore and the Rhode Island Coast**) provide good opportunities for the bird-watcher and botanist alike.

The white-circle trail leads from the parking area through an oak-hickory forest and over a boardwalk, crossing a low-lying red-maple swamp (**A**) (see **#13**). This wetland, and others at Westwoods, are believed to have originated as small glacial ponds, which have been gradually filling in. There is no assurance, however, that an orderly process of succession will occur with the wooded swamp evolving into a drier but still-moist low-slope community (red oak, tuliptree, white ash, hophornbeam, and so on). Ecologist Neil Jorgensen writes that certain natural disturbances, such as beaver damage, blow-downs, and flooding have probably kept most red-maple swamps open enough to allow for the germination and growth of the sun-loving saplings. In those rare places where the canopy remains undisturbed, however, one would suspect a low-slope forest very slowly to take hold.

The swamp is a good place to observe migrant warblers, especially during the first 2 weeks of May. Though one might see any number of different birds during this exciting period, look for species usually associated with wetlands. These include the yellow and yellow-throated warblers, redstarts, waterthrushes, and blue-gray gnat-catchers (see **#96** for more on migration).

Find the yellow-circle trail to the right at the end of the boardwalk.

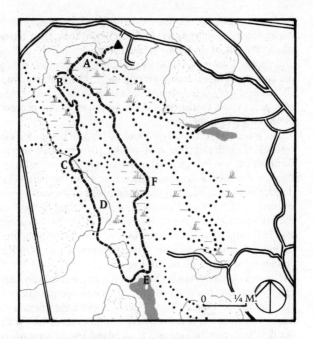

As the trail ascends the ridgeline, it navigates the first of a long string of narrow, rocky clefts and passageways (**B**). You'll soon find yourself stooping and bending through the jumble of tremendous granite boulders. These outcroppings are part of the larger Stony Creek granite formation, a 600-million-year-old domelike wedge of igneous rock. A series of faults, activated by nearby but ancient seismic activities (see **#83**), and the actions of frost within the rock fissures have produced the dramatic splits and caves. Notice the pink orthoclase feldspar crystals, along with translucent quartz, dark biotite mica, and silvery muscovite mica.

Many glacial erratics have been left stranded here on a large exposed rock dome (**C**) (see **#85**). A close look will tell you they are of the same composition as the surrounding bedrock and are probably pieces broken off from nearby ledges and then deposited by the glaciers as they melted. Some however have been transported from as far away as Durham—about 10 miles to the north.

Notice also the incredible process of soil formation going on right before your eyes (see **#85**). Several trees are growing, surprisingly enough, on a very thin mat of lichens, mosses, and soil all seemingly woven together. You can actually lift up the edge of the mat a bit if you try. It is entirely possible that the development of these few inches of soil atop this bare ridge has taken thousands of years, beginning with lichens (see **#88**) on naked rock, then mosses colonizing the bits of earth blown into the cracks. As the rootlets spread and captured more soil and as preceding generations of vegetation died and built up the mat with organic matter, higher plants such as shrubs and trees could spread their own shallow roots and make a stab at survival. Evidence of differing stages in this process can be observed here on the ridge.

The forest at Westwoods is about 50 percent hemlocks, somewhat unusual considering that only about 10 percent of the forests in Connecticut are evergreen (**D**). According to forester Michael Pochan, a number of reasons may account for the hemlocks' abundance here: the devastating chestnut blight of the early years of this century, which reduced competition; the cutting of hardwoods for the brickyard kilns of North Haven; and the 1938 hurricane, which toppled many taller trees. These factors, plus the original presence of hemlocks in the ravines here, have contributed to making this lovely conifer Westwoods' dominant tree.

The yellow-circle trail eventually ends at the northern edge of Lost Lake, a brackish body of water connected to a larger salt marsh by a channel under the railroad tracks (**E**). Before the railroad was built many years ago, Lost Lake was a true salt marsh (see **#29**). Now the flow between the lake and Long Island Sound is greatly reduced, and the water is quite shallow, thus limiting any resident fish population. Various worms and other invertebrates, however, provide a good food source for shorebirds, and during low tide one can scan the exposed mudflats from this high bluff with binoculars or a scope and look for sandpipers, yellowlegs, and associated species.

The orange-circle trail is much gentler than the yellow trail and traverses flatlands, swamps, and some rocky terrain. Red foxes make their dens among the caves and holes of Westwoods (**F**) and are occasionally seen. Observation and identification of their scats (droppings), however, may be the most reliable method of ascertaining their presence. A typical fox scat is about 2 to 3 inches long, twisted, and pointed at one or both ends. It usually contains hair, from rabbits or other small mammals, and sometimes berries. Foxes tend to leave their scats at noticeable places along the trail, such as an exposure of flat bedrock in the midst of a forest or on a mound of earth. It is believed that this practice is connected to the marking of their territorial boundaries.

Remarks: *The walk takes a good 4 hours. The yellow-circle trail takes longer than the returning orange-circle trail because it involves more climbing. For those who choose not to walk the yellow trail, the white-circle trail is somewhat less demanding, and the green-circle trail is easiest of all, each* taking about 1½ hours. Westwoods is connected to the 350-acre Stony Creek Quarry Preserve by the green-rectangle trail. Remnants of old quarrying operations are evident there in the form of stone piles, granite spoils, and old railroad beds. There is still an active quarry operation at the northwest corner of the property. A detailed map of Westwoods is available at Bishop's Orchard (see Directions) or at the town clerk's office in Guilford. Because the trail system here is so extensive (40 miles), one must be careful not to confuse the circular blazes with the rectangular ones, nor get lost on the other unmapped paths. Great Harbor Salt Marsh can be reached by following the white-circle trail to the south. Camping is available at nearby Hammonasset Beach State Park in Madison.

41.

Bluff Head

Directions: **North Guilford, Conn. From New Haven, take I-95 (Connecticut Turnpike) east about 13 miles to Exit 58. Go south on Route 77 toward Guilford 0.5 mile. A small, primitive parking area is on the west (right) side of the road, among the trees. There are no signs.**

Ownership: **Guilford Land Conservation Trust.**

Hawk-watching from the top of this 765-foot-high basalt ridge is excellent during the fall migration, with as many as five thousand broadwings flying by in one spectacular late September afternoon. During the rest of the year, Bluff Head provides good birding for other species, and fine views of the Coginchaug Valley and Long Island Sound. The Mattabesset Trail, one of Connecticut's longest hiking routes, passes through the preserve on its way toward the Massachusetts border.

Follow the blue blazes up a steep hillside, and proceed through a dry oak forest along the eastern side of the bluff. Eventually you will come to a series of open lookouts, the second being the highest and the best (**A**). On a clear day you can see north to the tall office buildings in distant Hartford, and south to Long Island Sound and Long Island's sandy shores. To the east are the rolling hills and valleys of south-central Connecticut. Directly below you is Meyer Huber Pond, a body of water that draws great blue herons, wood ducks, kingfishers (see **#46**), and other aquatic species.

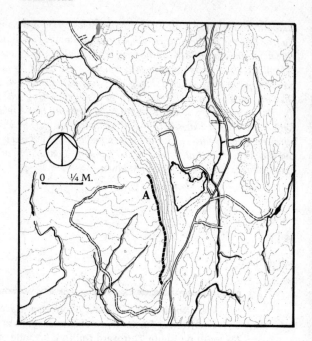

Hawk-watching is generally better in the fall than in the spring for complex reasons, some of which can be addressed here. The number of birds heading north is usually less than the number of birds heading south, partly because of wintering mortality rates, but also because the surviving chicks born up north swell the populations as the migratory procession travels south. Also, the nesting or sibling groups tend to fly south together, producing a more concentrated effect. Finally, the weather patterns of fall often produce a wind-funneling effect, which the birds use to their advantage (see **#96** for more on migration).

To save energy, the hawks tend to congregate near physical features that provide deflective uplift; they fly along mountain ridges such as this one that deflect the wind upward, creating conditions conducive to a soaring flight. The best hawk watching is usually after the passage of a cold front accompanied by brisk northwest winds. The deflection of these winds makes for exciting bird watching.

Thermals, or bubbles of rising warm air, are also important factors during hawk migration. A thermal occurs when the sun heats the air near the ground, usually in an open environment, forcing that air to rise. Broad-winged hawks, in particular, use the thermals as a means of flying great distances with a minimal expenditure of energy. They let the thermal lift them, sometimes thousands of feet, and then as the thermal dissipates, they soar downward and toward their destination, seeking other such bubbles of rising air along the way. It is not uncommon to see broadwings soaring in large groups, or kettles. Using their keen eyesight, the birds quickly move toward kettles that have already been discovered by others. On September 14, 1979, over 21,000 broadwings were seen from Hawk Mountain, Pa. (see **Mid-Atlantic Inland volume**).

Prominent topological features, such as the Atlantic coastline, the Appalachians, or the shorelines of the Great Lakes, also help determine what route the hawks will take. The birds tend to follow a long natural landmark, which ornithologists call a diversion or leading line, for at least two basic reasons: they are reluctant to cross large expanses of open water, and they can obtain good uplift along the mountaintops.

The broad-winged hawk is roughly the size of a crow. It breeds throughout most of eastern United States and Canada and feeds on frogs, toads, small mammals, and some species of insects. Broadwings are members of a group of soaring hawks called *buteos*, which have chunky bodies, broad wings, and wide, rounded tails. Another common member of this subfamily one is likely to see here is the red-tailed hawk.

A considerable number and variety of birds breed on Bluff Head. Worm-eating warblers nest on the hillsides, and solitary vireos find sites in the hemlock–mountain-laurel woods here along the edge. The entire area has been cited by Connecticut bird-watchers as being prime territory, with one party recording seventy-five species in a single spring day.

Remarks: *The walk up Bluff Head takes about 20 minutes. Wear sturdy shoes with good traction for the crumbly slopes. One can continue on the blue trail west over several ridgetops. Consult the* Connecticut Walk Book, *published by Connecticut Forest and Park Association, 1010 Main St., East Hartford, Conn. 06108. The area is popular and may be especially crowded on warm, sunny weekends.* Twenty-five Birding Areas in Connecticut, *by Noble Proctor, offers further information about Bluff Head. Camping is permitted at nearby Hammonasset Beach State Park (see* **#42**).

42.

Hammonasset Beach
State Park

Directions: **Madison, Conn. From New Haven, take I-95 (Connecticut Turnpike) east about 18 miles to Exit 62. Go about 2 miles south to the entrance tollbooth. Drive south and east for approximately 1.7 miles to a parking area on the left and a sign that reads "Picnicking." This is just before Meig's Point.**

Ownership: **Connecticut Parks and Recreation Unit.**

Although 918-acre Hammonasset Beach State Park is one of the most popular recreation areas in Connecticut, it is also one of the state's better birding spots. Salt marsh, mudflat, open water, and wooded thickets attract many different types of birds, from migrating warblers to breeding clapper rails. A number of species unusual for the region have been sighted here, including snowy owls, red phalaropes, and black-legged kittiwakes.

An unmarked trail begins at the northeastern corner of the picnic area and heads into the thin woods (**A**). This little oasis of oak, sassafras, and maple is surrounded by many acres of salt meadow (see **#29**). During fall migration from early September to mid-October these trees serve as perching, resting, and feeding spots for countless songbirds that are heading south. Towhees, sparrows, kinglets, thrushes, numerous kinds of warblers, and other birds stop here. Many birds migrate at night, especially those smaller species that may be vulnerable to predation by gulls, hawks, and falcons. During the day they can frequently be found seeking insects, seeds, and berries. On a fall day you'll find birds flitting about from almost every limb and branch (see **#96** for more on migration).

Continue walking toward the salt meadow, scanning the area from a small bridge (**B**). Great egrets and seaside sparrows nest alongside the ditches and channels, and clapper rails among the higher meadow edges, and snowy egrets in the trees along the edge of the marsh.

Clapper rails are large grayish-brown birds whose laterally compressed bodies aid them in running through the thick marsh grasses. They feed on mudflats in low tide, making use of a long bill that is well adapted for catching crabs, snails, worms, fish, aquatic insects, and other marine organisms. The clapper rail breeds along the Pacific, Gulf, and East coasts, as far north in our region as Cape Cod (see **#27**).

Rails in general are secretive birds and, as ornithologist Roger Tory Peterson states, "more often heard than seen." The clapper is no exception, and its harsh and loud clatter is one of the more familiar salt-marsh sounds. Listen, especially at dusk, for a *kek-kek-kek* or *cha-cha-cha*.

A narrow beach, fringed by salt-marsh cordgrass, is littered with shells, stems, pebbles, and other mostly natural debris (**C**). The variety of birds in the bay varies seasonally. During migration you are apt to see many species of ducks and waterfowl. In summer, local breeders such as gulls, common terns, and possibly least terns fly close by.

The ubiquitous presence of herring, and to a lesser extent, great black-backed gulls is a fairly recent phenomenon and is due both to man's influence and to the behavioral characteristics of the birds themselves. Their population levels have grown tremendously during the middle of this century, partly because of their aggressiveness

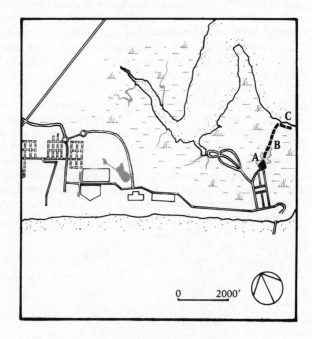

and their ability to live near human activity. Also, food has been readily available from burgeoning garbage dumps, sewage outlets, and processing plants (see **#17** and **#77**).

Historically, gulls were not the dominant East Coast seabird they are today; there were greater varieties and numbers of other birds until widespread hunting in the nineteenth and early twentieth centuries almost wiped them out. By the 1870s herring gulls were a rare bird along the New England coast. After most migrating birds were protected by the passage of the Migratory Bird Treaty Act of 1918, the gulls slowly rose to the position they are in today, primarily because of their great scavenging ability and the readily available food supplied by man's activities. The roseate tern and other members of the tern subfamily never regained their former status.

Great black-backed gulls are readily identifiable because, as their name implies, the tops of their wings and their backs are very dark, while their underparts are white. The birds gain this plumage when they are about 3 years old, changing from the deep mottled gray of immaturity. This large gull is noted for its domineering and sometimes deadly behavior toward other seabirds, often attacking eggs and chicks in order to feed its own young. This usually occurs near the gull's nesting colony and near the nests of other seabirds such as terns, frequently on a secluded sandbar or offshore island.

The beach is intersected by a narrow channel that cuts up into the marsh, and you will have to turn around unless you wade across. If you choose to do so, keep walking toward Long Island Sound and Meig's Point. The higher topography there provides a good viewing point.

Remarks: *The actual walk to the bay beach takes about 10 minutes or less, but can be extended for quite a while by intensive bird-watching. If you walk over to Meig's Point, allow another 10 minutes or so each way. The park itself is likely to be too crowded during the warmer months for topnotch birding. Visiting here in the spring and fall is much quieter and more rewarding. For more information on the other birding areas within the park—and they are considerable—consult Noble Proctor's book,* Twenty-five Birding Areas in Connecticut. *A scope is useful here for viewing waterfowl. Camping is available at the park; call (203) 245-2785.*

43.

Hurd

State Park

Directions: **Middle Haddam, Conn. From Hartford, take I-91 south about 10 miles to Exit 22 for Route 9. Go southeast on Route 9 about 5 miles; go east across the river on Route 66 and continue about 5 miles to Cobalt. Turn south (right) on Route 151; after 2.4 miles bear right at a sign for the park. Continue 0.5 mile to the entrance. Turn right and continue for 1.1 miles to a small parking area on the right, opposite the Split Rock Trail sign.**

Ownership: **Connecticut Parks and Recreation Unit.**

Two distinct and differing vantage points of the Connecticut River are accessible by foot at this picturesque 884-acre state park. One trail leads to rocky bluffs high above the eastern shoreline, providing good views of the river and surrounding hills, while another ends at the water's edge, where an interesting variety of floodplain trees line the bank (see **Long Island Sound's North Shore and the Rhode Island Coast**).

Yellow blazes and a small sign reading Split Rock Trail-River Vista point the way through a mixed-hardwood forest to a steep granite ridge that overlooks the river (**A**). Bear Hill, at an elevation of 640 feet, stands across the river to the left. Notice the pitch pines and chestnut oaks here among the cliffs, growing in exposed and dry places where other trees cannot survive.

Split Rock, a massive block of granite with a 25-foot-deep crevice, lies a short way downhill to the right. It is situated in such a way that one can peer directly down into the crack. Frost action within the joint plane may have been responsible for this phenomenon. Purplish crystals of smoky quartz can be found throughout the rocks here. Local radiation at the time of formation was responsible for the coloring.

To get to the river bottom, one must return almost to the road until the purple-blaze trail is intersected on the left. Follow this downhill past some very large black birches, some red oak, shagbark hickory, and beech to a grassy plateau bordering the river (**B**). Perhaps 100 feet wide, this flattened plain represents the buildup of

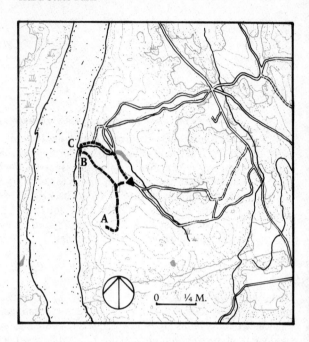

sand, silt, and other flood-propelled material over many years. A group of trees here are varieties one usually finds within a floodplain habitat. They prefer moist, well-drained soils and must be capable of living through periodic flooding, but also drier conditions during summer and fall. In fact, the main difference between a floodplain community and a wet-meadow community is that the former dries out seasonally, whereas the latter usually remains quite moist year-round.

Cottonwoods, silver maples, and sycamores are three of the more notable species, and each displays at least one unique or identifying characteristic. The cottonwood, for example, produces great quantities of white cottonlike material that is attached to the seed catkins in spring. This aids in seed dispersal by the wind and can frequently be found in small heaps along the ground. Silver maples have the largest winged seeds of any native maple and are also known for their somewhat delicate and deeply cut leaves, which look silvery white on the undersides. You will often find grass growing under silver maples, because enough sunlight can penetrate the moderate foliage. Sycamores are among the largest deciduous trees in the eastern United States and are easily recognized by their mottled creamy-white-and-brown flaking bark. Their fruit is the familiar round "itchy ball."

The Connecticut River is the longest river in New England, flowing 407 miles from its source in northern New Hampshire to Long Island Sound near Old Lyme (**C**). Like the Hudson, it is partially tidal and has a lower portion that is brackish. It is also a major fishery for the American shad, a chunky member of the herring family that returns from the ocean to freshwater spawning grounds.

Shad are a migratory fish, spending their winters along the southeastern seaboard, their summers north around the Bay of Fundy, and their breeding months in various northeastern rivers. They usually enter the Connecticut River in early April when the average water temperature is about 55 degrees and swim to the shallow mouths of tributary creeks, where they mate. The female lays about 25,000 eggs. The larvae, or fry, hatch out in the remarkably brief time of 5 to 7 days and remain in the river until the fall, when they migrate south. In about 4 years they come back to their natal waters to spawn and begin the entire cycle again.

It is estimated that about a hundred commercial fishermen on the Connecticut use drift nets to catch the shad, which average 3 to 5 pounds. Countless other sport fishermen use various lures during the often hectic spring run. Shad are considered to be relatively free of the toxic chemicals and contaminants that other fish, such as carp or perch, pick up, mainly because the shad are transients whereas the others are permanent residents.

After exploring the river's edge for a while, find a returning trail to the left of the little feeder stream and take it uphill to the entrance road. Your car is to the right several hundred yards away.

Remarks: *The walk to both spots takes about 1¼ hours. Camping is available along the river here, but it may be limited to boaters. Call (203) 526-2336 for information on accessibility, permits, and fees. The park is fairly popular, so time your visit accordingly. Cross-country ski trails are marked here.*

44.

Devil's Hopyard
State Park

Directions: **East Haddam, Conn. From Hartford, take Route 2 southeast about 22 miles to Exit 19, then continue south on Route 11 about 6 miles to Exit 5. Turn right and**

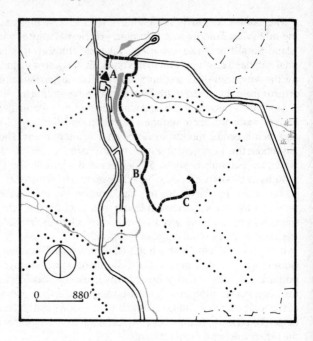

go about 3 miles, then turn south (left) on North Plain Rd. to the parking area near Chapman's Falls.

Ownership: Connecticut Parks and Recreation Unit.

Set in the rural and hilly valley of the Eight Mile River, Devil's Hopyard State Park contains Chapman's Falls, a 60-foot-high flow of water that cascades through a rock channel pockmarked by a number of potholes. The river valley is a natural flyway for migrating birds, and until 1977 this was the only known nesting site in the state for the Acadian flycatcher. Other features include several scenic overlooks, a small cave, hemlock woods, and access to the trout-stocked waterway.

Over a century ago, Chapman's Falls was the site of a mill, but now it is free flowing and accessible (**A**). The river has cut its channel through a bedrock of schist, a metamorphic rock that tends to weather somewhat easily because of the platelike and elongated shape of its component minerals. You can see this typical layering or foliation of schist in those exposed portions of rock along the edge.

During low water one can also see the circular potholes that have been carved into the riverbottom by eddying pieces of rock (**A**). In a high-energy environment such as this one, where large volumes of water often crash through the channel and over falls, swirls and eddies may form, especially at the base of a plunge pool or where the cascading water drops and strikes. As bits of sand, pebbles, and even small boulders are churned around and around, a drilling motion occurs, and a hole is slowly created. Although most potholes are a yard or less in width and about a foot deep (as these are), huge ones up to 60 feet wide and 18 feet deep are occasionally discovered.

Cross over the top of the falls at Foxtown Rd. and down along the other, or eastern, side where you will pick up a trail that parallels the river. Scarlet tanagers and rose-breasted grosbeaks are frequently heard singing in the tops of the trees here. Both of their songs sound like variations on that of a robin—a long, clear two or three note whistle. Hooded warblers nest along the hillsides. A small covered footbridge once crossed the river here below the falls but was washed away in a recent flood. A replacement is being made.

As you walk along the boulder-strewn shoreline and eventually reach the large hemlocks, (**B**), keep a sharp eye on the lower limbs of these conifers for the little greenish-yellow Acadian flycatcher. Although only a pair of these birds nested in the park prior to 1977, the numbers have gradually increased since then. According to Dave Rosgen, coordinator of the *Connecticut Breeding Bird Atlas*, there are now about six pairs in this area, and several dozen statewide. The reasons for this range extension are unknown, but it represents a complete reversal of an earlier regional decline. In 1933 ornithologist Ludlow Griscom wrote, "Since 1900 the Acadian Flycatcher is definitely known to have abandoned the greater part of its northeastern breeding range." Then, writing in 1964, John Bull continued the story by stating that the "reasons for its disappearance are not clear but like certain other species on the periphery of their ranges the Acadian flycatcher has withdrawn from its northeastern limits." Whatever the reasons may be for its comeback, bird-watchers throughout the state are excited by its presence.

Because the Acadian flycatcher closely resembles at least two other breeding flycatchers in southern New England, the only sure way to identify it is through its short but diagnostic song. Roger Tory Peterson describes this as "a short explosive pit-see! or wee-see!, [with a] sharp upward inflection."

The basket-shaped nest of this little bird is usually near a river gorge or stream bottom. Here in Devil's Hopyard the birds nest on this side of the river where hemlocks are most numerous. They lay 2 to 4 eggs and incubate them for about 2 weeks. The young birds take their first flight approximately 2 weeks later and slowly start catching their own insects and spiders.

Among the other birds in the vicinity that can usually be seen or heard during the warmer months are Louisiana waterthrushes, Canada warblers, veeries, and wood thrushes.

An indistinct side trail to the left of the main path leads up to Devil's Oven, a narrow cleft in the rock that reminds one of a large, old-fashioned outdoor oven (**C**). The cave is about 8 feet long and 3 feet wide and may have been created during a minor faulting or slippage of the surrounding schist. The region is known to be an active one for minor earthquakes, and such tremors may have moved these rocks around. If you walk to the right of the cave and around and above it, you will find a small clearing offering good views of the nearby countryside. It may also be possible to see coyotes or wild turkeys, which have occasionally been sighted here.

Return to the falls and parking area the way you came in or consult the map for a loop trail.

Remarks: *Walking time is about an hour. There are a number of other trails to explore here. Noble Proctor describes more of the birdlife of the park in* Twenty-five Birding Areas in Connecticut. *Camping sites are available here, but the park is popular and may be crowded during the summer. For further information call (203) 873-8566.*

45.
Bluff Point
State Park

Directions: **Groton, Conn. From New London, take I-95 east about 4 miles to Exit 88 and take Route 117 south for 1.1 miles. Turn west (right) on U.S. 1 and continue 0.3 mile to the Groton town hall. Turn left onto Depot St. and go 0.4 mile, where it dips under a railway bridge. The road then turns to dirt and continues beside the bay for 0.3 mile to the parking area.**

Ownership: **Connecticut Parks and Recreation Unit.**

Through the years, development along the Connecticut coastline has been both extensive and destructive, severely limiting public access to coastline properties. Yet, there exists a large 778-acre tract of land now protected by its status as Bluff Point State Park. Bluff Point is

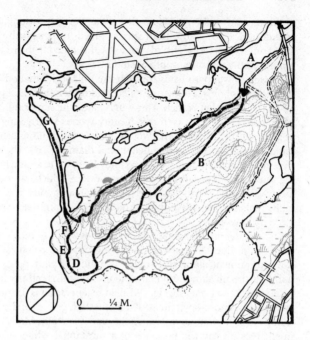

0   ¼ M.

exceptionally rich in variety, with upland hardwoods, old-field regeneration, a half-mile-long sandspit, extensive boulder beaches, and
impressive bluffs. It stands as a good example of a relatively undisturbed piece of Connecticut coast (see **Long Island Sound's North
Shore and the Rhode Island Coast**).

Take a moment to scan the bay along the road, as a host of
waterfowl may congregate here to feed and rest. Depending on the
time of year, you may sight greater and lesser scaups, mute swans,
mallards, and buffleheads, among others (**A**).

Scaups are perhaps the most impressive of these waterfowl, especially with respect to number. During the winter, they may gather
in flocks of up to 50,000 on favorable feeding grounds in saltwater
bays and estuaries. Members of the diving-duck family, they are
known to dive up to 20 feet for crabs, barnacles, and other crustacea;
they also eat wigeon grass and sea lettuce, which are plentiful in the
bay. Some say that the bird's name derives from one of its characteristic calls, a loud, discordant *scaup*. The male scaup can be recognized
by its pale-bluish bill, solid dark head and neck, and white underparts. The female is a uniform brown with a sharply defined white
mask at the base of her bill. Only subtle differences, such as length

of white wing stripe and head sheen, can serve to distinguish the greater and lesser scaup. Both species breed further north, and by late April the majority of birds have left this area for their breeding grounds, only returning south again in October.

A wide gravel path leads through the upland hardwoods out to the rocky shoreline. Follow the gated road until it forks and proceed along the upper left branch. This winds along the center ridge of the peninsula through a mixed oak-hickory woods with young stands of gray and black birch. The woods age as you climb, indicated by the dramatic increase in tree height and diameter (**B**). These older trees have not been disturbed as recently by man. In spring listen for the loud, whistling call of the northern oriole, which can help you locate this orange beauty as it perches high in a trailside tree. Certain individuals stay to weave their pendulous nests and raise young in these open woods.

The vegetation changes as the forest fades into a thick tangle of shrubs and vines. Stone walls indicating previous colonization become prominent along this stretch of trail. On your right, a pure stand of smooth sumac gradually blends into thick catbrier, oriental bittersweet, and honeysuckle. Old-field regeneration is further demonstrated by more-open areas of tall bluestem grasses and scattered clumps of redcedar, hawthorn, and cherry (see **#60**). Many of these small trees display the presence of a substantial white-tailed deer population (**C**); notice that buds and twigs have been chewed off and that lower branches and trunks have been stripped of bark.

In the last few decades, with protection and management, deer populations have increased dramatically in the Northeast. Deer are essentially a forest-edge species, favoring thickets and old abandoned fields, where they browse on twigs, buds, bark, and fruits such as apples and cherries. They occasionally graze on grasses and lichens as well. Thus, Bluff Point's many successional stages create an ideal habitat for deer.

As the fields continue to open up, the trail forks again. Proceed along the left branch. Shortly, the road forks once again out toward the water, and you should stay to the right here. You now get your first good views of the water since leaving the protected bay along the entrance road.

At this point, head back up to a small footpath that winds through thick perennial vegetation such as bayberry, salt-spray rose, and beach plum. On the upper beach here, above reach of even the highest waves, perennials can safely establish themselves. Their bright spring flowers paint the shore, and later the fall fruits serve to nourish many birds. Bayberry (**D**), for example, has glossy oval leaves and stiff gray branches that carry thick clusters of gray fruit. Tree swallows and yellow-rumped warblers gorge themselves on this fruit during migration, and deer eat the buds and twigs throughout the winter. Traditionally, people have also used these berries in candle-making. The berries are boiled until the waxy coating melts and floats to the surface of the water, where it can be skimmed off. This wax is then used to dip candles of a very subtle gray-green color.

The trail drops down along the shore again shortly before the bluff. The rocky coastline is evident here—large boulders stand out against the smaller cobbles and gravel. The bedrock is primarily metamorphic, composed of Paleozoic gneiss and schist (rocks over 225 million years old). Beach pea and seaside goldenrod are two annuals that proliferate among the cobbles in early summer and bring added color as they bloom. Beach pea has showy deep-purple flowers, while goldenrod displays rich yellow spikes later in the summer.

A huge boulder (**E**) over 15 feet high, predominantly gneiss, stands perched on the outer edge of the beach. It was probably transported by the glaciers that moved through this area (see **#85**) and subse-quently was exposed by waves that ate away at soft, loose till that covered it. Recent wave-erosion effects can be seen in the pits and grooves on the seaward side of the boulder.

The trail again becomes a wide gravel path and takes you to the edge of the bluffs (**F**). The top of the bluff stands about 30 feet above sea level, with a nearly 90 degree rock face of light-colored gneiss and schist joining the boulder beach below. Geologists believe this area to be a *drumlin*—a smooth, elongated hill composed largely of till and shaped by glacial forces (see **#63**). When water reaches the base of the drumlin, it eats into the seaward edge, forming a cliff that becomes higher and higher as it progresses into the sloping hillside. Thus, the metamorphic till derived mainly from local bedrock is well exposed here.

The bluffs are the best spot from which to view this section of Long Island Sound. Numerous bodies of land can be seen from this point: Groton Long Point and Groton Heights are to your left and right, respectively; Fisher's Island lies in the center, and the terminal moraine at Watch Hill, R.I., is on your far left. Further portions of Long Island can be seen on exceptionally clear days. Waterfowl, gulls, terns, and migrating shorebirds may be seen from this elevated spot.

Continue down off the bluffs and out onto a narrow, ½-mile-long sandspit (**G**). Spits are formed on a gently sloping shoreline where shallow depths far offshore cause the waves to break. The movement of the water is thereby slowed, and sediments settle out. Gradually, the bottom along the breaker line builds into a bar and, if connected to land, is termed a *sandspit*. This sandspit opens into Bushy Point at low tide and has built up small dunes along its center ridge, held together by strong strands of beach grass. Here in the dunes, spotted sandpipers are afforded enough protection to nest.

Along this last stretch of road, sassafras (**H**) is the most common hardwood. A generally small tree, the sassafras here has grown to a considerable, hardy size. The trunk bark is deeply furrowed and red-brown in color with bright-green twigs. But perhaps its most distinctive features are the unusual differing leaf patterns, which occur on the same tree and even the same twig; some are oval with smooth edges, others mitten-shaped, and others three-lobed. You can identify the sassafras by chewing on a twig, since no other native tree has its characteristic spicy flavor.

Of little value as a timber tree, sassafras is famous for a tea made by boiling the root bark. This oil produced from the roots is also used in soaps and rubbing lotions. In addition, an extract of the bark is said to produce a subtle orange color on wool.

Remarks: *Walking time is approximately 2½ hours. There are many interesting side trails if you wish to explore further. The park is open from 8:00 a.m. to sunset year-round, with a limited area available for swimming during summer months. This is an ideal spot for birding during summer and fall migrations, when many birds stop here. Camping is available at Rocky Neck State Park about 12 miles away in Niantic. The park is open from April through September. For information contact Rocky Neck State Park, Box 676, Niantic, Conn. 06357; (203) 739-5471.*

46.

Barn Island
Wildlife Management Area

Directions: **Stonington, Conn. From New London, take I-95 east about 10 miles to Exit 91. Head south on Taugwonk Rd. for 0.3 mile. Turn left and go 1.6 miles on North Main St. Turn left again on U.S. 1 and continue 1.8 miles to the light at Greenhaven Rd. Turn right here and again at the next intersection onto Palmer Neck Rd. Follow this 1.7 miles to the parking and boat ramp.**

Ownership: **Connecticut Wildlife Unit.**

Nestled in the easternmost portion of Connecticut's coastline is a nearly-100-acre wildlife management area of fields, thickets, pockets of woodland, and extensive coastal marsh. Over 50 percent of Connecticut's original coastal marshlands have been lost in this century alone, and thus, the Barn Island Wildlife Management Area stands as an important parcel of protected critical habitat. With the surrounding fields and woodlots, the area is a haven for migrant and nesting birds, prime feeding grounds for herons and shorebirds, and home to many aquatic organisms that find refuge in this sheltered environment.

Begin your exploration along the east side of the road, where a trail leads from just above the rustic rest-room facilities through thickets and upland hardwoods of oak, birch, and scattered redcedar. This tract is alive with migrant birds during spring and fall, attracting hundreds of such colorful species as yellow warblers, rufous-sided towhees, and prairie and blue-winged warblers (see **#96**). Many will stay to nest, among them the bright and vocal yellow-breasted chat. Although classified as a warbler, the chat stands apart from others because of its larger size, heavy bill, and loud voice. The long series of disjointed noises and constant whistles it makes will no doubt allow you to locate this bird. Similar patches of low woods frequented by landbirds are found in scattered segments along the dike that leads across the salt marsh and four impoundments.

Although Barn Island still holds substantial salt-marsh acreage, human interventioin in this area is evident. Altering of the marsh environment began almost as soon as human beings came into close contact with it, largely due to the exceedingly high insect populations. The salt-marsh mosquito in particular made it nearly impossible for people to live in the vicinity of the marsh. Thus began a long campaign to control the insect population—the side effects of which often caused irreparable damage to much of this fragile habitat.

The salt-marsh mosquito is a very hardy and well-adapted inhabitant here. The female is humankind's major offender as she searches for the meal of blood she needs for nourishment to produce her eggs. The eggs are laid, usually hundreds at a time, along the damp mud, where they begin to develop immediately. The larvae, however, require rain or spring tides to submerge them and allow for final development to an adult mosquito. Because standing water may not accumulate for some time, the eggs have the ability to live for weeks or even months in the mud, ready to hatch into larvae with the first water.

The necessity of standing water for successful mosquito development led humans to drain salt marshes by means of evenly spaced ditches, evident here along the wide Barn Island marsh. In a major eradication drive in the 1930s, Barn Island and many other East

Coast marshes were extensively ditched. Ditching, however, only made a dent—and a brief one at that—in the mosquito population and subsequently compounded the problem due to increased loss of other wildlife species, including mosquito predators, which had previously also taken advantage of the pools of standing water. Barn Island's waterfowl population was especially hard hit.

In an attempt to rectify the troubles brought on by ditching, impoundments were created to try to solve both problems concurrently. Dikes were built to hold in water and control fresh- or salt-water levels. Impoundments create side effects of their own, such as reduction of suitable areas for the growth of salt-marsh grasses and, consequently, the protected sites for young and larval stages of countless organisms. Yet they did open the area up to waterfowl and other bird species once again. The four impoundments on Barn Island are currently undergoing experimental studies to determine their efficiency and productivity.

The first impoundment (**A**) has recently been opened up to the natural rhythms of an estuary (see **#59** and **#72**) and is in the beginning stages of salt-marsh restoration (see **#29**). Yet the contrast is still evident; on your right lie extensive flats of salt-meadow cordgrass (*Spartina patens*), lined along the water's edge with

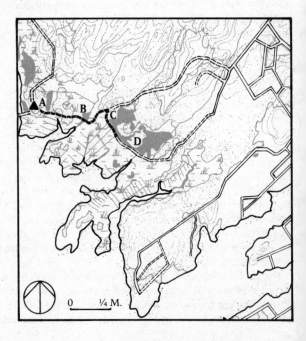

the taller salt-marsh cordgrass (*Spartina alterniflora*) and up the upland edge with thick stands of switchgrass (*Panicum virgatum*) (see **#14**). The impounded section to your left holds cattails, phragmites, and open mudflats. The mudflats and cattail cover allow for heavy use from shorebirds such as the greater and lesser yellowlegs, killdeer, and spotted sandpiper. Open water at higher tides also attracts fish-eating waders, such as herons and egrets.

The small green heron is one of the long-legged waders you might see here. The smallest North American heron next to the least bittern, its yellow legs contrast with its squat, dark body. Unlike most other herons, which nest in large colonies, the green heron can be a solitary nester and will build a frail stick nest in a dense foliated tree. Green herons nest here in the woods that border the marsh and come to the impoundments to feed on killifish, minnows, crayfish, and numerous insects. Watch for a tremendous display of patience as this little heron searches for food—it may freeze in odd positions for considerable amounts of time as it stalks prey.

The second impoundment (**B**) receives daily tidal flushing and has considerable water at high tide and mudflats at low tide. These flats again attract substantial numbers of shorebirds—according to the noted ornithologist Noble Proctor, the rare European ruff has been spotted here. Osprey platforms are visible to the east and have been very successful in local efforts to repopulate this species. Listen for the ospreys' loud cries, and watch for dramatic feeding forays as they hover more than 50 feet above the water in search of fish, diving from this height when they spot their prey (see **#22, #50,** and **#99**).

Yet another bird that may be seen hovering in this area, especially along the wide ditches, is the kingfisher. It is easily recognized by its large head, heronlike bill, and loud, rattling call. Both sexes are dark gray above and sport a broad rusty breastband, and the females have an additional rusty band. As their name implies, kingfishers are primarily fish eaters and are quite adept at capturing them with their long, sharp bills.

The kingfisher's life-style is unusual—it excavates a nest chamber in the side of a bank. Just past the third impoundment (**C**) you can get a firsthand look at nest-chamber entrances in an old abandoned gravel pit. Both sexes excavate, using their bills to dig and their feet to remove soil. The nest tunnels are usually 4 to 5 feet in length, with a small enlargement at the end where the five to eight eggs are laid. Once the chicks hatch, the adults must fish day and night to satisfy the nestlings' ravenous hunger.

Impoundments 3 and 4 are currently being controlled to keep the water level high enough to attract waterfowl. Impoundment 3 is brackish water and attracts many of the shorebirds, along with added waterfowl. Impoundment 4 (**D**) is fresh water, and you should look for gadwall, pied-billed grebe, coot, and Canada geese along here. Note the thick, towering phragmites along the water's edge, evidence of previous disturbance since this is a species that readily invades open areas.

As you retrace your steps along the dike, concentrate on the seaward and marsh side. Thick salt-marsh cordgrass along the dikes holds nesting seaside sparrows, sharp-tailed sparrows, and the occasional clapper rail. But aside from all the more obvious wildlife in the marsh, particularly birds, there are many creatures living out a more secretive existence among the mud and salt-marsh grasses. Innumerable larval forms and minute plants exist here, and if you look closely at the base of the marsh grasses, you should see a number of small holes. These holes lead to burrows inhabited by fiddler crabs.

Fiddler crabs are so named because the male has one disproportionately large claw that he waves in such a way as to remind one of a violinist playing a fiddle. These crabs emerge from their burrows at low tide to feed on the minute plants and tiny organisms on the mud surface. During mating season these large claws play an important role: The male stands at the entrance to his burrow for hours, waving his claw frantically to gain the attention of passing females. When he is successful, the pair mates underground, and the female fiddler then carries her eggs on her abdomen. She will move down to the creeks at hatching time to release her young into the water, which thus continues to proliferate one of the many life forms in the salt marsh (see also **#27**).

Remarks: *The entire walk takes about 2 hours, but you will need at least 4 hours to bird this area. Binoculars and a spotting scope are a must for birding open water. Low tide is probably the prime time for birding, as shorebirds and waders will be feeding. The management area is open to hunters in season, so check the state Department of Environmental Protection office to get official dates. Salt-marsh grasses are very sensitive to trampling, so please exercise restraint on the open marsh flats. Camping is available about 15 miles away at the Burlingame Management Area in Charlestown, R.I. This 2,600-acre site has 755 campsites open all year. For information telephone (401) 322-7337, or write to Rhode Island Department of Environmental Management, 83 Park St., Providence, R.I. 02903.*

47.

Pachaug State Forest

Directions: Voluntown, Conn. From New London, take Route 32 north 5 miles, then Route 52, the Connecticut Turnpike, about 18 miles to Exit 85A. Go east on Route 138 about 6 miles to Voluntown, then turn north (left) onto Route 49. Go 1 mile to the main entrance, on the left; enter and drive 0.7 mile, bearing left at the Y, to the parking lot just beyond. The trail is to the right, marked by a sign saying "Rhododendron Sanctuary."

Ownership: Connecticut Parks and Recreation Unit.

The largest forest in the state system, Pachaug covers approximately 24,000 acres in six towns. One particular wetland, an Atlantic white-cedar–giant-rhododendron swamp, is an excellent example of an uncommon botanical community. Another natural feature, Mount Misery, affords fine views of eastern Connecticut. The forest is also known as a good birding spot, especially for warblers.

From the dry pine and oak woods near the parking area, descend slightly to a unique coniferous swamp (**A**). Two different woody plants immediately catch the eye: the sprawling giant or rosebay rhododendron (*Rhododendron maximum*) and the tall, stately Atlantic white-cedar (see **#30**). The rhododendron is especially striking because of its large evergreen leaves, and in July its magnificently showy pinkish flowers.

A swamp such as this one is unusual for several reasons. Most of New England's Atlantic white-cedars were cut down during the past three centuries, because the wood's resistance to moisture made it an extremely useful building material for boats, fence posts, shingles, and railroad ties. Many of the wetlands that were not cut or that have grown back have suffered from drainage and filling. Proper soil and vegetational conditions must be present for such a swamp to form (see the following explanation). And, finally, the giant rhododendron is considered a rare plant within the entire range of this guide, growing only in scattered colonies. It grows abundantly in the central and southern Appalachians.

The ecological conditions that led to the formation of the swamp can only be theorized, since the long-term history of the area is unknown. However, we do know that the giant rhododendrons as well as the thick base of sphagnum moss are plants found in highly

179

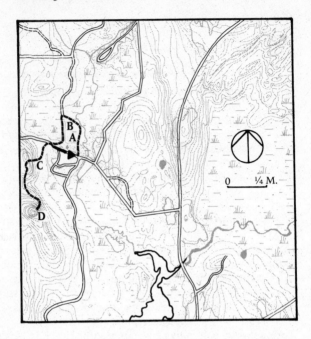

acidic conditions. The only trees that can tolerate this acidity, which was caused originally by a combination of the chemistry of the underlying rock material, the humid climate, and the surrounding vegetation, are conifers or red maples. What might the area have been before the cedars were here? One possible answer is that it was a bog. Bogs occur in places where there is little inflow and movement of water, where the nutrient and dissolved oxygen levels are low and thus dead plants decay only slightly, and where the basement debris is derived from acidic granite bedrock (see **#56**). As the bog filled in over a period of years, trees such as Atlantic white-cedars replaced the plants and shrubs, and a wooded swamp developed. Red maples may not have had a nearby seed source or were shaded out by the densely growing cedars.

The trail follows blue blazes off the main path and into the thickest parts of the swamp itself, where you must carefully pick your way through the young trees (**B**). A diminutive mammal, the southern bog lemming, is believed by state ecologists to be present in this type of habitat, though information is somewhat sketchy because of the animal's secretive habits. The southern bog lemming is a member of the rodent order and is distributed locally over most of the northern and central states and eastern Canada. It is listed as rare in the state of Connecticut, although it may very well be abundant in small, hard-to-locate colonies. It prefers low, damp bogs or meadows, where it eats leaves, stems, grasses, seeds, and other succulent greenery. Occasionally one finds smaller heaps of cut grass stems along with piles of bright-green droppings that betray its presence. Look for these signs near surface runways and tunnels.

When the trail emerges from the swamp onto a narrow dirt road, go left until you meet a paved one. Follow the blue blazes to the right and then left into the woods. As the trail ascends and the slope gradually sharpens, notice the change in tree variety (**C**). In the moister flatlands, hemlocks and white pine share the area with oaks, but as you climb and as available moisture decreases, the oaks and other hardwoods predominate almost completely. At the first lookout, a gnarled, twisted, and almost-grotesque pitch pine struggles to survive in the thin, rocky soil. The tree may have been the victim of a previous fire. Here, too, is bearberry, a low, creeping evergreen shrub of the north country, found mostly in sandy and rocky terrain.

After the trail dips down into a small stream valley, it climbs briskly to the summit of Mount Misery (**D**). From this exposed vantage point one can see more of the vast acreage of Pachaug State Forest, a swamp off to the east, and the village of Voluntown to the south. Mount Misery, at 441 feet in elevation, is part of eastern Connecticut's rolling uplands. Its granite composition is more durable than the schist and other weaker rocks that make up a good deal of the valley below.

Look along the forested slopes for worm-eating warblers, small olive birds with two parallel black stripes on a lighter colored head. The late ornithologist Arthur Cleveland Bent suggests that the name hillside warbler might be appropriate for this bird, because it "shows a decided preference for wooded hillsides covered with medium-sized deciduous trees and an undergrowth of saplings and small shrubbery." A usual nesting place for the worm-eating warbler is on the ground, well concealed among dead leaves, tree roots, or other natural cover. Its song closely resembles the dry trill of the chipping sparrow.

Remarks: *The walk takes about 1¾ hours. Wear rubber footwear for swamp conditions. Camping is available on the grounds.*

48.

Ninigret
National Wildlife Refuge

Directions: **Charlestown, R.I. From Providence, take I-95 south about 11 miles to Exit 9. Follow Route 4 south about 12 miles and continue south and west on U.S. 1 another 16 miles to Charlestown. In Charlestown, turn off U.S. 1 at the exit sign for Ninigret Park, and go straight on Old Post Rd. to the entrance. Follow the signs to the Frosty Drew Nature Center at the refuge entrance.**

Ownership: **U.S. Fish and Wildlife Service.**

Ninigret National Wildlife Refuge lies on a 404-acre tract of broad coastal plain bordering the northern edge of 1,711-acre Ninigret Pond, the largest salt pond in Rhode Island. Four miles long and one-half mile wide at its broadest point, Ninigret Pond (also called Charlestown Pond) is the most prominent coastal lagoon pond in a string of eight salt ponds that line Rhode Island's south shore. These salt ponds are separated from the sea by an almost continuous ridge of barrier beaches stretching from Point Judith in the southeast to Watch Hill in the southwest, though many of the ponds—including Ninigret—are flushed twice daily by ocean tides entering through narrow, man-made breachways cut through the outlying beaches.

The wildlife refuge occupies the site of an abandoned U.S. naval air base. At present, its remaining macadam runways provide foot access across the refuge's gentle terrain of grassy meadows, brush, and shrub uplands, and to the north shore of Ninigret Pond. Marked hiking trails and self-interpreting nature walks will soon be established here.

Ninigret Pond is truly a "cradle of life," for the salt pond is an unusually productive ecosystem that serves as breeding ground and nursery for a wide variety of aquatic organisms. Because a salt pond's tidal salt water is diluted with inflowing fresh water from upland streams and groundwater springs, it can nurture both brackish species like oysters and saltwater creatures like quahogs, scallops, and flounder. Ninigret Pond is more saline than some coastal ponds, so oysters are relatively scarce and restricted to the most brackish areas of the lagoon.

The luxuriant growth of aquatic vegetation in salt ponds like Ninigret provides a rich food source for finfish and shellfish. This high fertility results from the ponds' characteristic shallowness. In a pond such as Ninigret, with an average depth of 4 feet, the flow of plant nutrients into the water from decaying organic matter on the bottom occurs far more rapidly than in deep ocean water.

Where the water is shallow, sunlight can also penetrate more directly to the bottom, promoting the growth of beneficial plants such as eelgrass. This rapidly growing aquatic plant forms extensive beds just below the low-tide level within protected bays and estuaries. Its thick root system binds and stabilizes the sandy or muddy bottom substrates, while its dense grass blades tend to trap floating sediments. In some instances, accumulated sediments make the pond shallow enough to allow cordgrass and other salt-marsh plants to develop. The rapid growth of eelgrass produces large amounts of decaying plant matter, which provides food for many organisms such as small shrimp. The Atlantic bay scallop depends upon eelgrass for its young to settle upon and grow. You may see scallop shells washed up on the shores of the pond. This shell, 2 to 3 inches long, has about eighteen raised ribs fanning out from a flattened base. Although few aquatic creatures feed on the living blades of eelgrass, it is an important food for birds like Ninigret's resident black ducks and its migrant brant geese.

The high productivity of the salt pond plays a vital role in supplying the deep ocean with many species of fish. For instance, Ninigret Pond and an adjoining lagoon, Green Hill Pond, supply Block Island Sound with as much as one-quarter of its winter flounder. The adult flounder migrate to the pond through the breachway from Block Island Sound to breed. The pond then serves as a nursery for the young until they reach the age of 2 or 3, when they join the adults on their return to the open ocean. Many young flounder are killed by predatory schools of bluefish—called "snapper blues"—which enter the ponds each summer. The bluefish rampage through the pond in "feeding frenzies," killing many more smaller fish than they can eat. Seagulls gather to feed on the dead fish washed ashore, or flock in the shallows to prey upon the young flounder and other fish that have sought to escape from the bluefish by swimming close to shore.

Much of Ninigret Pond's aquatic life is hidden from human eyes. For example, the most abundant shellfish in the pond, the soft-shelled clam, may lie buried to depths of two feet in the mud. The very common quahog burrows into mud and sand just below the low tide level, where it may live as long as 25 years.

Far more conspicuous at Ninigret Pond are the winged predators that search for food along the mudflats and beaches. Among the numerous water-loving birds that appear here are two beautiful migratory birds, the snowy egret (see **#74**) and the glossy ibis. The snowy egret is a slender, long-legged heron whose elegant, pure white plumage was once so highly prized for hat decoration that it was hunted almost to extinction. Its distinguishing marks are its black bill, black legs, and yellow feet. Unlike most herons, the snowy egret is a highly animated forager, darting around shallow waters in pursuit of fish. A common summer resident at Ninigret, it rarely appears north of southern New England and migrates to the southern United States in winter.

The glossy ibis is another long-legged wader that inhabits shallow brackish ponds and marshes. Its bronzed plumage is tinged with green and gray on the wings and back. With its long, downward-curved bill, it probes in the mud for mollusks, crayfish, and frogs, as well as feeding on fish and insects. In contrast to the herons, it flies with its long neck outstretched and with more rapid wing-beats. Watch for this species in grassy areas of the shoreline in the summer.

The brush-and-shrub upland areas of the refuge are also habitat for many birds and mammals. One animal you are likely to see in the summer is the woodchuck, the largest New England member of the squirrel family. The woodchuck is often active in the early morning and late afternoon, when it feeds on grasses and clover. One of its natural predators, the red fox, is also resident here.

Other wading birds that have been recorded at Ninigret include the great blue heron, green heron, and black-crowned night heron. Greater and lesser yellowlegs, as well as the double-crested cormorant and various sandpipers, are other waterbirds of this site. Nesting waterfowl include the mute swan, mallard, black duck, and wood duck. Migratory waterfowl are varied and numerous, including the common loon, gadwall, canvasback, green- and blue-winged teal, bufflehead, common eider, greater and lesser scaup, scoter, and merganser. Many types of songbirds can be enjoyed in the wooded areas of the refuge.

Remarks: *The refuge's gentle terrain allows easy hiking. Trail orientation is provided by a full-time naturalist in summer months. Inquire at the Frosty Drew Nature Center, which is located at the refuge entrance in Ninigret Park. The center offers interpretive programs and a wide spectrum of nature-related activities for children, including school groups. Maps for hiking trails that are currently being planned can be obtained at the nature center. The refuge is open throughout the year; the nature center in summer, and other times by appointment. For further information write*

Frosty Drew Nature Center, Ninigret Park, Box 131, Charlestown, R.I. 02813.

No license is required for saltwater fishing in Rhode Island. Nonresidents must obtain licenses for shellfishing; Rhode Island residents must obtain licenses for shellfishing in commercial quantities. For more information on fishing and camping contact the Rhode Island Department of Environmental Management, 83 Park St., Providence, R.I.

Nearby Places of Interest

Ninigret Conservation Area: Charlestown, R.I. Take East Beach Rd. south off Route 1, just west of the National Wildlife Refuge exit.

This 174-acre tract is on Charlestown Beach, the 2-mile-long barrier beach that encloses Ninigret Pond from the sea. Access is by soft-sand beach roads suitable only for foot travel and oversand (four-wheel drive) vehicles. Saltwater swimming, surf-casting in the ocean, and saltwater fishing in the pond are permitted. Lifeguards are on duty in summer from 9:00 a.m. to 6:00 p.m. Overnight camping facilities include 50 shoreline sites for self-contained trailer units only.

Charlestown Breachway: Charlestown, R.I. Take Charlestown Beach Rd. south from Matunuck School Rd., east of Charlestown center. The breachway is the channel between Block Island Sound and Ninigret Pond. This state-owned area has a shoreline campground with 75 sites for self-contained trailer units. There is a boat ramp. Fishing is permitted in Ninigret Pond or from the breachway.

Burlingame State Park: Charlestown, R.I. Located off Route 1 west of Charlestown center. This 2,600-acre state campground has 755 tent and trailer sites. Freshwater swimming, fishing, and boating are permitted at Watchaug Pond. There are several ocean beaches nearby.

49.

Trustom Pond

Directions: **South Kingston, R.I. From Providence, take I-95 south about 11 miles to Exit 9. Follow Route 4 south about 12 miles and continue south and west on U.S. 1 another 10 miles to South Kingston and the Moonstone Beach exit. Follow this road 1 mile and turn right onto Mantunuck Schoolhouse Rd. The refuge entrance is 0.7 mile on the left.**

Ownership: **U.S. Fish and Wildlife Service.**

As Rhode Island's largest protected coastal pond (160 acres), Trustom Pond serves as a refuge for a wide variety of birds and waterfowl, which pass by on the Atlantic flyway during seasonal migrations (see **#96**). This shallow, brackish body of water, surrounded by open fields, old orchards, and scrub forest, is protected from the open Atlantic by a long and narrow barrier beach (see **Long Island Sound's North Shore and The Rhode Island Coast**). The habitat provides an abundant supply of food and nesting sites, and it is not unusual to see as many as two thousand birds at a time during migrations. A colony of about two hundred mute swans enjoys the pond and its resources year-round.

An old farm lane leads from the parking lot to the pond. It passes through an old hayfield, a remnant of the refuge's past incarnation as a working farm. The alfalfa is still harvested, primarily to maintain the open field as a habitat for small mammals, insects, and birds. If left alone, the field would soon succumb to the forces of forest succession (see **#38** and **#60**).

As the path comes to a stone wall, this reclamation process is evident (**A**). Thick clumps of blueberry, shadbush, tatarian honeysuckle, and raspberry have grown up here in another old field. All of these plants have taken easily to the sandy, acidic soil that is common in coastal New England. They are important sources of food for many birds, including the ring-necked pheasants and grouse, which you may startle out of the underbrush.

As the trail moves on, the wild fruit trees and bushes grow taller and more dense. This area of the farm was abandoned to brush some years earlier. Robins, thrashers, catbirds, and orioles are some of the most common birds competing for berries here. Their drop-

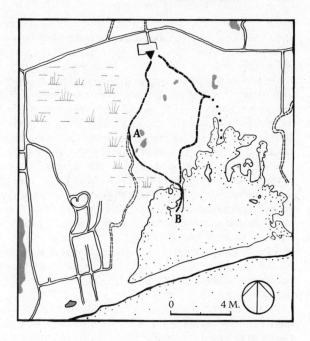

pings, which contain the seeds of their food, are a major reason for the new growth of these plant species throughout the refuge.

Continuing toward the pond and the ocean, the path leads to a small forest of scrub oak and pitch pine, quite common in sandy, windswept coastal areas. These trees grow slowly under such relatively poor conditions, and they will never get much larger than the biggest ones here. You are now on one of the narrow necks of land that jut out into Trustom Pond (**B**). From here you can watch the thousands of birds that swim and fly around the open water, especially in late spring and fall. Among the ducks commonly seen here are mallards, pintail, teal, canvasback, eider, and bufflehead. Notice the difference in feeding movements between the diving and the dabbling varieties. Canada and snow geese are also here from spring through fall.

The most established and impressive residents are the mute swans, gliding gracefully through the water. Mute swans are not native to North America, but were introduced from Europe as ornamental park birds—the once-common whistling swan having been largely eliminated from New England through hunting and human encroachment on its native habitat. However, the mute swans, which are indeed mute, have become established in the wild over the last 75 to 100 years. However, their increased populations have occurred at the expense of the native waterfowl, which must compete for food and habitat with the large swans. In mid-June, you can see the adults here, accompanied by the fluffy young cygnets which ride on their parents' backs. Although the cygnets can swim and feed themselves from birth, they stay very close to their parents for about 9 months, growing into graceful long-necked birds that feed on reeds, grasses, and other aquatic plants. When swans migrate, in the spring and fall, they form long lines or V formations just like geese.

Above the water and its shores is an entirely different community of birds. Marsh and red-tailed hawks soar over the open field and marshland searching for rodents or young birds away from their parents. Cormorants, egrets, and gulls (see **#17** and **#77**) glide high over the pond and scan the water for fish. In the late afternoon, it is common to see a heron standing in the shallow water, carefully stalking its prey. Summertime often finds ospreys at the pond (see **#22, #50,** and **#99**). This uncommon coastal hawk swoops over the water's surface and abruptly dives to grab a fish in its sharp claws.

Most of the vegetation around the pond is a brackish water plant called *Spartina* (see **#77**). It produces rich nutrients for the fish and birdlife in the pond and can live in varying levels of salinity found in coastal ponds. Unlike other pond/barrier-beach complexes, there is no natural breachway to the ocean. Instead, when the water level becomes high, usually in the spring, an artificial breach is cut through to the ocean, draining the pond and allowing for flushing and re-charge action. Although this human intervention may seem unnatural, it helps bring new life to the water that would otherwise become stagnant and relatively lifeless.

Remarks: *This 2½-mile walk takes about 2 hours. A bird guide and binoculars will add to the enjoyment. Camping is available at nearby Ninigret Beach (see* **#48***).*

50.

Great Swamp

Directions: West Kingston, R.I. From Providence, take I-95 south about 11 miles to Exit 9. Follow Route 4 south about

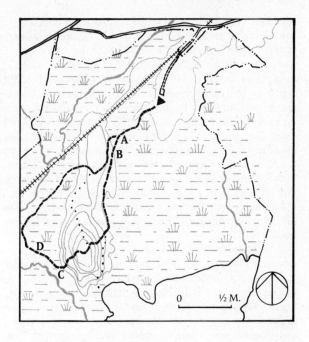

12 miles and continue south on U.S. 1 about 4 miles. Turn west (right) onto Route 138 and go about 6 miles. In West Kingston, turn west (left) onto Liberty Lane; go 0.9 mile to the refuge entrance.

Ownership: **Rhode Island Division of Fish and Wildlife.**

The Great Swamp of Rhode Island lives up to its name by being the largest swamp in New England. Stretching for acres, it harbors a wide variety of woody swamp vegetation, including American holly, which is rarely seen in New England. It is also home to a diverse population of birds, including the osprey, the large fish-eating coastal hawk whose population has been diminished by human encroachment and the use of pesticides, but is now coming back. Here these birds can be seen in their giant nests on top of dead trees or swooping over the water and diving for fish.

Although the swamp is only 5 miles from the ocean, it differs greatly from the marshes that are common to coastal wetlands: swamps are dominated by woody vegetation, whereas marshes are grassy habitats. This contrast is clearly visible when you reach the open water and marshland in the center of the swamp. Vegetation is usually very dense in swamps, making them difficult to explore. But here, a dirt road winds through the swamp, allowing the hiker to avoid the wet muck that covers most of the preserve.

As you walk away from the parking lot, there is an area of young forest that is dominated by an understory of blackberries, huckleberries, paperbush, and blueberries. Here the earth is drier than most of the swamp; note the contrast between this spot and the swampy area on the left a little further on (**A**), which is dominated by dead trees. The constantly high water level has drowned the trees, whose decay has led to an increase in acidity. On the right side of the road is a stand of American holly trees, which are very near their northern limit, occurring in significant numbers in New England only here and on Cape Cod. The proximity of the ocean, with its moderating influence on temperatures, and the predominantly sandy soil found in the nonswamp areas combine to provide a good habitat for the holly (see **#25**).

Beyond the power line clearing is another area of dense woods—primarily black cherry, red and swamp maple, and blackgum (**B**). The cool, damp soil, almost mudlike in places, is ideal for these moisture-loving trees. It also supports a rich variety of ferns, including bracken, cinnamon, sweet, and hay-scented ferns, which fill the understory. Look here for two types of club moss—creeping Jenny and prince's pine. Club mosses are closely related to ferns, being vascular plants that reproduce by the dissemination of tiny spores rather than seeds or flowers. They are often mistakenly thought of as conifers because of their needlelike leaves and the fact that they are evergreens. They are frequent inhabitants of wet, lowland habitats, requiring the same high ground moisture that most ferns do.

Wildlife is abundant throughout this area, and it is not uncommon to see deer and rabbit tracks in the muddy soil. Grouse, quail, and woodcock browse through the underbrush, and their calls are frequently heard in spring and early summer.

Continue walking on the gravel trail and follow the grassy lane that leads uphill to the right. You will pass some open fields and come to a second gravel road. Turning downhill to the left, you will come to a long dike, which was built in the 1950s to create these marshlands by impounding several small streams and thus provide a good habitat for waterfowl (**C**) (see **#46**). The lush growth of grasses, such as sweet gale and cattail, dominate the area, and lilies ring the edges, blooming in midsummer.

Although there are usually large numbers of Canada geese and a variety of ducks in and around the water, and an occasional otter swimming across the surface, the major attraction here is the ospreys. With wingspans as large as 4½ feet, they are easy to spot as they fly over the water and catch fish by dropping suddenly, feet first. A good place to observe their activities is from the wooden boardwalk (**D**) that goes under the power lines. Ospreys were rapidly approaching extinction in the 1950s and 1960s because the pesticide DDT entered their bodies through the food chain and caused their eggshells to weaken and crack before offspring could be born. Ever since DDT was banned, these birds have been making a comeback, returning to the coast of New England in small but increasing numbers.

Each spring and summer ospreys migrate from the Gulf states to breed here. Their huge nests can be seen on top of the dead trees and utility poles that stretch across the pond, and in recent years as many as six have been inhabited. Ospreys generally prefer an existing nest but will construct a new one if none is available. After mating, the female lays two or three eggs over the course of several days. The incubation period is 37 days, during which time the male does all the hunting while the female sits on the eggs. When the young birds are hatched, the male continues to be the food provider for the whole family. The female eats some of the fish brought by the male and breaks the rest into pieces to feed the newborns, who grow quickly and can stand and flap their wings after 3 or 4 weeks. They take their first flight at around 7 weeks old, but stay with the parents another couple of weeks, through mid-August, to sharpen their flying and hunting skills. Although they will then set out on their own, they will not mate until they are 3 years old (see also **#22** and **#99**).

The dike continues along the edge of the marsh, past stands of dead trees and marsh grass on the right and thickets of pussy willows, maples, and rushes on the left. In the shallow shore area, look for green herons stalking fish and kingfishers hovering in the sky waiting to dive. Kingfishers look like large blue jays with long, sharp beaks for spearing unsuspecting fish (see **#46**).

The dike road returns to the woods, going uphill through an open area. After passing under the power line, you will reach the main gravel road, which returns to the parking area.

Remarks: *The distance of the full circuit is 5 miles. Allow 3½ to 4 hours for the walk. Binoculars are recommended for bird-watching. A good way to explore the swamp is by canoe, which offers closer views of the marsh habitat, including waterfowl. Put in at the Chipuxet River, 2 miles west of Kingston on Route 138. Paddle 4 miles to Worden Pond. Or on the Usquepaug River, 3 miles west of Kingston, put in 2 miles south on Route 2. Paddle downstream to the Charles River, then 2 miles upstream to Worden Pond in the Great Swamp. Camping is available nearby at either Burlingame Management Area (see #46) or Ninigret National Wildlife Refuge in Charlestown (see #48).*

51.

Long and Ell Ponds
Natural Area

Directions: **Hopkinton, R.I. From Providence, take I-95 about 33 miles south to Exit 2. Turn right from the exit ramp and go 0.1 mile north; turn southwest (left) onto Route 3 and go 0.5 mile. Turn (right) onto Canonchet Rd.; go 2.1 miles to the dirt parking lot on the left.**

Ownership: **The Nature Conservancy; Audubon Society of Rhode Island; Rhode Island Department of Environmental Management.**

Situated in the rural countryside of western Rhode Island, this 340-acre reservation contains an array of rare plants and spectacular geological formations concentrated around the adjacent Long and Ell ponds. Long Pond lies in a preglacial valley with bare cliffs of pink granite rising 70 feet above its waters. Its deep gorge is joined to the smaller Ell Pond, a glacial kettle-hole lake, by a deep, rock ravine. Ell Pond is surrounded on three sides by an Atlantic white-cedar and red-maple swamp (see **#30** and **#13**), and by a quaking bog mat of sphagnum moss. Long Pond, the more accessible of the two, has a smaller bog mat that extends into the connecting ravine. Its most distinctive botanical features are its extensive colony of rare native rosebay rhododendron and an old grove of towering hemlock trees known as "the Cathedral."

The major trail begins to the right of the sign at the parking lot. For its entire length this trail threads its way across steep, craggy rock ledges and heavily forested slopes that form the walls of the gorge cradling Long Pond. The trail leads a short distance into an oak forest, where it quickly forks in two directions. Take the path that veers sharply to the right (north), following the yellow blazes as it swings west through a bouldered area cloaked in eastern mountain laurel. This stretch of the trail features vegetation that is characteristic of upland oak forest. Herbaceous plants such as trailing arbutus and wild sarsaparilla grow beneath a dappling canopy of gray and yellow birch and chestnut and other oak trees. The trail cuts across a narrow, slanting bedrock ledge and then weaves around trees and rocks as it skirts the high, forested slope of the valley's south wall. At several points, gaps in the trees to your right provide glimpses of the impressive cliff, "the Bluffs," on the north side of the valley, though here the foliage is too dense to allow more than a brief glimpse of the pond that lies below.

The lichen-covered surface of a crumbling stone wall soon appears to the left of the trail, and standing just beyond it are three massive glacial boulders. These huge rocks, called glacial erratics, were transported to this spot by glacial ice that plowed across the landscape during the Ice Age. The ice sheet tore both small and large rocks from bedrock ridges and cliffs and scattered them across the frozen land for distances ranging from as little as a few feet to as much as several hundred miles. The cliffs and ledges at Long and Ell ponds are heavily glaciated, their granite surfaces scarred and shattered by the ice. The landscape is strewn with numerous erratics that in some instances have been heaped into jagged, obstructive piles.

The path dips into a steep hollow and climbs again into the open air at the top of a broad exposed ledge. Conical crowns of young hemlock trees rise up from below the ledge to form a luxuriant screen of arching boughs. Their short evergreen needles, white underneath and glossy green above, dangle from a profusion of slender, roughened twigs.

The trail gradually descends through a dense, sunless stand of hemlock, where understory plants are completely absent. In dense forest groves hemlock retains its lower foliage for a longer time than most trees, blocking out the sunlight required for the growth of most small plants and shrubs. Even more important, few plants can tolerate the high soil acidity produced by a thick carpet of hemlock needles. Hemlock naturally thrives in areas underlaid by acid types of bedrock like granite, and because its needles are acidic in themselves, the soils are made even more inhospitable for small plantlife.

Pick your way down the steep side of a high outcrop to the bottom of a moist hollow. On your right stands an impenetrable thicket of rosebay rhododendron. This is one of New England's rarest shrubs; the large colony here is one of only a few scattered stands found in the entire region. The rhododendrons at Long and Ell ponds are exceptionally tall, some reaching the species' maximum height of 15 to 16 feet. Their leathery oval leaves are 4 to 6 inches long, curling at the edges when the temperature drops below freezing. Their large, showy clusters of pinkish-white flowers bloom in July. The rhododendron, like its relative the mountain laurel, usually prefers moist, cool habitats, where it forms crooked, tangled thickets.

The path winds uphill and weaves through another dark, crowded stand of young hemlocks before it reaches the brow of a high, bouldered slope. Below you lies an open, spacious hollow, overspread by a canopy of lofty hemlock trees. This area embraces a large portion of the Cathedral where some of the oldest and tallest of the hemlocks on the reservation are located. Tree-ring counts on fifteen hemlocks at the Cathedral found that the majority ranged between 80 and 130 years old. Several trees in the sample fell between 180 and 189 years old, and the oldest specimen was about 200 years old. Hemlocks of this age are rare in Rhode Island. Although hemlock has not been a major component of the Rhode Island forest since at least colonial times, forest researchers believe it was more prevalent 200 years ago. Extensive clearing of the land for agricultural purposes, which peaked at about the middle of the nineteenth century, may have eliminated hemlock from many areas where it had existed prior to colonial settlement. Periodic forest fires may also have reduced its numbers. Unlike hardwoods, hemlock cannot sprout from stumps on cutover lands, and the elimination of mature trees as a seed source would have had a greater impact upon its abundance and distribution than, say, upon the so-called sprout hardwoods like oak, maple, and other dominant trees in today's woodlands. Although researchers investigating this stand found no evidence of cutting or fire, they did find that fires and logging had occurred in surrounding areas where hemlock is now scarce.

The trail continues to head west, surmounting several high, rocky outcrops before plunging to the floor of the wet ravine that connects Long and Ell ponds. The moisture and acidic soils of the ravine support many plants that also grow in wooded swamps at the edges of bogs. In fact, some of the plants here have invaded from the bog mat beyond the ravine's mouth on the western edge of Long Pond. As you cross the log footbridge across the ravine, look for sweet pepperbush, swamp azalea, and sphagnum moss, which forms small hummocks on the ravine's saturated, muddy floor. Rosebay rhododendrons are found here on the somewhat drier banks at the ravine's edge. Red maple, a common tree of woodland swamps, and Atlantic white-cedar, a common bog tree in southern New England, also grow here. You can easily identify the Atlantic white-cedar by its bluish-green foliage and fibrous bark.

Cross the footbridge and climb up a steep rocky cleft that divides an overhanging cliff. At the top of the cliff, turn right and follow the footpath to the east. On your left you will see a branch trail heading north that leads out of the reservation. This trail returns to the road, but first walk east along the path as it skirts the ledges overlooking the Bluffs. Notice the difference in the vegetation on this side of the pond. Its warmer southern exposure, coupled with the dry soil conditions created by rapid runoff, supports oaks and pitch pine rather than species of cool, wet climates like hemlock.

A short walk brings you to the top of the Bluffs, a sheer bedrock cliff that offers a commanding view of the entire pond. To the south the high hemlocks of the Cathedral are visible. You can also clearly discern the low-lying, floating bog mat at the southern end of the pond, with its rim of Atlantic white-cedar trees wedged into the mouth of the ravine. Enjoy the scenery before retracing your steps to the branch trail.

The branch trail to the north leads a short distance to a dirt parking lot on the edge of the road. Turn right on the dirt road, which soon turns to pavement as it curves southward. Look for Canonchet Rd. on your right, and follow it back to the parking lot at the entrance.

Remarks: *Allow 3 hours to hike the trail around Long Pond. Yellow blazes on trees and rocks are clearly marked throughout its length. The terrain is steep, rugged, and rocky. The surfaces of bedrock ledges and boulders can be very slippery underfoot. Hikers should wear footwear with gripping power (not sneakers). The ravine may become swollen with runoff in the spring, and its log footbridge is narrow and requires caution. Ell Pond lies a short distance west of Long Pond. There are no marked hiking trails from the Long Pond trail, but an informal footpath leads along the high southern ledges overlooking the ravine and moves westward to the edge of Ell Pond. This path is densely overgrown, and not recommended. Hikers should be alert for signs of mammals that have been reported at Long and Ell ponds, including raccoons, bobcats, gray squirrels, and especially otters. The area is open all year, daily, from one-half hour before sunrise to one-half hour after sunset. For information on nearby camping areas, see* **#50**.

52.

Napatree Point

Directions: **Watch Hill, R.I. From Providence, take I-95 south about 40 miles to Exit 1. Take Route 3 southwest about 4 miles, then continue south on Route 78 for about 4 miles more. Turn south (left) onto Route 1A; in Avondale, turn southwest (right) onto Watch Hill Rd. Follow the road into Watch Hill center; park at the meters at the end by the town beach.**

Ownership: **Watch Hill Fire District.**

Napatree Point is one of the best areas along the southern coast of Rhode Island to watch the fall hawk migration (see also **#41**). A narrow, shifting sandspit stretching into the sea off Watch Hill, this long, vacant peninsula forms the extreme southwestern tip of Rhode Island. To the north of Napatree Point, Little Narragansett Bay lies sandwiched between the Connecticut mainland and the point itself, its waters sweeping into Fisher's Island Sound in the west. To the south, the vast blue wash of Block Island Sound forms the sprawling margin of the coastal flightpath along which many of New England's fall migrants stream southward for the winter.

New England's two most common hawks—the sharp-shinned and broad-winged—are among the most numerous birds sighted at Napatree in the fall. The sharp-shinned hawk, measuring only 10 to 14 inches long, belongs to a family of woodland hawks, the accipiters, which have short, rounded wings and long tails. In flight, it alternately beats its wings rapidly and soars. It has a gray back and wings, and a russet breast with white cross-stripes. The sharpshin's winter range extends into the northern states. The broad-winged hawk is the smallest member of the buteo family, which have broad wings and broad, rounded tails. The broadwing, like the sharpshin, is no bigger than a crow, only 14 to 18 inches long. Distinguished by two white bands on its dark tail, it typically soars in wide circles in the sky. Broadwings winter from Florida south into the tropics.

The American kestrel, or sparrow hawk, is another hawk commonly sighted at Napatree. This small falcon is only 9 to 12 inches long, with pointed, streamlined wings and a long tail. Unlike most hawks, it often hovers in one spot by rapidly beating its wings. Its reddish-brown tail is unique among small hawks. The male has a gray back and wings; the female is rusty brown. Both sexes have a reddish spot on the crown, and black-and-white face markings.

You may well see the double-crested cormorant, a common cormorant of the Atlantic shore, which is abundant here (see **#95**). This long-necked bird is sometimes confused with geese or loons, but its tail is much longer. Like geese, cormorants fly in formation, but their wingbeats are more rapid and their necks more extended. They winter along coasts in the south.

Other birds that may appear at Napatree include the marsh hawk (northern harrier), osprey, and merlin (pigeon hawk), and less frequently, the red-tailed hawk. Common loons and great cormorants have been reported in small numbers during migration. Many unexpected woodland birds also appear here during the peak of the fall migration in late September and early October. The third and last weeks of September are traditionally the best period for watching hawks. Migratory hawks and waterfowl also fly over Napatree in the spring.

Throughout its history Napatree Point has been battered by fierce storms that periodically attacked Rhode Island's south coast. In modern times the point was devastated by the tidal wave accompanying the great hurricane of 1938, which completely swept away the summer beach residences that had lined its shore. Before the hurricane struck, the peninsula was more extensive and sicklelike in shape; its extreme northern tip, then called Sandy Point, reached further north toward the Connecticut mainland. The tidal wave broke through the base of the outer point, severing it from the southern portion of the peninsula, so that today Sandy Point stands as a separate island in the middle of Little Narragansett Bay.

Napatree Point is also the site of the ruins of Fort Ninigret, a defensive shore installation built in 1898 by the federal government. The fortification, consisting of fifty buildings, never saw combat and was sold in 1927 to local residents, who razed the structures, leaving only their dune-swept, fortified concrete walls.

Remarks: *The trail is a sandy footpath that leads to the end of the point. It begins beyond the Watch Hill Beach and the Yacht Club to the west. The trail is moderately difficult, with soft sand and no trees for shade. Allow 3 hours to walk to the end and back. Parking is limited to metered spaces on the main road. The Watch Hill Beach parking lot is restricted to residents only. Napatree Point is open all year. Camping is available at Ninigret National Wildlife Refuge in Charlestown (see #48), and at Burlingame Management Area (see #46).*

53.

Beavertail
Point
State Park

Directions: Jamestown, R.I. From Providence, take I-95 south about 11 miles to Exit 9. Follow Route 4 south about 12 miles; take Route 138 east and south about 7 miles. From Jamestown center, take Beavertail Rd. south about 4 miles to the park entrance.

Ownership: Rhode Island Department of Environmental Management.

Beavertail Point forms the southwest headland of Conanicut Island, a narrow 9-mile-long strip of land stretching northward into Narragansett Bay from Rhode Island Sound. The state park encompasses a tract of open, windswept land on the point—or tail—of the beaver-shaped landmass that makes up the southern portion of Conanicut. This is connected to the larger part of the island by a narrow neck of land at Mackerel Cove. From Beavertail's rocky shores, which rise 50 to 60 feet above the water, you can see Rhode Island Sound in the south, the seaside resort city of Newport in the east, and the tree-mantled coastline of the Rhode Island mainland in the west.

Narragansett Bay, a beautiful stretch of salt water, occupies more than 200 of Rhode Island's 1,497 square miles, extending inland for a distance of 28 miles from the open waters of the sound. The geological origins of the bay are complex, but several aspects of its formation are revealed in the rock ledges ringing the shoreline of Beavertail Point. An impressive outcrop of hard metamorphic rock, these ledges stand in contrast to the comparatively softer sedimentary rocks that dominate the greater area of the Narragansett basin. They represent a small intrusion of the hard bedrock that underlies the southern portion of Conanicut Island, as well as portions of the other islands in Narragansett Bay. To the west and east of Conanicut are deep, submerged channels that were created by the glacier and its meltwater streams some 20,000 years ago at the end of the last ice age. These erosional channels were cut from the soft sedimentary shales and slates that formed in the Narragansett basin some 200 million years ago during the Pennsylvanian coal-forming period. Although the great earth upheaval that faulted and folded the Appalachian Mountains buried much of this sedimentary rock, some of it remained exposed in troughs between the folds of the earth—such as the Narragansett basin—where millions of years later it was eroded by glacial activity. The intrusions of more resilient bedrock were less affected than the sedimentary rock by erosion from glacial ice and water. When the sea level rose after the Ice Age ended, these areas of hard bedrock, like Beavertail Point among them, remained above the water level of the bay as isolated islands.

Today, the shore ledges produce a magnificent spectacle in heavy seas, when high surf crashes upon the rocks. The scratches, grooves, and fractures in the rocks are reminders of the power of the glacial ice that rode across the land (see **#85**).

The rock ledges at Beavertail serve as resting places for harbor seals, which seek the protection of the sheltered waters of Narragansett Bay in winter months. The harbor seal is the most common Atlantic seal off southern New England, where it frequents coastal waters, harbors, rivers, and estuaries. The adults are most active in the water at high tide, when they pursue their diet of fish, shellfish, shrimp, and squid. At low tide, they climb ashore on rocky ledges or beaches to rest and sleep; this is the best time to watch them. Remain at a distance on the rock ledges, since these shy animals will dive into the water if you came too close. (see **#97**). The male and female look similar, but the male is slightly larger. Adult seals measure 4 to 6 feet long and weigh 100 to 300 pounds. Their coat is yellowish-gray, with black and brownish spots and white rings and loops. Although clumsy on land, harbor seals can swim at speeds up to 13 knots and may remain underwater for as long as 15 minutes.

In winter, waterfowl may also be seen in Narragansett Bay from Beavertail Point. Species include scoter, brant, eider, and other common cold-weather ducks and geese.

Since 1749, when a lighthouse was erected near the present granite tower at the end of the point (only the third established in America), Beavertail Point has served as the oldest lighthouse site on the Rhode Island coast. The standing beacon, Beavertail Lighthouse, was built in 1856 and today is a visitor center for the state park (see **#80** for more on lighthouses).

Remarks: *Beavertail Point has no formal hiking trails, but footpaths descend to the rock ledges from various parking overlooks. These are located at intervals along the state park road that circles the point. Use caution when walking on the rock ledges, since these may be extremely slippery underfoot. Recreational activities at the park include saltwater fishing, picnicking, and sunbathing. A park ranger conducts nature-education programs and tours in July and August from the visitor center at Beavertail Lighthouse. The park is open all year.*

Nearby Bay Island State Park encompasses 23,000 acres of islands in Narragansett Bay. Facilities for group campsites on the southern end of Prudence Island and individual campsites on Dutch Island are by permit only, for a maximum stay of three nights. For information, contact Rhode Island Department of Environmental Management, Division of Parks and Recreation, 83 Park Street, Providence, R.I. 02903. Other scenic state parks on Narragansett Bay include Fort Wetherell State Park, Jamestown, on the southeastern tip of Conanicut Island; and Brenton Point State Park and Fort Adams State Park, Newport, both located on the southwest end of the island of Rhode Island. Wetherell and Brenton Point offer sightseeing and picnicking; Fort Adams features saltwater swimming in the bay.

54.

Purgatory Chasm

Directions: **Middletown, R.I. From Newport go east 2.4 miles on Memorial Blvd. to the intersection of Paradise Ave. Turn right and park in the area just up the road on the left.**

Ownership: **Rhode Island Department of Environmental Management.**

Rising high above a sandy beach and looking out over the Atlantic Ocean near Newport is a mass of strangely colored and textured rock. A deep ravine slices through it, dropping 50 feet to the ocean waves. Purgatory Chasm shows us the combined effects of erosion, glacial activity, and the upward thrusting of the earth's crust. It is also a fine place to watch gulls, (see **#17** and **#77**) cormorants, and other seabirds swooping and soaring over the bay.

About 125 million years ago, much of this land was thrust upward along fault lines during great upheavals of the earth's surface (see **#83**). At that time the crack, known as a fracture zone, that has become Purgatory Chasm first appeared. It was most likely only a few inches wide, considerably less than the present 10 feet. As the earth moved through several ice ages, beginning about 3 million years ago, a sedimentary rock was formed over the existing bedrock. It was composed of small granite stones carried by the ice and bonded together by the intense weight and pressure of the huge ice mass (see **#74**). Although the formation of this conglomerate rock, commonly known as pudding stone, happened throughout New England, the rock found here is unique, due to its blue-gray, almost purple, color, and is found only in the Narragansett Bay region.

After the glaciers melted, the erosional effects of the ocean continued to work on the fracture zone, widening and deepening the cut. The continual pounding of the waves and their tremendous force can be heard echoing between the walls of the chasm as it continues the age-old process (see **Cape Cod to Portland**).

Remarks: *The chasm is just a few hundred feet from the parking area. A small footbridge spans the chasm, providing an excellent view of its size and shape. Allow 15 to 30 minutes to visit. On the opposite side of the bay is the Sachusett Point Wildlife Refuge, which is worth a visit if only for the view back across the bay to Purgatory Chasm. From there the rocky cliffs appear strong and impenetrable, except for the large gap of the chasm. A public beach lies just east of the chasm.*

55.

Norman
Bird Sanctuary

Directions: **Middletown, R.I. From Providence, take I-195 east about 7 miles to Exit 2 in Massachusetts. Take Route 136 south about 15 miles to Portsmouth, R.I. Take Route 138 south for about 5 miles, over the Middletown line. Turn left onto Mitchell's Lane; go south to the end of the road and go straight through the intersection onto Third Beach Rd. Look for the sanctuary entrance on the right.**

Ownership: **Audubon Society of Rhode Island.**

The windswept coastal marshes, woodland swamps, and shrub forests at the Norman Bird Sanctuary in Middletown constitute one of the richest bird-watching areas in Rhode Island. The 250-acre sanctuary is located on the south coast near Sachusett Point, bordering Block Island Sound and the Saknonet River. The sanctuary features 5 miles of hiking trails, including several high scenic overlooks across the salt marshes and coastal ponds where flocks of migratory waterfowl gather in the spring and fall migrations.

The hiking trails originate at the nature center at the sanctuary's entrance. Take the major southeast trail as it descends the field to the rear of the nature center and enters a shrub forest dominated by black cherry, birch, and other scrub vegetation. Many branch trails radiate from the main path, but continue ahead until you encounter a scattered stand of redcedar trees growing amidst a leafy thicket at **A**. This area with its low, dense shrub cover and weedy clearings is habitat for many birds, including sparrows and warblers. You may glimpse the dazzling red plumage of the male cardinal here, the only red bird with a crest. The female is light brown, but shares the male's red crest and its stout, finchlike bill.

The trail soon emerges in a wet forest dominated by red maples.

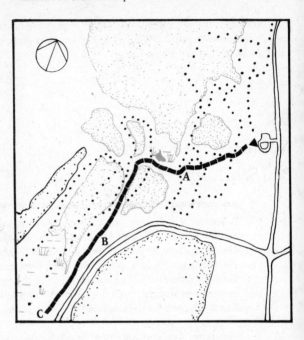

Watch and listen here for the woodcock. This squat bird can sometimes be flushed from its hiding places in thickets and woodland
swamps. On ascent into the air, its beating wings produce a whistling
or trilling sound. The woodcock is 10 to 12 inches long, brownish,
and has short legs, rounded wings, and an extremely long bill.

The trail now leads across a bridge over a dry swamp. Stepping
stones serve as a pathway before the trail comes to a fork. Follow
the red blazes to the left for the Hanging Rock Trail, which leads
through a cool, shady forest of tangled vines, shrubs, and ferns and
skirts a cedar grove before finally emerging at the base of a small cliff
at **B**. Ascend the natural footholds in the ledges of the cliff, which
rises to a breathtaking overlook at the top of a long, finger-shaped
rock ridge stretching between two deep valleys to the shoreline of
Block Island Sound.

Follow the trail to the left as it heads toward the sea. As you walk
along the ridge, take note of the rough, pebbly surface of the bare
rock ledges underfoot. These ledges are composed of a type of sedimentary rock called conglomerate. Conglomerate rocks have a coarser
texture than, say, a sedimentary rock like limestone, which has a
fine, smooth grain. Like all sedimentary rocks, conglomerates are

formed from fragments of preexisting rock that were deposited by wind, water, or ice. The size, shape, and arrangement of the rock fragments that compose a sedimentary rock determine its texture. Conglomerates consist primarily of rounded stones, and the type found here goes by the popular name of "pudding stone" because the colors of the pebbles on the rock's surface contrast sharply with the duller color of the rock in which they are imbedded.

The trail reaches its southern terminus at Hanging Rock (**C**), overlooking the sea. From this outcrop you can view migratory waterfowl in the low-lying marshes and ponds to each side of the ridge. At this distance you can best enjoy the aerial formations, colorations, and profiles of the geese and ducks in flight as they land or take off from the water and tall grasses. Canada geese's familiar V formation is a common sight in the skies over the refuge. Brant geese form a looser, more irregular line as they beat along the shoreline or circle in the air before landing. The black duck displays flashes of white beneath its wings in contrast to its distinctive black belly and dark upper body. The slim-bodied mergansers hold themselves in almost rigid horizontal profile as they fly low over the water in line formations before braking in the water to dive for fish. The green- and blue-winged teal can be identified by their small size; the mallard, with its glossy green head and white neckband, has a slow, deliberate wing-beat. Many migratory waterfowl return to New England as early as March, while the southward exodus in autumn stretches from late September into late November.

Enjoy the view from Hanging Rock before retracing your steps to the sanctuary entrance.

Many of the common waterfowl along New England's south coast appear at the sanctuary, including goldeneye, scaup, bufflehead, old squaw, and scoter. Canada geese are year-round residents. Several other sanctuary trails skirt the marshes and ponds where waterfowl may be seen from a closer vantage point.

Remarks: *The Hanging Rock Trail is a 90-minute walk over difficult, rocky terrain. (Other sanctuary trails have easier terrain.) Trail maps and other information are available at the nature center, which has varied nature exhibits on display. Trails are well marked, with colored blazes and signs at intersections. The sanctuary is open daily, 8:30 a.m. to 5:00 p.m., throughout the year.*

56.
Bowdish Reservoir

Directions: **Glocester, R.I. Take U.S. 44 west from Providence about 25 miles to Chepachet. Continue west on U.S. 44 about 6 miles to the campground entrance of the George Washington Management Area on the right.**

Ownership: **Rhode Island Department of Environmental Management.**

Bowdish Reservoir is an unusual example of a quaking sphagnum bog, for here, the natural process of bog succession has been permanently reversed by human engineering. This man-made lake contains several remnant floating bog mats surviving as islands in a freshwater basin that was formerly a natural bog. Here one finds characteristic bog flora, as well as two plant species—black spruce and dwarf mistletoe—that are uncommon in Rhode Island. The bog mats are only accessible by boat from the public boat landing at the campground in the George Washington Management Area, which encompasses 3,153 acres of forest conservation land in the rural countryside of northwestern Rhode Island.

The typical or "classic" sphagnum bog in New England forms in a wetland basin where high levels of acidity and deficiencies of oxygen retard the normal decay of organic matter (see **#75**), producing an environment that is extremely poor in plant nutrients. Thus, only plants that can tolerate such impoverished conditions are involved in the ecological succession of a pond or lake into a bog. Of these the major plant is sphagnum moss, which takes root in accumulations of partially decomposed organic matter—the source of peat—along the shores of a freshwater basin. This floating mat of sphagnum is joined by other small bog plants as it creeps inward upon deeper, open waters, finally covering the entire pond or lake. Gradually, larger vegetation, such as acid-loving heath shrubs and tall conifers, invades the mat. Their presence signals the beginning of the bog's succession to swamp forest and perhaps eventually dry upland.

This typical process of succession was interrupted at Bowdish Reservoir, where only a remnant of a former bog exists. In order to form a pond in the management area, the state flooded the reservoir basin, thereby detaching the developing bog mats from the old shoreline. Set adrift by the rising water level, the original mat was broken into several small islands in the middle of the lake. These quaking sphagnum "islands" will probably survive here indefinitely.

Bowdish Reservoir's bog mats still retain the specially adapted flora that, in many instances, is exclusively associated with sphagnum bogs. Among these are insectivorous sundews and pitcher plants, rare species that obtain vital nutrients by capturing insects. (See **#58** for more on these species and on bog succession.)

There are black-spruce trees at Bowdish, though they occur infrequently in southern New England, growing only at about a dozen sites in Rhode Island. Also called bog or swamp spruce, this conifer is the most common tree to invade northern New England bogs, where it may form almost pure stands. The warm climate in southern bogs, on the other hand, favors Atlantic white-cedar trees, which at Bowdish grow alongside the black spruce. Botanists offer opposing theories to explain the presence of the black spruce in southern New England. For many years they believed the stands of black spruce to be relic colonies remaining from a time when the climate was cooler, but more recently they are suggesting that the black spruce may be migrating southward in response to a long-term cooling trend. In southern New England the black spruce is usually an irregular, short tree, seldom attaining 30 feet in height. Its needles are stiff and pointed, appearing blue-green at a distance, while the Atlantic white-cedar has light-green, slightly flattened, scalelike needles.

The black spruce at Bowdish serves as host for an even rarer plant, the semiparasitic dwarf mistletoe (*Arceuthobium pusillum*). This tiny evergreen shrub, which lacks roots but contains chlorophyll, receives at least a part of its nourishment from the spruce branches, the only place where it can grow. (It also appears on white spruce.) Its range is restricted to northern bogs, where it has been recorded as far south as New Jersey and Pennsylvania and west to Michigan. The dwarf mistletoe has thin, scaly leaves and yellowish-green stems, which spread irregularly in many directions. Flowers and fruit appear from early July to late September. The seeds are dispersed by birds.

The sphagnum "islands" at Bowdish contain other, more common bog plants, such as bog laurel (also called pale laurel) and bog rosemary. Bog laurel measures about 2 feet high, with pink flowers, similar to those of the more familiar mountain laurel, that are borne at the ends of the stems. It is the least common of the three laurel species native to southern New England. Bog rosemary is a short shrub, whose narrow leaves have rolled margins. Its small pink flowers are bell-like in shape and droop in clusters from the stems.

Remarks: *The quaking bog mats at Bowdish Reservoir can be reached quickly by boat from the public boat landing at George Washington Campground. Allow roughly 15 minutes to reach the islands by nonmotorized craft. There are no boat rentals here. Exercise caution when walking on the bog mats, since holes may occur and the trampling underfoot of rare plants such as sundews and pitcher plants can permanently alter the delicate ecological balance that allows these species to survive here. George Washington Management Area has seventy-two tent and trailer campsites and two shelters in a wooded area overlooking Bowdish Reservoir. Campsites are available on a first-come, first-served basis. Other facilities include a recreation building, a swimming beach, and hiking trails. The Walkabout Trail (about 8¼ miles) was built by the Australian crew of the H.M.S. Perth while on a layover in 1965. The reservoir is open from April 15 to October 31.*

57.

Lonsdale Marsh

Directions: **Lonsdale, R.I. In Providence, take I-95 northeast to Exit 23. Take Route 146 northwest about 4 miles, then take Route 123 east 3 miles to the traffic light at Route 122 (Lonsdale Ave.). Turn south (right) and go 0.2 mile to an unmarked dirt road on the left, opposite Lower Rd. Park at the barrier at the end of the dirt road beyond the softball field.**

Ownership: **Towns of Lonsdale and Valley Falls.**

Typical of freshwater marshes throughout New England, Lonsdale Marsh displays a carpet of grasses, sedges, cattails, and pond lilies, threaded by meandering streams. It is habitat for numerous waterbirds, mammals, reptiles, and amphibians; indeed, the freshwater marsh is one of nature's most complex ecosystems.

Situated in the floodplain of the Blackstone River, 25-acre Lonsdale Marsh forms a natural oasis in the heart of eastern Rhode Island's thickly developed industrial belt. The Blackstone River was harnessed as a power source for nineteenth-century mills and has been one of the most heavily used waterways for manufacturing in the region. It flows southeastward 40 miles from central Massachusetts through a densely populated industrial corridor before draining into the Seekonk River a few miles north of Rhode Island's Narragansett Bay. Surrounded by this urban sprawl, Lonsdale Marsh has suffered water pollution and serious encroachment from building development. Parts of its wetlands have been filled. Yet its abundant wildlife, including numerous nesting birds and a large muskrat population, shows that wild creatures can persist amidst urban development if allowed suitable and sufficient natural habitat.

Lonsdale Marsh lacks designated hiking trails, but informal footpaths lead off the dirt access road that begins at the parking-lot barrier. Running along the western edge of the marsh, this straight road terminates at the marsh's southwestern perimeter. To the left side of the road are small, weedy clearings, alternating with dense stands of shrub vegetation and trees, through which footpaths lead to the banks of the marsh. From the edge of the water you can observe the wildlife in the marsh and see many of its common aquatic plants.

Many of New England's marshes have developed along the broad, open floodplains of slow-moving rivers, where water is widely dispersed along the flat margins of the stream channel. "Riverine marshes" are among the largest marshes in the world, such as those found along the flat bottomlands of the Mississippi Delta. Other types of marshes form along the shallow fringes of lakes, like the extensive marshes that occur along portions of the Great Lakes and the major waterfowl marshes of the massive prairie lakes in Manitoba. Marshes may also develop in depressions in the land fed by a network of tributary steams, which sometimes mark the sites of extinct glacial lakes.

Lonsdale is a riverine marsh, and the small valley in which it lies is a glacial formation created by a huge block of stagnant ice. Buried beneath a stream of sand, gravel, and other sediments released by glacial meltwaters as the ice sheet began to withdraw from New England some 11,000 years ago, this massive ice block later melted and left a cavity in the land that has been modified by centuries of erosion. This type of glacial formation, called a kettle hole, is fairly common throughout the southeastern Coastal Plain of New England.

The freshwater marsh represents a "successional wetland," meaning that it is a temporary plant community that will eventually be replaced by different kinds of vegetation. In the typical evolution of a freshwater marsh, open water very gradually becomes dry land. The herbaceous aquatic plants that colonize the shallow waters of the marsh die back in the autumn and, by their decomposition, release vital nutrients that will fuel the growth of new spring plants. Over time this yearly cycle of birth, death, and decay produces increasing accumulations of organic matter in the form of muddy soils on the shallow marsh bottom. A gradual elevation of the bottom is first seen in the emergence of small islands, or tussocks, above the surface of the water. As they expand and grow higher, they offer rootholds for an invasion of woody shrubs such as buttonbush, willow, alder, and red maple. These plants make up a somewhat drier wetland environment, the shrub swamp forest. Examples can be seen in areas along the edge of Lonsdale Marsh, and these species may someday predominate in the swamp. The succession to swamp forest can take many centuries, however, while climatic factors like extended periods of drought or higher-than-normal rainfall may shorten or prolong the life-span of a freshwater marsh.

You can observe the wildlife at Lonsdale Marsh more easily if you first recognize its major plants, since birds and other creatures tend to favor particular types of vegetation for nesting cover or for food. Marshes are divided roughly into vegetation zones, which generally represent a major plant group's affinity for shallow or deep water. Various sedges, or bulrushes, grow in the shallow water beyond the marsh's banks. Sedges include a large variety of grasslike plants that form elevated tussocks along the marsh edges. These islands of sedges may be the first areas to be invaded by woody swamp vegetation in the marshland succession. The most common sedge in New England is the tussock sedge, which grows 2 feet high and has extremely narrow leaves. Another common aquatic plant of shallow areas is pickerelweed, which grows 1 to 4 feet high. It has a single heart-shaped leaf and a spike of blue flowers that blooms from June to October.

The shallow marsh edge is a common habitat for the red-winged blackbird. In spring, it often gathers in large flocks within Lonsdale Marsh. The male's red shoulder patch is the only spot of color on its black plumage.

The cattail colonizes the deeper waters of the marsh. This easily recognized plant grows 3 to 9 feet high, with a distinctive brown spike of flowers at the tip of the stem. Highly nutritious, cattails are a major source of food for muskrats and are raw material for their mound-shaped lodges, which are composed of such vegetation and mud. The muskrat is the most aquatic member of the rodent family, spending most of its active hours in the water. Though it is primarily nocturnal, the muskrat is often abroad during the day. It eats fish, mussels, and frogs, as well as cattails and other plants. It is a prolific breeder, and occasional population explosions result in the extensive defoliation of large areas of the marsh. Yet the muskrat more often plays an important ecological role by promoting marsh longevity: the animals continually cut back the cattails, thereby keeping the water open and preventing swamp vegetation, such as trees, from moving in. A sizable array of predators, including mink, raccoon, hawks, and owls as well as snakes, snapping turtles, and even large fish, hunt the muskrat as food.

A rare denizen of the cattail stands is the Virgina rail. There are at least eight nesting pairs of these shy birds at Lonsdale, which seldom emerge from the dense cattail cover where they breed. This bird is small, 9 to 11 inches long, with a long bill and distinctive gray cheeks. If startled from its hiding places in the dense plant cover, it emerges into the open air and flees a short distance before disappearing again within the marsh.

Other common birds at Lonsdale include marsh wrens, yellow-crested flycatchers, and a spring migrant, the black-crowned night heron. Snapping turtles are also plentiful.

Remarks: *The footpaths along the marsh's edge are dense with vegetation—including poison ivy and brambles—and can be soggy in areas. Be prepared for a considerable degree of bushwhacking, for footpaths may end abruptly and require impromptu trail-making. However, it is impossible to get lost, for the area is bounded on the west by the access road and on all other sides by the marsh. The area west of the marsh described here was once used as a town dump, but landfilling and cleanup have been largely completed. Proposed recreational development of Lonsdale Marsh by the state of Rhode Island may improve its accessibility and potential as a nature-study site. Among the ideas under study are the establishment of marked hiking trails and the continuation of a cross-state bikeway through the property. Lonsdale Marsh can be visited throughout the year; however, spring floods may submerge large areas. Lincoln Woods State Park, Lincoln, R.I., which is located off Route 123 between Lonsdale and the junction with Route 146, is a recreational day-use area with facilities for picnicking, hiking, and horseback riding. Fishing, boating, and freshwater swimming are permitted at Olney Pond.*

Cape Cod to Portland: Rocky Beginnings

The farther north one travels from the front of the last ice sheet at Long Island, the less evident the rubble and sand leavings of the glaciers. Heaped-up glacial debris is replaced increasingly by landscapes derived from the sheer physical impact of the ice, which pressed down the land and scoured bedrock naked. The transition is gradual, starting on the Connecticut shore and becoming more obvious north of Cape Cod, although in many places between the Cape and northern Maine the beginnings of New England's truly rockbound coast are still masked.

Morainal hills of rubble and glacial debris are prominent, for instance, just north of the Cape. Strewn about are boulders—among them Plymouth Rock—that were carried by the ice sheets from inland and summarily dropped, as if in memorial of the glaciers' passing. Coves and estuaries shelter salt marshes, especially on the coast of northern Massachusetts, and in places such as the lower Scarborough River, south of Portland, Maine, where as the glaciers melted the rising sea level flooded low, fertile plains.

Much of the seaside south of Portland, moreover, lacks the hard, granitic aspect of the jagged headlands and cliffs to the north, virtually all bedrock. Between Portland and the Cape, the sea has smoothed out the face of the shore to a much greater degree than in northern Maine, where the visage the land presents to the waves is much more impervious to their assaults. South of Portland, the coast is relatively even, although it has myriad small coves with marshes and some sandy beaches.

Even so, a stony finger of land pointing seaward just south of the Massachusetts border testifies that the shore between Portland and the Cape does indeed belong to New England's truly rock-ribbed edge. It is Cape Ann, where at places such as Halibut Point Reservation the massive granite ramparts that typify the northern coast loom over the waves.

Along this coast dwell communities of seashore life that grow increasingly spectacular as the rocks dominate. The animals inhabiting a rocky shore—such as limpets and chitons—must be able to cling to a hard, ungiving surface and hold on even amidst the fiercest pounding of surf. Unlike creatures of the sandy beach, they cannot burrow for shelter below the surface on which they live. But they do find it in the countless cracks and crannies, where some of them wedge themselves so tightly it would take hammer and chisel to remove them.

One creature in particular has adapted so well to anchoring on rocky shores that it spreads everywhere and becomes virtually part of the landscape. It almost seems as if the barnacle becomes part of the rock itself, and some people who visit the shore do not even think of it as animate.

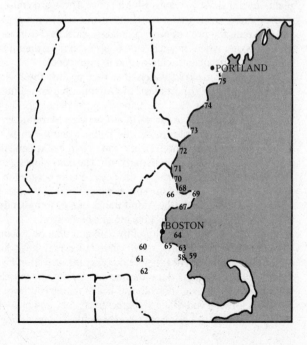

The barnacle begins life as a minute larva, freely swimming for a time before it settles down on rock or some other hard surface. The young barnacle makes contact with the rock headfirst, and cements itself fast with a glue secreted by tiny glands shaped like goblets.

Then the barnacle secretes lime, which takes the shape of a cone-like shell around its body. Its sharp edges a bane of barefoot beach-combers, the shell has a valve atop that opens when the creature feeds. To gather food, the barnacle extends feathery legs and sweeps them through the water, as if kicking food into its mouth. The shell is so strong that it remains long after the creature that made it dies, whitening the rocks in great beds.

While not always as evident as barnacles, other animals of the rocky shore are found much more easily than their sandy-beach counterparts because of their inability to hide beneath the surface. Some of the most fascinating can be found in tide pools, water stranded in rocky basins when the tide recedes. Those on the coast north of the Cape are among the most spectacular in North America. Plum Island, in particular, is noted for the rich abundance of its tidal pools.

Tide pools are ruled by the same ecological laws as the broader ocean beyond them. Sunlight promotes the growth of minuscule plants in the shallow waters of the pools. These are consumed by grazing animals such as sea urchins or mussels, some of which in turn become the prey of other animals—sea stars, for instance—or are scavenged when they die. Tide pools even have their own complement of fish, such as sculpins and mummichogs.

Fish teem in the cold waters that rage against the rocky shore north of the Cape, a portion of the Atlantic that constitutes a vast bight known as the Gulf of Maine. A great depression in the sea floor, the gulf reaches as far north as Canada's Maritime Provinces. Stretching for 200 miles along the gulf's western rim is Georges Bank, 100 miles wide, rumpled into shoals in the north and flattened into a broad undersea plain in the south. The bank slopes gently into the gulf but descends sharply to the deeps on the ocean side.

The cold-water fishes of the gulf, especially around Georges Bank—and beyond the gulf on the Grand Banks of Newfoundland—make the waters off northern New England one of the world's great fishing grounds. The gulf is the realm of the cod and pollock, halibut, haddock, redfish, and whiting. Their abundance may have lured the Vikings to North America; before the Pilgrims arrived at Plymouth, Georges Bank regularly drew Basque and Portuguese vessels across the Atlantic. New England colonists began taking cod from inshore waters before the end of the seventeenth century and by 1748 were bringing their catch back from Georges Bank. Today, fishing vessels from around the world fill their nets in these waters to such an extent that the abundance of the past may become a memory if the harvest of the sea is not controlled.

Toward the shore, the abundant fishery is already a thing of the past, its decline beginning almost in colonial times, as people took what they could with little thought for the future. Furthermore, inshore life has suffered drastically in more recent times from pollution.

Boston Harbor, for example, had a wealth of fish and shellfish when Europeans first settled on its shores, but it has become a virtual sewer for human and industrial wastes. Researchers have found heavy concentrations of toxic metals in sediments near Deer Island, along parts of Dorchester Bay, and in the northern part of the Outer Harbor. Hundreds of thousands of gallons of sludge filled with solids from human waste were pumped into the harbor daily. Recently, however, environmental controls have started to take effect, and the upgrading of sewage-treatment facilities has resulted in a slow cleansing of the harbor, although it is still an eternity from a pristine state.

Peddocks Island, for instance, just west of Hull, had turned into a dump after three centuries of habitation. Closed to the public in 1947, it was reopened as a place where visitors can observe nature and examine ancient Indian archaeological sites. The restoration of the island was carried on by the Peddocks Island Trust, and eventually the New England Aquarium in Boston hopes to establish a seal colony there.

Human activities have also changed the look of the land immediately behind the shoreline. The strip of coast between the Cape and Portland is heavily urbanized. Southern Maine, logged long ago, has fewer conifers than in the past but increasing stands of birch and maple. South of Cape Ann, once largely oak forest, a mixture of oaks and pines now predominates. As long as the sea beats on the shore, however, the coast will retain a touch of wildness. This is never more true than when a nor'easter churns the waves and the sky turns as gray as the sea.

Edward Ricciuti

58.

Black Pond
Nature Preserve

Directions: **Norwell, Mass. From Boston, take I-93 south to Exit 25, then Route 3 southeast for about 12 miles to Exit 31. Take Route 53 north for 0.6 mile. Turn east (right) onto Route 123 and follow it about 3 miles into Norwell. Turn north (left) onto Central St.; go 0.9 mile. Turn right onto Old Oaken Bucket Rd.; go 0.2 mile and turn left onto Mount Blue St. Go 0.7 mile to the parking lot on the left.**

Ownership: **The Nature Conservancy.**

The rare and unusual flora of the quaking cedar bog represents one of the most specialized plant communities in New England. The 80-acre Black Pond Nature Preserve in Norwell is an outstanding example of this unique ecosystem, where only a small array of plants are specially adapted to the intensely acidic conditions characteristic of the sphagnum bog. Among these plants—many of which are not found outside the bog habitat—are some of the most fascinating species in New England: the insect-eating sundews and pitcher plant, the delicate rose pogonia and calopogon bog orchids, and Atlantic white-cedar trees.

A short trail begins at the chained gateway, located across Mount Blue Street from the parking area. It runs for a few yards through shrub thicket to a grassy clearing, where a path leading into a bordering woodland appears on the left. The path winds through a forest grove containing American beeches, oaks, and eastern hemlocks before joining a boardwalk on the right. The boardwalk spans the sodden floor of a swamp forest, dominated by a belt of Atlantic white-cedar trees growing at the pond's edge. Soon it emerges in the open air on the periphery of the treeless, floating bog mat—a deep-green circle of sphagnum moss and other plants ringing the dark, still waters of 1-acre Black Pond.

Black Pond, like many sphagnum bogs, occupies a glacial kettle hole. This spring-fed depression, which was created from a block of stranded glacial ice at the end of the Ice Age, lacks the oxygen and plant nutrients that are normally introduced into ponds and lakes by inflowing tributary streams. In addition, the presence of underlying mantle rock that is poor in nutrients, such as sand or gravel, further contributes to the shortage of nutrients that characterizes all bogs.

The most important factor in the development of bogs, however, is a cool, moist climate. The sphagnum bog serves as an insulating microclimate where the cold of winter is more or less retained throughout the year, providing a congenial habitat for various plant species, such as Labrador tea or leatherleaf shrubs, that normally grow only in the cold Arctic tundra.

Because bogs are so deficient in oxygen and nutrients that are necessary for the normal decomposition of organic matter, the potential number of plants that can survive in such acidic conditions is severely limited. Yet these bog species play a vital role in the development of this slowly changing ecosystem. For bogs, like marshes or swamps, are successional in nature. According to the classic pattern of bog succession, the sphagnum bog transforms open water into woodland swamp, and perhaps ultimately, dry land.

Black Pond is a relatively young bog, yet even here the stages of bog succession are readily apparent. This is because bogs evolve incrementally through space; that is, they grow inward from the shores of a pond until the entire expanse of open water has been completely engulfed by a floating mat of sphagnum moss, which serves as a platform for increasingly larger vegetation to take root.

The first phase in the evolution of a bog involves the formation of the floating bog mat at the fringes of the pond. Beneath the sphagnum lie accumulating layers of partially decomposed organic matter, which are sources of peat once the bog mat dries out. If climatic conditions are sufficiently cool and moist, the bog mat will completely overspread the open water and at the same time thicken to depths that allow larger plants to take root, including the well-known insectivorous species. Closer to the pond's edge at the periphery of the forest the bog mat is invaded by shrubs, such as leatherleaf and other members of the acid-loving heath family. Together with ferns and cotton grass, these shrubs separate the sunny reaches of the bog mat from the shady woodland.

The swamp forest represents what the entire pond will someday become after it has disappeared beneath the encroaching circle of the sphagnum mat. The Atlantic white-cedar (see **#30**), which serves as a common pioneer tree species in bogs in this southern coastal region, will eventually creep across the bog mat where open water now stands. But in time even the white-cedar will succumb to the pressures of succession: because young cedar seedlings cannot mature in dense understory shade beneath parent trees, red maples and other wetland species common to woodland swamps in this area will replace the cedar as the dominant species here.

Bog vegetation is specially adapted to overcome high acidity and lack of adequate nutrients. The most unusual species are the insectivorous sundews and the pitcher plant, which obtain vital nutrients by capturing insects. The pitcher plant is perhaps the better known of these indigenous insect-eaters. Its numerous tubular or pitcher-shaped leaves grow up to 8 inches long and are green and purplish in color. The leaves form a rosette at the base of the plant, from which a globular, drooping red flower stands 8 to 24 inches high on a separate stalk. The mixture of water and sticky fluid contained in the hollow leaves attracts insects which become trapped by small hairs on the leaves that allow them to enter but block their escape. The trapped insects soon drown in the liquid, and their soft body parts are absorbed by the leaves of the plant. The nutrients stored in the insect thus allow the pitcher plant to survive in an environment where relatively few other plants can compete.

The round-leaved sundew is the most common member of this family in the region. It has round leaves on slim stalks that form a rosette at the base of the plant. This more inconspicuous insectivorous species is small, measuring only a few inches in diameter across the leaves at the base. Its white or pinkish flowers grow in a one-sided cluster on single stalk that measures 4 to 9 inches high. Sundews capture small insects by exuding a sticky substance on their leaf hairs. Once an insect becomes stuck in this fluid, the leaves enclose it and absorb the nutrients from the carcass.

Bog orchids, like other members of the large orchid family, are highly specialized. Each species of orchid depends upon a specific insect for pollination. The largest flower petal usually serves as a landing pad for insects seeking the orchid's nectar gland. The germination of the orchid's tiny seeds is another example of this family's high evolutionary position in the plant kingdom. The embryonic orchid seeds have evolved a symbiotic relationship with particular kinds of fungi. These fungi provide nourishment for the developing orchids until they have produced their first leaves for photosynthesis. Such exacting ecological requirements explain the rarity of these beautiful plants.

Among the most uncommon orchids are those of sphagnum bogs and acidic wet meadows, which serve as habitats for the two species seen here. Grass pink (*Calopogon pulchellus*) has loose clusters of two to ten flowers on a stem, ranging in color from purple to pink to white, which bloom in July. A yellow-crested lip lies uppermost on each flower. The slender stem is sheathed in a single narrow leaf at the base.

The showy pink flowers of the rose pogonia are borne singly, one to a stem, which grows up to 20 inches tall and displays a single broad leaf. Its unique, unmistakable lip is fringed with yellow and veined with red. Its flowers bloom from June to August.

Retrace your steps from the boardwalk to the parking lot.

Remarks: *The short trail is a 30-minute walk over easy terrain. The various plant species can be enjoyed from the boardwalk, but hikers should refrain from walking in the bog because of the fragility of the vegetation. Visitors must contact the Massachusetts Audubon Society, which operates Black Pond Nature Preserve for The Nature Conservancy, for permission to enter the property and to arrange guided tours of the bog. Write or call Massachusetts Audubon Society, North River Wildlife Sanctuary, 2000 Main St., Marshfield, Mass. 02050; (617) 837-9400. Parking facilities are closed unless arrangements have been made in advance.*

59.
Albert F. Norris
Reservation

Directions: **Norwell, Mass. From Boston, take I-93 south to Exit 25, then Route 3 southeast for about 12 miles to Exit 31. Take Route 53 north for 0.6 mile, then turn east (right) onto Route 123 and follow it about 3 miles. Go through Norwell center; turn right on Dover St. Turn left onto West St.; the reservation sign and parking lot are on the right.**

Ownership: **Trustees of Reservations.**

Some 5 miles inland from the Atlantic Coast the historic North River curves eastward from the south as it skirts the town of Norwell. Streaming through the grassy expanses of a windswept salt marsh, this estuarine river forms a vista of extraordinary scenic beauty as it embarks upon its final course to the sea. Along the ½ mile of river frontage at Albert F. Norris Reservation, the blue waters and shimmering marsh grasses are flanked by the gentle slopes of an upland wood. White pine, redcedar, and American holly occupy a forest bordering river and marsh, which also contains two ponds set within the watershed of Second Herring Brook. Situated just outside Norwell center, this 100-acre tract has quite understandably become a popular site for hiking and nature study.

From the parking lot an unmarked but well-defined trail leads rather quickly to the first of the reservation's two ponds. This mill-

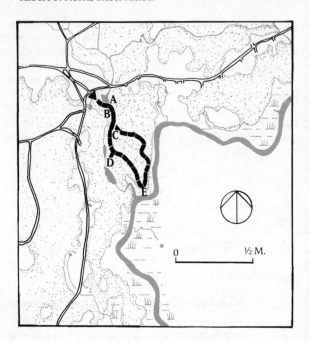

pond (**A**) was the site of an historic grist and saw mill built in 1690. Crossing the millpond's stone dam, the trail affords a view of the water as it rushes through the dam's spillway and resumes the course of Second Herring Brook below the pond. Many ponds and lakes in New England were created by damming the numerous rivers and streams so characteristic of the region's hilly topography. Generating power for early industries, many of these bodies of water were abandoned around the turn of the century or earlier. Today millponds such as this one serve as secluded refuges for waterfowl and other wildlife.

At **B** the trail leads through a shady grove of mature white pines and redcedars, familiar pioneer tree species that invade disused agricultural lands (see **#60**). These pioneer tree species, coupled with the presence of stone walls throughout the reservation, provide evidence of previous land use. This grove is a habitat for the familiar gray squirrel, whose nests may be seen in the lofty branches of white pines on the right. These large aerial nests are constructed of leaves and twigs and are clearly bigger than those of birds (see **#73** and **#83**).

Soon the trail forks to the southeast and the southwest (**C**). Take the latter route (right), watching for the American-holly tree scattered throughout the understory off the trail on the left. A deciduous evergreen whose glossy-green, spiny-pointed leaves and bright-red berries are favored as decorative branch cuttings for the Christmas holiday season, the American holly is also common as an ornamental in gardens. Usually regarded in New England as a species of the southeastern Coastal Plain, it ranges over areas of Cape Cod and Martha's Vineyard, as well as portions of the Rhode Island and Connecticut coasts (see **#25**). At Albert F. Norris it is only a few miles from the northern limits of its range, south of Boston. In the wild the American holly usually grows no more than 30 to 40 feet in height; here it rarely exceeds 20 to 25 feet. An understory tree, holly prefers moist, well-drained soil, such as that found in this upland tract bordered by a waterway.

A branch trail on the right leads to the edge of the reservation's other woodland pond (**D**), where Canada geese and black ducks may be seen.

Return to the main trail, which winds through a forest consisting of mixed hardwoods and white pine. At **E** a grove of American beech, easily identified by its smooth, light-gray bark, occupies the edge of the reservation's frontage along the North River and its adjacent salt marsh. The superb view from this vantage point encompasses a stretch of the river flowing northward through a small valley of marshy wetlands bounded on each side by forested slopes. Gulls and hawks may be seen soaring over this grassy expanse, and waterfowl should be watched for in the open river or among the marsh grasses.

The North River is an estuarine waterway, which means that salt water flows into the river channel from the tidal action of the nearby ocean. The resulting mixture of fresh and salt water is necessary for the development and survival of a salt marsh and its particular types of vegetation. This unstable environment is characterized by extreme temperature changes and salinity fluctuations. While such instability severely restricts the range of marine species that can survive, it does support such saltwater plants as salt-meadow cordgrass (or salt hay), salt-marsh cordgrass, spike-grass, and other vegetation that has adapted to the high level of salinity and frequent flooding. In turn, saltwater plants provide food for waterfowl and many shorebirds. Marsh vegetation grows on muddy sediments that are rich in organic matter produced by decaying plants. During periods of low water these muddy substrates are exposed above the waterline in the river channel. An especially good view of the saltwater marsh sediments at low water appears just ahead on the trail as it begins to swing northward. At this point the marsh becomes narrower on each side of the river's channel, and the soil underlying the surface of the marsh is clearly exposed on the opposite side of the water. This dark, rich sediment lies beneath a layer of peat, which separates the muddy substrate from the living plants. The peat is composed of partially decomposed roots, in which the living vegetation has rooted itself. Over time this layer of peat accumulates as new generations of the sáltwater marsh plants continue to root in the decomposing remains of their predecessors (see **#29** for marsh development).

Proceed along the trail as it follows the bend in the river and traverses a low, 50-foot hill. Here and there you may glimpse the river between tall white pines, as it curves away to the east; then the trail veers away from the water and returns to the fork of the trail loop. Retrace your steps to the parking lot.

Remarks: *This is a short, 50-minute hike over easy terrain, especially well suited for walks with children. Black Pond and Bog is situated nearby.*

60.
Henry L. Shattuck Reservation

Directions: **Medfield, Mass. From Boston, take Route 109 southwest from Exit 59 off I-95 (Route 128); go about 7 miles. Opposite the cemetery in Medfield, turn left onto Causeway St., which becomes a dirt road and crosses a wooden bridge. Look for unmarked iron gates in the stone wall on the right side of the road; at the second gate (about 2 miles from Route 109), stop and park; an unmarked trail leads into the forest.**

Ownership: **Trustees of Reservations.**

A lovely white-pine forest and wetland meadows lie along a southern portion of the Charles River. Shattuck Reservation encompasses a 283-acre parcel on the river's eastern bank, where a short, unmarked trail wanders through woodlands to the river's edge. The successional forest, crisscrossed by stone walls and bordered by wetlands, displays several species of woodland wildflowers and serves as habitat for a variety of wildlife, including the great horned owl.

Evidence of past agricultural usage is apparent throughout the trail, beginning at the iron gate situated on Causeway St. Stone walls

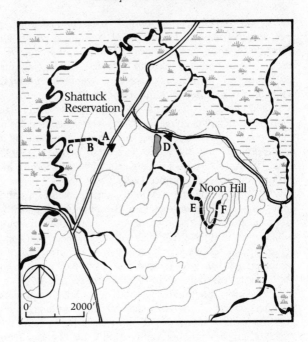

and pioneer tree species, chiefly white pine and eastern redcedar, are common indicators in southern New England of farmland that is reverting to woodlands. Several specimens of eastern redcedar, a dark-green conifer of either conical or pyramidal form, appear on the right (**A**) at the outset of the trail. Redcedar and pioneer conifers such as white pine and common field juniper require open space and plentiful sunlight to grow. They invade abandoned pastures before other trees and may even appear while livestock still grazes there. White pine and common juniper are distasteful to livestock, as are the redcedar's sharply pointed needles, which become scaly with age. The appearance of any of these conifers prior to the abandonment of a pasture gives them a competitive advantage over other vegetation that may appear later. However, in former hayfields, the trees may take root only after an initial takeover by shrubs, which, unlike conifers, can sprout from cut stems after mowing has ceased. Redcedar and white-pine seeds germinate well in the grassy turf of hayfields, and either one may quickly become dominant if the shrub cover is not too dense.

The white pine is the dominant tree at Shattuck, reaching heights of about 60 feet or more along the trail. It is the tallest eastern conifer and its potential life-span of 400 years is exceptional among pioneer species, which are usually short-lived. Yet only a very few isolated stands in New England are even as old as 150 or 200 years. The tree's value as timber resulted in its widespread logging during colonial times and the early decades of the twentieth century. Colonial white pine was cut for ships' masts for the king's navy. Later, a new generation grew up on abandoned farmlands as New England agriculture declined after about 1840. This later generation of "old-field white pine," as it is known, was extensively logged around the turn of the century, and many trees were destroyed in the 1938 hurricane. The vast majority of the region's white-pine forests, including this one, have grown up since 1900.

White pine germinates well in dry, sandy upland soils and abundant sunlight. However, there must be a mature pine nearby to act as a source for seed. Its tiny seeds can be carried by the wind as far as one-third of a mile. The high volume of seeds that can be dispersed over a relatively wide area by one or several mature trees, combined with the tree's rapid rate of growth when young, are important factors in its success as a pioneer species.

At a clearing about midway down the trail (**B**), the understory of the forest on the left reveals small white-pine seedlings. Gaps in the high canopy have allowed sunlight to reach these smaller seedlings, which otherwise could not survive. Notice, too, that smaller oak and maple hardwoods are also thriving in the sunlight. These hardwoods will probably constitute the next generation of trees in this forest. Once a stand of pine begins to die, it is very unusual for a new generation of pine to replace it. The great number of pine seedlings here, however, will probably ensure that at least some will flourish among the emerging hardwoods.

This upland forest is also the habitat of the great horned owl, the only large owl with ear tufts resembling small horns. Reaching almost 2 feet in length, the great horned owl has a very prominent white throat collar and large head. An impressive, though noiseless, bird in flight, it often favors pine as a roost, sometimes living in hollow tree trunks or abandoned hawk's nests. Its prey includes small mammals, such as rabbits, squirrels, mice, and rats, as well as wild birds and poultry. It is a common species in southern New England and a permanent resident throughout its range from Labrador and Hudson Bay south to Florida, Texas, and Mexico. One horned owl has been sighted here regularly.

Continue along the path as it slopes gently downhill and emerges upon the bank at a bend in the river (**C**). The hardwood trees that had been scattered among the more dominant pines are now more prevalent. With their trunks and branches arching into the sunlight over the open water, such trees as pin oak and red and silver maple can withstand the higher springtime waters that follow thawing snow and heavy rains. Also notice the grapevines twining up the trunks of trees on the riverbank. Common to wet areas, grapevines often form tangled, invasive thickets that can slow the growth of other vegetation. They may also damage or destroy smaller trees, as in the case of the small pine seen standing next to the trail some 6 feet from the water. Grapevines have almost completely overspread the tree, threatening to pull it down or strangle its slender trunk.

Retrace your steps back along the path. As you go, watch for Canada mayflower growing along the forest floor. It is a member of the lily family and emerges in late April or early May, its two light-green leaves and dainty white or yellow flowers standing only about 3 inches high, though it can spread by underground runners to form an extensive ground cover. Also visible in places is the well-known pink lady's slipper, with its easily recognizable single pink flower and oval leaves. Both Canada mayflower and pink lady's slipper prosper in the acidic soil of the oak and pine forest.

If you wish, stray off the path for a short distance to the left, where through gaps in the trees a wet meadow marsh is visible beyond a stone wall. Stop for a moment at the edge of the higher ground and enjoy the sunny view before returning to the trail leading back to the road.

Remarks: *The unmarked trail is a short, 20- to 30-minute hike over gradually sloping terrain. The Shattuck Reservation entrance on Causeway St. is unmarked, but management regulations are posted on trees at intervals along the road and aid in identifying Trustees of Reservations property. Inquire at nearby Rocky Woods Reservation, Medfield, for further information and assistance, or at the Trustees headquarters at 224 Adams St., Milton, Mass. 02186, (617) 698-2066. Noon Hill Reservation (Noon Hill St., off Causeway St.) is located within 1 mile of the Shattuck Reservation. These two Trustees of Reservations properties can be explored together for a morning or afternoon hike.*

61.

Noon Hill

Reservation

Directions: **Medfield, Mass. Follow directions for #60. After Causeway St. crosses the wooden bridge, take the first**

left onto Noon Hill St. Proceed to an unmarked iron gate
on the right just beyond a small pond. Park there; an unmarked trail leads into the forest.

Ownership: Trustees of Reservations.

Noon Hill rises to 369 feet above sea level, with views across the
woodlands and meadows of the floodplain of the Charles and Stop
rivers. The reservation comprises 52 acres of white-pine and oak
forest, and a path leads past a woodland swamp and over rocky
slopes. Local tradition asserts that Noon Hill was named by early
settlers who marked the midday hour when the sun appeared over
its ridge. Today stone walls and abandoned cellar holes at Noon Hill
attest to the former presence of these early Medfield pioneers.

This unmarked trail winds along the western slope of Noon Hill
before ascending from the southern end of the hill. Before starting
down the trail, however, walk to the edge of the small, but scenic
pond (**D**), a few yards to the right of the gate. Holt Pond was once
the site of a grist mill and is fed by a brook that continues north to
become a tributary of the Stop River. As you walk from the edge of
Holt Pond to the gate, an abandoned cellar hole is visible. Trees are
now growing in the cellar hole, a familiar occurrence on such abandoned sites when seeds take root on the packed-dirt floors. As a
remnant of New England's heyday as an agrarian society, such scenes
are a reminder of the resurgence of the region's forests in the wake
of agricultural clearing.

Proceed down the trail through an area of white-pine forest—a
common pioneer tree species that quickly invades forsaken agricultural lands (see **#60**). Walk for about 15 minutes until the stone
walls that mark the boundaries of former fields and pastures are left
behind. Soon the trail dips downhill as it winds around the base of
Noon Hill's western slope.

An expanse of woodland swamp (**E**) stretches away to the right
of the trail. Red maple is the dominant tree in this wet area, in
contrast to the white pines and oak prevalent on the higher slopes.
Often called swamp or scarlet maple, it is usually associated with
boggy areas, where it can form pure colonies. Unable to withstand
the constant submersion of its roots in standing water, it often grows
on hummocks elevated slightly above the boggy soil. Red maple is
the only variety of maple capable of growing on the very dry ridges
or dry upland slopes in southern New England (see **#13**). The silver
maple inhabits damp floodplains, and the sugar maple moist upland
soils and valleys. An early-autumn-foliage tree, the red maple's leaves
turn a deep scarlet on acidic soils and varying degrees of orange and
yellow elsewhere. It is the most widely distributed tree from

north to south in the eastern United States. Although relatively short-lived, it sprouts vigorously after logging or fire.

As the trail curves southeasterly, it forks uphill to the north and downhill to the east. Veer left to the north, ascending to the top of Noon Hill. A small footpath on the right leads over a solid rock ledge to the edge of a cliff (**F**). White pines rise up from below the cliff; in the open gaps between them are views to the east and southeast of Noon Hill. Return to the trail, walking a short distance to a second footpath on the right, which again leads over the ridge. Eastern redcedars have grown up in areas of thin soil at intervals on top of the rock. Views to the east across the countryside can be enjoyed here, before returning to the trail and retracing your steps back to the road.

Remarks: *This unmarked trail is a 40-minute hike over relatively easy terrain. Other unmarked trails and paths crisscross Noon Hill, sometimes joining or crossing the trail described here. To avoid confusion, stay on the main trail, which always continues straight ahead, until it finally veers left and climbs up the southern slope of Noon Hill. Henry L. Shattuck Reservation (see #60) is located within 1 mile of Noon Hill, on Causeway St. Inquiries for information and assistance can be made at nearby Rocky Woods Reservation, Medfield (see #62).*

62.
Rocky Woods
Reservation

Directions: **Medfield, Mass. From Route 128 (I-95), which circles Boston, take Exit 59 onto Route 109. Go south 1.8 miles and turn west (right) onto Hartford St. Go 2.7 miles to the reservation entrance on the right.**

Ownership: **Trustees of Reservations.**

Rocky Woods lies in the low, granite hills of eastern Massachusetts. White-pine and oak forest, ridges of solid rock, and four freshwater ponds are the chief attractions within the reservation's 473 acres of boulder-strewn, crested terrain.

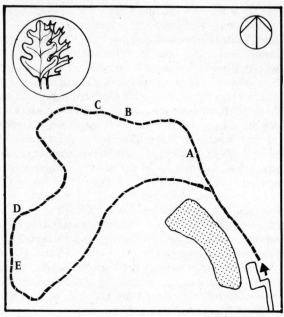

Inset: White & red oaks

The bedrock of granite and related igneous rocks that determines the shape of Rocky Woods's landscape, and also strongly influences its soil composition and vegetation, is the dominant natural feature of the landscape. Because it is more resistant to erosion than other types of bedrock, such as marble or limestone, granite often gives substance to hills, ledges, ridges, and other areas of terrain higher than the surrounding land. Very frequently, the granite bedrock has been exposed in these high places where erosion has stripped away the topsoil. Where a topsoil is present, it is likely to be thin, highly acidic, and may contain loose rocks that range in size from small stones to large boulders.

The Hemlock Nature Trail at Rocky Woods contains geological features typical of granite bedrock, as well as many plant species likely to be found in rocky, acidic soil. Starting from the access road running along the east side of Chickering Lake near the parking lot, the wide, well-kept trail forms a loop, with numbered posts keyed to an interpretive trail guide. Where the trail forks, veer to the right, walking in a northwesterly direction.

Oaks are the dominant trees at Rocky Woods. At **A** compare the white oak at the trail's edge, its leaves with characteristically rounded lobes, to the red oak visible behind it, which has more sharply pointed leaves. The southern New England oak forest occupies many areas with acidic soils similar to Rocky Woods. Soil acidity is determined by the underlying bedrock and the nutrient content of decaying leaf litter. Oak leaves, for instance, are themselves highly acidic and generally increase soil acidity. The fungus and bacteria that are largely responsible for the decomposition of leaf litter and other organic matter in the forest cannot tolerate highly acidic conditions. As a result, decomposition is slow, and organic matter accumulates in a layer or carpet of leafy debris. This carpet is known as *mor humus* and, as seen beneath the oak trees here, can easily be distinguished from the underlying mineral soils.

Igneous rock, a type that includes the granite bedrock of Rocky Woods, tends to break down into acidic soils. Rocks of igneous origin solidifed from a molten state about 200 million years ago. At **B** are two kinds of igneous rock closely related to granite: Dedham granodiorite, of a pinkish color on fresh surfaces, and Salem gabbrodiorite, which is darker colored.

The eastern hemlock (**C**), clustered among the boulders and ledges on top of Hemlock Knoll, is one of the few shade-tolerant conifers. It is a common species of tree in areas of acidic soil and rocky terrain. Its short needles are themselves highly acidic, like oak leaves, and permit few plants to survive beneath its branches. The hemlock prefers the cooler habitats of ravines and shady slopes, and its shallow root system enables it to survive in thin, rocky soil.

Pipsissewa, or "prince's pine" (**D**), is an ericad, meaning that it is a member of the heath family. Like many of the other small ground flora common to the oak forest, such as wintergreen, pipsissewa is an evergreen that spreads by underground runners to form colonies. It has glossy, dark-green leaves; white or light-pink flowers bloom in July. It belongs to the limited group of herbaceous plants that have adapted to acidic conditions. Reproduction by underground runners allows this perennial to flourish where annuals (which must produce new generations every year) would quickly disappear. Annual seed germination is difficult in the oak forest because the thick humus layer prevents seeds from reaching the soil beneath it. Moreover, long centuries of ecological development have seen herbaceous plants and shrubs come to require rather precise levels of soil acidity in order to prosper and multiply as individual species.

The underlying bedrock at Rocky Woods is dramatically displayed at the Whaleback Ledge (**E**). Erosion occurring over millions of years probably exposed this ledge before the last ice-age glaciers (see **Long Island, Cape Cod, and the Islands**) scoured and smoothed its surface, some 10,000 to 15,000 years ago, molding it into the rounded form of a "whaleback."

Remarks: *Hemlock Knoll Nature Trail (1 mile) is a 45-minute walk over easy, if sometimes stony, terrain. All other trails at Rocky Woods are undergoing renovation and rerouting at the time of this writing. Reservation personnel will assist hikers and visitors with updated trail information. In the last several decades, Rocky Woods has seen a number of its former swamps dammed to create four bodies of water. These quiet scenic ponds or lakes, which will certainly be included along the modernized trail system, are Notch and June ponds, situated in the watershed of the Charles River, and Echo and Chickering lakes, located in the watershed of the Neponset River. A popular recreation area, Rocky Woods provides facilities for picnicking, winter ice skating, organized games, and numerous trails for hiking, horseback riding, and cross-country skiing.*

63.
World's End
Reservation

Directions: **Hingham, Mass. From Boston, take I-93 south to Exit 20, then follow Route 3A southeast about 12 miles through Hingham. Turn east (left) on Summer St.; go 0.5 mile. Turn north (left) onto Martin's Lane; follow it about 0.6 mile to the reservation entrance.**

Ownership: **Trustees of Reservations.**

Situated on the Massachusetts coast some 14 miles southeast of Boston in the historic South Shore town of Hingham (settled 1635), World's End consists of two adjoining drumlin islands separated from the mainland by a narrow marsh. Bounded on the west by Hingham Harbor and on the east by the Weir River, the reservation's 251 acres embrace wooded shores, hilltop meadows, salt marshes, rocky coves, and beaches. Graceful, tree-lined roads designed by Frederick Law Olmsted (1822–1903), America's first landscape architect and pioneer conservationist, highlight harbor views that rank among the most beautiful in all of coastal Massachusetts.

The two island hills that together make up World's End are known to geologists as *glacial drumlins.* The hills' gentle, rounded shapes are characteristic of all drumlins, which are easy to recognize because they contrast sharply with the rugged, irregularly shaped bedrock

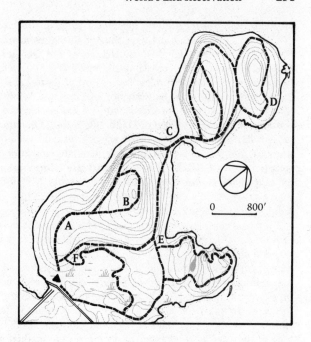

hills and ridges that dominate the New England landscape. Drumlins are comparatively young land forms on the scale of geologic time. They are the products of the ice-age glaciers that began to creep south over New England about 1 million years ago and only began to withdraw some 15,000 years ago. Drumlins were created when glacial ice sheets ground regions of soft bedrock into rock flour (silt and clay), which was then gathered up by the moving ice and deposited in a mass beneath the glaciers. As the ice sheet eventually moved over these trapped deposits, they were molded into something like their present-day forms.

Drumlins are generally distinguished by their low, elongated profile and smooth contours, which usually measure no more than several hundred feet high and 1 mile long. They are often oval-shaped, with the lee slope, which faced away from the oncoming glacier, higher and steeper than the stoss slope on the other side. Drumlins are usually concentrated within a geographical area, called a *drumlin field,* and groups of drumlins are referred to as *swarms* or *clusters.*

The Boston Basin, an area that encompasses the city's outlying suburbs (including World's End) and harbor, is a well-known drumlin field. Many of the historic hills and islands in this region are drumlins, including Charlestown's Bunker Hill, Newton's Chestnut Hill, and Boston's Meeting House Hill, as well as Georges Island, Thompson Island, and Deer Island, among others.

A number of island drumlins in the Boston Basin have become linked together through the formation of sandspits. Before the sea level rose as a result of the melting of the ice-age glaciers, the Boston Harbor Islands were hills on dry land. But with the flooding of the present-day harbor basin, the ocean waves eroded the slopes of these drumlins and then deposited the loose material in the form of sandspits (see **Long Island, Cape Cod, and the Islands**). Such bars are called *tombolos* (see **#78**). Nantasket Peninsula, lying less than a mile east of World's End, is a tombolo composed of five drumlins linked together by sandspits.

The island closest to the mainland includes Pine and Planter's hills. From the warden's office at the entrance gate, turn left and walk across a short causeway spanning the extreme western tip of the marsh. On the left stands one of the two dikes that enclose the salt marsh from the harbor. These dikes were built in pre-Revolutionary times so that the marsh could be drained for the harvesting of salt-meadow cordgrass, or salt hay. Proceed straight ahead from the causeway as the road climbs 50-foot Pine Hill (**A**). Go right at the fork in the road beyond Pine Hill to ascend the gradual slope of Planter's Hill (**B**), which at 120 feet is the reservation's highest point. Stone walls line the roadside, bordering a field on the right in which eastern redcedars, pitch pines, and scarlet sumac trees are scattered. As you reach the brow of the hill, a superb seascape unfolds below the broad field on the right. To the southeast the narrow peninsula of Nantasket Beach across the Weir River curves northward and disappears from sight, while beyond it the vast Atlantic stretches into the distance.

After the road circles the summit of Planter's Hill, it rejoins the main road, which leads north (right) across the low-lying sandbar (**C**) that links up with the reservation's outermost island. The bar was constructed by early settlers in order to travel between the islands at high tide. The road climbs the south slope of the outer island from the bar. The roads here form two interlocking loops circling the island's two rounded peaks, the first loop bisected by a crossroad that leads over the summit of the island's most landward hill.

The tree-lined roads that crisscross the reservation are World's End's most elegant feature. In the nineteenth century, World's End, so named because it is located at the end of the peninsula, was part of a seaside country estate owned by John R. Brewer, a prominent Boston businessman. In 1890 Brewer commissioned Frederick Law

Olmsted, designer of New York City's Central Park, to design the roads as part of planned subdivision of the land for house lots. The proposed homes were never built, but Olmsted's tree-lined lanes were generally constructed according to his original plan. The trees were planted in staggered, double rows, in order to create the visual effect of a solid foliage screen or natural green wall enclosing the roads. This scheme is still evident along many stretches of the road, and some of the original trees still survive today.

Oaks, maples, and horsechestnut trees dominate the lanes. The horsechestnut was widely introduced during colonial times as an ornamental and street tree in the United States and has become naturalized in some parts of the Northeast. The species has a spreading rounded or elliptical crown, with dark-green leaves. It bears white flowers in the spring, and its late-summer fruit takes the form of brown, spiny capsules containing one or two poisonous seeds.

The northernmost part of the outer islands is the most heavily forested area of the reservation. At **D** a large American-beech tree stands surrounded by small beech saplings that have sprung up from shoots around the old tree. The brushy thickets bordering the fields serve as habitat for fox, rabbit, quail, and pheasant. Gray squirrels can also be seen throughout the reservation (see **#73** and **#83**).

At **E** a footpath leaves the road that winds along the east side of Planter's Hill on the landward island. It wanders through dense stands of eastern redcedar that grow in patches of turf clinging to the bedrock ledges of Rocky Neck. The bare outcrops of conglomerate and volcanic rock at Rocky Neck stand in stark contrast to the smooth beaches that largely surround the islands. The footpath at Rocky Neck overlooks the Weir River, where a splendid view of the outer islands can be enjoyed. Shore and sea birds may be seen in the tidal channel of the river, before the trail curves westward and connects with a road that returns to the entrance gate.

The boardwalk through the marsh (**F**) is also a fine birding spot. Turn right after crossing the causeway beyond the entrance gate and look for the footpath on the right of the road.

Remarks: *World's End has no formal trail system, but hikers can roam freely over its unpaved lanes, several footpaths, and a boardwalk in the marsh. Allow about 3 hours for a full circuit of the reservation's two islands and Rocky Neck at a leisurely pace over easy terrain. Minimum distance is about 4 miles. Picnicking and swimming are prohibited. Limited parking facilities require early arrival by car on warm-weather weekends and holidays. This is a popular hiking spot among residents of Boston's densely populated metropolitan suburbs. An admission fee is charged. The reservation is open all year, from 10:00 a.m. to 5:00 p.m.*

Nearby Places
of Interest

Boston Harbor Islands State Park: This park, which includes 195 acres on thirteen islands in Boston Harbor, offers wilderness camping, fishing, historical study, and varied recreational and sporting opportunities.

Wompatuck State Park: Union St., Hingham, Mass. There are four hundred public campsites in this 2,877-acre park. A one-mile self-guiding nature trail is located near the park's visitor center. Forest Climax Grove features some of the oldest forest stands in southeastern Massachusetts, with white pines, hemlocks, and American beeches as old as 175 years. Many varied recreational and sporting activities, including 10 miles of additional trails.

64.

Whale Watch

Directions: Aboard the *Ranger IV,* leaving from the New England Aquarium, Central Wharf, Boston, Mass. The aquarium is located off Atlantic Avenue, two blocks east of the Faneuil Hall marketplace.

When wondering about the largest creatures that have existed on earth, one often thinks of dinosaurs and the huge skeletal models that can be found in natural history museums. However, the largest creatures were not dinosaurs but whales, and they are still roaming the ocean depths as they have for several hundred thousand years.

Public interest in whales and their behavior has grown since the early 1970s when people realized these magnificent mammals were being hunted to extinction. Protection in the form of international quotas and a total ban on whaling in the United States have given new hope for their survival. Today one can observe whales close up at sea on any of several "whale-watch" expeditions that operate from Long Island to northern Maine. From late spring to mid-fall day-long expeditions leave daily from the New England Aquarium in Boston, accompanied by a naturalist who speaks about whales and seabirds.

Whale-watching is best in New England between late spring, when the whales migrate north from southern waters, and early fall, when they return. They are drawn to the North Atlantic by the warming waters and the abundant food supply that increases in the spring and summer. One of the richest feeding areas is the Stellwagen Bank, a steep underwater plateau about twenty miles east of Boston between Provincetown and Cape Ann. The bank is a geological extension of Cape Cod, with a sandy bottom, about 100 feet below the surface, covered with a lush growth of plants that thrive on the intense sunlight that warms the relatively shallow water. The sides of the plateau drop steeply to depths of 200 to 300 feet. When ocean currents hit the clifflike walls, they rush upward to the surface carrying rich food and nutrients from the bottom. This draws large schools of fish, which feed on the plankton, and the fish in turn attract the whales, which feed on them (see **Cape Cod to Portland**).

As the boat leaves Boston Harbor, several common seabirds may be seen around the small islands and over the open water. Black-backed gulls, herring gulls (see **#17** and **#77**), and cormorants follow the boat looking for food. A flock of eider ducks may fly in formation low over the water. After about 2 hours, you enter the Stellwagen Bank area and begin looking for whales. The boat's captain looks for seabirds feeding off the water, a sign of possible whale activity, since whales often bring fish with them to the surface when they blow. Different whale-watch boats also communicate by radio for reports of whale sightings.

Although about five of the twenty-one species of whales, and the closely related porpoises, can be seen off the New England coast, by far the most common are the humpback and finback whales. On a spring trip you might well see both species, including pairs of mothers and calves. The boat draws close enough for you to clearly see the differences between the two types and to observe them feeding and "playing" at some length. Finbacks average about 65 feet in length and weigh up to 60 tons. They have a dark back and light underside with two pale stripes, or chevrons, along the back. When a finback surfaces, it shows a lot of its back, and the dorsal fin near the tail—hence its name. It dives to feed for 2 to 10 minutes then returns to the surface to breathe, blowing water and air from its blowhole up to ten times, at 20-second intervals, before diving again. On a windless day, the waterspout can be 10 to 20 feet high. Both the finback and the humpback are known as baleen whales, which refers to their method of eating. Instead of teeth, they have long fingernail-like plates hanging down the sides of their mouths with hairs that act as a strainer while feeding. The whale locates a school of fish and opens its mouth, taking in hundreds of fish and a large amount of water. It then closes its mouth, expels the water through the strainer, and swallows the fish. It is a very efficient system for satisfying such a large appetite.

Finback calves are born between December and April, after a 1-year pregnancy. The calf nurses on its mother's milk for 7 months, each day consuming some 700 gallons and gaining 30 pounds. It then feeds on planktonic crustaceans before beginning an adult diet of fish at about 1 year. By that time it will be about 40 feet long, and may grow as large as 70 feet during its approximately 30-year life-span. Whales reach sexual maturity and mate at the age of 5 or 6 years. The finbacks, numbering about 7,200 in the North Atlantic, are not considered an endangered species. They are the fastest swimmers among whales, a characteristic that served them well during the heyday of whaling and earned them the nickname of "greyhounds of the sea."

The other commonly seen whales off New England are the humpbacks. They are the most acrobatic and friendly of the whales, often putting on a show for viewers and coming up to the side of the boat. The humpback is the easiest whale to identify, distinguished by the knobby "stovebolts" on its head and its humped back. They are not as slender as the finbacks, and are smaller, weighing about 50 tons and averaging 45 feet in length. They have very long white flippers on the lower front sides of their bodies, which they use for propulsion and control of movement. As you may discover, they also use them to wave at visitors while rolling on their backs. The whales are very playful, and often breach, jumping completely out of the water. When they dive, their tail fins show above the water, and scientists have found that the markings on the tail are unique to each whale. Like fingerprints, no two are alike, and this has allowed observers to identify and name individual whales. With photographs of the tail markings, whales can be tracked to determine their migration and feeding patterns. Many of the same whales return year after year, although only about 200 of the estimated 10,000 humpbacks in the northwestern Atlantic have been catalogued.

Without seeing whales, it is difficult to fathom their size and fully appreciate their grace. On a New England whale watch, you may well sight a pod, or group, of whales close up and perhaps a solicitous mother watching her calf as it approaches the boat.

Remarks: *There are over a dozen regularly scheduled whale-watch cruises from Montauk, Long Island, to Mount Desert Island, Maine. They gener-*

ally run from the middle of May to the middle of October, but this can vary. Trips generally last between 6 and 8 hours. Warm clothes are recommended, since it is often 20 degrees colder out at sea. Sunglasses, binoculars, and cameras are good equipment to have along. If you are prone to seasickness, consider appropriate medication. Some boats sell food, others require that you bring a lunch. Many whale-watch trips are accompanied by a naturalist, who can enhance your understanding and enjoyment; inquire about this when selecting a boat. Some trips also feature birding. Most boats will go out rain or shine—whales like rain—but storms can cancel trips. All the Massachusetts whale watches go to the Stellwagen Bank area. Although there are no guarantees that you will see whales on a given trip, you are likely to find the cruise informative and enjoyable just the same. A selected few of the cruises are listed below:

Plymouth, Mass.:	*The Captain John and Son,* with The Web of Life; (617) 746-2643
	The Cape Cod Princess, (617) 747-2400
Provincetown, Mass.:	*The Ranger,* (617) 487-3322
	The Dolphin Fleet, with the Center for Coastal Studies; (617) 487-1900
Gloucester, Mass.:	*The Daunty,* (617) 285-5110
Boston, Mass.:	*The Ranger IV,* with the New England Aquarium; (617) 742-8830
Mount Desert Island, Maine:	Maine Whalewatch, (207) 244-3575 or (207) 244-7429

65.

Peddocks Island

Directions: **Boston, Mass. The island can be reached by boat from Long Wharf in Boston, next to the New England Aquarium off Atlantic Ave. two blocks east of the Faneuil Hall marketplace. Water-taxi service is also available from other Boston Harbor Islands. Information can be obtained at the wharf.**

Ownership: **Massachusetts Metropolitan District Commission.**

Among the scattered islands of Boston Harbor, within sight of the city skyline, is an island that offers a unique mix of natural and human history. Peddocks Island, the second largest in the harbor, contains salt marsh, mudflats, mature forest, and the diverse marinelife of the harbor. Since 1982 the 185-acre island has been managed by the Peddocks Island Trust, a nonprofit consortium of educational and scientific institutions that plans to maintain the island's natural diversity and make it more accessible to the public. They also intend to restore the graceful turn-of-the-century brick buildings of the military fort on the island's East Head.

Peddocks Island is composed of five distinct drumlins connected to each other by a series of narrow spits of land called tombolos (see **#78**). All of the Boston Harbor Islands are drumlins, glacial deposits of gravel, clay, and other materials that had been carried by the ice. However, unlike the deposits at the terminal moraine of the glacier, drumlins were formed under the ice and became elongated and elliptical in shape as the ice moved over them. This streamlined shape enables us to see the direction of the ice flow. The various Boston Harbor Islands have different directional orientations, which is mysterious—theoretically they should all be the same. A possible explanation is that glacial ice moved into the harbor from several different directions, but we may never know the answer for sure. (See **#63** for more on drumlins.)

The Harbor Islands are the only drumlin field in the United States that intersects the ocean's shoreline. As such, they closely resemble islands found in Northern Ireland, but are quite unlike the typical barrier island found along the Atlantic Coast. After the melting of the glacier, Peddocks' five drumlins were separated by water and

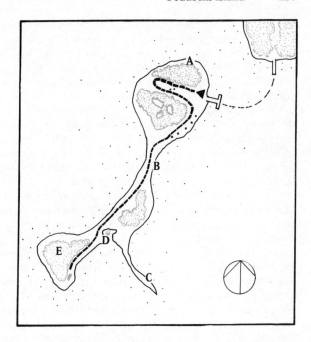

formed a series of hills overlooking a broad coastal plain. About 5,000 years ago the sea level began to rise, and the process of land erosion and building began that has shaped the island into what it is today.

As you approach Peddocks Island on the boat from Boston, you will see the high eroded cliffs of the East head (**A**), which is made up of the island's two largest drumlins. At 125 feet above sea level, this is the highest point of land in Boston Harbor. This end of the island is exposed to the currents and storms coming from the northeast. Over the years the land has been carried off the East Head and swept in a circular pattern around the drumlins. This material began to collect and build up as spits connecting the drumlins. They are like little barrier islands but they are actually tombolos (**B**), which are spits that are connected to the mainland at both ends. These tombolos are composed of gravel rather than sand, which is much more common. As a result, no sand dunes are developing with their accompanying vegetation, which is important to the survival of most islands. Theoretically, this would put the island at a disadvantage in its continuing battle against the effects of erosion and a rising sea level, since dune complexes generally protect the land area behind them and build up the vertical height of the land. However, these tombolos are increasing in size due to storm action, which erodes one part of the island (the drumlins) and builds up another (the tombolos). The type of flat gravel that is most prone to being carried ashore in storms is a shalelike rock known as Cambridge ardulite, which underlies the entire Boston Harbor area.

There is one part of Peddocks Island that is disappearing due to the forces of the wind and sea. Prince Head (**C**) is the smallest drumlin on the island and is eroding rapidly at the rate of about 6 inches per year. Geologists say that it will be gone in the foreseeable future. It can be reached at low tide by walking (barefoot) over the shallow flats. However, as Prince Head erodes, its gravel is being carried around to the West Head and is building up the shoreline there. The extinction of Prince Head, although a natural occurrence, was helped along by the military who used it as an artillery target during World War II.

A variety of birdlife can be seen on Peddocks Island. The small salt marsh (**D**) near Prince Head is home to several species of sandpipers and dowitchers. The West Head drumlin (**E**), thickly covered with sumac, maple, and dense thickets of poison ivy, serves as a wildlife refuge where nesting birds go undisturbed. The trail out there ends at a small brackish pond frequented by herons and egrets. Black-crowned night herons have nested in this area, and a great horned owl has been sighted.

The Middle Hill section of Peddocks is a small village of summer cottages, many inhabited by the descendants of Portuguese fishing families that settled here in the mid-nineteenth century. Back on the East Head (**A**) where the boat docks is a relatively mature forest surrounding old Fort Andrews. The higher elevation and better soil here enabled the maples, cherries, and oaks to reach greater sizes than their counterparts on the West Head. In the early 1900s, botanists from Boston's Arnold Arboretum planted many foreign plant species as an experiment. Most of them survived, and a self-guided nature trail leads through such trees as Japanese bittersweet and chokecherry. The island is also an excellent place for foraging for edible wild foods. Lamb's-quarters, wild mustard, milkweed, cattail, and European cranberry abound. There are also over 20 varieties of apples that were planted by the military. They are a treat to enjoy while waiting for the return boat to Boston.

Remarks: *Schedules and fares for boat service to Peddocks Island can be obtained by calling the Bay State Cruise Line on Long Wharf, (617) 723-7800. The Peddocks Island Trust has major plans for developing educational programs and exhibits on the island in the years ahead. An aqua-*

culture program is planned, and the New England Aquarium may estab-lish a center for the treatment and release of injured harbor seals. For more information contact the trust at 127 Lewis Wharf, Boston, Mass. 02110, (617) 523-1184. Camping is permitted on the island, although you must purchase a permit in advance from the trust office. Swimming is also permitted, but it is unsupervised. Fishing is good; bluefish and flounder are a common summer catch from the dock. The island has a very healthy growth of poison ivy, and caution is advised when walking the trails. Mosquitoes are also abundant in the summer. The other islands in Boston Harbor are part of the Boston Harbor Islands State Park and offer a variety of activities including historical tours, picnicking, swimming, and fishing. For information telephone (617) 749-7160.

66.
Ipswich River
Wildlife Sanctuary

Directions: **Topsfield, Mass. From Boston, take I-95 north about 5 miles beyond the Route 128 beltway. At that point, follow U.S. 1 as it splits off from I-95; continue about 3 miles north. Turn southeast (right) onto Route 97; follow it to a traffic light. Turn left onto Perkins Row and con-tinue for 1 mile to the sanctuary on the right.**

Ownership: **Massachusetts Audubon Society.**

This scenic and accessible refuge is home to an unusually large va-riety of birds and waterfowl, which are attracted by the area's diver-sity and isolation. The 2,400 acres contain over 20 miles of trails that pass through upland meadow, marsh, old pine forest, sphagnum bog, and mature mixed forest. There are also several interesting nonnatural features, remaining from when the land was a private estate. These include an elaborate rockery, a wildflower garden, and several exotic oriental plants and trees.

Scattered throughout the sanctuary, which is three-fourths wet-land, are many ponds and marshes that resulted from the disruption of ancient rivers by the last glacier, 15,000 years ago. As the ice advanced over the soft-shale bedrock, it created a *drumlin*—a streamlined, oval-shaped hill composed of rocks, clays, and boulders

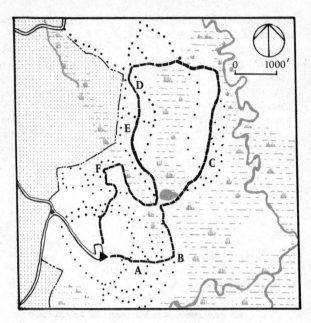

called glacial fill (see **#63**). This high ground at the sanctuary's entrance is known as Bradstreet Hill and is one of the largest drumlins in eastern Massachusetts.

Kames are another glacial formation that can be seen throughout the sanctuary. They are relatively steep-sided hills of random shape that were formed as material collected in the openings of stagnant ice. When the ice melted, this layered material remained as a hill (see **#28**). They are now islands in the marshes, primarily in the Great Wenham Swamp area along the Ipswich River.

The third major geological feature are two *eskers*. These are long, sinuous ridges composed of stratified sand, gravel, and boulders called outwash. They mark the former courses of meltwater streams flowing in tunnels or cracks in stagnant glacial ice. The streams deposited their load of debris beneath the ice, and when the ice melted, these raised stream beds were left standing as ridges. These eskers are outstanding examples and allow the visitor to imagine the size and power of the glacier that formed them.

Leaving the parking area, follow Bradstreet Lane down the east side of the drumlin. In a meadow on the right is the wildflower garden (**A**). Although it did not occur naturally, it contains only spring wildflowers found in the immediate area. These include pink and yellow lady's slippers, trailing arbutus, jack-in-the-pulpit, and hepatica. The full variety and beauty of the flowers are best seen in late May and early June. The garden has been planted in a glacial pothole, an appropriately named area dug out by the moving ice and rocks (see **#44**).

Bradstreet Lane continues to the South Esker (**B**), which rises abruptly from the road. Turn left and walk along the ridge. Notice the loose sand-and-gravel composition of the soil. This is the outwash that filled the streambeds under the glacier (see **Long Island, Cape Cod, and the Islands**). Across the marsh toward the Ipswich River are two islands that are actually kames. The trail descends from the esker and continues to a junction at Pintail Pond.

Turn right onto Averill's Island (**C**). The tall cattails and rice cutgrass on the left are part of Hassocky Meadow, a large marsh that is an ideal summer habitat for mallards, black ducks, and Canada geese, which feed on the leaves, roots, and leaves of aquatic plants. From here, one can often see these birds taking off or landing on the open water. As you continue onto Averill's Island, you enter an excellent ·example of a mature New England forest. This part of northeastern Massachusetts lies in an area between the ranges of southern oak forest and northern hardwood forest. The growth on the island is mostly mature white pine (see **#60**), indicating that this land was once open, as white pine is a prolific colonizer of open spaces. Since white-pine seedlings are eventually shaded out, the forest is succeeding to shade-tolerant hardwoods. American beech and eastern hemlock are abundant, along with some red, white, and black oak, paper and yellow birch, and red maple. At **D** is a rare stand of mature red pine, one of the few naturally occurring stands in Massachusetts. It is usually found only to the north, but the cool, moist, and sandy soil conditions have allowed this stand to become established. Also nearby is a pure stand of beech. Large holes made by pileated woodpeckers can be seen in dead trees throughout this area. At the north end of the island are some unusual mature hemlocks that escaped the cutter's axe when this area was settled over 200 years ago.

Cross the dike over the marsh. There is an abrupt change in vegetation to an immature forest of beech and maple. This area was logged about 40 years ago. Notice the abundant understory here that was absent on the shaded forest floor on Averill's Island. White ash, red maple, and European linden grow in dense clumps wherever the sunlight reaches the forest floor.

After passing through a planted pine grove, the trail turns left onto the North Esker (**E**). The trail along the ridge affords a good view of marshes on both sides where waterfowl are commonly seen. Rejoining the road, follow the signs to the Rockery. The trail circles a small pond that was planted with thick stands of mountain laurel and rhododendron, as well as cedar trees. On the west side of the pond is the Rockery (**F**), an impressive maze of rocks built at the turn of the century into paths, bridges, and tunnels. Since the glacier did not leave many boulders in the immediate area, these rocks had to be imported from several miles away.

Turn right after the Rockery, as the trail continues through a small marsh and a high, open meadow, returning to the top of Bradstreet Hill.

Remarks: *This is an easy 3-mile walk, which takes about 2 hours. Obtain a trail map of the entire sanctuary at the headquarters and explore some of the other trails. An observation tower and duck blind for bird-watching are located on Bunker Island. There is good canoeing on the Ipswich River. Cross-country skiing and snowshoeing are permitted in winter. For camping information see* **#70.**

67.

Agassiz Rock

Directions: **Manchester, Mass. From Boston, take Route 128 northeast from the point where I-95 splits off to go north; continue about 15 miles to Exit 15. Go north 0.6 mile on School St. toward Essex. There is a small parking area on the right.**

Ownership: **Trustees of Reservations.**

The two large boulders called Agassiz Rock and Swamp Rock are dramatic examples of the power of the glacier that moved over this area 15,000 years ago. The boulders are known as glacial erratics because they were transported by glacial movement and haphazardly deposited here when the ice melted (see **#85**). The trail leading to the rock passes through a variety of typical New England woodland habitats, including beech and maple forest, hemlock grove, and red-maple swamp. There is also an excellent view of Massachusetts Bay, and in the distance, Boston, from the top of Beaverdam Hill.

The trail, marked by white blazes on trees, begins at the parking area and passes through a young mixed-hardwood forest consisting mainly of maples and beech. Notice along the trail the many boulders scattered around, well rounded by the effects of glaciation and erosion. At **A** a high face of rock ledge is exposed, and a variety of ferns and lichens thrive in the shadows thrown by its westerly face. Hemlocks become more prominent throughout this area as the trail rises past more outcroppings of ledge. Mosses thrive here, too, indicating a relatively thin topsoil that is somewhat alkaline in nature due to the closeness of the rock to the surface. These rocks are composed largely of marble, which as it decomposes neutralizes the more naturally acidic soil commonly found in this area (see **#62**).

As the forest opens up at the top of Beaverdam Hill, Agassiz Rock (**B**) sits rather precariously balanced on a smaller rock beneath it. Notice that the erratic is pinker and of a more granular composition than the more grayish bedrock that forms the hill. They are both granites, but they obviously come from different areas, the erratic apparently from the north, as it is similar in composition to rock found along the coast of Maine. The path around the top of Beav-

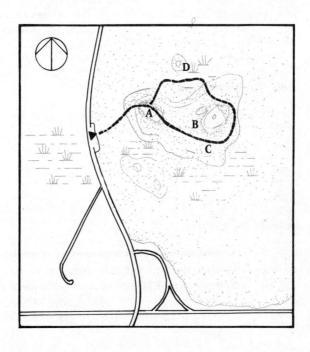

erdam Hill leads through a variety of vegetation normally associated with more northerly climates, including lichens, mosses, and bear-berry. The bedrock outcrop retains the coolness of the earth, which in turn influences the vegetation around it. Juniper, blueberry, and hemlock also grow here, but strong winds off the ocean keep the vegetation low and the appearance rather barren. The exposed bed-rock along the trail here reveals a number of glacial markings. At **C** the large expanse of bedrock shows long grooves, or glacial scrap-ings, made when the ice dragged rock composed of harder minerals across this spot. The series of small indentations, known as shatter-marks, were caused by very large boulders being slammed down by the ice and bounced across the surface. Several large cracks have opened here where water in the grooves froze and expanded, again demonstrating the power of ice (see **#85**).

The trail continues behind Agassiz Rock and descends through an area of hemlock and oak and through many smaller, moss-covered erratics. The trail enters a lower, swampy area of ferns and young red maples. Turn sharply to the right at the large hemlock tree (**D**) and walk 50 feet to Swamp Rock, a larger erratic than Agassiz that came to rest here in the lowlands. Once again, the familiar leafy lichens (see **#88**) cover the mostly shaded western side of the boul-der, being intolerant of direct, intense sunlight. Swamp Rock is of a grayer color and smoother texture than Agassiz and was most likely brought here from an entirely different location.

Going back to the main trail, continue uphill through a stand of disease-ravaged hemlocks. The trail will soon meet the main trail; turn right and descend back to the parking green.

Remarks: *Total time for the hike is about 40 minutes. The trail is steep in spots. For camping information on the north shore, see* **#70.**

68.
Crane's Beach

Directions: **From Boston, take Route 128 northeast from the point where I-95 splits off to go north; continue about 7 miles to Exit 20. Take Route 1A north about 9 miles to Ipswich. After passing the hospital, turn right onto Essex**

Rd. and then take the second left onto Northgate Rd. Turn right at the junction with Argilla Rd., and follow it to the reservation entrance at the end.

Ownership: **Richard T. Crane, Jr., Memorial Reservation, Trustees of Reservations.**

A sweeping coastal dune complex is the highlight of Crane's Beach in Ipswich. A part of the 1,352-acre Richard T. Crane, Jr. Memorial Reservation at Castle Neck, the beach and dune area stretch 4 miles along the shoreline of Ipswich Bay, offering superb sandy beaches for swimming and a hiking trail (see Remarks).

The geological history of the sand dunes at Crane's Beach and the peninsula of Castle Neck dates back to the Ice Age. Castle Neck, which protrudes eastward into Ipswich Bay from the mainland, is composed of three glacial drumlins that are joined together by sandspits. Glacial drumlins (see **#63**) are gentle, rounded hills, consisting of silt and clay, which were molded beneath the glacial ice that began to retreat from New England some 15,000 years ago. The melting of the ice sheet, which flooded the Coastal Plain, exposed the soft sediments of these newborn hills to a rising sea. Ocean waves eroded the seaward sides of the drumlins, and their eroded sediments settled beneath the hills to form sandspits. Meanwhile, other glacial sediments that had been deposited along the New England coast to the north of Castle Hill were swept southward by shore currents. This sandy material was washed up on the neck's beaches, which have long since been modified by waves and winds into the shoreline you see today .

The expansive dune fields at Crane's Beach evolved long after Castle Neck had been built up from sediments left by shore currents and waves. At one time the coast was fertile and forested, but erosion by the wind greatly expanded the original beach through its continuous movement of the sands. Dunes embody the power of the wind over loose sand. They initially develop when an obstruction such as a shrub or tree begins to trap windblown particles of sand. Over time sand accumulates in increasingly larger amounts, until finally a steep ridge develops where before a flat beach or perhaps a grassy shore meadow had stood upon the edge of the sea. The dune ridge may migrate inland as prevailing ocean winds blow sand from its seaward slope over its crest and down its landward side. At Crane's Beach the prevailing winds are from the northeast, and so the dunes are slowly encroaching upon the lands that lie to the southwest.

Walking across the dunes, you can see plants that have adapted to the dry, windswept conditions of the shifting sands. Many play a vital role in stabilizing erosion. The stiff-bladed American beach grass (see **#79**), called "the anchor of the dunes," is the most abundant plant on the windy seaward slope of the dune ridge. Its roots spread over wide areas gathering moisture, and its spiky shoots trap wind-blown sand. On the crest of the dune the beach grass is joined by other plants like beach pea, beach plum, seaside goldenrod, and dusty miller. Beach pea is similar to the common garden pea, but smaller. It keeps nitrogen in the soil, which helps to promote the growth of other plants by adding vital nutrients to the sterile sands. The woolly hudsonia (also called beach heather or false heather), a ground-hugging evergreen, forms dense, sprawling mats that bind the sands in sunny, sheltered areas of the dunes. Its tiny, scalelike leaves minimize evaporation of precious water. In June and July its minute flowers carpet the dunes with yellow blossoms.

Animal life in the most exposed, barren areas of the dunes is restricted to just a few creatures. The most interesting is the dune wolf spider (*Lycosa pikei*). This dark brown spider hunts without use of a web, stalking insects across the sands. It burrows a deep, narrow hole in the sand where the female nurtures the young.

Far more favorable for animals is the sheltered pitch-pine forest that lies behind the dunes. Its resident red squirrels gather seeds from pine cones, which are stored in large underground caches. Favoring conifer forests of the north, this small, reddish-brown squirrel is less common in the extensive oak woodlands of eastern Massachusetts than the larger eastern gray squirrel. A pile of discarded pine cones on the ground or a large aerial nest made of pine cones, leaves, and twigs are typical signs of its presence. Furthermore, it is not shy about announcing itself to intruders. Noisy and aggressive, it chatters loudly and shakes its tail when disturbed. Other common mammals include the eastern gray squirrel, eastern chipmunk, raccoon, and white-tailed deer.

Remarks: *The Pine Hollow Interpretive Trail is a self-guiding nature walk that explores the various ecological communities of the dunes. The 1-mile hike starts on the south side of the parking lot and crosses the dunes, before making a circuit through the pitch-pine forest and a red-maple swamp. A trail guide and map keyed to numbered markers can be obtained for a small fee at the parking-lot entrance booth. The terrain is moderately difficult, with soft sand and high sun exposure. Crane's Beach offers salt-water swimming, with bathhouses, lifeguards, and a refreshment stand in the summer. Beach and dune access is from the parking lot. The beach is open daily from 8:00 a.m. to sunset year-round. For information on camping on the north shore, see* **#70.**

69.
Halibut Point
Reservation

Directions: **Rockport, Mass. From Boston, take Route 128 northeast from the point where I-95 splits off to go north; continue about 23 miles to Exit 9. Take Route 127 north 2 miles to Rockport; from the junction with Route 127A, continue north on 127 (Granite St.) for 3.6 miles. Turn right onto Gott Ave.; go 0.2 mile to the parking lot on the left beyond the reservation sign.**

Ownership: **Trustees of Reservations.**

Halibut Point, a rocky headland at the northern tip of Cape Ann, is located in the historic fishing village of Rockport on the state's north shore. The point was originally called "Haul-about" by nineteenth-century sailors who had to tack around Cape Ann, which thrusts east into the Atlantic some 12 miles beyond the median coastline of the state.

The outstanding feature of the 12½-acre Halibut Point Reservation is a shore bluff of naturally fractured granite shelves that rises about 50 feet above sea level. This isolated, windswept bluff, which stands exposed to raging surf in prevailing northeast gales, looks north across Ipswich Bay to the New Hampshire shoreline and, on clear days, to Mount Agamenticus in southern Maine. Note the quarry drill marks preserved in the granite ledges; in the nineteenth century a thriving industry mined the valuable granite bedrock that makes up nearly 90 percent of Rockport's area.

The granite bedrock that underlies Cape Ann gives the peninsula its unique natural character. Cape Ann is the largest outcrop of rocky headland on the southern New England coast between Cape Cod and Maine's Cape Elizabeth, and the only one of any considerable size and geographical significance. The greater part of the southern New England coast consists of sandy beaches and sea cliffs of soft rock, which furnish the eroded sediments necessary for the formation of its characteristic sand spits, bars, dunes, and salt marshes (see **Cape Cod to Portland**). In contrast, Cape Ann's rocky shores, like those of Maine, are far more resistant to wave erosion. These granite headlands will remain unchanged for many centuries after the region's soft, sandy shoreline has been substantially transformed by the sea.

Cape Ann, like other areas in New England where hard bedrock exists, has an abundance of glacial boulders. The moving glaciers of the Pleistocene Ice Age tore loose rocks and ledges as they rode over the landscape more than 15,000 years ago. These boulders, or glacial erratics, now litter the inland regions of Cape Ann (see # 85). At Halibut Point the force of the ice sheet reveals itself in the fractured bluff of toppled ledges that have since been stripped bare of till by the surf. These granite shelves have a slablike form and layered appearance, since granitic bedrock tends to break along parallel cracks, or sheet joints.

Halibut Point's rocky shore represents a harsh habitat for life, where extreme environmental stresses arise from exposure to winter ice, summer heat, wind, surf, and tidal action. Most of the marine plants and animals that survive here are able to cling to rock surfaces while adapting to conditions in various intertidal zones ranging from the highest to the lowest areas of the shore. These marine organisms are visible at low tide when the ledges become fully exposed. Barnacles, starfish and blue-green and brown algae are a few of the plants and animals that adhere to rocks or remain in the small tidal pools on the ledges (see **Portland North**).

The reservation is also a popular observation point for migratory sea and shore birds on the Atlantic flyway (see **#96**). Among the species reported here are common eider, gannets, purple sandpiper, kittiwake, guillemots, and, in all seasons, gulls.

Halibut Point's terrestrial vegetation, which can be enjoyed all along the trail leading to the bluff, includes asters, bayberries, blackberries, and wood lilies.

Remarks: *A short trail runs from the parking area to the bluff. Follow the private road adjacent to the parking area to the sign for the Halibut Trail. Exercise caution when walking on the ledges of the bluff during low tide, where it is often very slippery underfoot. The reservation is open from April through November. For information on camping on the north shore, see* **#70.**

70.

Parker River

National Wildlife Refuge

Directions: **Plum Island, Newburyport, Mass. From Boston, take I-95 north about 22 miles beyond the Route 128 beltway. Take Route 113 east about 3 miles to Water St. in Newburyport. Turn left on the Plum Island Turnpike; after crossing the bridge onto the island, turn left onto Northern Blvd. to the refuge headquarters, or right onto Sunset Dr. to the refuge gate.**

Ownership: **U.S. Fish and Wildlife Service.**

Parker River forms 6 miles of coastal wilderness at Plum Island, one of the few natural barrier-beach-and-dune complexes along the New England coast north of Cape Cod (see **Cape Cod to Portland**). Situated north of Cape Ann at the mouth of the Merrimack River, this 4,650-acre refuge features sandy beaches, dunes, salt meadows, and both freshwater and saltwater marshes. Hiking trails cross windswept, sparsely vegetated dunes, weave through sun-filtered stands of pitch pine and redcedar, and dip into shadowy wetlands lush with shrubs and trees. The wealth of plantlife and unique geological features within a small radius comprise the typical habitats of a New England barrier island, which support large communities of marine life, mammals, and birds. Plum Island is particularly famous among bird-watchers for the over 270 species of local and migratory birds that feed in its marshes and meadows (see **#96** for more on migration). Waterfowl, including some rare species, are especially numerous; and during peak migratory periods such species as Canada geese can number over 6,000.

Plum Island is a legacy of the retreating Wisconsin ice sheet of 15,000 years ago, and a living testament to the natural forces of wind and water that continue to shape it. Some 6,300 years ago Plum Island began to form as the sea level rose in the wake of the melting glacier. A complex series of changes in the land–sea elevation eventually produced erosion of the coastal moraine—ridges of clay, sand, and rocks created offshore by the ice sheet (see **Long Island, Cape Cod, and the Islands**). By 6,000 years ago Plum Island was merely a sandspit composed of this eroded sand and

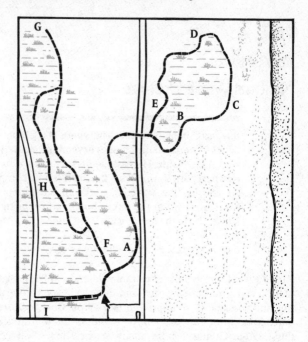

gravel that had begun to collect on top of a deposit of glaciomarine clay. As the rising sea level began to abate some 4,300 years ago, Plum Island gradually became anchored to a group of nearby drumlin islands, which now compose part of the island's surface. During this process, salt marshes formed on the island's landward side and, in ensuring years, overspread the open water that once separated the expanding island from the mainland (see **#29**). The ocean beach and sand dunes have meanwhile continued over the centuries to undergo dynamic change from wind erosion and, to a lesser degree, from overwash by storm waves.

Hellcat Swamp Trail is the lengthiest of three nature trails at Parker River and provides the most extensive tour of Plum Island's representative features. Access to the trail is from parking lot 4, where an observation tower with a panoramic view of the surrounding marshes, dunes, ocean, and mainland allows visitors to orient themselves to the landscape.

The trail begins on the north side of parking lot 4 and then quickly forks into east and west directions. The eastward trail (**A**) winds for a short distance through areas of scrub growth and pockets of freshwater swamp. Freshwater swamps form where the level of the land surface dips below the freshwater table. When rain or melting snow percolates into the ground, it eventually reaches a level where the soil is thoroughly saturated, which marks the water table. Because fresh water is less dense than salt water, the two liquids will not mix. In effect, fresh water floats on top of the salt water beneath ground, because it is lighter. Usually the fresh groundwater will extend far below sea level, to a depth of about forty times greater than the height the water table reaches above sea level.

Here the trail crosses the road that divides the island and becomes a loop that rings Hellcat Swamp, a freshwater habitat surrounded and interrupted by sand dunes. Wooded thickets along the trail reveal an assortment of trees that have become established in the more protected environments some distance away from the beach. These trees of the maritime forest generally fall into two broad categories: trees of the upland dunes, such as black oak, black cherry, and redcedar; and trees of the wet hollows lying between the dunes, such as alder, black tupelo, hackberry, and hoary and pussy willow.

A 50-foot-high dune (**B**) provides a commanding view of the island and allows observers to study the physiography of the barrier island. The island can, in essence, be divided into five major zones—three dunes areas plus salt- and fresh-water marsh—each of which constitutes a different habitat for vegetation and other life (see **#33**). From east to west across the island, the beach is the least hospitable habitat for plant life. Only such hardy species as beach grass, spikegrass, and wild radish can survive the ocean exposure and shifting sands. The foredune area can be seen bordering the beach as a barrier ridge of dunes. Salty spray, wind, and extreme temperature variations again severely limit the growth of plantlife to such vegetation as beach grass. The foredune area blends into the interdune, a zone of young sand dunes interspersed with small freshwater swamps situated in low hollows, some of which contain cranberry bogs.

As you walk a short distance down the trail, a typical feature of the interdune becomes visible. A *blowout* (**C**), where wind erosion has scooped out a depression in the dunes, shows how difficult it is for plants to gain a foothold here. False heather, a dominant plant of the interdune that produces brilliant yellow flowers in the spring, is seen along this stretch of the trail, carpeting areas of limited sand drift.

The interdune area gives way to the backdune, an older and more stable area where the dunes reach their highest and the forest is well developed. Here, as in the interdune, low hollows known as *wet swales* extend below the water table and support freshwater swamps, like Hellcat Swamp itself. At **D** a freshwater swamp displays the typical plants of this sheltered habitat. Bayberry, blackberry, Virginia creeper, and many of the lowland trees already mentioned can thrive here. Further along the trail (**E**) a second freshwater swamp reveals another assortment of vegetation common to the wet swale, such as blueberry and winterberry, which are natural food for many birds.

Return to the fork in the trail near the parking lot; the western trail (**F**) skirts the freshwater marsh and leads to a wildlife-observation blind (**G**) where many waterfowl, such as black duck, can be appreciated quietly at close range. Small mammals, such as rabbits, are very common in this area.

Taking the loop in the trail after leaving the observation blind leads to the freshwater marsh (**H**). Created by the construction of a dike by the refuge management in order to attract a greater variety and number of shorebirds, wading birds, and waterfowl, the freshwater marsh is blanketed by plants such as cattail, reed grass, and purple loosestrife, an invasive plant that creates a dazzling carpet of purple color in late summer.

Return to the observation tower (**I**) after leaving the trail. The salt marshes are visible to the west beyond the dike, where salt hay is harvested for commercial mulch. The mowed marshes are popular feeding grounds for waterfowl. Many species of shorebirds can be observed from the tower in the saltwater estuary and freshwater pools on each side of the dike.

Two other shorter trails are worth mention, since they display features of a New England barrier island not present along the Hellcat Swamp Trail. Both can be walked in a brief time.

Pine Trail contains Plum Island's largest stand of pitch pine, a common conifer of sandy coastal regions in the East (see **#9**). It is often associated with fire-subclimax forests because of its ability to sprout from stumps after fires. Within this forest is the largest of several small stands of naturally occurring pitch pine; other stands were introduced. Historical research has revealed that Plum Island was naturally forested with pitch pine in colonial times. But by the end of the eighteenth century, the forests had vanished, whether destroyed by a violent storm or cut down by inhabitants remains unknown.

Also worth noticing at spots along the trail are the effects of salt spray on redcedar. Branches on the windward side of the cedars are either dead or misshapen as a result of extreme chloride concentrations from the salty ocean winds; the leeward branches have survived because of less exposure to the prevailing sea breezes. Access is from parking lot 5.

Kettle Hole Trail circles a low depression behind High Sandy, one of the higher ridges in the backdune region of the refuge. This basin is not a kettle hole in the geological sense, meaning that it was formed by glacial ice during the Ice Age (see **#99**); rather, it is a low point situated in a curve of the backdune ridge. The wind has scooped sand from this area to build up the crest of the ridge, a process called *deflation*. Often these depressions are called blowouts.

This more hospitable environment is the site of the oldest and largest forests on Plum Island. Because of the protection from salt spray and sand afforded the forest by the height of the dune, some trees as high as 50 feet have managed to survive the rigors of the coastal environment. An oak 10 inches in diameter, at breast height, was 45 years old at the time of this writing, an 8-inch black cherry 36 years old. Access is from parking lot 3.

Remarks: *Hellcat Swamp Trail (2 miles): takes 1½ hours for a casual walk over easy terrain. The trail is easy both to follow and to walk, since planks have been laid for the entire length over marshes and sand dunes. An interpretative trail guide available at the refuge headquarters is keyed to numbered trail markers, which are easily overlooked and must be carefully watched for. A second observation tower at the southern end of Plum Island has ocean and mainland views, as well as glacial drumlin formations: Bar Head, Grape Island, Cross Farm Hill, and Stage Island. Access from parking lot 7. These points, as well as beaches and other areas of interest, can be located on a map of Plum Island available at the refuge headquarters, which is located on the northern end of the island outside the refuge. Also available is information on wildlife, including a list of over 270 bird species observed at the refuge. Surf-fishing is a popular recreational activity at Plum Island, with striped bass a favorite catch of sportsmen. Swimming beaches are open to the public within Plum Island State Reservation, which is located at the island's southern tip and owned by the Massachusetts Division of Forest and Parks. Public camping areas are few in this densely populated north shore region of Massachusetts. Salisbury Beach State Reservation is located just north of Plum Island, on Route 1A, with 150 campsites open all year. For information contact Salisbury Beach State Reservation, Salisbury, Mass. 01950; (617) 462-4481.*

71.

Hampton Harbor
Marsh

Directions: **Hampton, Hampton Falls, and Seabrook, N.H. From Portsmouth take Route 1A south about 15 miles, crossing the Hampton Harbor Bridge. The parking area for**

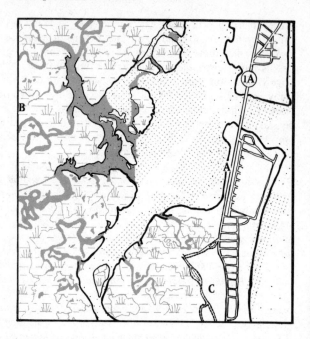

access to the beach and mudflats is on the west side of 1A, 0.3 mile south of the bridge and just north of the Hampton Police Department.

Ownership: **Numerous public and private owners, including the New Hampshire Division of Parks and Recreation and the Audubon Society of New Hampshire.**

A few miles north of Plum Island, just across the New Hampshire border from Massachusetts, is the largest salt-marsh complex in New England. The Hampton Harbor marsh area comprises over 8,000 acres of mudflats, salt marsh, and sandbars, which draw large populations of shorebirds, particularly between July and September. The marshland is highly accessible, for although much of it is privately owned, it is surrounded by highways (Routes 1, 1A, and 101A) offering numerous vantage points for viewing birds at fairly close range. Driving around the marsh also gives you a feel for the enormous size of this wetland and for the influence it has on the three communities in which it is situated.

The best time and place to begin a bird-watching trip is at low tide on the mudflats of Hampton Harbor Inlet (**A**). Here you can walk out to the shoreline of the Blackwater River and see birds in the marsh on the opposite shore or feeding on the flats in the shallow water and tide pools. A pair of binoculars or a viewing scope is highly recommended. Clam diggers are common along the mudflats, for the nutrient-rich waters of the estuary make these the finest clam beds in New Hampshire.

Moving over the flats, you can't help but notice the striking contrast between the natural beauty of the blue water and green marsh grass and the stark and imposing presence of the Seabrook nuclear power plant, still under construction, on the west side of the marsh (**B**). Since the mid-1960s, environmentalists have opposed the plant, for it is not yet known what its effects on the sensitive marshland will be. There are many opposing theories about how the intake and expulsion of water for cooling will influence the estuary. A change in the water temperature in the harbor could affect the breeding grounds of fish, such as flounder, and of mollusks, such as clams and mussels. The plants and small organisms of the estuary could also be affected by a change in the water level or temperature. Any such change would most certainly also affect the bird population, which relies on these other life forms for sustenance.

Along the flats, it is common to see clusters of black-bellied plovers, semipalmated plovers, and whimbrels, a type of curlew distinguished by its long, downward-curved bill. These birds feed on small aquatic insects and sometimes on the mussels that grow in clumps on the mud. Both mussels and clams are popular with the herring gulls and great black-backed gulls that are constantly overhead, screeching loudly across the harbor. In 1983, a black skimmer, a rarity this far north, was seen feeding on the opposite shoreline. More commonly found to the south, the skimmer has gradually expanded its range northward in search of new feeding and nesting areas. This sleek and agile bird has a unique way of feeding. It flies swiftly over the water with the lower half of its scissorslike bill skimming the surface in order to catch fish.

Also on the opposite shore, in front of the power plant, is Hunts Island, the only place in New Hampshire where remains of the great auk have been found. This penguinlike, flightless bird was once abundant along the New England coastline. Beginning with the European settlement of North America, it was heavily hunted for food, feathers, and fish bait. Humans also collected the birds' eggs to eat. The great auk populations diminished rapidly, its disappearance accurately described as senseless slaughter. By 1840 this unusual and beautiful bird was extinct.

Many other sea and shore birds that are seen here on the mudflats were once needlessly hunted for sport, feathers, and bait. Market hunting of such birds as the yellowlegs and dowitchers, which scamper along the shoreline here, gave rise to the Audubon movement and led to the passage of a national bird protection act in the early part of the twentieth century. Had it not been for these two developments, it is quite probable that many more species of shorebirds would be extinct today.

As you walk northward along the tide line, there is a sandbar visible in the harbor inlet that is often heavily populated by cormorants and common terns. These small, black-capped birds nest in the higher elevations of sandy areas and were once common on the sandspit near the harbor bridge. However, human disturbance of their habitat drove them away and decreased their numbers. Efforts along the New England coast to provide secure nesting sites for terns have met with success, and their numbers are increasing.

Also seen on the flats are sanderlings, ruddy turnstones, least sandpipers, knots, and white-rumped sandpipers. Most of these shorebirds begin to migrate south in early September when the food supply dwindles and the weather turns colder, the adults leaving first and the young birds following in a week or so. Somehow, the young birds always manage to make the journey without adult direction and to be reunited with their own flock in their winter habitats. If you are watching birds here, be aware of the incoming tide, which can leave you stranded.

In addition to the excellent birding on the flats, there are three other areas of interest close by. South on Route 1A about 0.7 mile from the parking area are the Seabrook Dunes (**C**). This approximately 50-acre area is the only dune complex in New Hampshire, for as we go north from here the coastline changes rapidly from sandy to rocky (see **Portland North**). These dunes have been severely damaged by dune buggies and foot traffic, but they still manage to support small colonies of dune vegetation. Two clumps of woods, primarily black cherry, shadbush, and maple, provide an oasis for small migratory landbirds such as swallows and wood warblers. Green herons have also been known to nest in these trees. The area is thick with poison ivy, beach pea, and bayberry, all of which provide food for the migrating birds. On the southern end of the dune complex is an unusual pitch pine that is an excellent example of layering—the process by which a tree grows horizontally rather than vertically in order to gain moisture from the arid ground. In order to explore the dunes and not add to the damage, stay on the trails and roadways that circle through them.

You may explore the marsh itself either from vantage points along the highways or by canoe or boat. A good spot for putting in is the sandspit near the bridge at the harbor inlet. On the marsh, in among the brackish water and tide pools, you are likely to see snowy egrets, great blue herons, blue- and green-winged teal, glossy ibis, and black ducks. Marsh hawks and rough-legged hawks commonly hunt over the grasses.

A short distance up Route 1A, 1.7 miles north of the bridge is Great Boar's Head. This rocky promontory jutting out into the sea is an excellent place for watching loons and grebes fly over the surf and dive steeply into the ocean to catch fish in their long bills.

Remarks: *Exploring the large marsh area, Seabrook Dunes, and Great Boar's Head can easily take the better part of a day, although a productive visit to the mudflats may only take an hour or two. Ocean swimming is available at Hampton Beach State Park on Route 1A, and at numerous other public beaches along the coast. For birding, an identification book and binoculars or a scope are useful. This is also a good area for bird photography. Camping is available a few miles south of here at Salisbury Beach State Reservation in Massachusetts. See #70 for more information.*

72.

Great Bay
Estuary

Directions: **Durham, N.H. From Portsmouth, take U.S. 4 northwest about 9 miles to Durham. Turn south (left) onto Route 108. After 2 miles, turn left onto Durham Point Rd. Proceed about 5 miles to the entrance gate to the Jackson Estuarine Laboratory and Adams Point, on the left.**

Ownership: **New Hampshire Fish and Game Department; University of New Hampshire; numerous private owners.**

Although the New Hampshire coast is only 20 miles long, the Great Bay Estuary is one of the largest in New England, covering an area of some 11,000 acres to the west of Portsmouth in the basins of the Piscataqua, Exeter, and Bellamy rivers. An estuary is an embayment where salt water meets fresh water that is flowing to the sea. This confluence creates wide and frequent variations in both salinity and water temperature, which place great stresses on plant and marine organisms. Nevertheless estuaries play a significant role in the complex web of marinelife, providing rich nutrients and breeding grounds for a wide variety of marine species. It is estimated that 70 percent of the commercial fish species in New England either inhabit or derive indirect nutrients from estuaries. Fish and small marine life that originate in the estuary are also an important food source for fish that do not originate here, such as the bluefish, and for marine mammals such as harbor seals and whales.

Adams Point in Durham offers an opportunity to walk along the shore of the estuary in one of the few places that is accessible to the public. You can also drive around the region on Routes 4, 108, and 101. This will give you a clear sense of the great size of the Great Bay area and of its influence on both natural and human conditions.

Estuaries in New England are all relatively young, having formed after the disappearance of glacial ice 10,000 to 12,000 years ago. The rising seas from the melting ice flooded valleys created by the glacier, and rivers began flowing through these valleys from the uplands to the sea. Rivers carry with them sediments that settle on the bottom as the speed of the river's flow decreases near the ocean. These sediment deposits build up, creating baymouth bars that may enclose the mouth of the river, which in turn causes the area behind the bar to become shallow as deposits accumulate there. Mudflats then develop, followed by salt marshes. The life cycles of both these habitats are heavily influenced by the tides, which extend up the mouth of the river and into the estuary impoundment. At Great Bay, tidal influences occur as far inland on the Exeter River as the town of Exeter, some 4 miles inland from the open water of the estuary.

Here at Great Bay off Adams Point, the salinity of the water can fluctuate at different times of the day from under 0.5 percent to about 20 percent, and fluctuations are relatively constant. The further upriver you go from the estuary, the more the salinity decreases. At the point the water temperature fluctuates as well, with cold ocean waters during the summer months meeting the warmer waters flowing from the interior. In winter, the situation is often reversed, as the ocean waters are sometimes the warmer of the two. In Great Bay, which is a fairly deep estuary, the bottom remains colder than the surface throughout the summer. This difference decreases in the fall as the surface temperature drops and the waters from different levels mix.

Despite these harsh fluctuations in salt and temperature conditions, many organisms thrive in Great Bay because of the high levels of nutrients, some of which are carried downstream by the rivers. Others are created from detritus, or decayed plants, such as seaweeds and salt-marsh grass. The nutrients in the deeper waters of the bay are also continually rising to the surface as the bay, which is filling in with sediments, becomes shallower. All of these factors combine to allow phytoplankton populations to remain very large and strong throughout the spring and summer seasons when young fish are hatching out and growing. The bay thus harbors an extremely important source of food for young and adult fish, and since different fish species spawn at different times, there is little competition for this food. Some of the nutrients are carried out to sea by the tides, where they support other populations of fish.

Some fish always remain in the estuary, while others enter and leave at different stages of their life cycles. White perch, tomcod, and smooth flounder are all fish that prefer to live in the brackish water within the estuary. More familiar to ocean fishermen are the migrant fish that leave the estuary for the open seas. These include Atlantic shad, Atlantic salmon, alewife, and striped bass. The striped bass matures in the ocean, where it survives on a diet of fish, crabs, worms, and clams. It reaches sexual maturity at about 4 years old, and then leaves the open ocean to enter the estuary to spawn. Striped bass lay their eggs in brackish water at the head of the estuary in the summer. The eggs are then carried down the estuary by the tides, and hatch in the tidewater, where the young grow and then enter the sea. Mature striped bass commonly range in size from 3 to 40 pounds, and average between 2 and 3 feet long. In the early days of colonization, striped bass of up to 125 pounds were caught off the New England coast.

Great Bay is a good area for viewing migrating birds during the spring and fall. Several hundred black ducks, scaup ducks, and upwards of 2,000 Canada geese fly over Adams Point during migration. For them Great Bay is a sheltered and protected stopover that provides rich feeding grounds, as it does for millions of marine creatures beneath the water's surface.

Remarks: *Boating is permitted in the entire estuary area, and small boats may put in along the entrance road to the point. There are no boat rentals here. The walk around Adams Point is very easy, and takes about 30 minutes. Fishing is permitted, with a license. At Adams Point is the Jackson Estuarine Laboratory operated by the University of New Hampshire. This marine research facility is studying the complexities of estuary life, and offers tours of the lab and slide shows if arrangements are made in advance. Contact the Marine Extension and Public Education Office, NEC Building, University of New Hampshire, Durham, N.H. 03824; (603) 862-1255.*

73.

Vaughan Woods
Memorial

Directions: **South Berwick, Maine. From Portsmouth, N.H., take U.S. 1 north 3 miles to Kittery, Maine, then take Route 236 northwest (left) about 9.5 miles toward South Berwick. At the junction with Route 91 (on the right), turn left onto Old South Rd. At the next intersection, turn left and go 0.3 mile to the park entrance (on the right). Park in the lot or, off season, beside the road.**

Ownership: **Maine Bureau of Parks and Recreation.**

Bordering the east bank of the Salmon Falls River, Vaughan Woods is a small woodland park where a number of trees grow at the northern edge of their species' range. A system of interlocking trails allows numerous choices for walking routes, one of which is described below.

The trailhead is at the edge of the picnic area, at the far end of the parking lot. Almost immediately, you encounter a tree species that does not grow much further north than here. The shagbark hickory (**A**) can be identified by the long, vertical strips of bark that peel away from the trunk at both ends. In the South this species tends to grow in deep, moist soils, whereas in the North it is found mainly on upland slopes and well-drained sites. Researchers have noted that the climate of Maine does not seem to favor sexual reproduction in shagbarks. They suspect that these individuals spread primarily through their prolific root-sprouting capabilities.

Follow the path down toward the river. Cross the wooden bridge over the brook, following the River Run sign. At the junction with the Porcupine Path, there is a large black, or sweet, birch on the right (**B**). Like shagbark, black birch is here at the limit of its range. The wintergreen taste of fresh black-birch twigs was popular among Indians and pioneers, who chewed them as a way of refreshing their mouths. The flavor is imparted by an oil that is identical in chemical composition to that produced by the wintergreen (a small ground-cover plant common in the New England woods.) This oil of wintergreen has been used as a flavoring agent and as an ingredient in liniments. When it was discovered that black birches could yield far

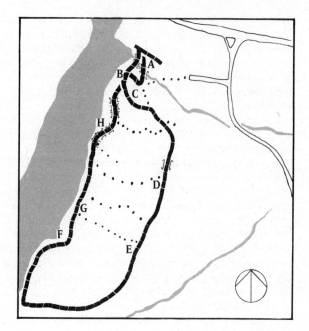

more of the oil than harvests of wintergreen could provide, large stands of the trees rapidly disappeared—it takes a hundred or more young black birches to produce 1 quart of wintergreen oil! Today the oil is produced synthetically. While black birches now live relatively free of oil hunters, they remain popular among some for their sap, which can be fermented and used to make birch beer, or boiled down to make syrup and candy.

Turn left and head up the Porcupine Path. Partridgeberry grows very densely on the floor of these moist woods (**C**). In the spring, you may see paired, four-petaled flowers at the ends of the creeping stems. The ovaries of these flowers are joined, and as they mature, each set forms a red, two-lobed berry. Although quite dry, seedy, and tasteless, these berries are listed in some guides as edible.

At the upper end of the Porcupine Path, turn right on the Bridle Path. Stay right at the Bridle Path Loop junction. At **D** there is a large white pine that splits into three trunks about 10 feet above the ground. This type of branching indicates that the major shoot, the trunk, was damaged, releasing the side branches to grow upward.

Continue along the Bridle Path. Beyond the head of the Old Gate

Trail, two gorgeous, big red-oak trunks stand joined at their bases like Siamese twins (**E**). In such a case, it is difficult to know the exact origin of the phenomenon. This might be a single oak that was damaged very early in its life and developed two major branches, which now grow like trunks, or it might be two oaks that germinated close to each other and bumped and joined as their girths expanded.

You may discover gray squirrels here, for acorns are among their favored foods. When the colonists arrived in this country, gray squirrels were abundant and provided a good food source for the pioneers that pushed westward. But the squirrels proved an annoyance to the settlers because they devoured corn crops as readily as they consumed acorns and beechnuts. In 1749, a bounty of three pence per head led to destruction of 640,000 Pennsylvania squirrels in one year. Continued hunting and clearing of forests took its toll. Decline in the gray-squirrel population was noted around the time of the Civil War, and by 1900, it was so low that conservationists were concerned that the species might become extinct. Forest and wildlife protection of the past century has allowed the gray squirrel to become reestablished in moderate numbers.

Although gray squirrels stay close to home, they are noted for periodic but unpredictable mass migrations. Not even rivers, lakes, or mountains stop them on these treks. Today the masses include only hundreds of animals, but in the past, the numbers were truly spectacular. In 1843, Ernest Thompson Seton, naturalist and writer, witnessed a 4-week-long migration in which he estimated close to a half-billion gray squirrels were involved. Biologists speculate that failure of nut crops or high population densities may give rise to these migrations (see also **#83**).

Continue to Trail's End, passing the old Warren homestead site, where a crumbling cellar hole and a number of worn stone grave markers remain as reminders of a time when these woods were cleared land. Go right, along the river. Cow Cove (**F**) was the landing site of the first cows and the first sawmill brought to this part of Maine in 1634.

Beyond the bottom of the Old Gate Trail, about 30 feet before the bridge, there is a bee tree, a large, living white pine on the right side of the trail (**G**). The hive entrance is a 6-inch oblong hole about 15 feet up the trunk. A bee returning to the hive can tell other workers where to find a good nectar source that it has discovered. It communicates the direction and distance to the source by a waggling dance it performs on the comb inside the hive. Direction is given in relationship to the polarization of light, which bees—unlike humans—can detect. By the odors on its body or in its honey, the bee can communicate the type of flower it has just visited.

Entomologists have discovered other ways in which bees see differently than humans. Bees' eyes are sensitive to the short wavelengths of ultraviolet light, but do not detect the long waves of red light; thus, a wood-sorrel flower, which to a human looks white and pink, appears ultraviolet and vividly veined to a bee. While bees seem to distinguish readily between minor differences in radially symmetrical patterns, they do not seem able to differentiate between a straight line and a wavy line. Thus, although you and the bees of this Vaughan Woods hive share the same physical world near the bank of the Salmon Falls River, you and the bees visually perceive two quite different environments. This difference is amplified when the picture pieces received through your and the bees' other senses are included. The world as an organism perceives it is called its *Umwelt*. Trying to understand an organism's *Umwelt* is an integral part of the search to understand the behavior of other organisms. The discovery that detection of polarization of light is part of a bee's *Umwelt* allows us a better understanding of how a bee can give directions to another bee without the use of words or a compass (see also **#100**).

As you follow the river path further upstream, you will pass the lower ends of the trails you intersected on the Bridle Path. Just beyond the bottom of the unmarked trail after the Nubble Knoll Trail junction, you come to Oak Point (**H**). There are numerous white oaks in the area. Look for the rounded lobes of their leaves, which readily distinguish them from Maine's more common red oak. The range of the white oak extends northward just into southern Maine. Populations growing at their range limits, often in pockets isolated from the main population, are of special interest to botanists studying genetics, adaptation, and evolution. These populations are living under conditions somewhat different from those experienced by the main body of the population, and therefore, sexual recombinations of genes and genetic mutations that might not survive elsewhere may survive here. The addition of these new combinations to the gene pool can give a species greater potential to survive environmental change. Alternately, if the fringe population is reproductively isolated for long enough, new combinations of genes *may* change future generations so much that they become classed as a new species.

Continue along the river, past the bottom of the Porcupine Path. Go right up the Shady Hill Trail, left on the Bridle Path, and then right back up to the picnic area and your car.

Remarks: *This is a 2-mile walk over basically level terrain. With some maneuvering by an attendant, the Bridle Path is accessible to those in wheelchairs. Day use only. Picnic tables present. The gate at the entrance is open from May 30 to Labor Day. During the off-season, the trails are still accessible with only a short extra walk. The Bureau of Parks and Recreation is working on a trail map of Vaughan Woods, which should be available in the near future. The area is a good one for watching migrating warblers and other songbirds. There is camping at Beaver Dam Campground, Berwick (May 15 to September 15). For other interesting areas nearby, see #74, Remarks.*

74.

East Point Sanctuary

Directions: **Biddeford Pool, Maine. From Portland, take U.S. 1 south about 17 miles to Biddeford. Go southeast on Route 208 and 9 toward Biddeford Pool; where Route 9 splits off going south, stay left on Route 208. In another 1.6 miles (0.1 mile beyond an A-frame building on the left), turn left again. In about 0.8 mile, swing right onto Ocean Ave., where limited roadside parking is available. The trailhead is some 30 yards back up Route 208, where a chain-link gate fronts an old dirt road.**

Ownership: **Maine Audubon Society.**

East Point Sanctuary is a 30-acre plot on the top of the Biddeford Pool peninsula. It was donated to the Maine Audubon Society in 1976 by a number of Biddeford Pool landowners. The sanctuary's field, thickets, and shoreline are alive with birds during spring and fall migrations. The point is also a good place for watching flocks of wintering ducks. Wood Island, to the north of the point, supports a nesting colony of herons and egrets, whose comings and goings are often visible from East Point. The rock features of the sanctuary, including several shingle beaches, are intriguing at any season.

From the chain-link gate, follow the dirt track as it curves around behind some houses, passing between them and the golf course on its way into the sanctuary. Just beyond the Audubon welcome sign, a side trail on the right leads down to the shore (**A**), where beautifully banded bedrock is exposed. The layers were originally laid down horizontally on a sea floor some 400 million years ago. Eons

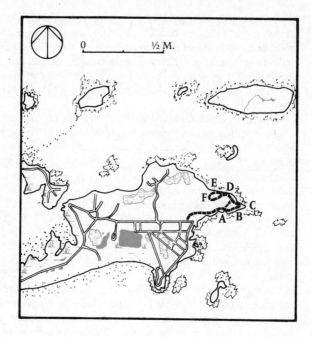

before that, numerous other processes were at work creating the raw materials—sandy and silty sediments—that formed the layers. As rocks of any sort are exposed at the surface, sun, rain, frost, and the air itself begin breaking them down again. This is called *weathering;* both chemical and mechanical (physical) processes are involved. Chemical weathering includes all breakdown from mineral reactions with oxygen, water, and soil acids. Physical weathering occurs when rocks are abraded by fragments carried by wind or water, when rocks are broken by the action of water as it freezes and expands in a crack (frost wedging), when a root in a crack grows enough to force the crack to widen (root wedging), or when inner earth tensions are released in an earthquake.

Once the rocks begin to disintegrate, running water, wind, and ice transport the particles to lower levels. This is called *erosion.* Streams and winds carry their loads until their velocity drops below a critical speed and the particles begin to settle, the larger ones dropping out first, the smaller ones carried great distances by almost imperceptible currents. These sediments build up in layers in valley canyons, on lakebeds, and on sea floors. As the accumulations become thicker and thicker, the loose grains are welded together by the pressure of the layers above them and by the deposition of cementing substances between the particles; finally, the loose grains form sedimentary rock. Some deposits of these rocks are thousands of feet thick. The sedimentary beds of sandstone, siltstone, and graywacke (formed from coarse, gray particles) at East Point have been metamorphosed and tilted on edge by tectonic movements (see **#83**) associated with mountain building.

Continue eastward along the shore rocks or on the grassy road above. The beach at **B**, formed mainly of flat-sided stones, is called a *shingle beach*. Such beaches form in areas where the fragments available for building the beach are derived from layered rock. When the pieces break from the bedrock, they generally have flattened faces, and as they are washed back and forth on the shore, they slide more than they tumble, emphasizing their flattened shape. There are also some round stones on the beach, formed primarily from granitic bedrock, which fractures into blocky fragments. These pieces roll and tumble as the waves wash about them, wearing down the corners and surfaces fairly equally and sometimes forming quite spherical stones.

During spring and fall, a flock of sparrowlike birds wandering in the short grass may explode in a white flurry of wings, veering and wheeling with precision as the birds move away and then settle on the ground again, at a safe distance. These are snow buntings. No other songbird has so much white in its plumage. Just as the snows begin to melt and patches of bare ground are exposed, snow buntings begin their journey to the Arctic, where they nest on the tundra. Although their wintering range reportedly includes the coast of Maine, we see them primarily as migrating flocks and individuals stopping to feed on seeds and insects (see **#96** for more on migration).

From the end of the point (**C**), you can see north to a string of islands. Wood Island, marked by the lighthouse on its eastern end, is also owned by Maine Audubon and is the site of an active heronry (a nesting colony). This is one of only a few Maine heronries that is occupied by a mix of species. At last census, snowy egrets, glossy ibises, and black-crowned night herons were the most common nesters. Many of them build their nests in the thick poison-ivy vines that clog much of the island and help protect the birds from human disturbance. Maine Audubon discourages visitation of the island during spring and summer, when the birds are breeding and rearing their young.

Although they may seem quite common now, snowy egrets were near the brink of extinction earlier this century because the long breeding plumes of herons were so popular in the millinery trade of the mid-1800s to early 1900s. All herons were persecuted, but the snowy egret may have suffered more than the rest because of the flexibility and delicacy of its plumes. Fortunately, individuals and organizations, such as the National Association of Audubon Societies, mounted educational and legislative campaigns that have led to protection of these birds while their populations were still large enough to recover.

It is when the young begin to wander from their nests on Wood Island that you will be most likely to see these graceful birds at East Point. In this period after breeding and before fall migration southward, egrets, mainly the young ones, disperse from the nesting site in all directions of the compass. Ornithologists suspect that this may be a way in which new territory is scouted and/or a way in which population pressures are relieved. An egret will hunt in either fresh or salt water, usually standing quite motionless in the shallows, waiting for its prey to come within striking distance of its long neck and bill. Small fish, snails, frogs, snakes, turtles, crustaceans, and insects are common fare.

Because East Point projects out into the Gulf of Maine, it is one of the places on the mainland where you may see pelagic (sea-dwelling) birds that have been blown landward by storms. Dovekie and common and thick-billed murres have been sighted here.

From the point, continue along the old dirt road, which soon turns into a trail. Stay right (there are a number of side trails leaving left), paralleling the shore (**D**). There are a number of domesticated fruit tree species growing in the thickets west of the field, a common sight in areas that have been used for or are near human dwellings. Among these species is the apple (**E**). There are about two dozen species of apple in the northern temperate regions of North America and Eurasia, some of them prized for their fruits, others sought as ornamentals, with their showy flowers in spring and attractive fruits in the fall. Cultivated since ancient times, the common apple is the parent of most of our domesticated apples. Its exact origin is unknown, but etymological tracing of the name suggests that it may have developed in western Himalayan vegetation and then have been carried westward via northern Persia, Asia Minor, the Caucasus, and the Mediterranean lands. Introduced to the United States from overseas, the apple has now spread from our cultivated orchards to roadsides, clearings, thickets, and borders of woods, where the fruits are eaten by numerous wild animals, including deer, bears, foxes, mourning doves and other birds.

The main trail swings inland at **F**, winding through more pitch pines, maples, quaking aspens, and cherries, until it completes a full loop, rejoining itself near the shore. Go right at the junction and then right again where the trail becomes an open grassy road. Cross the field and head right, toward the welcome sign and your car.

Remarks: *This is a ½-mile walk over primarily level terrain. The shore is rocky. Poison ivy is present but easy to avoid. The trail around the major area of the point is an old road accessible by wheelchair, although you will have to fold the chair to get it around the chain-link gate. Day use only. No picnicking. There are numerous beaches open to the public, from the Scarborough area south to Kittery. Camping is available at Sea-Vu Campground, Wells (May 15 to October 1); Ten Acres Campground, Kennebunkport (Memorial Day to October 15); Willey's Hideaway, Saco (May 20 to October 1); Stadig Mobile Park, Wells (Memorial Day to October 1). At low tide, the mudflats surrounding the Biddeford Pool are an excellent place to watch migrating shorebirds. The Maine Audubon Society owns an 8-acre piece of the shore of the pool, just southwest of the A-frame building mentioned in the directions for East Point (#74). Other places worth visiting are Vaughn's Island Preserve, on the coast east of Kennebunkport; Blowing Cave, a popular roadside stop on the southeast edge of Kennebunkport; the Webhannet Marsh, just east of Wells; the Rachel Carson Wildlife Refuge, 1 mile northeast of Elms on Route 9; and Mount Agamenticus, west of Ogunquit, 1 mile north of the Mount Agamenticus Rd. Brief descriptions of many of these areas are included in Dorcas Miller's* The Maine Coast: A Nature Lover's Guide.

75.
Scarborough
Marsh

Directions: **Scarborough, Maine. From Portland, take Route 1 and 9 south about 8 miles to West Scarborough. Turn southeast (left) on Route 9 and drive 0.8 mile to the parking lot at the nature center, on the left.**

Ownership: **Maine Wildlife Management Area.**

All rivers run down to the sea, but some take their own sweet time about it, meandering in broad curves, doubling back and looping around as if they cannot decide whether to meet the salty waters or not. Such are the Dunstan and Nonesuch rivers, which join together to form the Scarborough River and then flow into Saco Bay. But Saco Bay waters also flow up the Scarborough River with each rising tide, so that the lower part of the river is an estuary (see **#59** and **#72**). Spreading over some 2,700 acres around this estuary and river system are the Scarborough marshlands, the upstream ones fresh and the estuarine ones salt. This entry is concerned with the salt marshes (see **#29**).

The best way to visit Scarborough Marsh is by canoe. From this perspective you can get a wonderful bird's-eye view of the marshlands. There is easy put-in access by the nature center (**A**). If you prefer to walk, a former roadbed (**B**) and an old railroad grade (**C**) provide solid pathways.

The relationship between people and the Scarborough marshlands has been long and varied. Indians trapped alewives and herring for use as food and fertilizer (see **#26**). They and the Europeans after them collected eggs of nesting waterfowl, gathered edible plants, and dug clams. Coastal fishermen of the 1600s salted and dried rich offshore catches of cod and haddock in fishing camps they established along the Scarborough River. They obtained the salt by evaporating seawater. Colonists grazed their cattle on the rich salt hay

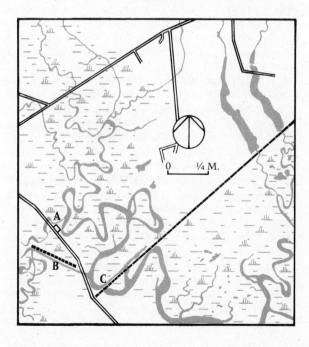

and then harvested the remainder to use for winter fodder. The old wooden posts standing in the marsh near the nature center are the remains of "staddles," post structures upon which the marsh hay was stacked until winter freezing allowed horse-and-wagon access onto the marshlands.

In the past several decades, there has been much pressure to drain and fill marshes with tilled fields, buildings, or sewage and wastes, or to dredge them to allow boat access from the sea. Some 60 percent of the wetlands in the eastern United States have met such a fate. Recently, though, biologists have begun to realize the important roles marshes play as wetlands. An estuarine marsh such as Scarborough is a nursery to the larval stages and young of hundreds of saltwater organisms, including about 70 percent of our commercially valuable fish and shellfish. The marsh also produces a tremendous amount of organic material, over three times as much per acre as a cultivated field of grain. Some of this feeds organisms in the marsh and some of it gets flushed out to sea by the river and the tides, providing significant nutrients to the organisms of coastal waters. In addition, the marsh is a catch basin for nutrients carried seaward by the river systems that feed it, the grasses and muck trapping some of the sediments and others settling out as the waters slow down in the winding marsh channels. Of the nutrients that get washed out to sea, some are used by the microorganisms in the upper layers of the water, and others drift to the sea floor, where they are buried away from the use of almost all living things for millennia. Marsh entrapment is one of the processes by which nutrients may be circulated longer in environments where they are available to life.

On top of all these roles, the Scarborough wetlands are a breeding ground and migratory resting-place for numerous species of waterfowl (see **#96** for more on migration). Some 15 years ago, sportsmen became concerned over the potential destruction of Scarborough Marsh as a habitat for waterfowl. Although food, water, cover, and living space would be available in a Scarborough housing complex or a field of cabbage, they certainly would not be of the proper sort for waterfowl. Each organism has its own specific habitat requirements, and if those critical conditions cease to exist in an area, individuals relying on them will either move to another suitable place, adapt to the new conditions if they are not too drastically different, or die. Recognizing that human uses of marshlands generally changed them beyond the short-term capabilities of waterfowl, sportsmen's groups began to urge the state to acquire and protect habitat for wildlife in the Scarborough Marsh. Today this area is managed by the Maine Department of Inland Fish and Wildlife. The Maine Audubon Society operates the nature center and offers walks, canoe trips, and marsh-ecology information in the summer (see Remarks).

If your excursion into the marsh is not at high tide, take a look at the muddy-bank cross-section. Exposed from top downward are living cordgrass, decomposing cordgrass and cordgrass roots (see **#77**), oozing muck (soggy, decomposing organic matter), and mud. After the glaciers scoured these shores and then scattered their loads of till (unsorted glacial debris), river and tidal sediments began to build up in areas where slowed currents dropped their loads. When these deposits reached a critical level below mean (average) high water, salt-marsh cordgrass was able to become established. As the grasses also began to trap sediments, the vegetated islands grew, until only shifting channels were left for the water. Each year, the stems and leaves of the cordgrass die, adding their decomposing mass to the sediment below and creating upward growth of the marsh as well as outward expansion. Some of the powerful odors of the marsh are related to this mass of decomposition. Methane gas is one of the products of anaerobic (without oxygen) decomposition, the common decomposing process in wet areas where water rather than air fills spaces in the mass of dead material.

You may also discover oily scums on the surface of the water, some from the natural processes of rotting plants and some from algae growing in the water. Bubble-gum-like pink scums are photosynthetic bacteria that use hydrogen sulfide and carbon dioxide, rather than water and carbon dioxide, when they photosynthesize. They operate in anaerobic environments, such as stagnant puddles. The orange color of scums is usually from the oxidation of iron. In the muck where oxygen is absent, iron particles remain black and add to the dark color of the mud.

Marshes can be thought of in terms of four broad habitat types: muddy bottom, open water, low marsh, and high marsh. The organisms that inhabit the bottom muds are often rounded or slender, shapes that allow them to move more readily through their dense environment. Worms and clams are common. Perhaps most intriguing are horseshoe crabs. Ancient relatives of spiders, they have been prowling earth muds for some 200 million years. Although they occasionally swim—rather awkwardly—they usually plow through the mud preying on worms and clams. Some shellfish operators claim that the horeshoe crab is a universal threat to clam populations, but since few quantitative feeding data for this species exist, these claims remain neither substantiated nor disproved. In either case, humans are still the major predator on adult horseshoe crabs, using them as fertilizer, as supplemental stock feed, for educational and research specimens, and as a source of blood cells for testing for the presence of toxins in blood and other fluids administered to hospital patients. The crabs are particularly vulnerable when they mass on beaches in late spring to breed. They are not known to breed in the Scarborough marshes, but their molted exoskeletons, or shells, are sometimes found along the shores (see **#7**).

In the open water of the marsh, many animals are adapted for diving and for swimming on or beneath the surface. They generally have webbed feet or other flattened appendages that aid them in moving through the water. Canada geese, teal and other ducks, muskrats, and fish are common examples. Other open-water species have long legs and long toes for wading and long slender bills for capturing fish, crabs, and mollusks. The white plumage of snowy egrets makes them conspicuous even from a distance (see **#74**). Herons and yellowlegs are also common. The glossy ibis is a special attraction. This darkly iridescent bird is primarily a Eurasian species, but in the fall, during its postbreeding dispersal, it is an inveterate wanderer. The individuals that travel as far as Scarborough are few but regular. You may see them probing the mud with their large, downward-curved bills, seeking crustaceans, mollusks, and worms.

A little higher than the open water is the low marsh, which includes mudflats and areas covered with salt-marsh cordgrass. Periwinkle snails prowl here, each on its broad, flexible foot (see **#101**). The birds that frequent the low marsh have webbed feet or long toes that facilitate walking on soft substrate. Many have sensitive beaks that allow them to locate prey in the mud, while the sharp eyesight of others helps them to catch insects and crustaceans on the surface. Sandpipers, often called "peeps," scurry along the water's edge, picking small organisms from the surface or probing shallowly into the mud like little sewing machines. Whimbrels and occasional godwits, with long, slender bills, probe more deeply. If you look carefully in the cordgrass, you may discover an American bittern which, having seen you first, is standing erect with its beak pointing skyward, its body camouflaged by its vertically streaked brown feathers. Its eyes are located so low on its face that even in its alarm posture it can watch the movements of intruders.

A bit further removed from the water is the high marsh, flooded only by the highest tides. It is characterized by fine salt-meadow cordgrass, or marsh hay, which often is bent over, forming dense mats beneath which numerous small organisms hide. If you part the grasses, you may find them interlaced with 1½-inch-diameter runways cut by meadow voles, mouselike creatures with short hairy tails. Living in grass- or grain-covered habitat in both wet and dry areas, the meadow vole is one of the most abundant mammals in New England. It is active year-round, feeding mainly on seeds, stems, roots, and tubers, and occasionally on meat when it is available. Females are prolific, producing several litters annually. It has been noted that under optimum food and cover conditions, meadow-vole populations increase to a maximum in about 4 years and then die off to low levels within a few months. The reasons for such dramatic die-offs are not known, but biologists suspect that food shortages, epidemic diseases, and behavioral and physiological changes due to crowding may be involved.

Birds that use the high marsh often have feet adapted for grasping blades of grass and beaks adapted for eating seeds and insects. Sharp-tailed sparrows and red-winged blackbirds nest here.

In both the low and the high marsh, pools and shallow salt pans form in depressions. Mummichogs and sticklebacks are small fish that often get trapped in the pools. During colonial times, grazing cattle periodically sank in them as well, making marshlands without such pools much in demand. The salt pans are shallow enough that rainwater and evaporation create wide variations in salinity (see **#14**). Glasswort (*Salicornia*) is one of the plants that can tolerate these conditions. Its fleshy, jointed stems are about the tastiest treats the marsh has to offer. Geese seem to agree on this point. In the fall, when glasswort reaches maturity, its seed-containing tips turn a lovely purple-red. Although it is the seeds that attract the attention of hungry ducks, it is the color that draws human eyes.

Remarks: *This trip can be either a walk or a canoe excursion, of whatever length you choose. The Maine Audubon Society operates the nature center on Route 9. Offerings include walks, canoe trips, a slide show, and exhibits. Canoes are available for rent. The season is mid-June through August (closed Mondays). Call (207) 781-2230 for information. Prout's Neck Bird Sanctuary and Scarborough Beach State Park (fee) are on the southern end of Route 207, on the far side of the mouth of the Scarborough River. Higgin's Beach, Two Lights State Park (fee), and Crescent Beach State Park (fee) are on Route 77, all within 20 miles of Scarborough Marsh.* The Maine Coast: A Nature Lover's Guide, *by Dorcas Miller, has brief descriptions of these areas. Camping is available at Bayley's Campground, West Scarborough (Memorial Day to Labor Day); Homestead Camp-ground, Biddeford (Memorial Day to September); Wassamiki Springs, Westbrook (May to October 15); Wild Acres, Old Orchard Beach (Memorial Day to mid-September).*

Portland North:
Rough and Rocky
Ramparts

If a new land were to rise rough and dripping from the sea, it would probably resemble the immense, rocky ramparts that gird the coast of northern Maine. Stark and bare, it is an ungentle coast of severe angularity, indented helter-skelter with inlets and bays that are often studded with stony islands. The estuaries of streams that issue from the rocks into the ocean are not lush and expansive but narrow and deep, as if hacked into the earth, rather like the fjords of Scandinavia.

The rawness of the coastline that begins north of Portland stems partly from the fact that the sea has not had time to smooth the hard rock of which it is built. The other reason is that after the melting of the last glacier the sea advanced much further inland in northern Maine than it did in southern New England, turning rugged interior highlands into the shoreline of today. The ice sheet that weighed down on the north country much more thickly than toward its margins in the south pressed upon the land until it warped and broke, sinking with a tilt toward the sea. The water moved up narrow river valleys, leaving only the tops of hills and mountains exposed, forming points and headlands like Penoquit and Pemaquid that today angle away from the shore, as well as islands such as Monhegan, which stand on what once was a coastal plain.

Geologists believe that much of Maine was depressed by the ice for several hundred feet, and more than 1,000 feet in some places. Even as the sea advanced, however, the land, free of ice, slowly rebounded. The sea edged back a bit, leaving behind deposits of marine clay now high and dry inland. Abandoned by the sea, rock surfaced that only a short while before (geologically speaking) had been submerged. At present, the level of the sea is far above what it was during the time of the glaciers, but below the peak of its advance after their weight was lifted from the land. Maine's craggy coast is the result.

Today the Maine coast still experiences a significant advance and decline of the sea, routinely, twice a day. More than any other part of the Atlantic seaboard of the United States, this coast experiences tidal extremes, with a gap of up to 20 feet or more between high and low water. The region between the extremes is the intertidal, or littoral, the interface of sea and land, a never-never realm, sometimes part of the ocean, sometimes shore, but neither for very long.

The organisms inhabiting the littoral must be highly adaptable, able to cope with continuous change as the tides ebb and flow. When submerged, they live under relatively stable conditions of temperature, moisture, and salinity. When the tide is out, they may bake under the sun or freeze in winter's chill. Fresh water in the form of rain or runoff may drench them, whereas at other times they may be subject to shriveling desiccation. Above all, in one way or

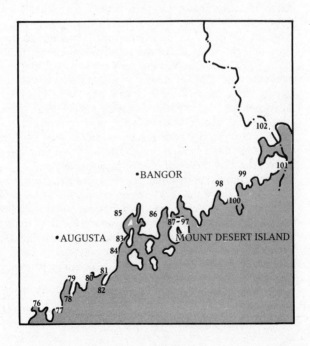

another, they must survive in both water and air, something few other plants and animals can manage. Some barnacles inhabit rocks so high in the littoral that they are washed by the waves only during the highest tides, several days apart. Rockweed must live lower in the littoral to survive because, although it can withstand moderate exposure to the air, it will eventually dry out and die if not covered by the sea.

This sort of situation has caused a zonation of life in the intertidal, seen best on rocky shores where life cannot disappear under sand or mud, and especially where—as on the Maine coast—the tidal range is great. Life zones of the intertidal can vary a bit from place to place, but generally the lowest on Maine's coast is known as the *kelp zone*, because of the seaweed that grows profusely there. Part of this zone is never totally above water, although its upper fringes are during the lowest tides. The upper margins of the kelp zone grade into one dominated by another alga, Irish moss, a reddish seaweed festooned with tufts. Blue mussels grow thickly amidst the plants, increasing in number with distance from the low-water mark.

Mussels continue to proliferate in the next zone, typified by lush growth of rockweeds. Above this belt is the zone most heavily colonized by barnacles, into which wander periwinkles from the zone above. The strip inhabited by periwinkles is covered only during the spring tides, which occur twice monthly, at new and full moon. When above water, the periwinkles retain moisture in their shell, which is sealed by a horny cover called an operculum.

The periwinkles also venture above their zone into the one that marks the upper reaches of the intertidal, the *black zone*—which gets its name from the slick carpet of dark blue-green algae that covers the rocks there. The colonies of algae are seldom under water except during storms. Their contact with the sea at other times is limited to splash and spray. Scientists speculate that the first living things to emerge from the ocean and colonize the land were blue-green algae, so the growth of these microscopic plants today may be a replay of one of the most important migrations in the history of earthly life.

Wheeling above the rocks, often perching on cliffs, and probing the waters of the Maine coast for fish are legions of seabirds—not just the terns and gulls commonly seen the length of the New England coast but those of colder, broader seas. In varying degrees of abundance and seasonality, the granite bulwarks of this coast play host to black guillemots, gannets, puffins, razorbills, parasitic jaegers, greater shearwaters, skuas, and dovekies.

Not far from where the seabirds fish live other birds, those of the spruce and balsam forests that grow to the inland margins of the rocks, even sometimes within yards of the sea and on many of the offshore islands. This is the world of great horned owls and gos-hawks, nuthatches and chickadees, pine siskins and evening gros-beaks.

Ranging right up to the sea, sometimes even prowling the beaches, are many of the mammals of the interior—porcupines, red foxes, coyotes, and white-tailed deer. The avian and mammalian fauna of the northern Maine coast is just a continuation of that inhabiting the north woods that stretch across inland Maine to Canada.

The white spruce and balsam among which the animals live are better able to grow cheek-by-jowl with the sea than many of the other trees—such as white pine, birch, and maple—that dominate the interior. Spruce in particular has roots so shallow they can grip tenaciously to rock even if it is covered with just a thin skin of soil.

Originally, the spruce and balsam of the coast grew with birch, beech, maple, and hemlock. Some of these trees still grow by the sea, but not in their previous abundance. Logging has cleared the forests of the coast several times since Europeans first settled there. Today, spruce and balsam are pioneering their way back to the northern shoreline so that again much of it is backed by cool, dark forests, mossy and damp. Maple and birch are returning to the southern shores of Maine, but they are still absent in numbers from the north.

While the rocky coast of Maine is linked geologically to southern New England shores, it also belongs in one sense to a different realm. The Maine coast is an outpost, a frontier of sorts. It is there, within the sound of seabird cries, that at its southernmost point the great northern wilderness meets the sea. On one side of the coast stretches a sea of water. On the other, in the still-numerous places where humans have not obliterated nature, is a sea of trees.

—Edward Ricciuti

76.

Wolf Neck
Woods

Directions: **Freeport, Maine. From Portland, take Route 1 north about 15 miles to Freeport. Opposite L.L. Bean, turn east (right) onto Bow St. Go 1.4 miles, bear right at the fork, and after another 0.9 mile, turn right onto Wolf Neck Rd. Go 2 miles to the park entrance on the left. In summer, park in the lot inside the state park; off season, park along the road *north* of the entrance (*not* in front of the gate).**

Ownership: **Maine Bureau of Parks and Recreation.**

Wolf Neck Woods, a small park on the southern coast of Maine, lies on a peninsula bounded on one side by the estuarine waters of the Harraseeket River and on the opposite side by the salt waters of Casco Bay. The network of trails here invites exploration of a variety of terrestrial and aquatic communities, each illustrative of the events that created it and continue to form it. Watch for ospreys circling overhead. Look for the creative effects of erosion and strong winds.

Begin at the western (right) trail entrance. Bear right twice in close succession onto the Harraseeket Trail. The woods in this first section (**A**) are composed of a variety of deciduous and coniferous trees, a common phenomenon in younger woods in areas of Maine where drainage is better and the soils are slightly deeper. Wintergreen, bunchberry, goldthread, club mosses, partridgeberry, pipsissewa, and bracken and wood ferns find niches on the forest floor. Some of the most luxuriant trailing arbutus to be seen in Maine grows in Wolf Neck Woods.

Pass the Hemlock Ridge Trail (left) and cross the Wolf Neck Rd. Feel the soft needles under your feet and look up at the almost-century-old pines towering overhead; these (**B**) are the largest in the park. Even from the ground, the long, stiff, and coarse needles of red pines are distinguishable from the shorter, soft, and fine foliage of white pines. Although the white pine tends to occupy cooler and moister sites than the red pine, here both are finding adequate conditions for growth.

At **C,** you are surrounded by a hemlock-dominated forest that a teacher's guide for the park labels "hemlock climax." This model of

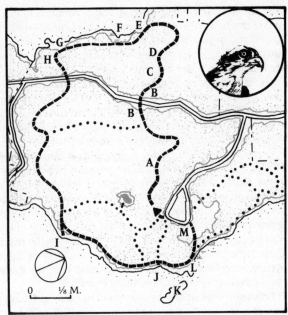

Inset: Osprey

succession, often termed *the deterministic theory* because it describes vegetation patterns in terms of predictable sequences, has been the most widely accepted one in the West over the past few decades. Like all models, it is based on numerous assumptions about how our earth systems function. Prominent among these are that a stable condition will be achieved in which certain predictable "climax" species will perpetuate themselves until disturbed by outside forces, and that fires, floods, and human interactions are imposed from outside the community.

Recent work by biologists suggests a new and equally valid model. It is often called *the probabilistic theory* because it explains succession as a matter of probabilities rather than foreseeable certainties. Two of the major bases in which this theory differs from the deterministic theory are in the following assumptions: (1) that conditions are always changing, even if the changes are so slow that we cannot see them from day to day; and (2) that fires, rainfall of all types (including floods), and human interactions are *parts of* a community. This model proposes that a forest is the expression of all the processes interacting at a site. According to this model, the forest here is one of many associations that will occur on this site; it is no more nor less "supposed to be here" than any other community that has lived or will live here. It is here in part because of eons of shifting climatic conditions, in part because of local soil characteristics, in part because of humans clearing the land, in part because of the kinds of seeds hemlocks, oaks, and pines produce.

As the trail dips and swings right around a coarse-granite boulder, look left for a very old yellow birch (**D**). Look to see whether the hole under its roots is being used by a small creature. Cobwebs and dead leaves in the entrance would suggest not. Fresh dirt, matted leaves, or bits of fur in the opening might signify yes.

Continue down to a granite overlook of the Harraseeket River (**E**). The estuary (see **#59** and **#72**) before you experiences a twice-daily influx of the tides. The nutrient-rich waters are able to support a large amount of life, yet all of it must be tolerant of both freshwater and saltwater conditions and thus also of frequent changes in the degree of salinity. At low tide, look for ducks feeding in the shallow water and gulls (see **#17** and **#77**) hunting on the exposed bars. These long, sinuous deposits of sediments, derived from erosion upriver, provide clues to current movements in the estuary, since bars accrete where water flow slows (see **#45**).

Sediments deposited at the mouth of the gully at **F** have provided substrate for a small pocket of salt marsh. The gully here and the ones further on, at **G,** are examples of erosional interaction where waterflow down a slope is greater than soil and vegetational capacities to absorb and percolate it.

On your right, at **H,** is an even-aged stand of soft-needled, young white pines that, even without the evidence of the stone wall you cross, suggests the former existence of a field here. White pines often get established on old fields in southern Maine: their seeds are heavy and work down well through grass mats to the soil below; the seeds have enough food stored in them to allow the seedlings to compete successfully with grasses; and the seedlings are resistant to the drought conditions imposed by competition with grass (see **#60**).

Recross the Wolf Neck Rd. and ramble through the woods to the shore, passing the Hemlock Ridge and Bog trails (left). A short spur-trail (right) at the Casco Bay Trail junction leads down to the water (**I**), where an old oak has fallen, its foothold undermined by the action of the sea. Footsteps have compacted the slope above, making it more susceptible to rainwater erosion. Both of these are natural processes, but in parks where we intend human influence to be minimal, we build trails and take various precautions in order to reduce erosion resulting from our presence there.

Follow the shoreline and then go right, down a flagstone path to the rocks (**J**). Low tide uncovers ridges of rock extending toward and into the water. These ridges are dikes of hard, granitic rock that were intruded into somewhat softer, more easily erodable metamorphic rocks during the Acadian Orogeny, a mountain-building period that occurred some 350 million years ago. Some sections of the contact zone are still intact.

Across from you, on Googins Island (**K**), the big broken pine near the shore has been the home of ospreys for many years. In 1982, strong, gusty winds broke the top off the dead snag, destroying the nest and killing the young. This is not an isolated incident: ospreys often build nests in tall trees near the shore, and these exposed trees sometimes do succumb to the power of coastal storms. It is a hazard ospreys face, just as people living on a floodplain risk the danger of flood to the house (see **#22, #50,** and **#99**).

In the woods at **L,** evidence of blowdowns still abounds. The thin soils here provide marginal foothold against the vigorous onslaught of storms. At the same time, what some might call an ugly mess of blowdowns creates new habitat spaces: openings for herbs and saplings, hiding places for small animals, food for decomposers and the animals that feed on them. The field and picnic area (**M**) you cross on your way back to the parking lot (next left) were established on the site of a concentrated blowdown.

Remarks: *The 2-mile walk is over level terrain, with some rocky and slippery footing. Day use only. The gate is open from May 30 to Labor Day. During off-season, access to trails from the main gate is a quarter of a mile. This is a popular park for school field trips. Contact the park manager in Freeport at (207) 865-4465. A teacher's guide and map are available.*

77.

Popham Marsh

Directions: **Popham Beach, Maine. From Portland, take I-95 and then U.S. 1 north and east about 34 miles to Bath. Turn south (right) onto Route 209. After about 7 miles, at the junction with Route 216, bear sharply left, staying on Route 209. Continue another 3 miles to a paved parking pulloff on the right, just past a wooden gate across a dirt**

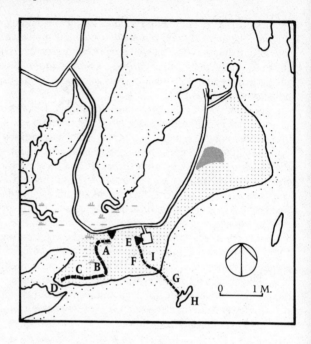

road on the right. The entrance to Popham Beach State Park is 0.3 mile ahead, also on the right.

Ownership: **Maine Bureau of Parks and Recreation.**

The Popham Marsh fringes the meanders of the Morse River estuary (see **#59** and **#72** for more on estuaries). The area is particularly interesting to botanists and geologists because the Morse River channel has significantly shifted course, and the end of the Popham sandspit (see **#45**) has visibly accreted *and* eroded in the past decades. This walk takes you across the busy backdunes, through the edge of the marsh, lush with a variety of salt-marsh grasses and wildflowers, and along the sandspit beach. Migrating shorebirds are common in the spring and fall (see **#96**).

The trail to the marsh begins at the wooden gate you passed 0.1 mile west of the parking space. Follow the wide, sandy track beyond the cable and into the dunes. Beware of the poison ivy that grows among the dune shrubs. The path swings around left, and the bushy vegetation of the backdunes gives way to beach grass on the hillock tops and salt-marsh species in the hollows in between (see **#79**).

The Popham Marsh is unusual in that it has a large, newly formed section that integrades with this dune field. The changes in vegetation from the tops of the hillocks down to the water channels reflect the gradation of environmental stresses. Salinity and flooding are among the major stresses affecting the terrestrial plants in the salt marsh. *Spartina*, a genus of grass with two species heavily represented in the salt marsh, illustrates a number of the kinds of adaptations that help plants tolerate these conditions: (1) it can excrete excess salt (look for cubical salt crystals on the leaves); (2) it can tolerate higher-than-average salt concentrations in its cell sap; (3) it has a thickened cuticle (surface covering), which inhibits evaporation; and (4) its roots can survive in wet, low-oxygen muds. Salt-marsh cordgrass (*Spartina alterniflora*), which is tall, with coarse stems and leaves, grows along the channel edges and in the wettest parts of the marsh, where it is flooded by each high tide. Salt-meadow cordgrass (*Spartina patens*), which is shorter, with fine stems and leaves, often bent down and matted, occupies sites that are drier and flooded only by the highest tides. One might suspect that salt-marsh cordgrass, flooded twice daily by salty water, would be the more salt-tolerant of the two *Spartinas*. Studies have revealed, though, that in the areas flooded less frequently, evaporation between floodings leads to salt accumulation, creating an environment even saltier than that of seawater. Salt-meadow cordgrass, which occupies this type of habitat, is the more salt-tolerant species.

On ground slightly higher and drier than the salt-marsh-cordgrass habitat, black grass, really a rush, becomes dominant, its flowering tops often giving a ruddy-brown tinge to this area, the edge of the marsh. Above, the sands are inhabited by dune and coastal-plain plants not specifically associated with salt marshes. Common among these are beach grass, seaside goldenrod, beach pea, and orache. The broad, succulent leaves of seabeach orache are among the tastiest edibles of the salt marsh. This succulence of leaf is another water-conservation strategy. A thickened leaf has a smaller surface-area-to-volume ratio than has a thin leaf, and all other things being equal, allows less water to evaporate than its thinner counterpart. A good illustration of plant distribution from cordgrass to beach grass is at **A,** where a new track bypasses a section of old track, which now gets flooded and acts as a marsh channel.

Where the new and old tracks rejoin at **B,** look to the right into a "field" of sea milkwort, which blends into salt-meadow cordgrass, sea lavender, and sea blite.

A late September day, just as a full- or new-moon tide (the highest of the month) is getting full, is a wonderful time to be at this spot. The fly and mosquito populations have dwindled. Pastel-purple patches of sea-lavender blossoms still hover over the grass. And if you listen carefully, you may hear the quiet hiss and bubble of the tide waters as they creep between the dunes. Lines of flotsam wind across the vegetation along the furthest reaches of the previous high tide.

Continue through the gap in the dunes and then walk along the shore to the right, west (**C**). In 1976, a spring storm deposited a 4-foot drift line (of seaweeds, etc.) along this beach. Soon afterward, thousands of sea-rocket seeds germinated. These plants trapped blowing and high-tide-washed sand grains. Within a few months, 1 foot of sand had been deposited, and by the end of the summer, the dunelet had grown to the critical level above high water that allowed beach grass to become established on it. As you proceed along the beach, you will pass numerous dunelets of varying sizes.

Notice that there are a number of places in which storm waves have breached the dunes. Overwashing of dunes can have either accreting or erosional effects, depending on the force of the waves and the height and shape of the dunes. In this area, both have occurred within the past 5 years.

The beach ends at the mouth of the Morse River (**D**). The spit on which you stand is a complex one, formed after a major shift of the Morse River channel in the 1940s. Researchers suspect that between 1862 and 1965, accumulation of 200 feet of beach on the west side of the river's mouth led to the deflection of the river channel. More recent changes have also been noted. When the shoreline was mapped in 1965, there were four small islands in the mouth of the Morse River. By 1977, they were no longer present, currents and waves, presumably, having eroded them away.

On the banks of the Morse River, on the sands of the beach, among the swells, or in the air, you are likely to see and hear herring gulls. While the adults are white-bodied with gray across their wings and back and black on the wingtips, the young birds sport various plumages of mottled brown and white. During most of the year, you will see herring gulls operating as rugged individualists, frequently joining a flock, but just as readily leaving it. In the spring, the adults that bred the previous year seem usually to pair up a couple of weeks before heading for their breeding grounds, and you may see such birds going everywhere in twosomes. Herring gulls seek fairly se-cluded places for breeding. In Maine, they usually use offshore is-lands that are free of mammalian predators. There they build nests on the ground, using grasses, seaweeds, sticks, shells, and feathers. Each year, there is a sizable population of gulls that do not breed. These often spend the summer feeding in garbage dumps or pilfering food from beach bathers. Herring gulls are omniverous, leaning heavily on the side of scavenging. Nestlings are fed by regurgitation. The red spot on the bill of the adult stimulates a pecking instinct in the nestlings, and this in turn stimulates the parents to regurgitate food. Even after a fledgling, as large as its parents, is well able to fend for itself, you may see it trailing one or both of its parents and begging loudly to be fed (see **#17**).

As you walk back up the beach, notice the variety of tracks in the sand: the webbed footprints of gulls, the unwebbed footprints of shorebirds and crows, the pad and nail prints of dogs, ripplemarks (see **#78**) and wrack lines of the waves, the concentric-arc tracings of windblown grass leaves, the sand castle of a child falling to the rising tide, your own footprints among those left by human visitors. Each set tells a story. Follow some bird tracks and see if you can deduce the activities of the maker.

Remarks: *This is a 1-mile walk over level, sandy terrain. Poison ivy is common in the backdune area, but the trail is wide enough to make avoidance of contact easy. Mosquitoes and deerflies can be wicked here in July and August. Wear protective clothing and use repellent. The Fox Island Tombolo hike begins from the Popham Beach State Park parking area. For other hikes in the region, see* **#76, #79, #80,** *and* **#81.** *Camping is available at Chewonki Campground, Wiscasset (mid-May to mid-September); Hermit Island Campground, Bath (Memorial Day to mid-October); and Ocean View Campground, Popham Beach (May 15 to October 15).*

78.
Fox Island
Tombolo

Directions: **Popham Beach, Maine. Follow directions for #77 through to the entrance to Popham Beach State Park. The parking lot is not far beyond the fee booth.**

Ownership: **Maine Bureau of Parks and Recreation.**

Popham Beach lies on a peninsula that pokes into the mouth of the Kennebec River. The beach area is highly unstable, making it an instructive place to study erosional and depositional sand features, which include parabolic dunes, dune scarps, an accreting beach, recently formed sandbars, and Maine's two sandy tombolo spits, each linking an island to the mainland. During spring and fall migration, you may see numerous species of shorebirds prowling the sands.

This walk begins on the trail that leaves from behind the outhouses at the southwest (far right, as you enter) corner of the parking lot. Wend your way through the scattered picnic table sites (**E**; this site is keyed to map, p. 286). The parking lot and the picnic places have been established in an area of parabolic dunes stabilized by pitch-pine forest. These dunes are called parabolic because of the curved shape of the depressions that have been scooped out of them by strong winds (see **#34**). These and many other parabolic dunes in Maine are unusual in that they have been excavated by offshore rather than onshore winds. These particular dunes were actively forming and migrating in the 1930s and 1940s, but they have been stable enough in recent years to become covered with pitch pine and even to develop a thin layer of soil. Where foot traffic is limited, beach heather, a short shrubby plant with scaly leaves and yellow flowers (summer), covers the sand surface. Although it is tolerant of water, salt, and nutrient stress, it is very sensitive to the disturbance of people walking on it, so please stay on the established paths. Like numerous other plants of dry habitats, beach heather has a layer of white, downy hairs on its leaves that helps it to conserve moisture. This species is not very tolerant of sand burial and can therefore only live where dunes are stabilized. At Popham, beach heather is near the northern end of its range in Maine.

From the picnic-area paths, head left and pick up any of the fenced walkways over the frontal dunes and onto the beach. To the left, the steep face of the dunes below the parking lot (**F**) shows the effects of recent wind erosion. Strong southwest winds have blown away much sand, creating a concave scarp on this side of the dunes.

Stretching seaward from the dunes is a wide, triangular-shaped area of beach called a *cuspate foreland*. Such features form in the lees of islands or where two currents come together; both are areas where low-energy waves deposit more sand than they erode. This foreland is attached to its sheltering island, Fox Island, by a *tombolo*, a sandy bar that connects either two islands or an island and the mainland. As with the cuspate foreland, the tombolo has formed in the lee, or protected, side of Fox Island. This and the Wood Island tombolo just to the north are the only two large, sandy tombolos in Maine. This one is flanked by two large nearshore bars, which are visibly changing from year to year. These bars and the cuspate foreland are particularly interesting to geologists because, while most of the shorelines in Maine are eroding in this period of ice-cap melting and sea-level rise, these features are accreting.

At all but high-tide levels, you can walk over the tombolo (**G**) to Fox Island. One of the unusual aspects of the sand that forms this tombolo and the beaches and dunes at Popham is that it is derived from the sediment load of the Kennebec River rather than from the reworked glacial till of which most of Maine's beaches are formed (see **#79**). Notice the magnificent and widely varying patterns of the ripplemarks in the sandy surface. These are formed by combinations of oscillatory motion of waves and the flow of longshore currents (see **#29**) and by the turbulent motion set up in wave backwash as it flows for long distances down gently sloped sand.

Fox Island (**H**) is a hill of resistant rock. Walk slightly left as you reach it, entering a sandy-bottomed inlet formed where schist was more easily eroded than the granite next to it. Notice the lovely orange-and-gray lichens on the rock surfaces near the shore. Even though none of the chlorophyll of their algal component is visible to us, it is indeed "visible" to sunlight, allowing these plants to make their food through the process of photosynthesis. The orange-and-gray pigments we see are those of the fungal component of the lichens (see also **#88**).

Higher on the island, numerous pegmatite intrusions are visible. If you look closely, you may find small garnets in them. Many of the bedrock joints and contact zones between two types of rock are sculpted by solution pits, some of them 8 or more inches deep. Especially in the earlier stages, the splitting action of frost wedging probably played a significant role in the development of these holes (see **#74**). Although solution pits can form in any depression that collects standing puddles of water, almost all the ones on Fox Island seem to be associated with depressions along weaknesses in the bedrock.

From the top of the island, you can view both its seaward and its landward slopes. The side facing the sea is very sparsely vegetated. Seaside goldenrod, found in sheltered cracks, and lichens are among the few plants that can survive the wind, salt spray, and lack of soil on this exposed slope. The side of the island facing the mainland is in the lee of strong onshore winds, and here sand and soil have been able to accumulate, providing sheltered foothold for a variety of typical coast inhabitants, including beach grass, meadowsweet, and yarrow.

As you walk back along the tombolo and beach, look for flocks of sanderlings darting after the edges of retreating waves. Picking small mollusks and crustaceans from the surface or just below it, they look like a flurry of clockwork toys. The palest of the sandpipers, sanderlings are distinguishable by their black shoulders and by the bold white stripe exposed on their wings in flight. This species has a circumpolar distribution. It nests on stony Arctic tundra, north of Hudson's Bay, and winters from the United States (south of Maine), Britain, and China to the Southern Hemisphere. In Maine, flocks of sanderlings are commonly seen engaged in very active foraging along the outer beaches and tideflats as they work their way north or south during spring and fall migrations.

Follow one of the trails that cross the dunes northward, back to the parking lot. The beach-grass area south of the dune privies (**I**) was part of the area overwashed by storms in 1975 and 1976. Botanists watched the regrowth of vegetation here and found that in only 7 weeks, the beach grass grew through over 10 inches of sand under which it had been buried. This tolerance of burial is one of the reasons beach grass can survive on the shifting substrate of the foredunes (see also **#79**).

Remarks: *This is a ¾-mile walk over sandy dune and beach terrain and onto a rocky island. The island access (tombolo) is exposed at most tide levels but not at high tide. There is a park entrance fee. For available camping in the area, see* **#77**. *The Popham Marsh hike begins 0.4 mile west of the state park entrance. The Rachel Carson Salt Pond Preserve is located near Pemaquid Point, in New Harbor. Fort Popham, an uncompleted, semicircular fort begun in 1861, is another mile up the road, at the end of the point; an entrance fee is charged.*

79.

Reid Beach

Directions: **Georgetown, Maine. From Portland, take I-95 and then U.S. 1 north and east about 34 miles. Cross the Bath bridge; at the east end, turn south onto Route 127. Go 10 miles, through Georgetown, and turn left onto Seguinland Rd.; go 2 miles to the entrance to Reid State Park. Follow the right fork to Todd's Point parking area.**

Ownership: **Maine Bureau of Parks and Recreation.**

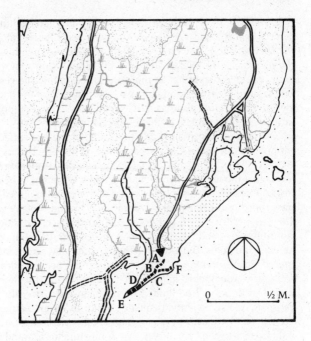

Reid Beach, the northernmost large, sandy-beach system in the state, faces into the Gulf of Maine, at the mouth of the Sheepscot River. Within the span of a short walk, it offers opportunities to enjoy and examine salt-marsh, dune, beach, and tidal sand-flat communities (see **#34**). A variety of sea and shore birds, including a few uncommon ones, frequent the area throughout the summer season.

The trail begins at the northeastern corner of the parking lot as an old dirt roadbed heading through the backdunes toward the shore. Bear right (straight) at the first junction and right again at the fork, passing between the dunes and the marshy area behind them (**A**). Although growing in very sandy footing, the plant species here are generally ones you might find in overgrown fields and along road edges the length and breadth of Maine: blackberry, raspberry, bayberry, meadowsweet, wild rose, yarrow, a little poison ivy, and gooseberries, whose dangling flowers grow into translucent, juicy berries, green in July, red and tasty with the coming of August. Within a species, some major differences between dune-dwellers and individuals that grow further inland are that the dune-dwellers have leaves that are more succulent (thickened and packed with water) and have thicker cuticles, both adaptations that help prevent desiccation.

As you pass along the boardwalk that cuts through the dunes (**B**), erosion exposes root systems of American beach grass, one of the few species able to live on a frontal dune ridge. Among the stresses it must be able to tolerate are sand burial and sand removal, salt spray, extreme changes in air moisture, and extreme changes in soil temperature, moisture, and chemistry. As is typical of the backdune species, beach grass also has a thickened cuticle. In addition, it has curled edges and sunken stomata (pores) on its leaves, which permit gas exchange (oxygen and carbon dioxide) at the leaf surface with minimal loss of water. Unlike most other plants, beach grass is very tolerant of burial by sand. In fact, it is reported to need a 3-inch coverage annually in order to survive, and it is known to be able to grow up from depths as great as a yard or more. When buried, beach grass sends out runners, or rhizomes, which send roots down and shoots up, every 6 to 10 inches or so. At the surface, the shoots trap more blowing sand, which stimulates the grass to produce more runners and roots and shoots. Thus, a dune may grow from the interaction of sand grains being blown up the beach and a single beach-grass root lodged in the sand during a storm. The dimensions of such a dune will be limited by the sand-grain size, the wind-transport velocity, and the frequency of storms. Frontal dune ridges like the one here act as buffers against storm erosion of backdune and marsh areas and are also storage compartments for sand, which replenishes beach supplies during storms.

Examine the sand itself (**C**). It is medium-to-fine in grain size and contains high concentrations of feldspar and schist fragments. These are clues that lead geologists to believe that, as is true of most beach material in Maine, this sand is derived from wave-washed glacial till and local bedrock fragments, rather than sediments brought to the coast by rivers (see **#78**). Longshore currents, which play extensive roles in the transport of beach-building sands in states farther south, play very minor parts up here (see **#29**).

If you have walked on Mile Beach, you may notice that the sand-grain size here on Half Mile Beach is smaller. This is because waves with lower energy deposit smaller particles on this part of the shore than farther north (see **#86**) and because this is the downdrift end of the small, two-beach system. Longshore currents are created when waves approach a straight coastline at an oblique angle. The net drift here is probably caused by storm waves from the northeast—the finest particles are transported the furthest to the southwest, in other words, to Half Mile Beach.

Walk to the right (southwest) along the beach (**D**). During much of the season, the fencing that helps protect the dunes from erosion from human-foot traffic continues seaward to include a large section of the backbeach. Here the fence serves to protect the beach as the northernmost nesting habitat on our continent for least terns (see **#23**) and also as the nesting habitat for piping plovers, which are uncommon (see **#39**). As recently as 1977, none was nesting here. One biologist suggested this may have been because the beach had been eroding for a number of years prior to that time and also because it was so heavily used. Whatever the reason, despite continued heavy visitation, a small number of least terns and piping plover have begun to nest here. The exposed beach environment offers few defensive nest sites—holes are very unstable, and foredune vegetation provides but meager cover. Both least terns and piping plover nest in shallow depressions on the open sand, the irregular blotchiness of their eggs and chicks breaking up the telltale outline of the shell and young and thus serving as camouflage protection, a type known as cryptic coloration. Ironically, this concealment has become a liability with the rise in popularity of beach recreation, because the eggs and chicks blend with their surroundings so well that they are often trampled unwittingly, by beach visitors.

In an effort to minimize nesting hindrance while still allowing for human enjoyment of the beach, the Maine Audubon Society is cooperating with the Bureau of Parks and Recreation in efforts to set aside a section of nesting habitat and to encourage the least terns to use it. Recent study of common and Arctic terns, which in Maine nest colonially on offshore islands, suggests that these birds are attracted to sites where they see others like them (either real or decoy). Although least terns nest in a widely spaced colony, researchers suspect that they, too, might respond to decoys. In the spring of 1983, least-tern decoys were placed in the more remote end of the protected area with hopes that the birds would be drawn there to nest. As of late May 1983, the little terns had returned from their wintering grounds off Brazil, and could be seen plunging into the surface waters to catch small fish. It remains to be seen whether or not they will join the decoys in the sand.

Offshore to the southwest, the beacon of the Seguin lighthouse perches 185 feet above sea level. The second oldest light in Maine, it was originally erected in 1795 and rebuilt in 1887. Its location is known for being one of the most foggy on the Maine coast (see **#80**).

At the far end of the beach, you reach the mouth of the Little River, a tidal reentrant in which sea-carried sands are deposited behind the frontal dune ridge, forming sand flats frequented at low tide by shorebirds searching for food (see **#78, #100,** and **#96**).

The end of the sandspit (**E**) visibly changes shape from season to season, as waves and currents fluctuate in force and direction. And as the relative sea level along this portion of the Maine coast contin- ues to rise (see **Portland North**), the spit and dune field are grad- ually migrating shoreward, incorporating old shoreline ridges into their mass.

Before you return to your car, walk up to the other end of Half Mile Beach, where a rocky headland juts into the sea (**F**). While the near portion is formed primarily of thinly banded schists glittering with myriad flat flecks of mica, the far part is mainly of granitic rock in a wonderful exposure of pattern and history—older, medium- grained, gray sections are crossed, recrossed, and crossed again by younger, often rather pink intrusions of pegmatite, coarsely grained, granitic rock formed of the same basic minerals as the grayer rock, but with a higher percentage of light colored minerals and a decid- edly larger crystalline structure. Notice that these pegmatite bands generally have smaller crystals at the edges, where they cooled more rapidly, in contact with the older rock. This is a good place to explore on hands and knees with a magnifying lens. Among the feldspar (pink and white), quartz (gray), mica (thinly sheeted, translucent, almost clear or almost black), and hornblende (black, rectangular), you may also discover small, reddish garnets.

Remarks: *This is a mile-long walk on sand and a bit of headland rocks. It is a fine chance to watch for shore and marsh birds and for sea ducks. The park season is from mid-April to mid-October, although the Half Mile Beach end may be open only on weekends during the early and late parts of the season. An entrance fee is charged. Picnic tables, grills, rest rooms, and bathhouses are available at both Mile and Half Mile beaches. No pets are allowed on the beaches.*

*About ¾ mile from the entrance station, on the Todd's Point road, marshland opens on both sides of the road, offering an expansive view of cordgrass and black grass (see **#77** and **#75**). Camping is available at Chewonki Campground, Wiscasset (May 15 to September 15). The Jose- phine Newman Sanctuary, containing a variety of coastal habitats and trails, is off Route 127, just east of the Georgetown bridge. Sherman Lake waters and marshlands are accessible from the Sherman Lake Rest Area on Route 1, which is 3.2 miles north of the Wiscasset bridge. Both sites are described in Dorcas Miller's* The Maine Coast: A Nature Lover's Guide.

80.
Pemaquid Point

Directions: **Bristol, Maine. From Portland, take I-95 and then U.S. 1 northeast about 53 miles to Newcastle; take Business Route 1 southeast into Damariscotta. Take Route 129 south for about a mile, then bear left onto Route 130; follow it through Bristol to Pemaquid Point, where the road ends. Park Here.**

Ownership: **Town of Bristol.**

Pemaquid Point is one of the numerous peninsulas that jut southward from Maine's highly convoluted coast (see **Portland North**). It forms the western headland of Muscongus Bay, identified from the sea for over a century by the beacon of its lighthouse. It offers an invitation to explore fascinating bedrock formations, intertidal lifestyles, and the human history of the area.

Dominating the view as you reach Pemaquid Point is one of Maine's prettiest lighthouses. Originally built in 1827, it was tended until 1934, when the light was put on an automatic system. The residence is now owned by the town and houses a Fisherman's Museum, which includes photographs of Maine's other lighthouses and displays of artifacts from Maine's fishing industries.

Watch the light as it flashes and is dark. Each of the lights in a particular area has a unique combination of color (red and/or white) and flashing pattern. These are indicated on navigational charts, making it possible to use a light not only as a warning device but also as a locating device. For instance, if you were disoriented by fog or storm in the Muscongus Bay area and you could pick out a white light that flashed every 10 seconds, you could orient yourself by noting that that pattern corresponds to the light on Pemaquid Point, and not, for example, to the one on Monhegan Island, which, while also white, only flashes once every 30 seconds.

Walk down onto the beautiful banded rocks below the lighthouse. These exposures were formed millions of years ago as thick layers of dark, muddy sediments and thin layers of pale, limey sediments (from the skeletons of microorganisms) were deposited on an ancient sea floor, gradually forming sedimentary rock (see **#74**). Later, when tectonic movement (see **#83**) folded the rocks and forced intrusions of magma between some of the layers, these rocks were metamorphosed, and although the banded structure remained, it was tilted on edge and highly warped in some sections. In the ridge that juts seaward below the lighthouse, where distorted layers mingle with granitic intrusions, one can get a vivid sense of the magmas having forced and melted their way into the overlying bedrocks.

The patterns of cracks and other places of weakness in rocks greatly influence the shapes into which land develops. Along the coast of Maine, from Pemaquid Point south and west to the Portland area, much of the bedrock is metasedimentary (metamorphosed sedimentary). In such rocks, the major planes of weakness run along the contacts between the bands, in a parallel series. The peninsulas and islands in the area reflect this and tend to be long and narrow. Further east, in the areas of Blue Hill and Mount Desert Island, the islands and headlands, reflecting the blocky fracturing characteristic of granitic bedrock, tend to be rounder and of higher profile. The rocks on the beach to the south of the lighthouse also reflect those differences in bedrock structure (see **#74**).

Below the wide no-man's-land of virtually barren rock, the intertidal zone occupies the fluctuating "edge" where sea, air, and land meet. Shaped like tiny volcanoes or Chinese hats, limpets are among the common creatures that prowl the mid to lower sections of this area. Like the snails to which they are related, limpets have a filelike radula, which they use to scrape algae off of rocks and other surfaces. Unlike snails (see **#101**), though, limpets have no operculum with which to close the open end of their shells. Instead, they are able to adhere to hard surfaces with tremendous force. This adhesion is so strong that if you want to pick one up to observe its underside without breaking its shell, you must be quick and sly. Slip a fingernail under one edge of the shell and then slide the limpet along parallel to the rock surface until its grip is completely loosened and you can pick it up; if it will not slide readily, leave it and look for another one, for damaging a limpet's shell leaves it vulnerable to desiccation and predation. In addition to their ability to cling tightly, limpets also rely on their shape for protection. The force of a wave is greatly dissipated by the low, conical shell profile.

Our Maine coast species of limpet is reportedly most active at night and at low tide. Each individual seems to establish its own home base, a place "tailored to fit" by rubbing shell against rock (that is, if the rock is harder, as is common here, the shell edge wears away to fit the rock contour, and vice versa). The limpet returns to this spot after browsing even as much as a few yards away.

In some of the tide pools and in the water below the low-tide line, find brown blades of kelp. These large algae (all seaweeds are algae) have prominent holdfasts, rootlike structures by which they attach themselves to hard surfaces such as mussel shells or rocks. Holdfasts are not true roots because they are not specialized to draw moisture and dissolved nutrients into the plant body. There is no need of that in an aquatic environment, where a soup of nutrients washes around the entire plant and can be absorbed by all its surfaces. True roots are the invention of complex terrestrial plants, such as the white spruces and seaside goldenrod that grow on the rocks above you. With most of their photosynthetic bodies surrounded by air, which not only cannot provide them with available mineral nutrients but also desiccates their tissues, such terrestrial plants have evolved roots and pumping systems to help solve the problem.

As kelps grow, they have the capacity to gather iodine from the sea. Iodine is an important element for humans and other animals who rely on a thyroid gland to produce hormones and to regulate metabolic rate; without iodine, the thyroid does not function properly. Kelp is commonly exploited for this element and also for substances such as alginates, sticky compounds that are used as additives in a wide variety of domestic and industrial products. Another less-well-known role kelp plays in our lives is also related to iodine. Kelp binds some iodine into a volatile form called methyl iodide. Some of this compound escapes from the seawater and travels through the air, where it decomposes, setting free the iodine. Iodine, too, is volatile and can stay in the air long enough to be blown across continents. Thus it gets spread over wide areas of land and can be absorbed by organisms (through their food) even if they live far from the coast.

Also down in the deeper parts of the intertidal zone, under the edges of boulders or overhanging ledges, you may discover some spiny, green pincushions. These are green sea urchins. Gently dislodge one and place it on your open palm. Do not worry; its spines are not poisonous (those of some southern species are), only sharp, so be *very* careful in handling them. Watch your urchin—it will begin waving those spines around in a seemingly erratic manner, but the effect will be that the urchin will begin to move slowly across your hand. Turn the urchin over, and in the center of its bottom side find a round mouth with five triangular, white teeth, which the urchin uses for grazing on algae. Urchins scrape algae from all sorts of surfaces, even those of lobster traps—but the lobstermen don't thank them, because the ambitious critters also scrape away the surface of wooden traps, hastening their decay. Place the urchin in a quiet and cold (remember, urchins live in the colder depths of the intertidal zone) pool of seawater. Purplish "worms" will begin to emerge from between the spines. These are tube feet. Like those on the arms of its cousin the starfish, these tentacles are little hydraulic suction cups, which the urchin uses to help hold itself in its crack or crevice, allowing added protection both from waves and from predators such as gulls, foxes, cod, and humans. (Some people consider the eggs a delicacy; in some cultures they are used as an aphrodisiac.)

Before you return to your car, dip your finger in the water and then lick it. As you probably expected, the water is salty. This is due to salt-forming ions, or atom-sized particles of elements that carry either a positive or a negative charge. The majority of these ions are sodium and chloride, which are washed into the ocean by the rivers and released into it by undersea upwellings of molten rock. However, if you were to estimate the amounts of salts delivered into the seas, you would conclude that the waters are *much* more salty than they actually are. The big question, then, is not why the seas are salty but rather why they are not *more* salty. Some scientists suggest that many salt ions may become trapped, carried downward, and buried by the rain of tiny skeletons that continuously drifts to the bottom of the sea as diatoms and other microorganisms die. At this time, though, the question remains one of our unsolved mysteries.

Remarks: *There is no particular trail for this ramble. The ledges available for exploration extend a couple of hundred yards seaward from the lighthouse. Caution: the rocks may be slippery even when they are dry. A parking fee is charged from May to October. The Fisherman's Museum is open from May to October; a fee is charged. Camping is available at Sherwood Forest Campsites, Pemaquid Beach (May 15 to October 15); Duck Puddle Campground, Nobleboro (May 1 to September 15); Lake Pemaquid Camping, Damariscotta (May 1 to October 15); and Little Ponderosa, Boothbay (May 15 to October 15). The Rachel Carson Salt Pond Preserve is on Route 32, on the northeastern edge of New Harbor (Pemaquid Beach is on the southwestern edge of New Harbor).*

81.

Hog Island

Directions: **Medomak, Maine. Follow directions for #80 to Damariscotta. On the northeast side of town (just north of the Damariscotta Plaza), turn east (right) onto Biscay**

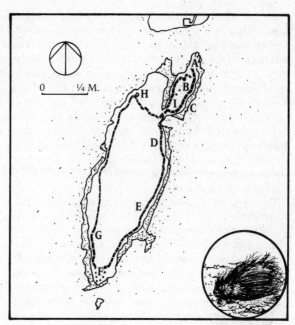

Inset: Porcupine

Rd. Go 5 miles and turn north (left) onto Route 32. Go 1.2
miles and turn right onto Keene Neck Rd. Where the tar
ends, turn left. Park in the lot at the top of the hill, on the
left. There is a small-boat access at the bottom of the hill.

Ownership: **National Audubon Society.**

Eleven islands along the coast of Maine today bear the name Hog
Island, an allusion to their ridgebacked shape or to the creatures
once raised on them. Hogs on the mainland often wound up being
a picnic for wolves, so islands without predators were often used for
raising them, especially if oaks—and a supply of acorns—were present.
No one seems to remember the hogs for which this Hog Island could
have been named, so perhaps it is one of those named for its shape.
Today, it is the home of the Todd Wildlife Sanctuary and the Audubon Ecology Camp in Maine. The trail around its perimeter passes
through habitats varying from dark spruce tunnels and lush fields of
hay-scented fern to rocky tide pools inhabited by such creatures as
star tunicates. Ospreys hunt in the bay, and the island vegetation is
alive with warblers and other songbirds, especially during May and
September migrations (see **#96**).

As you travel the waters around Hog Island during the height of lobstering activities (July to November), you are likely to see more lobster buoys per square mile than anywhere else on the Atlantic seaboard. Muscongus Bay is well known not only as lobstering ground but also as a retreat for many species of deeper water fish, which come here to spawn (see **#82**). The name of the bay itself alludes to this—*muscongus* is an Abnaki Indian word meaning "the fishing place." The favorable conditions are created by a combination of factors: the shallowness of the bay with its slightly higher temperatures than the Gulf of Maine, the slightly lower salinity created by the large amounts of fresh water introduced into the bay by its four major rivers, and the large amounts of nutrients also carried into the coastal waters by the rivers.

Once you have landed on the island, walk up into the grassy area surrounded by buildings. On the south side of the Fish House (the building on the northeast side of the grass) stands an old elm (**A**) which sports a strange, metal skirt. For some reason, Hog Island porcupines love to munch on the leaves and twigs of this tree, and as you can see, they have pruned it severely. The skirt discourages them from climbing up the trunk, but sometimes they manage access anyway, perhaps via other trees' branches. As you hike the island today, keep your eyes open for these rather awkward but fascinating creatures. As long as you do not try to pet one or scare it in any way, a porcupine is quite harmless. It cannot throw its quills, but it can slap its tail around with surprising rapidity, and the barbed quills readily detach from the porcupine once they penetrate something else. Generally, you will find porcupines to be quite placid, shambling along through the woods, calmly eating bark or greenery, or curled up in the fork of a branch, looking much like a large, twiggy nest. Also look for their slightly curved, inch-long scat, which is often concentrated around the base of a tree; their pigeon-toed footprints in the mud; and their large-toothed gnaw marks on tree trunks. A hungry porcupine can kill a tree by girdling it—that is, chewing away the bark and cambium around the entire circumference of the trunk. The tree dies because there is no longer any food-carrying connection between the leaves and the roots.

From the east side of the Bridge (the dining hall building), follow the footpath south. At the fork with the No Smoking sign, bear left onto the trail, which follows the east shore. Beyond the camp buildings, the trail passes through the first of a number of dense and dark spruce tunnels (**B**). Feel the coolness and moisture. In such places, mushrooms are likely to abound. Of the many species that inhabit the Hog Island woods, the tiny *Marasmius* mushroom is one of the most enchanting. Each small beige cap, about ¼ inch in diameter, perches atop a dark, slender, and pliable stalk. Where you find one, you are likely to find a whole troop of them sprouting out of the duff, or thick humus, each rising out of a single decaying spruce needle. I discovered a warbler nest lined with dark and copper-colored filaments, which on close inspection turned out to be *Marasmius* and haircap-moss stalks. Mushrooms, particularly the larger species, are also popular as food among woodland creatures. Notice that many of them have holes where they have been nibbled. Slugs (see **#101**) mice, red squirrels, and white-tailed deer commonly feast on mushrooms.

At **C**, where the trail skirts the land side of a rocky outcrop, take a side trip to the shore. At low tide, numerous tide pools are exposed along this section (see **Portland North**). Among the most special creatures to be found here are star tunicates, primitive chordates (the larval stage has a notochord) more closely related to humans than any other tide-pool inhabitants except fish! Arranged in flat circles, each patterned with dark, radiating lines, they form stiff, jellylike masses on Irish moss, mussels, or rocks. Up close, they remind one of exquisite African batik designs. Each circle is a colony. Each radiating individual sucks in its own stream of seawater, straining microscopic food from it. The water is expelled from the communal center. Star tunicates are most commonly accessible in the pools at the southern end of this rocky point.

Rejoin the trail, continuing past two small coves and then entering the woods. At the junction, go left. Near the upper end of the salt-marsh-edged inlet, go left again, to the shore. Walk right along the beach. Notice the wind-thrown trees, all blown over in the same direction. As you will see, the southeast side of Hog Island is subject to strong winds. Near the end of the beach, go right and return to the main path, bearing left twice to follow the East Shore Trail. Beyond the next creek and salt-marsh crossing, you enter woods that are composed of a birch overstory and a spruce understory (**D**). Since birch seeds do not germinate well in duff, this area was likely cleared at one time, either for a field or by a clear-cutting logging operation. Although the birches are much taller than the spruce, they may be approximately the same age—spruce grow much less rapidly than birches. Foresters use a tool called an increment borer to determine the age of a tree. With it they can withdraw a small core from the trunk and then count the rings, which reveals the tree's age. Keep an eye open to the left for ghostly communities of Indian pipes, a flowering plant which gets its nutrients from dead organic matter in the soil rather than through the process of photosynthesis.

From here to the end of the island (**E**), enjoy the lush growths of lichens (see **#88**) and mosses. Deer, hare, and fox signs are common. Black-throated green and black-and-white warblers sing from the trees. How do all these organisms get onto an island? Spores and seeds of many plants may be blown over the water, carried by animals, or float across on logs or even in the water. Mammals can swim the narrows or walk across on winter ice. Birds can fly, of course, but some species are loath to fly over water, so you will not find them here, at least not in any large numbers. Slugs and amphibians may arrive in either egg or adult form, but they are very sensitive to desiccation from salt water and spray and to exposure to sun and wind. They may travel to sea islands, especially the ones further offshore, concealed in lumber or other supplies sent by boat from the mainland.

As you emerge into the open at the southern end of the island (**F**), you are in osprey territory (see **#22, #50,** and **#99**). Please spend little time in this area if the osprey are flying around and calling. Too much disturbance can cause them to abandon their nests. As you cross over the top of the field, keep an eye out for meadow voles scurrying from the cover of one grass tunnel to the next (see **#75**). Also note that there is some nettle present.

As you head back up the west side of the island, you pass through large fields of hay-scented fern (**G**), which have grown up in old blowdown areas. The high density of ferns here, as opposed to herbaceous or woody vegetation, leads some botanists to infer that the trees were probably more frequently snapped off than root-sprung, leaving the duff and soil layers relatively intact. Hay-scented fern, which reproduces readily through underground stems, can colonize such an area much more rapidly than plants that must grow from seeds, especially those that have difficulty penetrating the duff to reach the soil they need for sustained growth. Rub the end of a frond and smell it. It sometimes smells like new-mown hay and sometimes like pepper. Often, the odor is so pungent that you can smell it in the air. Sweeping down across these fields wherever a trickle or brook flows toward the sea are swaths of skunk cabbage, the first wildflower to bloom each year in Maine. Its spring may begin when the ground is still frozen. Related to the jack-in-the-pulpit, the skunk cabbage has a hooded flowering part that pushes above the ground before the leaves appear. The skunk cabbage is able to generate heat and keep its developing ovules warm, a feat usually associated with warm-blooded animals. The process is not well understood, but it seems that the skunk cabbage is able to produce heat by rapid respiration, or breathing; it uses oxygen to break down sugars and release energy. All green plants respire, but few of them do so rapidly enough to produce heat, and if they do, it generally is dissipated quickly into the air. The skunk cabbage not only generates heat, but also keeps it right where it is needed—around the flower-bearing spadix—and insulated by the hoodlike cowl, which is formed of tissues packed with air chambers, similar to the closed-cell styrofoam used to make hot-drink cups. One researcher reported that an individual spadix could maintain a temperature 36 to 63 degrees above the air temperature.

At **H** you pass the Bingham Cottages, summer homes of two generations of former island owners. It is to the energies of Millicent Todd Bingham and her mother, Mabel Loomis Todd, that Hog Island owes its sanctuary status. When Mrs. Todd first sailed past the island in 1908, a 40-acre strip had been cut over, and rumor had it that a similar fate awaited the entire island. In succeeding years, Mrs. Todd and a friend managed to buy all of Hog Island except for the peninsula on the northern end. In 1933, a year after Mrs. Todd's death, the owners of the inn and bungalows on the peninsula decided that they had to sell their property. Millicent Bingham, sharing her mother's love for the island, decided that Hog Island would be an ideal place for a nature camp, housed in the peninsula buildings, with the rest of the island as a laboratory. Two years and much intense work later, she was introduced to John Baker, newly elected director of the National Audubon Society. The Audubon Ecology Camp in Maine opened the very next summer, dedicated to sharing with teachers (and today, with any interested adults) insights into natural history and ecology.

When you reach the head of the salt-marsh cove, turn left at the junction (to camp); keep going straight to the junction where the trail joins from the east side of the peninsula. At **I**, go straight, following the West Shore Trail to a dirt court. Go left, down to the camp buildings. A right and then a left will put you on familiar territory once again.

Remarks: *This is a 4½-mile hike around the perimeter of a nearshore island. Most of the trail is on the soft ground of the woods. It is liberally sprinkled with wet places, so wear footgear you don't mind getting wet and muddy. Please check in at the office in the Bridge (dining hall) building before you begin your walk. Day use only. No fires may be built. No pets are allowed on the island. The visitor center and the Hockomock Trail, a self-guided nature trail, are on the mainland section of the sanctuary. Check for information about guided nature walks and other programs for the public (summer months only). Descriptions of the Audubon Ecology Camp program and historical information about Hog Island are available during the summer season. At other times, write to the National Audubon Society Camp Office, 4150 Darley, Suite 5, Boulder, Col. 80303. For camping in the area, see* **#80**.

To reach the island, you must cross a quarter-mile of saltwater bay. There are no boat rentals, but there is small-boat access at Hockomock Point. Please remember to park your vehicle at the top *of the hill. Be careful of winds and tidal currents on your crossing. On Hog Island, tie your canoe/kayak/rowboat to the southern side of the small (righthand) float. If you arrive by larger boat,* do not *drop an anchor—it may snag underwater pipes and power lines. Please request a mooring.*

82.

Monhegan Island

Directions: **Monhegan, Maine. From Portland, take I-95 and then U.S. 1 about 75 miles northeast through Thomaston, then turn south onto Route 131. Go about 13 miles to Port Clyde, at the end of the road. The ferry dock and parking are to the left of the general store.**

Ownership: **Private and land trust.**

"Once you've slept on an island, you'll never be quite the same." That was Rachel Field's opinion. Certainly, whether you sleep on Monhegan or not, a trip to this outermost of the Muscongus Bay islands is a fascinating treat. It offers opportunities to explore the ecology of islands and to experience the remoteness and relative isolation of being entirely surrounded by water.

As you travel out to Monhegan and the mainland eases into the distance, you skip past island after island, the numerous inner ones and then the more scattered outer ones, ranging randomly in size from small, rocky ledges frequently overwashed by storms to broad and sometimes high islands of over a mile in length. Some of them are barren, some covered with grasses and shrubs, others mantled with forests. The diversity of life on these islands varies widely, influenced by combinations of factors such as the distance from the mainland—most organisms spread less readily to islands further offshore; the size of the island—larger islands frequently have a wider diversity of habitats and niches; and the extent of human influence,

Inset: Puffin

such as logging and livestock grazing. Accounts of early European exploration suggest that forest diversity was greater on some of the islands (Monhegan, for example) before European usage. Some botanists suggest that heavy-seeded species, such as oak and beech, may reseed on islands very slowly after available stocks are cut especially since the saplings from their seeds are subject to destruction from grazing.

After you pass between the wooded slopes of Burnt and Allen islands, look westward. On a relatively clear day, you should be able to see some low-profile, ledgy islands: Little Egg Rock, Eastern Egg Rock, and Western Egg Rock (perhaps with binoculars), named for the egg collecting common on them during the 1800s. At the beginning of the egging season, the collectors would break all the existing eggs in order to ensure that future gatherings would be of fresh eggs. Heavy egging, combined with hunting (for meat and plumes) and general habitat disturbance, had disastrous effects on the Gulf of Maine coast and seabird populations. In this century, protection from much of these activities has allowed gradual reestablishment of numerous nesting colonies, especially those of gulls (see **#17** and **#77**). Some species, though, did not return.

Atlantic puffins, one of the most abundant species in the North Atlantic, once nested on five or six Maine islands, but by the early 1970s they remained breeding in this state only on Matinicus Rock. This situation caught the interest of ornithologist Steve Kress, who, with the aid of numerous research interns, has spent some ten summers attempting to establish a puffin nesting colony on Eastern Egg Rock (the one with the two small buildings). For a number of years, teams brought puffin nestlings from Newfoundland, placed them in puffin-type burrows, which they had excavated in the thin soil of the island, fed them, banded them for identification, and watched them take off to sea in August. Puffins tend to return to breed on the islands where they were born. Would these puffins remember Eastern Egg Rock as home when they were ready to breed 4 or 5 years hence? In 1981, the first birds returned to nest—five pairs of them. In 1982, fourteen pairs bred on the island. This may indeed be the exciting beginning of a new puffin colony in Maine, and some of the research techniques developed on Eastern Egg Rock have been put to use in such distant places as Hawaii.

When you reach Monhegan, get a trail map from the Island Spa and find the Cathedral Woods Trail (trail 11) by taking left forks on the village roads. As you wander along the trail, you will see that the species here are the same as those you can find elsewhere in Maine. A difference you may notice in early summer is that plants such as starflower, which are early bloomers, tend to bloom later here than on the mainland. This is because, being surrounded by a large buffering body of water, which heats up much more slowly than does a landmass, Monhegan's spring temperatures rise later. (Also, it is cooler here in summer than it is inland, and the autumn frost is delayed.)

The Cathedral Woods (**A**) are an almost-pure stand of red spruce, whose trunks rise like smooth pillars for tens of feet before being crowned with branches and needles. Growing conditions here are rugged enough that few trees have reached a diameter of 10 inches, even though the forest is quite old. A count of the rings of one 11-inch spruce indicated that it was over 90 years old.

Near the junction of trails 11 and 12, look for intricate twig and bark "fairy houses" built by Monhegan residents to entice these folk (see the Monhegan Island brochure, "What to See," point c). Continue straight ahead on trail 11 (**B**). Especially after a rain, the low ground on the right is full of pools, brown from leached tannins and, in early summer, populated by thousands of ½-inch-long "worms" that wiggle around a great deal. Watch one as it floats to the surface, tail end up, and hangs motionless for a few moments. It is breathing through its snorkel-like tube. These aquatic creatures are the larvae of mosquitoes. Like birds and other organisms that either fly or are carried on the winds, mosquitoes fairly readily find their way from the mainland to islands.

You are likely to find footprints of another animal that frequently colonizes islands—white-tailed deer. The ones that were not born here either were transported by humans or swam the 10 miles from the mainland, moving from island to island. Although deer hooves are not very speedy propellers, they are adequate for slow locomotion. And in the water, a deer's center of buoyancy is a bit further forward than its center of gravity, so it can swim with its head well above the surface, generally avoiding mouthfuls of brine.

At the next junction, where the Cathedral Woods Trail ends, go left on trail 1. At one of the first two wide viewpoints (**C**), look southward beyond the shore of Monhegan, into the Gulf of Maine. One day in the late 1500s, some seafaring fishermen, pursuing the cod fishing grounds ever westward across the North Atlantic, made the leap from the Grand Banks off "New-found-land" to the banks of the Gulf of Maine, thus opening up a busy new chapter in Maine life. Later, sometime after 1600, on another unrecorded adventure, other fishermen discovered the winter inshore spawning ground of the cod and turned the cod fishery into a year-round business—look northward (and eastward) of Monhegan. The practice was to arrive in the Gulf of Maine before March and, if possible, by Christmas, for the best catches were to be had in January and February. Stages (racks) for drying the salted fish were set up on Monhegan and other offshore islands, as close to the fishing areas as possible. Cured loads of fish were shipped back to Europe and to cities farther south. With the introduction in the late 1850s of the technique of longlining from dories (peapod-shaped rowing boats with a pointed bow and narrow stern), full catches on a good voyage could be made in a single month rather than two, and handlining from the decks of fishing vessels became a thing of the past.

As you continue along the perimeter of Monhegan, enjoy the wildflowers and raspberries. Pass the shore ends of trails 18 and 17, and wend your way out onto Green Point (**D**), on the northern end of the island. Just offshore is Eastern Duck Rock. The waters and rocks of this area are frequented by ducks and other seabirds, among them delightful, red-footed black guillemots, which are relatives of the puffin. Their black summer plumage, with large, white wing patches, is striking. Members of the auk, or Alcidae, family, these chunky birds swim under water using their wings, rather than their feet, for locomotion as they pursue fish, eels, and crustaceans, or browse on algae and mollusks. In the air, their rapid wingbeats and often low, veering flight look like hard work. Compared with gulls, the relatively short wings of the Alcidae are better adapted for swimming under water, whereas the long, pointed wings of gulls make gliding flight easy and graceful.

Continue along the shore, passing trail 15, then go left on trail 14, the Pebble Beach Trail (**E**). The trunks and branches of many of the spruces here swell with lumpy burls and densely branched "witches' brooms." Botanists suggest two possible causes for these: infection by a nonlethal virus, and physical irritation by salt crystals blasted into the bark by storm winds. Keep going straight where trail 1 joins from the right, and turn right when you reach trail 10, a fire road that leads you past the Cathedral Woods trailhead and back into the village.

Remarks: *With its ups and downs and ins and outs, this is a 2-mile walk. The trails are wet, narrow, and rough, especially along the shore, where they are marked with rock cairns. The trail labels are small—wooden numbers affixed to tree trunks. Trail 1, along the shore, is sometimes difficult to follow. The White Head and Burnt Head trails are recommended if your time on the island is limited. No camping is allowed on Monhegan, but there are several inns open mid-June through mid-September. It is wise to make reservations in advance.*

> *The Trailing Yew (opens mid-May), (207) 596-0440*
> *The Monhegan House, (207) 594-7983*
> *Off-Shore Inn, (207) 594-2321*
> *The Island Inn, (207) 596-0371*
> *Hitchcock Cottage, (207) 594-8137*

Camping is available on the mainland at Atticus Hill Farm Camping Area, Thomaston (May 15 to October 15). The ferry to Monhegan is the Laura B., *Monhegan's mail boat, which runs year-round from Port Clyde; twice-daily runs mid-June to mid-September; (207) 372-8848. Other suggested points of interest on Monhegan are Burnt Head for sunrises, Lobster Cove during shorebird migration, the Meadow in the center of the village for deer-watching and birding, the lighthouse, and the Monhegan Museum. See also the Monhegan Island brochure. For more information on the Puffin Project, contact Dr. Stephen Kress, Cornell Lab of Ornithology, 159 Sapsucker Wood Rd., Ithaca, N.Y. 14850. For more information on Maine islands, see* Islands in Time, *by Philip W. Conkling.*

83.

Mount Megunticook

Directions: **Camden, Maine. From Portland, take I-95 and then U.S. 1 about 88 miles northeast to Camden. Continue on U.S. 1; about 1.8 miles north of the junction with Route 52, the entrance to Camden Hills State Park is on the left. Park in the lot next to the headquarters, just beyond the fee booth.**

Ownership: **Maine Bureau of Parks and Recreation.**

The Camden Hills cluster on the western shore of Penobscot Bay, the largest of the many bays that indent the coast of Maine and the home of many islands (see **Portland North**). One of the nicest points from which to view this mosaic of water and islands is Ocean Lookout, on the ridge of Mount Megunticook. The hike passes from stately deciduous forests sheltered on the mountain's flanks to stunted oaks and coniferous trees on the windswept ridge. It is a pleasant walk, even on a foggy day, when you may enjoy the sights close to hand: the patterns in the rock surfaces, a red-eyed vireo sitting motionless on its nest, a gray squirrel leaping from tree to tree.

The white-blazed trail begins as a woods road in the campground between sites 102 and 84. Follow the signs left onto another dirt road and then left again onto an old gravelly road. In this deciduous forest (**A**), the rich odor of damp leaves and humus mingles with the salty tang of sea air. Red-bellied, ring-necked, garter, and milk snakes, none of them poisonous, are the common species of the woods in this part of Maine, although they usually do not stay visible long enough for you to see them closely. The ring-necked snake is an elegant little animal, dark with an orange belly and a narrow, orange-to-yellowish band around its neck. It will eat just about any small creature around which it can stretch its mouth, including other snakes (see **#98**).

Join a trickling brook (left) and go up a set of log steps.

If you are here in the spring or early summer, you may hear abrupt, short, robinlike phrases of birdsong in monotonous repetition, with brief pauses between them. A male red-eyed vireo announces his territory. More commonly heard than seen, he is probably sitting high in a deciduous tree, where his drab plumage allows him to conceal himself easily. His mate is likely to be nearby, build-

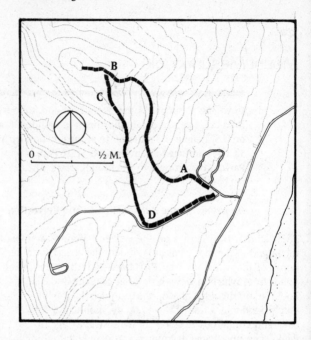

ing her nest or incubating eggs. The nest is a beautiful work. Hung by its rim in a horizontally oriented twig fork, it is woven of delicate materials, including birch-bark strips, filaments from weed stems, and the silk of spiders and insect larvae. These nests, rarely more than 15 feet above the ground, are often within eyesight, but the female sits so still that she draws little attention to her inconspicuous home. Although quiet, she is not always meek, as jays and crows that approach too closely discover. She will quickly join the male in diving attacks to drive away the larger birds.

From Ocean Lookout (**B**), you can see southwest to Mount Battie, a typical stoss-and-lee land form; east into Penobscot Bay, dotted with islands; and south over Camden and Rockport to the Gulf of Maine and the Atlantic Ocean. As you gaze out to sea, imagine being able to pierce the lightless depths with your eyes and see the bottom. A little more than halfway across to Europe, you would come across the Mid-Atlantic Ridge, where material from inside the earth is continually rising and spreading eastward and westward, forming new sea floor. This is the edge between two of the large, free-floating plates of which the earth's crust seems to be made. Continents ride on top of some of them; thus as you stand on the ridge of Mount Megunticook, you are moving slowly along with the sliding plate that underlies North America. Geologists call the widely accepted theory that describes this phenomenon *plate tectonics*.

The plates of crust do not all move at the same rate or even in a single direction, and they sometimes bump into one another. When this happens, one plate seems to dive diagonally beneath the other, melting into the mantle material that lies between the earth's crust and its core. This creates tensions that often result in volcanic action, intrusion of magma into crustal rock, or upheaval and folding of the surface into new mountains. As far as geologists can tell, the North American and European plates have collided at least three times, most recently about 350 million years ago, creating the Acadian Orogeny. (An *orogeny* is a period of mountain building; this one is called *Acadian* because it was first studied in Acadia, the region from Nova Scotia to eastern Maine.) During that period, the metamorphic rocks that are beneath your feet, at that time still sedimentary rocks (see **#74**), located on the sea floor, were thrust above the water. Concurrently, the granitic rocks of Deer Isle, Isle au Haut, and the southern part of Vinalhaven (all in Penobscot Bay) were intruded as masses of magma, which squeezed into the older sedimentary rocks. The heat and pressures involved in all this upheaval metamorphosed the sedimentary rocks. In the years between then and now, thousands of feet of rock have been eroded from the surface, exposing the rocks you see today. The myriad islands of Penobscot Bay are the tops of hills and mountains that are still tall enough to poke above the water. Along the coast of Maine, there are also tremendous numbers of submerged hills, as well as hills that are covered by water at high tide and uncovered at low tide.

These ledges, rocks, and islands make navigating the Maine coast a treacherous proposition. If the wind is coming off the water, you may be able to hear bell buoys clanging their warnings from positions near navigational hazards. Although terrestrial roads have replaced the waterways as the primary avenues of mobility, the bay and the sea remain a vital focus of life in this area. Lobstering, shrimping, scalloping, and deeper sea fishing are major industries (see **Cape Cod to Portland** for more on fishing), and in the summertime, pleasure sailing on windjammers (small schooners) is a popular part of the tourist trade. Numerous people still live on the islands year-round, and many more come here to spend their summer months in relative tranquility and isolation.

The loop trail back down to the parking lot heads first toward Mount Battie, on the Tablelands Trail. Descend on exposed ledges where mats of juniper lie flattened against the rock surface, as much out of the wind as possible. Glacial striations cross the flat ledge surfaces at **C**, evidence of the glacier's southward passage.

Traverse from bench to bench down into the saddle between Bat-

tie and Megunticook. At the junction, go left on the Nature Trail
(**D**), paralleling the Mount Battie toll road. A rapid scraping of claws
on bark may announce the presence of a gray squirrel scrambling
up and around a tree trunk to a place out of the range of your vision.
Gray squirrels spend a good deal of their time in trees, where they
have a better chance of avoiding their numerous predators, which,
besides humans, include foxes, coyotes, bobcats, large owls, and
hawks. As they run and leap from branch to branch and tree to tree,
the squirrels use their bushy tails like balancing poles. They do venture to the ground, primarily in search of food. Nuts, berries, tree
seeds, mushrooms, and insect larvae and cocoons are common items
in their diet. They also gnaw on old bones and antlers as a way of
getting the calcium required to build their incisors, which are always
being worn away and must continuously grow. Gray squirrels are
active all year-round, nesting and rearing their young in tree cavities
and building big leafy nests high in the branches in summer. In late
summer and fall, you may find them busily caching food in the
ground. Biologists suspect that they use both memory and sense of
smell to relocate the caches (see **#73**). When you meet Mount Battie
Rd. near the campground, go left to the headquarters parking lot.

Remarks: *This is a 2½-mile hike over both gentle and somewhat steep
terrain. The true summit of Megunticook is another few tenths of a mile
beyond Ocean Lookout. It is wooded and offers no views of the bay or
mountains. The Camden Hills State Park campground and the Mount
Battie toll road are open from May 15 to November 1, during which period
a park entrance fee is charged. There are no advance reservations for
campsites except for organized groups. Mount Battie is a good place for
watching hawk migrations in September. The larger islands in Penobscot
Bay are wonderful places to explore. They are served by ferries from Lin-
colnville, Rockland, and Stonington. There is a bridge from Sargentville to
Deer Isle.*

84.

Maiden Cliff

Directions: **Camden, Maine. From Portland, take I-95 and
then U.S. 1 about 88 miles northeast to Camden. Turn
northwest (left) on Route 52; go 2.7 miles to a small, raised
parking lot on the right, just before the road begins to
border Megunticook Lake.**

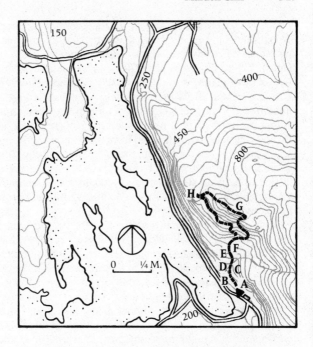

Ownership: **Maine Bureau of Parks and Recreation.**

Maiden Cliff looms an abrupt 800 feet above Megunticook Lake. The rocky trail passes through a variety of habitats from cool riparian woods to windswept ridgetop. The trail begins at an old logging road at the end of the parking area. Occasional red spots of paint mark the route; white blazes begin within a quarter of a mile. After you cross an old stone wall, the road becomes an eroded trough with stony soil profiles exposed in the sides (**A**). This is a place where "water bars" might have helped to control erosion. Water bars are made of stones or logs placed across the roadbed in such a manner that water running down the road is caught behind them and directed off to the side into uncompacted soil, where it can be absorbed.

A large boulder on the left (**B**) is almost completely covered by crustose lichens (see **#88**). About the only place where you can see the rock itself is in the crack. The unlayered, crystalline structure reveals that the rock is granitic, of igneous origin. Since virtually all the bedrock in the Camden area is metamorphosed sedimentary, it is unlikely that this boulder is derived from the cliffs above. Probably it was brought into this area by glacial ice (see **#85**).

At **C** is a lovely little cascading stream. Look for pinedrops here. Though they have no chlorophyll and therefore cannot make their own food, pinedrops are still classified as angiosperms (flowering plants), like roses and violets. Their sender rootlets penetrate the roots of other plants, absorbing sugars that are stored there.

At **D**, the bank on the opposite side of the stream is large, vertical outcrops supporting lush growths of dark-green mosses and light-gray-green-brown rock tripe. This leathery, foliose lichen has been used as a survival food, although from the texture and composition of it, it probably does little more than fill a hungry belly. The colors and textures are particularly beautiful on wet or foggy days, when the lichens have absorbed quantities of moisture: their colors brighten, and they become rather rubbery in texture. These wet days are also their growing days.

Beyond the creek crossing, on the left (**E**), small-crowned white pines are pocked with old pileated-woodpecker holes. With its long, stout beak, the pileated can expose insects deep within a tree. The small downy woodpecker tends to feed nearer the surface. A flicker will often feed on the ground. In this way, species occupying similar niches minimize competition from each other.

Notice the gorgeous, even, rather rigidly interwoven furrows of bark on the two big trees in the middle of the trail (**F**). This characteristic alone is enough to identify them as ashes. White ash is our upland forest ash. Its strong and resilient wood is highly prized for making tool handles, paddles, baseball bats, musical instruments, and numerous other items.

At the junction, go right via the Scenic Route. As you ascend, openings offer some glimpses over Megunticook Lake.

Stay left at the junction and walk through openings alternating with flat-canopied, wind-shorn woods. A stone "seat" tops the open ledges at **G**. Glacial striations and scour marks are still visible on some surfaces (see **#85**). Crack gardens are crowded with mosses, sedges, three-toed cinquefoil, and woody herbs. Behind the seat is a wide and shallow pit. Two kinds of chemical weathering are apparent here: (a) dissolution of the bedrock caused by the weak carbonic acid of rainwater; and (b) oxygenation of the iron in the wet, granitic stones, resulting in rust (see **#74**). On a typical Maine summer or fall day, you may be able to sit up here and watch the fog roll in from the bay to the east.

From the high point with the quartz intrusion, descend over broken ledges to Maiden Cliff (**H**). (You will pass the junction with the other Maiden Cliff trail at the large, flattened cairn: this will be your return route.) The big cross is erected near the spot where young Elenora French plunged to her death in 1864. The cliffs below were formed as the glaciers plucked tons of rock fragments from this "downstream" side of the mountain. Across from you are the more gentle "upstream" slopes of Bald and Ragged mountains.

Megunticook Lake spreads out below you. Notice that the headlands and islands seem to be arranged in lines. Indeed, they are the tops of bumpy ridges of more resistant rock dipping below and rising above the lake water level. The cove above which you parked is a flooded valley.

Climb back up to the junction at the flattened cairn and go right. This route traverses the wooded slopes below the ridge you followed on the ascent. The canopy is formed by trees with large crowns made possible by the fact that they are living on sloped terrain; here more of each tree's upper branches are exposed to sunlight than would be possible on flat terrain, where only the very top of the tree is exposed.

At the final trail junction, continue straight to return to the parking lot.

Remarks: *The walk is a 2½-mile loop. Trails are pretty rocky throughout; the rises are mainly gentle, with a few steep sections. For other hiking in this area, see Mount Megunticook (#83); Mount Battie, Bald Mountain, and Ragged Mountain are also nearby. Camping is available at Camden Hills State Park, May 15 to November 1; and at Warren Island State Park, May 30 to September 30. Camden is a lovely little town, well worth a ramble. The harbor is exquisite and is frequented by windjammers sailing the coastal waters during the summer.*

Acadia
National Park

Some 350 million years ago, beneath the salt waters of a shallow sea, masses of molten rock pushed their way into the layers of ancient rocks that formed the sea floor. Today, those invading rocks lie exposed on the surface of the earth—they are Mount Desert Island. Surrounded by the blue waters of Blue Hill and Frenchman bays, mantled with dark and bright forests, and dotted with fishing villages, its jewel is Acadia National Park. Here you can immerse yourself in rugged beauty, serenity, or storm, as well as expand your understanding of coastal boreal communities and life-styles.

Mount Desert Island has attracted people for thousands of years, from groups of Indians hunting swordfish long ago to millions of modern tourists from around the world. The name of the island comes from an early 1600s explorer and navigator, Samuel de Champlain. On his maps, he marked the island *L'Ile des Monts Deserts*—the island of the deserted or barren mountains, which we have Americanized to Mount Desert Island.

Contemporary with the exploratory expeditions of the 1600s came wave after wave of hopeful fishermen. Competition between the British and the French for control of the New England coast, expressed most dramatically during the French and Indian Wars, discouraged settlement of the area until 1759, when the French finally succumbed to the British near Quebec, allowing the new entrepreneurs to establish themselves in relative peace. Trees, furs, granite building stones and cobblestones, and boats joined the fish as exports from Maine. In the 1840s,

Mount Desert Island captured the eyes, hearts, and imagination of a growing number of artists and scientists. In the late 1800s, the high society of cities to the south discovered the beauty and tranquillity of Mount Desert Island, ushering in the era of the "million-dollar cottages." Today, Acadia National Park occupies about one-half of the island, attracting some 3 million visitors annually, mostly in July and August. Yet even at the height of the summer season, a short walk can take you to spots where the wildlife is plentiful and the visitors are few.

The establishment of Acadia as a park is intimately linked with the invention of the portable sawmill, a machine that opened vast, previously inaccessible woodlands to the lumber industry. In the early twentieth century, in order to protect at least a portion of coastal Maine for future generations, a number of families that owned land on Mount Desert Island, led by George B. Dorr and Charles Eliot, formed the Hancock County Trustees of Public Reservations. Their aim was "to acquire by devise, gift, or purchase, and to own, arrange, hold, maintain, or improve for public use lands in Hancock County, which by reason of scenic beauty, historical interest, sanitary advantage or other like reasons may become available for such purpose." Over the next 20 years the state-chartered trust acquired some 6,000 acres, primarily through George Dorr's devotion and energy, his generosity and that of others. In 1913, when the charter was challenged by a bill introduced in the legislature, Dorr decided the lands needed better protection. He went to Washington, D.C., and upon discovering Teddy Roosevelt's National Monument Act of 1906, set about to convince President Wilson to use his powers of presidential proclamation to accept the Mount Desert lands. In early July 1916, a month and a half before the National Park Service was established, the lands in the Hancock trust became Sieur de Monts National Monument, named for the captain of Champlain's ship. Three years later, the U.S. Congress voted the monument national park status, under the name of Lafayette National Park. In 1929, when the lands on Schoodic Point were donated, the park was given its current name, Acadia being a corruption of the French term La Cadie, or L'Acadie, used during the 1600s and 1700s to designate the coast from Cape Cod to Newfoundland.

Most of the park lies on Mount Desert Island, but even there it is not a continuous tract, because almost all the parkland was donated by fellow citizens, an unusual case in the national park system. Today, the wilder lands of the park form a delightful mosaic with the fishing villages and great estates.

Acadia National Park, some 35,000 acres in extent, includes a wide variety of environments tucked into a small area. Granitic rocks, many of them tinged a beautiful pink, form the heart of the park, rising in ancient, rounded peaks across the island and lying rough and ragged along the shoreline. Traces of the glaciers are visible in the saltwater fjord of Somes Sound, which nearly cuts the island in half, in perched boulders such as Bubble Rock, in the U-shapes of valleys such as that holding Jordan Pond, in boulder beaches now stranded over 250 feet above sea level on Day Mountain, and in the shapes of the mountains and islands. Mantling the slopes of the mountains are forests of dark, dense spruce and fir, and of maple, beech, oak, and birch. Southern and northern species meet as the curly forms of Dorr Mountain's pitch pines and Schoodic Head's jack pines vie with winds on summit ridges. Acadia Mountain supports an unusual stand of bear oak. The younger forests, which are repopulating the area burned by the big 1947 fire (see **#87**), offer glimpses into vegetational changes due to yet another of the island's environmental factors. Between the mountains lie valleys with clear, deep-blue lakes, communities of bogs and heaths, and small brooks, frequently impounded by beavers, one of the species whose numbers have risen dramatically as postfire growth has created appropriate habitat. The rocky coastline appears in many forms, rising in vertical cliffs on the Otter Point peninsula, sporting boulder and cobble beaches and the wave-built, stone seawall south of Manset (near Seawall Campground), while at Sand Beach it lies buried beneath a sandy beach and dunes. Elsewhere it spreads in broad storm-washed ledges, as at the tip of Schoodic Point and on the southern shore of Baker Island, or is dissected into myriad coves and inlets, chasms, and large bays. The moody Gulf of Maine, dotted with drowned-mountain-top ledges and islands, stretches southward. It meets the edge of the sky-dome overhead, sometimes enormous and exuberant with the distant, clear light of stars or sun, sometimes close with a soft fog through which forms loom suddenly and then disappear again.

The parklands lie in three major areas: on Mount Desert Island and adjacent smaller islands, on the Schoodic Peninsula, and on Isle au Haut. The visitors' center, the park headquarters, and the bulk of the park are on Mount Desert Island. For an excellent introduction to the area, stop at the visitors' center. There you can see the relief model of the island, and watch the park's introductory film for a preview of the variety of the outdoors environments. The visitors' center also has an Acadia National Park map of the island. The Park Loop Road, a 20-mile road that lies entirely within the boundaries of the park, includes such attractions as Ocean Drive, Thunder Hole, Gorham Mountain, Jordan Pond, and a spur road to the top of Cadillac Mountain. The four entrances to the Loop Rd. are Hull's

Cove, Sieur de Monts, Stanley Brook, and Cadillac Mountain. Note that the section from Sieur de Monts to Stanley Brook is one-way and that at three points Loop Rd. passes either under or over Routes 3 and 233 rather than intersecting with them. Use your map—the roads on Mount Desert Island are not laid out in grids and can be confusing. During the off-season (mid-October to mid-June) park maps, information, and publications are available at the park headquarters, about 3 miles west of Bar Harbor on Route 233.

Over 120 miles of trails provide fine hiking within the Acadian parklands. In the lowlands, the trails are gently sloped, with footing varying from almost smooth to quite rocky. Mountain trails, while short—Mount Desert Island's highest elevation, Cadillac Mountain, is 1,530 feet—tend to be rather steep and rough, especially where erosion has gullied them severely. In a few especially steep places, most notably on the Precipice Trail, iron bars have been embedded into the rock to aid hand and foot holds. Be aware that rocks may be loose and that sand, dirt, and moss on rocks may make them slippery. Two trails in the park, at Ship Harbor and Jordan Pond, have self-guided-nature-tour brochures keyed to markers along the route (see **#93**).

In addition to the hiking trails, there are some 40 miles of carriage paths in the park that are open for walking and other nonmotorized (wheelchairs excepted) adventures. Two loops have been specially graveled for bicycling (see **#89**). Maps and booklets about the trails and carriage paths are available at the visitor center (summer) or park headquarters (winter). The Philips map, printed by the chamber of commerce, is the best map of the hiking trails.

For those who would like to explore Acadia accompanied by a naturalist, from mid-June to early October the park naturalists offer an excellent selection of nature walks, mountain hikes, evening programs, and narrated boat excursions. Schedules are available at the visitor center, park campgrounds, and in a number of the free, local summer news sheets and pamphlets.

If you prefer to visit the park via automobile, the visitor center has cassette-tape tours available for rent or sale. You can also purchase an auto-tour brochure. Both will guide you on the Park Loop Rd. and Sargent Dr.

Another popular way to visit Acadia is by boat. There are a number of boat companies that offer tours of the bays and islands, some of them narrated by park naturalists. In addition, you are welcome to sail, paddle, row, or motor on your own in the bays, lakes, and salt marshes (Bass Harbor and Northeast Creek). Beware of sudden strong and gusty winds. Check on tides and tidal currents, especially in the Bass Harbor area. There are saltwater boat ramps in most of the towns and freshwater ones at Eagle Lake, Jordan Pond, Echo Lake, and Seal Cove Pond.

Picnic areas with tables are located at Thompson Island, Bear Brook, Seawall, and Pretty Marsh. There are shelters over some of the tables at Pretty Marsh. Fires are permitted only in the grills provided in the picnic areas and campgrounds.

Camping on Mount Desert Island is allowed only in designated areas, none of which are in the backcountry. There are two campgrounds inside the park. Blackwoods, 5 miles south of Bar Harbor on Route 3, is open year-round, and reservations may be made from March 15 through Labor Day. Seawall Campground, 4 miles south of Southwest Harbor on Route 102A, is open during the warmer months and operates on a first-come-first-served basis. Tents, campers, trailers, and recreational vehicles are accommodated (no hookups). There are group sites at both campgrounds and a number of walk-in sites (which are cheaper) at Seawall. Reservations for Blackwoods are accepted by mail only, and not before about April 20. For information and forms, write to Campground Reservations, Acadia National Park, P.O. Box 177, Bar Harbor, Maine 04609. In addition to the park campgrounds, there are about a dozen privately run campgrounds on Mount Desert Island. Many of them have recreational vehicle hookups. Listings are available at the park visitor center and from local chambers of commerce. In the villages, there are numerous motels, hotels, and rooming houses. Summer is a busy time on Mount Desert Island—make plans early; reservations are highly recommended.

Swimming areas with lifeguard services are located at Sand Beach (salt water) and Echo Lake (fresh water). Most of the other large lakes are public water supplies, and swimming is not allowed.

Saltwater fishing is permitted without any license. Freshwater fishing is under the auspices of the State of Maine and requires a license.

Pets must be either leashed or kept in check while in the park.

Winter activities include cross-country skiing, snowshoeing, winter hiking and walking, ice fishing, and snowmobiling (restricted to unplowed *roads*). Walkers should stay off the ski tracks. The winter season is from November to April. Snow cover is variable, so you should check on the conditions just prior to heading for Mount Desert Island.

Wildlife at Acadia can be elusive, but a little patience and persistence on your part may be well rewarded. Beavers are the most commonly sighted larger mammals. Look for them at dusk at Fresh Meadow, which is north of Sieur de Monts Springs, on the Jesup Trail, and at many of the marshy ponds in the Witch Hole Pond area. Intertidal organisms crowd all the shores. Some of the more accessible tide pools are on the end of Otter Point, along the Seawall picnic area, and at Wonderland.

Bird species from the north and the south, from the sea and the land, can be seen on Mount Desert Island during the course of the year. Look for bald eagles in the air or in tall evergreens near the water in the Somesville Library area, especially when the alewives are running (May and June); they are also frequently seen on Frenchman Bay Co. and Island Queen boat cruises (summer). Woodcocks display in the northern edge of Fresh Meadow and other open areas (April/early May). Non-breeding loons often can be seen off the northwestern end of the Blagden Preserve (spring through fall). A couple of likely spots to view raven acrobatics are from the top of Beech Cliffs and Cadillac ridges when there are strong up-drafts.

A wide variety of migrants also appear on Mount Desert Island, spread out over some 8 months of the year. Look for shorebirds feeding during low tide at the Bar Harbor Bar, Wonderland, and the Thompson Island picnic area (May and mid-July through September). Songbirds are most active in the early morning and late afternoon; watch at Sieur de Monts, Wonderland/Ship Harbor, and the field and forest areas at (**I**) on the Shore Trail map (see **#95**) (May and late August/early September). Hawks travel and hunt by day and can often be spotted from the Sunset Parking Area on Cadillac Mountain and from Beech Mountain (April/May and September/October). Look for nighthawks either day or evening out on Cape Rd. in Seal Cove, near the Tremont Public Landing (August/early September). Harlequin ducks gather off Isle au Haut (March/early April), so keep an eye out for them if you are in those waters.

Local plants are grown in the Acadia Wild Gardens at Sieur de Monts Spring. They are planted in the kinds of associations in which you may find them in the park, and they are labeled. Also at this location is the Abbe Museum, which houses displays of Indian artifacts and cultural history.

Isle au Haut, as its name implies, is a high island. Rising well above its neighbors in Blue Hill and Penobscot bays, it has been a landmark and an inspiration for many generations of explorers, residents, and visitors. It is a charming place to sample island communities and a good place to watch birds on spring and fall migrations. Although it is only 15 miles southwest of Mount Desert Island, access to Isle au Haut is via ferry from Stonington, at the tip of Deer Isle, a good 1½-hour drive from Bar Harbor. The summer ferry schedule makes single-day visits to Isle au Haut possible, but in winter boats no longer run twice a day. A network of trails and a loop road, primarily dirt, invite exploration of rocky headlands, coves, boreal forests, swampy lands, and small mountains. There are six lean-to shelters near Duck Harbor, for summer-season overnight use. Since these are the only backpacking campsites in Acadia National Park, they are in high demand. Reservations may be filled during the first day or two they are accepted, but there are usually a number of last-minute cancellations during the season. Contact the park in February or March to find out when the deadline will be. Ask also for the map brochure about Isle au Haut.

Schoodic Point, approximately a 50-mile drive east of Bar Harbor, is a rugged peninsula on the far side of Frenchman Bay. It is skirted by a one-way road. Among its more prominent features are the Raven's Nest cliffs, large basaltic dikes, an impressive storm "beach," and one of the few stands of jack pine in this part of Maine. It is an excellent area for watching surf during southeast storms and also a fine place to look for wintering sea ducks. A number of short trails provide access to the high point of Schoodic Head, rising 440 feet. There are no camping facilities in this section of Acadia National Park.

Remarks: *For information about Acadia, write to: Superintendent, Acadia National Park, Bar Harbor, Maine 04609: or telephone (207) 288-3338. See the* **Bibliography** *for useful books about Acadia.*

The Natural History Museum at College of the Atlantic is a good place to explore various elements of natural history, particularly marine mammals, through a unique program combining the summer museum and a number of outreach projects. A 25-foot minke-whale skeleton arches across the main hall, where superb taxidermy, living, and graphic exhibits explain biologies and ecologies of seabirds, plants, and mammals of Mount Desert Island and the Gulf of Maine. The museum is open from mid-June through Labor Day, and there is an admission fee.

The Oceanarium, on the Clark Point Rd. in Southwest Harbor, features intertidal and sea creatures, including a touch tank where you may watch and handle the organisms. There is also a room devoted to lobsters and lobster fishing. The Oceanarium is open during the summer tourist season, and an admission fee is charged.

The Gilley Museum, on Herrick Rd. in Southwest Harbor, houses a collection of intricate, hand-carved and hand-painted, life-size models of Mount Desert Island birds. Days and hours vary through the year. During the summer tourist season, the museum is open daily except Mondays. In spring and fall, it is open Friday through Sunday, and from January to March, it is open by appointment only. For further information, telephone (207) 244-7555.

Birdsacre Sanctuary and the Stanwood Homestead Museum, on Route 3 just south of the strip in Ellsworth (as you head up the hill heading toward Mount Desert Island), offer a woodland sanctuary with trails, ponds, and a bird rehabilitation center, as well as the furnished museum house of ornithologist Cordelia J. Stanwood. The museum is open from mid-June to mid-October; the sanctuary is open year-round. Telephone (207) 667-8460 for information.

The Bass Harbor Head, Baker Island, Egg Rock, and Bear Island lights are beautiful examples of Maine lighthouses. Although none of them is open to the public, you can drive to the one on Bass Harbor Head, and you will hike past the one on Baker Island if you go on the Baker Island naturalist cruise and the weather permits landing on the island.

Also highly recommended are the whale and seabird cruises aboard the Island Queen, *run by Maine Whalewatch from the main dock in Northeast Harbor. The habits of wildlife are variable, but Capt. Bob Bowman is very good at finding whatever animals are around. In addition, he and his crew will discuss current research and understandings concerning the biologies and ecologies of the creatures you encounter. Trips are run June through September. A fee is charged.*

85.

Jordan Pond and
Penobscot Mountain

Directions: **Mount Desert Island, Maine. From Bangor, take U.S. 1A southeast about 27 miles to Ellsworth. Go east about 1 mile on U.S. 1, then turn south (right) onto Route 3. Go about 9 miles, crossing the causeway onto Mount Desert Island, and bear left beyond the Thompson Island picnic area, staying on Route 3. The national park visitors' center is at the Hull's Cove entrance to the park, about 8 miles farther along Route 3; turn right and then right again.**

To reach Jordan Pond and Penobscot Mountain, turn right off Route 3 into the Hull's Cove entrance and follow signs for the Park Loop Rd. In 3 miles, bear right toward Jordan Pond House Park in the Jordan Pond parking area, 1.5 miles beyond the Bubble Rock pulloff and 0.1 mile before the Jordan Pond House.

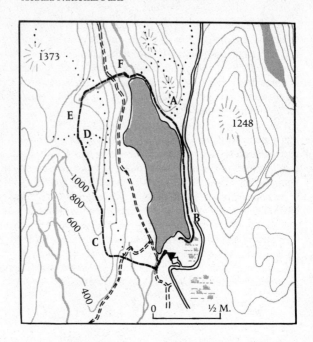

Ownership: **Acadia National Park, National Park Service.**

This area is rich in geological evidence of the power of the glaciers that covered the region 10,000 to 15,000 years ago. The trailhead is at the Penobscot Mountain parking lot, just north of the Jordan Pond House on the two-way section of Park Loop Rd. At the top of the gravel boat ramp, face the pond: just below you, on your right, is a woods trail. Follow it to the shore of Jordan Pond and then head around the lake in a counterclockwise direction, along the eastern side. The lake-edge boulders seem piled almost deliberately. In winter, when Jordan Pond is covered with ice, freezing and thawing around the edges causes expansion of the icy layer. Boulders at the perimeter of the ice slowly get pushed up on shore.

The two Bubble Mountains rise at the north end of the lake. These mountains partially blocked the movement of the glacier, making its flow more intense around them. The faster-moving ice carved the striking U-shaped valleys you now see flanking the mountains, and the steep banks and basin of Jordan Pond as well.

Since most bedrock is riddled with cracks, glaciers were able to pluck off many chunks and carry them southward. When the glaciers "retreated," they did *not* go backward, they simply melted faster than they were advancing. They left their rock loads strewn across the countryside, sometimes perched in odd positions. A rather ominous erratic (**A**), a "foreign" boulder, its crystals different in size and composition from Mount Desert Island bedrocks, perches on the east side of the South Bubble.

Just before the end of the lake, a talus slope (**B**) (where boulders have fallen from the cliffs above) meets the shore. The large number of unbruised trees, the heavy cover of lichen (see **#88**) on the rocks, and the absence of rocks with newly broken edges indicate little recent activity of this talus. Compare it with the very active slope on Park Loop Rd. above Jordan Pond.

As you round the end of the lake, find Penobscot Mountain Trail (0.9 mile). A finger of the 1947 fire (see **#87**) reached the slope you ascend here. Look for the limits of the fire's reach as you move back into the older forest. The trail crosses the stream twice just below a beautiful double-arched stone carriage-path bridge (see **#89**). Cross the carriage path and follow Deer Brook Trail. The lower portion is an excellent example of what happens when trails follow steep slopes. Footfalls compact the soil, which makes the trail the easiest place for runoff water to flow. Rather than seeping in, it rushes straight down the slope, picking up particles and eroding the soil as it goes.

At the four-corners, follow Sargent Mountain Pond Trail. After the steep bank beyond the second creek crossing, the trail levels out. Look here for glacial striations on the surface of a flat rock in the trail (**C**). The striations appear as shallow scratches all running in the same direction, similar to rake scratches. They were made by rocks dragged across the surface of the bedrock by the glacier.

Follow Penobscot Mountain 0.1 mile to the summit (**D**). If the sunlight is at the proper angle, you should be able to find remnants of glacial polish on the bare ridges. Sand and gravel carried by the glaciers and the sheer weight of the ice itself abraded and metamorphosed the bedrock surface to a near-mirror smoothness, slowly pitted and eroded since then. Numerous erratics of strange and wonderful compositions (curly-banded schists and gneiss, chaotic-looking breccias, Lucerne granite with large pink and gray crystals) dot the open ridges as well.

Imagine how Mount Desert Island might have looked 10,000 or 20,000 years ago when the ice melted away—all former vegetation uprooted, rocks and soil by the ton dumped into salty waters. Crustose lichens, able to live on bare rock surfaces, were probably the first plant inhabitants to arrive after the glaciers melted. Soil began to form: tiny dissolved particles released from the bedrock by standing water and lichen acids; particles wedged loose from cracks by the action of frost (frost wedging); dust blown in from elsewhere. These materials accumulated in low places such as cracks and valleys. Today crack gardens support moss and three-toed cinquefoil (**E**). These early plants become part of the soil-making process, adding organic material and root-wedged rock bits. The larger and more fertile the pockets of soil grow, the larger and more demanding are the plants they can support. Each pocket on Penobscot Mountain's ridge illustrates this process in miniature, beginning at the edge of the soil and proceeding to the center. Sheep laurel, juniper, blueberries, and huckleberries are the dominant ground cover. A small pond to the right of the trail supports cotton grass and other moisture-needing species. Just beyond a shallow, gorgelike depression, there is a lucious patch of mountain cranberry.

Notice the growth form of the spruces on the exposed ridge—very long low branches, short and stubby upper ones. Wind breaks vegetation and also dehydrates it. The trees here can maintain a large photosynthetic area only in their lower, better protected portions. As the trail enters more heavily wooded ground, look to the right for a clump of flat-bottomed northern white-cedars. These are arborvitae: the tree-of-life. Deer browse here in winter to the highest levels they can reach.

The trail now makes a sharp left bend and drops over the side of the ridge. Cliffs hold hanging gardens. Seeps, or small springs, provide homes for sphagnum and other mosses.

Cross the carriage path; after the footbridge turn right. The old mixed forest in the cool, protected stream canyon is especially beautiful in late-afternoon shafts of sunlight. Cross Jordan Stream and follow the carriage path around to the left toward Bar Harbor. You are now walking on top of a moraine (**F**), a heap of rocks of all sizes left by the last of the melting glaciers (see **Long Island, Cape Cod, and the Islands** and **#99**). It acts as a dam across the valley, making Jordan Pond a lake instead of a stream.

At the end of the lake, pick up the east-shore trail on the right. Notice the cement dam. It keeps Jordan Stream from eroding the lip of the moraine and allows human control of the water level in the lake, which is the public water supply for Seal Harbor.

Shoreline woodlands between the Jordan Pond House and the lake have succumbed to visitation and the cultural tradition of maintaining a picturesque, manicured view. Follow the shore (Pemetic and Bubbles direction) to the gravel boat launch below the Penobscot Mountain parking lot. Imagine this valley with ice a mile thick slowly, inexorably flowing southward.

Remarks: *This 4-mile hike passes over wet and gentle terrain with some rocky, steep places.*

86

Sand Beach and
Great Head

Directions: Mount Desert Island, Maine. Follow directions for #85 to Hull's Cove entrance. Enter the park and follow the signs for Park Loop Rd. and Ocean Dr., turning left onto the Loop Rd. after 3 miles. Continue about 6 miles, then park at the Sand Beach lot, on the one-way section (often called Ocean Dr.) of Park Loop Rd. (In winter, when the inland park roads are closed, pass the Hull's Cove entrance and stay on Route 3 through Bar Harbor, then bear left onto Schooner Head Rd. Go 3 miles and turn right at the stop sign and then left onto the one-way section of Park Loop Rd. Go about 0.3 mile to the Sand Beach parking lot.)

Ownership: Acadia National Park, National Park Service.

Acadia features one of the few sandy beaches in eastern Maine and one of the highest headlands along the entire Atlantic seaboard. Wandering across Sand Beach and over Great Head, one passes through the ancient history of Mount Desert Island, written in rock and sand and in plantlife.

From the parking lot, walk down the pathway and stairs to the beach (**A**). Sand Beach has one of the highest volumes of sand per area of beach in eastern Maine. Pick up a handful of sand and examine it up close, with a magnifying lens if you have one. It is unusual in two ways: most of it is apparently of bedrock rather than glacial-till origin (see **#78** and **#79**), and some 30 to 40 percent is from shell and other carbonate structures. These sources are dominant in tropical areas but generally play a lesser role in Maine. Look for fragments of green-sea-urchin spines, iridescent blue mussel shells, and pink potassium feldspar crystals, these last from the granitic bedrock of Mount Desert Island.

Of the factors that must combine to create a beach, three major contributors are a relatively low-angle shore; a source of beach material such as sand, gravel, or boulders; and a mode of transport for the materials, that is, waves and currents. Higher-energy waves can pile larger fragments onto steeper beaches. Compare Sand Beach with the boulder beach at Monument Cove, a mile farther down the shore (see **#95**). Monument Cove may not have sand because there is no source of supply, or because the waves and currents are not of the appropriate configuration to bring it there.

The dunes at the back of the beach are born from the union of the beach and the winds. They are very fragile. Please do not walk on them. Grain by grain they grow and shift, protecting the area behind them from the lashing of storms. But dunes are not totally impregnable, and there are gaps where waves from big storms have breached the sandy barrier.

Notice that the brackish pond behind the dunes (**B**) is slightly higher than sea level. At times, there is no apparent outlet to the pond; however, water does escape through the beach sand, and you may see it seeping in tiny rivulets over the lower sands at ebb tide. At other times, a stream flows across the eastern end of the beach. The variation is due to the fact that the profile of a beach changes from season to season. During the warmer months, when storms are smaller and waves have less energy, sand accumulates on a beach, building a high, broad *berm*—the relatively level area above the mean high-tide line—which at Sand Beach frequently closes the pond outlet. In winter, storm waves have such high energy that they carry away from the beach more sand than they bring, eroding the

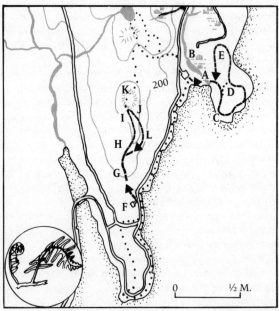

Inset: Polypody fern

beach into a steep profile and often cutting into the seaward face of the dunes. The Sand Beach pond frequently has an outlet to the sea during these months.

Examine the ledges at the east end of the beach (**C**). This area is part of the *shatter zone,* an area in which fragments of old rocks, broken by an upwelling of molten minerals hundreds of millions of years ago, fell into the melt and became fused into it as it solidified. Look for breccias, rock composed of varied-sized chunks of ancient sedimentary rock, that are embedded in a matrix of granitic material.

At the southeast edge of the pond is a flagstone stairway that begins Great Head Trail. Go right at the top of the steps, past staghorn sumac with its fuzzy branches, through a grove of aspen, and up a steep series of ledges to the top of the ridge. Follow the trail southward. Old Soaker, another part of the shatter zone, lies waiting off the southern end of the point. In 1911, the schooner *Tay* was wrecked against it, casting debris to the nearby shores. Part of her keel and ribs still lie embedded in Sand Beach and are sometimes exposed by the shifting sands.

As you round the point, look for patches of orange wall lichen (see **#88**). Just beyond, the main trail goes up to the left on a rock. A side trail goes down to the left through a notch. Follow this trail to the "amphitheater" below (**D**). Large patches of ancient rock seem to ooze within the darker young granites. A collection of colorful oxides, created by chemical weathering decorate the rock surfaces. Hard, gray diorite caps the outcrop above, holding the lid on the formation, as it is less easily eroded than the rocks below.

Geologists have found evidence that the Mount Desert Island area was a sea floor at least three times, accumulating sediments that under their sheer weight turned into rock (see **#74**). After each period of sedimentation, forces within the earth, associated with the movements of tectonic plates of the earth's crust (see **#83**), raised the sea floor above the level of the water. There rains, winds, and waves proceeded to erode most of it away again (see **#74**). Beneath the third series of layers, a large chamber of magma pushed its way upward, metamorphosing (changing by heat and pressure) some of the older rocks. Others were fractured and mixed into the molten minerals, squeezing into cracks between layers of the older rocks. The entire mass rose above the sea some 350 million years ago, a folded set of sedimentary and metamorphic mountains with a hardened core of granitic rocks, perhaps as tall as the Rockies are today. Since then water, frost, and wind have been at work chipping away thousands of feet of rock. More recently, glacial sculptors took their turn (see **#85**). Today, we walk on the granitic hearts of the ancient mountains.

Climb back up to the main trail and continue to the summit of the headland (**E**). Notice how the pockets of vegetation vary: patches of bayberry (see **#97**), meadowsweet, blueberries, goldenrods, asters, and alder predominate in the wetter areas; taller vegetation in the sheltered spots with thicker soil. The ruins at the summit are from a "tea porch" where, decades ago, one might have sat under cover and enjoyed scanning the view from Egg Rock Light over to Schoodic Head, up to the Porcupine Islands, and along Champlain and Gorham's ridges to Otter Point and Baker Island.

Leaving the summit, head inland through predominantly spruce and birch forest, where the trail is badly eroded. Continue straight (right) past the arrow sign to Sand Beach, through dense spruce woods and into a lovely, tall grove of big-toothed aspen. Watch the leaves as they flip back and forth in a breeze. Pick up a leaf and feel its stem right at the base of the leaf blade. It is flattened sideways, rather than round, allowing the stem to bend readily sideways but not very easily up and down. This structural feature permits the characteristic "tremble" of both big-toothed and quaking aspen leaves.

At the T junction, go left on the old gravel road, where larger trees survived Mount Desert Island's big 1947 fire (see **#87**). Stay on the gravel (left) at the fork. At the millstone, descend the steps to Sand Beach and descend again to Sand Beach where the sands shift on the shores in dunes and sand castles. Come again in midwinter, when stepping off the stairs from the parking lot you are likely to find yourself on "Boulder Beach," winter storms having carried offshore the sand that covered Sand Beach's base of boulders.

Remarks: *This is a 2-mile hike across a sandy beach and on rocky trails that include a few steep sections where you may need to use your hands a bit. The nearby Precipice Trail is a* steep *but wonderful climb to the top of Champlain Mountain. Vertical sections have iron rungs and ladders attached into the rock so they may be scaled by hikers without ropes or other mountain-climbing gear. The trailhead is on the one-way section of the Park Loop Rd., about 1¾ miles after the Sieur de Monts Exit. There is also access to the summit via the north ridge of the mountain and via the Bowl or Gorham Mountain.*

87.

Gorham Mountain

Directions: **Mount Desert Island, Maine. Follow directions for #85 to the Hull's Cove entrance. Enter the park, and follow the signs for Park Loop Rd. and Ocean Dr., turning** left onto the Loop Rd. after about 3 miles. Continue about 8 miles more; 0.2 to 0.3 mile after Thunder Hole, park at the Gorham Mountain lot on the one-way section of Park Loop Rd. (In winter, go past the Hull's Cove entrance and stay on Route 3 through Bar Harbor, then bear left onto Schooner Head Rd. Go 3 miles and, at the stop sign, go right to the one-way section of Park Loop Rd., then left to Gorham parking.)

Ownership: Acadia National Park, National Park Service.

This site offers a delightful chance to walk from the edge of the sea to the peak of a mountain and to witness the process of forest succession following a fire.

Enter tall forest at the end of the parking lot opposite the entrance (**F**; this site is keyed to map, p. 330). Notice the humus underfoot in the cool, shadowy depths. These spruce-fir woods are about 70 to 100 years old, having escaped the path of the 1947 fire. The many mosses and lichens here are among the species that can tolerate the cool, shadowy, and acidic conditions that prevail beneath this thick, coniferous canopy. Notice that there are openings in the canopy: a branch gone here, a tree fallen there. If you look carefully, you may discover a pile of "sawdust" at the base of a tree. The carpenter ants that have dropped it are undermining the tree's physical strength by destroying the dead rings of wood inside it. The ants are but one of the factors that help produce openings for other organisms in the forest. Wind is another factor, as is the life-span of the trees themselves (see **#97**).

Return to the parking lot and head up the Gorham Mountain trail. The area in which you now stand was burned in the big Mount Desert Island fire of 1947. Look for an open area dotted with fairly large, older pitch pines (3 needles per bundle), which survived the flames (**G**). It is easy to assume that what is growing adjacent to a burned area (i.e., the spruce-fir forest below) also grew on the burned land, and sometimes that is correct, but the older-than-1947 pitch pines on these ledges indicate a different story here.

At the junction with the Cadillac Cliffs trail, stay on the main trail to Gorham's summit. As you travel higher and higher, look behind you from some of the rocky outcroppings. You should be able to catch sight of the fire line: tall dark-green trees meeting shorter bright-green (or in winter, gray) trees.

The 1947 fire got started in or near a dump north of the Acadia National Park Visitor Center. It was a difficult fire to fight because it would smolder underground and pop up again unexpectedly after it was thought to be out. It began after three months of remarkably dry weather, as well as after years of active fire suppression had allowed quantities of fuel materials to accumulate as the aging forests dropped needle upon branch upon trunk. One day, gusty winds whipped the smoldering Hull's Cove fire into flames and chased them for 9 days down the island, rushing along the ground and through the crowns of the trees, until they were blown out to sea as the winds shifted or curled around the southern shores of Mount Desert Island.

People were concerned that the naked soils would be washed away unless they were speedily replanted. By the time the paper-work was done, however, nature had taken care of it herself, and that is what you see here. There are a great number and variety of seeds on any forest floor, just waiting for an opening, a chance to germinate and grow, and the 1947 fire created such an opportunity. In addition, the seeds of other species have been blown or otherwise carried in. The diversity of plant species here (**H**) includes quaking and big-toothed aspen, gray and white birch, red and white spruce, balsam, fir, huckleberry, red oak, pitch and white pines, sweet fern, cherries, blueberries, sheep laurel, and asters.

As you continue, notice large sections of rotting trunk, sawed into lengths (**I**). The fire moved so quickly that, though it destroyed leaves and buds, the wood inside the trunks was left unscathed. On many private lands, the dead trees were sawed into lumber and sold. The trunks here may have been cut for safety and/or aesthetic rea-sons. They are now on their way to becoming soil. As new vegeta-tion grows, succession will continue. Some biologists predict that after herbs and shrubs recolonize the area, deciduous trees will fol-low, and then finally coniferous species will germinate in the shade of the pioneer trees and become the dominant forest. Here, though, all these groups are growing together at the same time, suggesting a different picture. Research in the 1947 burn area indicates that, though the spruces and firs are only one-half to three-quarters as tall as the aspen and birch with which they are growing, they are all roughly the same age: The conifers must have seeded and sprung up without waiting for the shade of deciduous trees. As biologists investigate the dynamics of such communities, new evidence often leads to new interpretations and new models of ecology (see **#76**).

As you reach Gorham's false summit (**J**), a short, steep section opens onto a broad granite ledge, with a wonderful view of Sand Beach edging Newport Cove, and Otter Point stretching out toward Baker Island.

From the summit itself (**K**), almost all you can see of Mount Desert Island was in the path of the 1947 fire. Conflagrations burn-ing tens of thousands of acres are unusual here, with small fires that burn only a few trees or acres being more common. There are, of course, many varieties of fire. The one in 1947 burned 17,000 acres in 9 days, traveling through the crowns and on the ground, killing most of the vegetation. A fire in Yosemite National Park in the mid-1970's, on the other hand, took 2 months to move across 3,000 acres, traveling almost exclusively on the ground and leaving most of the larger trees, and a few of the smaller ones, alive.

Over the last two or three decades, research on the roles fire plays as part of environments has led to increased use of fire as a management tool: to reduce fuel levels in forests and thereby reduce the chance of high-intensity fires; to encourage the reproduction of certain species that, like pitch pines and jack pines, seem to germinate better after fire; to return nutrients to the soil at a faster rate; to maintain meadows and blueberry fields free of tree growth; to increase the nutritional value of forage for deer; to produce or maintain habitat for specifically desired species.

From the summit, return to Gorham Mountain parking, either (1) by the way you came up, (2) by descending the north ridge and looping down past the Bowl to the Park Loop Rd. and the Shore Trail, or (3) by following the Cadillac Cliffs Trail, which you passed on the way up (this way is more rugged than the ridge trail but well worth walking).

Return along the ridge to the upper Cadillac Cliffs junction. Descend the first bit of the cliffs trail (being careful not to skid on the sand and dirt on the rocks) and enter the shadowy abode of the goosefoot or striped maple. This is commonly an understory tree, but it frequents these cool mountainside ledges as well.

An iron rung and some cleverly built stairs lead down a talus slope to the base of the cliffs. These boulders and chunks of rock have broken off from the cliffs above and fallen here. Continue past delicate hanging gardens, dripping (when it's not too dry) mossy seeps, and rock polypody ferns in nooks and crannies. The large, overhung "cranny" (**L**) is an old sea cave, and the rounded boulder that is wedged in the back was bounced smooth by waves, like those on the beach at Monument Cove (see **#95**). Not only did the glaciers remove and restore waters to the oceans, but they also weighted and unweighted the land, pressing it down and then allowing it to rebound (see **Portland North**). This former shore cave is now over 200 feet above sea level.

Cross a pile of large boulders just before rejoining the main trail to return to the parking area.

Remarks: *This is a 2-mile walk over moderately steep terrain, with some scrambling here and there. It is a fine hike for those who would like to climb a small mountain. The trailhead for hiking Beehive Mountain and the Bowl is opposite the entrance to Sand Beach parking.*

88.

Dorr Mountain

Directions: **Mount Desert Island, Maine. Follow directions
for #85. Continue on Route 3 past the Hull's Cove entrance and through Bar Harbor. About 0.4 mile beyond the
Jackson Laboratory, turn right at the Sieur de Monts entrance. Go left at the stop sign, and park in the Sieur de
Monts lot.**

Ownership: **Acadia National Park, National Park Service.**

The trails around the base and on the slopes of Dorr Mountain
provide some vigorous and highly scenic hiking as they pass through
a variety of different habitats: young deciduous woods, glaciated
pond, beaver marshes, cascading stream, open mountaintop, hemlock woods, and older mixed forest. This diversity suggests that the
environment is always in the process of changing, its forests and
geological features slowly evolving. Both the beauty of Dorr Mountain and the power of this changing force are impressive.

The Tarn Trail begins at a wooden footbridge behind the nature
center and just before the Abbé Museum entrance. As you enter the
forest, notice how spindly most of the trees are (**A**). The entire area
of this hike was in the path of Mount Desert Island's fire of 1947
(see **#87**). The young forest of beech, maple, aspen, oak, and birch
is punctuated by large, older hemlocks and pines that survived the
flames. These woods are particularly special in wintertime, when the
dead beech leaves, many of which cling to their branches all winter
long, rattle in the wind.

The Tarn pond (**B**) lies in a depression left behind when the
continental glaciers melted. Like other ponds and lakes, the Tarn
gradually accumulates silt brought by mountainside streams. It is
shallow and fertile enough from these sediments that water lilies and
pond lilies can grow all across it. As it ages, it may become a meadow
or perhaps a bog, depending on many factors, including the amount
of sedimentation, the acidity of the water, and the flow of the water
(see **#56**).

Follow the Tarn's shoreline trail and look for Labrador tea, meadowsweet, and sheep laurel. Sweet gale, a relative of the bayberry
used in making candles and soap (see **#97**), also grows here. Rub
your fingers on the smooth, gray-green leaves and note the sweet,

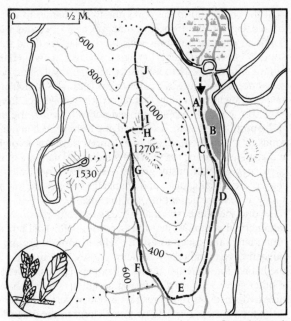

Inset: Sweet gale

resinous odor. All of these plants are able to tolerate a certain amount of sogginess around their roots. Where the trail winds through the talus slope (**C**), a field of rocks broken and fallen from the cliffs above, there are plants that prefer predominantly dry conditions. Rock gardens of polypody fern and crustose lichens of many colors cling to the boulders. The lichens, each a combination of an alga and a fungus, are the first plants to colonize bare rock surfaces. The alga photosynthesizes; the fungus provides structure and absorbs the moisture and dissolved nutrients needed for photosynthesis. This is an example of symbiosis, two organisms living together. While some botanists call it a parasitic symbiosis because the fungal component can never live by itself, other botanists interpret the association as a mutualistic symbiosis because both partners perform necessary functions in the lichen organism. As a result, lichens can often live under conditions that neither the alga or the fungus could survive alone. The lichen grows when it is wet and remains dormant when it dries out. As the pockets on the talus rocks gradually fill with soil, larger plants will be able to find a home here; eventually, if the talus is not bombarded too frequently by boulders, it may become a steep-sloped forest.

At the south end of the pond, the trail is harder to find. Follow the red tags on the trees; the trail will again become well worn. Continue past the junctions with the Ladder Trail and the trail to Route 3 parking lot. Look for signs of beaver activity (**D**): pointed stumps and sticks with tooth marks, a lodge, small dams, ponds that were once forests, and drag paths (see **#102**). This stretch of bottomland is changing so rapidly that differences can be seen from season to season. Look for recently formed ponds in which the trees, part of the postfire regrowth, are now dying or have recently died; older ponds in which the trees are in advanced stages of decomposition; and abandoned ponds in which the lodge and dam are in disrepair, often covered with bushy growth (see **#89**). The activities of the beavers are affecting plant and animal life throughout this area, and it may look very different in years to come.

Beyond the ponds, the trail curves westward, rises onto a higher flatland, and continues past the Dorr Mountain Trail junction. The young birch-and-aspen forest (**E**), with its tangled ground cover of blueberry, sheep laurel, sweet fern, grasses, and bracken fern, is a fine habitat for white-tailed deer. Their populations, as well as those of other species attracted to young deciduous growth, have greatly increased since the 1947 fire. This is due in part to the accessibility of the food—the leaves and twigs are closer to the ground—and in part to postfire growth producing very high quality forage for a number of years.

From the upland, the trail drops down to Canyon Brook, meeting it where the water slithers over large granite slabs edged with cedars. Follow the Murray Young Trail upstream (**F**). A creek-canyon forest clings to the steep banks, while the brook bounces and cascades toward the sea carrying bits of the mountain with it and gradually moving its headwaters upstream. Notice that many of the trees have a curve at the base, from being bent downslope by winter snows early in life.

As the trail reaches the glacially plucked "amphitheater" just below the notch (**G**), you'll find more evidence of beaver dams. Look carefully for the red arrows on the west (Cadillac) side of the ponds. Cross the creek on the old beaver dam, then follow the two red tags on trees. Beyond that, the trail follows the east side of the creek and then winds up at the center to the notch. Be sure to turn around and catch the magnificent views out to the Cranberry Islands.

The notch (**H**) lies between cliffs that clearly show the blocky pattern into which granite fractures as it cools, is stressed by tectonic shiftings inside the earth (see **#83**), or is released from the pressure of rocks above it when these rocks erode (see **#92**). The cracks are widened today as water freezes and expands in them, breaking off bits of crystals. The birch and oak here appear stunted due to the strong winds that blow through the gap. At the junction in the notch, look for small sections of glacial polish (very smooth surface) and glacial striations (very shallow, north-to-south-oriented scratches) on newly exposed surfaces of rock (see **#85**). It may seem barren here today, but imagine what it might have been like 10 or 20 thousand years ago when the glaciers had just melted. From the summit you can enjoy a 360-degree view of Mount Desert Island.

Descend toward the Park Loop Rd. and Kebo Mountain, following the large cairns down the north ridge (**I**). The trail passes through islands of pitch pines (three needles per bundle), which can tolerate infertile soils and high winds in most creative ways. Morphologically—that is, in the physical characteristics they exhibit—plants are very plastic or flexible, more so than most animals. This quality can be vital, given a plant's lack of mobility once rooted.

In the young deciduous forest farther down, note the very large sections of trunk lying on the ground—remains of an older spruce forest killed but not consumed by the fire (**J**).

Cross a seepy creek and go right at the trail junction. Recross the creek and descend into hemlocks, which thrive in such cool places as canyons and northern mountain slopes. Meet Hemlock Rd. and head to the right. From here it is a 5- to 10-minute walk back to Sieur de Monts Spring, through a band of older hemlock, sugar maple, and birch and through younger mixed forest.

Remarks: *This hike is a 5-mile loop on terrain varying from flat and smooth to steep and rugged. The Acadia Wild Gardens, displaying local plants in the groupings you might find in the wild, the nature center (housing natural history displays and an information desk), and the Abbé Museum (with displays about Maine Indians) are all located near the Dorr Mountain trailhead at Sieur de Monts Spring. The trailhead for Huguenot Head (and Champlain Mountain) is on Route 3, just south of the Sieur de Monts entrance, on the left. The north ridge trail on Champlain Mountain leaves to the right from the Park Loop Rd., beyond the Bear Brook picnic area and beaver ponds. Kebo Mountain is accessible via the Hemlock Rd. and Trail from Sieur de Monts Spring and from a trailhead on the Park Loop Rd. about half a mile northwest of the Kebo Rd. There is a trail to the top of Cadillac Mountain from Blackwoods Campground.*

89.

Witch Hole Pond
Carriage Path

Directions: **Mount Desert Island, Maine. Follow directions for #85. Enter the park at Hull's Cove; park in the visitors' center lot, on the right just past the entrance.**

Ownership: **Acadia National Park, National Park Service.**

The Witch Hole Pond Carriage Path, solid enough to support bicycles and wheelchairs (attendant advisable), offers easy access to the world of beavers (see **#102**). The beaver's ecological role includes eating bark and aquatic vegetation, perhaps being eaten by a coyote or an otter, creating ponds out of forests or carriage paths, and making a catch basin that may become a pocket of soil. The Witch Hole Pond Trail is an invitation to explore these and other aspects of beaver life-style.

Begin at the gravel trail at the far end of the parking lot. Note the wide variety of plant species. The Mount Desert Island fire of 1947 (see **#87**), which burned most of the Witch Hole Pond area, was a major force involved in the establishment of these species. Beavers are among the animals that, finding favorable habitat in the new, young forests, have greatly increased in numbers. Evidence of their activities abounds on the eastern part of Mount Desert Island.

Tucked in among the dense ground-cover growth, especially after warm rains, you may find numerous mushrooms, including some large members of the *Boletus* genus (look for pores rather than gills on the under surface of the cap). Many of the mushrooms have holes or depressions where they have been nibbled by woodland creatures. While the deer, squirrels, and mice that feed on them rarely stay around long enough for you to watch them at their work, you may see the small, slow slug on top of, but more commonly beneath, the umbrella cap. Watch how it uses its "horns." The longer pair is stalked eyes, the shorter pair sensitive feelers. As far as biologists know, a slug can perceive only very nearby objects, and although it has eyes, those eyes certainly do not focus images with as much detail as ours. On the right side of the slug's body, near the head, is a round hole that is sometimes open and sometimes closed.

A slug has no bronchial tubes or lungs; it takes air in and out of a cavity beneath its mantle (the textured forward section of its body). For eating, the slug, like its shelled cousins the snails, uses a filelike tongue or radula for rasping away at both living and dead organic material. If you put the slug on your hand and let it roam a bit, it just might tickle you with its tongue. Don't worry about the "slime"— it is a mucous coating secreted by glands in the slug's skin. The film inhibits desiccation of its soft body and protects it as it slides over the rough forest floor. Experimenters have discovered that a slug can crawl up and over the edge of a razor blade without being damaged!

Just beyond the junction at the top of the hill (**A**), where you go right, is a grove of red maples growing in water. This pond was abandoned by beaver for many years, during which time woody growth returned as the area dried. But beaver occupied the area again in 1980, and the maples are now flooded; they cannot survive this way for long (see **#13**).

Witch Hole Pond itself lies in a depression scoured by the glaciers (**B**). (Beware of poison ivy here. There is very little of it on the island, but at this junction it is healthy and abundant in the grasses and among the rocks.) Imagine the succession here as sediments

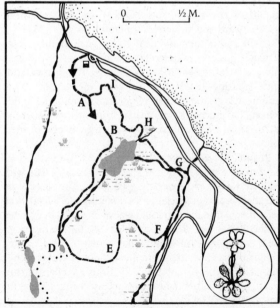

Inset: Sundew

continually accumulate on the pondbottom and plants are able to grow further and further toward the center of the pond. At the top of the second rise beyond Witch Hole (**C**), a short trail on the left leads to the shore of a rather special pond. In 1979, the center section of this most wonderful of beaver dams broke and slid during a heavy rain. The pond drained, and for some reason, the beaver did not rebuild. With the new environmental conditions came new inhabitants: terrestrial plants began to invade the exposed sediments of the pondbottom. In the fall of 1980, beaver reinhabited the area and began a new center section for the dam, reflooding the area.

Carefully examine the gravel of the old bottom or some of the large, wet trunk sections. You may be able to find some strange little plants with spoon-shaped leaves covered with red, gland-tipped hairs. These are sundews, which have adapted to low-nitrogen conditions (common in boggy areas) by becoming carnivorous. The gland-tipped hairs attract, trap, and absorb insects for nourishment. Look for swallows here as they fly around, mouths wide open to catch insects. The dead snags provide numerous nesting places for them.

Halfmoon Pond lies just before the junction (**D**) that leads to Eagle Lake (and the Eagle Lake parking access—see Remarks). Notice the series of smaller dams, downstream from the main pond dam, which provide the beaver with aquatic passages to food supplies downstream. Like ponds, these smaller impoundments are important protection for a mammal that is skilled at evading predators in the water but awkward and vulnerable on land.

At the end of the pond nearest the junction, there is another type of water passage, a canal, opposite the foot of a drag path (left), along which the beaver haul their logs. This particular drag path is quite amazing—it extends 100 yards up the hill. Its considerable length suggests that danger of predators is minimal in this area. The beavers have been drawn this far from their protective pond by an aspen grove on the hillside—aspen bark is one of their preferred foods.

Beyond the pond, bear left toward Bar Harbor–Duck Brook. At the top of a long, gentle rise is an open area (**E**) with views to Cadillac and Dorr mountains (see **#88**). The slabs of granite here still show traces of glacial times. Look for glacial striations (roughly perpendicular to the path) and glacial erratics, large stones deposited by the glacier (see **#85**). Look also (on the northwest side of path) for the gray band of diorite dike, where minerals oozed into and solidified in a crack in the granite millions of years ago. While you're still close to the ground, look for British soldiers, a shrubby gray-green lichen with bright-red sporecase caps. Blueberries are also prevalent here.

Continue to the stone bridge (**F**) (Duck Brook Rd. access—see Remarks). During the 1910s and 1920s, in response to recently granted motor-vehicle access to Mount Desert Island, John D. Rockefeller orchestrated construction of carriage paths through his wooded lands. When he later gave much of the land to Acadia National Park, he included the stipulation that the carriage paths remain for unmotorized use. This native stone bridge is one of seventeen uniquely different bridges, which are the pride of the carriage-path system. It seems to grow out of the creek canyon itself. Stalactites—"icicles" of calcium carbonate leached from the mortar between the stones—grow slowly under the arches as water evaporates and leaves the minerals behind. Staghorn sumac, with its furry younger branches, and honeysuckle grow near the base of the stairs. Spotted sandpipers frequent the banks of the stream, busily seeking insect and crustacean foods.

What the park rangers do when beavers flood a carriage path is demonstrated at the bottom of the hill (**G**). In the past, resource managers trapped the offending beavers and moved them to another location. However, finding a new location for the beavers is problematic: Another habitat might be unable to support them or might already be another beaver's territory, where the newcomers would be unwelcome. Other options are (1) to periodically break a section of the dam, being careful to allow the beavers enough pond so that they can still exit from their lodge and swim under the ice in winter; or (2) to put a long, hollow box through the dam, which will regulate the level of the water.

Beyond the next rise (**H**), find Witch Hole Pond on your left and an old marsh on your right. The beaver lodge in the marsh is attached to the bank. Sometimes, where there is enough soil, beavers make their homes in the bank itself.

At the junction go right, following the Paradise Hill–Hull's Cove Loop to discover views out over Hull's Cove, Frenchman Bay, and the Gouldsboro Hills (**I**). The bike trail to the visitor center is the next right. Come again at dusk. If you are quiet and patient, you may be able to see some of the beavers that make the plentiful signs you have been investigating.

Remarks: *This is a 3½-mile loop of carriage path with three access points. The visitor center access, described in this entry, is a half-mile moderate hill. The Duck Brook Bridge access, on the Duck Brook Rd., next to the pumping station, is only a bridge-span in length. The Eagle Lake Parking access, on Route 233 across from the northern end of Eagle Lake, is 1 mile of gentle ups and downs. The loop has similar terrain and a gravel surface, which is good for walking and bicycling. No motorized vehicles, other than wheelchairs, are allowed. There are nearly 50 miles of carriage paths in Acadia National Park. From Eagle Lake parking (access 3), another specially graveled carriage path loops 6 miles around Eagle Lake, while a rougher dirt branch forks right, toward Aunt Betty Pond. When there is snow, the carriage paths are wonderful for cross-country skiing and snowshoeing. Winter walkers are requested to make a pathway separate from the ski tracks. Northeast Creek, on Route 3 just northwest of Salisbury Cove, is a pleasant tidal estuary for a canoe or kayak paddle.*

90.

Flying Mountain

Directions: **Mount Desert Island, Maine. Follow directions for #85, but after crossing the causeway, do not bear left on Route 3; instead, go straight on Route 102. Go south about 10 miles toward Southwest Harbor. Turn left on Furnald Point Rd. at the bottom of the hill as you enter town. Go about 1 mile to the first dirt road on the left beyond the cove.**

Ownership: **Acadia National Park, National Park Service.**

Flying Mountain is a small and lovely mountain that juts out into the clear, deep waters of Somes Sound. The Abenaki Indians claim that it used to be the top of nearby Saint Sauveur Mountain until raging winds broke off the peak and brought it here. Geologists, on the other hand, believe it derived from molten minerals buried deep inside the earth.

The first part of the ascent winds through the stillness of a tall spruce-fir forest (**A**). Underfoot, the needles accumulate faster than they decompose, building a soft duff layer. The low illumination on the forest floor, the acidity of the soil, and the high competition for water and nutrients from the well-established root systems of larger trees allow few chances for undergrowth other than lichens and mosses. Only where blowdowns have opened a hole in the canopy and in the soil below, can one find dense clusters of saplings competing for survival.

Beyond an open ledge the forest grows shorter and contains more deciduous species (**B**). Notice, too, that the trail is worn down to the bedrock and the soil is very thin. A short, rocky scramble brings one

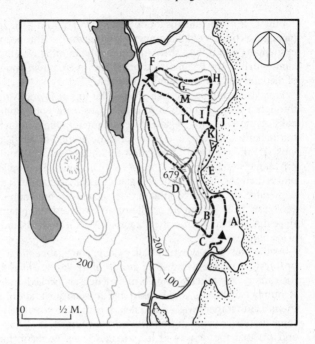

to the top (**C**). At only 284 feet, the stunting effects of exposure and little soil are evident in the sparse and short vegetation. The open ledge surfaces are so covered by crustose lichens that it is difficult to tell the color of the bedrock. The color of the lichens derives from pigments in their fungal components (see **#88** and **#78**).

Below and to the southeast lies the grassy expanse of Fernald Point, where, in 1613, a group of forty Jesuit missionaries established the first European colony on Mount Desert Island. It was one of the early settlements in what the French called La Cadie, the lands between Cape Cod and Newfoundland. Unfortunately for the French, the British called that same area New England, and within a few weeks of its establishment, the Jesuit settlement was destroyed by the British. Archaeological teams have unearthed some evidence of the Jesuit camp, as well as an old Indian midden, or shell heap.

The earliest Indian groups in the area date back some 6,000 years. When the Europeans came to these shores in the 1600s, they were greeted by the Abnaki Indians, "the People of the Dawn." Those early interactions here apparently were fairly peaceful, though not without typical manifestations of the value differences between the two cultures: Greening Island, which lies beyond Fernald Point, was "bought" from the Indians for one-half gallon of rum—the Indians, having no concept of land ownership, thought the Europeans were exchanging goods for a share in reaping the hunting benefits of the land, whereas the Europeans thought they were buying possession of the land and the sole rights to its use.

From the summit, the trail crosses the top of Flying Mountain, through a forest association of conifers scattered with birches and oaks, typical of this region. Sheep laurel, juniper, blueberries, huckleberries, lichens, and moss form the ground cover. The overlook (**D**) offers an end-to-end view of Somes Sound, the only fjord on Maine's Atlantic coast (see **#91**). The long, deep valley was plucked and sculpted by the last glacier. Look also at the long east-west ridge of Acadia Mountain, the second up the sound. Some geologists believe it to be a relic of an east-west mountain-range ridge that stretched across the breadth of Mount Desert Island before glaciation.

As the trail drops down to Valley Cove, you again enter a spruce-fir forest. There are two distinct groups of trees: one older, forming the canopy; the other young, forming a densely packed understory. A number of factors could contribute to such a situation, among them: (1) that there was an excellent seeding one year, or in two or three successive years, during which these young trees all got started; and (2) that the density of trees makes it very difficult for other generations to get started.

Access to the cove shore (**E**) lies beyond the footbridge. In years past, Valley Cove was, for good reason, known as Echo Cove. Join the truck road just up the slope. As you walk back to the trailhead, notice the variety of growth forms that can occur in a single species such as spruce. Because growing conditions vary so much from spot to spot, it is not possible to judge a specimen's age by girth or height alone. In a young conifer, you can make a rough estimate of age by counting the whorls of branches: one whorl per year plus several years for whorls at the base that have died, broken off, and become obscured by the growth of the trunk bark. Find an old stump and try to read the history revealed in its rings. Each pair of light and dark rings represents one year of the tree's life; the former is rapid summer growth, the latter slow spring growth. Since a tree grows in girth from the cambium layer just beneath the bark, the oldest rings are in the center of the stump. Rings that are broader are indicative of more rapid growth, which might occur after a neighboring tree was blown down, allowing release from some nearby competition. Look also for charred fire scars and radially arranged stubs of broken branches. Sometimes you will discover that they are contained totally within the stump wood, indicating that the tree grew enough to seal off the break in the bark surface.

While you enjoy the trees, listen also for ravens. The biggest members of the crow family, they share their cousins' ability to make a wide variety of vocalizations—sometimes they even sound like a troop of apes hooting in the treetops. It is wonderful to watch ravens at their aerial acrobatics: barrel rolls, wingtip to wingtip soaring, riding the air currents *upside down!* The best places to look for them in action is from a ridge or cliff area where there are strong updrafts.

Remarks: *This is a 1½-mile loop over moderate terrain. The hike can also be extended by combining Flying Mountain with Acadia and the Saint Sauveur Mountains (see #91, Remarks). Beech Cliffs and the Cadillac Mountain ridges are excellent places to look for ravens in flight.*

91.

Acadia Mountain

Directions: **Mount Desert Island, Maine. Follow directions for #85, but after crossing the causeway, do not bear left on Route 3; instead, go straight on Route 102. Go about 4 miles to Somesville; continue about 3 miles more to Acadia Mountain parking, on the right.**

Ownership: **Acadia National Park, National Park Service.**

This is a delightful little mountain with a loop of trails and old truck roads that wind through lowlands covered with shadowy forests, across slopes studded with windswept pitch pines, and over rocky outcrops overlooking the deep waters of Somes Sound, New England's only fjord. A short side trail to the mouth of Man-of-War Brook reveals, when there isn't a drought, a cascade of water falling to the sea.

The Acadia Trail rambles a bit at first, then crosses the truck road and begins to ascend the relatively gradual northeast flank of the mountain. The lower parts of the slope (**F**; this site is keyed to map, p. 345) are sheltered enough and have accumulated adequate soil to support a mixed forest of large trees. As you ascend, notice how soil, exposure, and vegetation change.

Leaving the large trees, head up a narrow granite stairway where a patch of rock tripe grows on the right-hand rockface. This brownish, leafy lichen, often resembling bits of old rubber, is classified as one of the *foliose* or leafy lichens. The lichens that form greenish, brown, or other colored crusts on the rock surfaces are classified as *crustose* lichens; the shrubby ones, like old-man's-beard (see **#95**) and British soldiers, are labeled *fruticose*. Rock tripe, a lichen large enough to gather, has been used as survival food (see **#88**).

Although Mount Desert Island's most common type of oak tree is the northern red oak, Acadia Mountain (**G**) supports another species as well. Here, in addition to the tree-sized red oak, one finds bear or scrub oak, which is shrubby in form. An unusual inhabitant in this area, its common range is from southeastern Maine to southern Virginia. Some botanists surmise that Acadia Mountain's bear oaks may offer a glimpse back to another era when glaciers no longer covered this area, yet their presence further north still maintained a lower sea level. Mount Desert "Island" was then "inland," the coastline probably as far away as the Georges Banks, now 100 miles offshore (see **Portland North**). This may have allowed the bear oak, not commonly found in coastal areas, to migrate here. Botanists continue to pursue the question why Acadia Mountain, alone on Mount Desert Island, still offers an adequate habitat for the little oak.

On the more open slopes (**G**), look for juniper, a low shrub that is an early inhabitant of open spaces. Its waxy, green (unripe) to dark-blue berries are used for flavoring gin.

From the summit (**H**), the trail heads eastward along the broad ridgetop of the mountain. There is a superb, but unmarked, overlook just beyond the summit marker, to the right of the trail. Somes Sound, the narrow finger of salt water below you, almost divides Mount Desert Island in half. It is a valley filled by the sea. Steep-sided and long, it is the only true fjord on Maine's Atlantic coast. Its U-shaped cross-section shows it to be one of the many gifts the glaciers left to posterity. (For more on glaciation, see **#85**). The mouth of the sound opens into the Great Harbor of Mount Desert, popular waters sheltered by the Cranberry Islands. Like many other islands "Down East" (which refers to downwind, from the prevailing southwesterly winds from Boston to Nova Scotia), the Cranberries were settled before the mainland by fishermen wishing to live as near their livelihood as possible. In those days the cash crop was codfish (see **#82**); lobster was used for bait and fertilizer—families so poor they had to eat lobster are rumored to have buried the shells in their yards, under cover of darkness.

A bit further on, there is a fine view north up the sound to Somesville, the first permanent European settlement on Mount Desert Island. At the northern base of the mountain next to the shore is Hall Quarry, a source of the pink Mount Desert Island granite, which was a popular building material before the era of cement and steel. (The old Philadelphia mint is built of Mount Desert Island bedrock.) The deep waters and steep sides of Somes Sound allowed schooners easy access to the heavy cargoes.

At the eastern end of the ridgetop, the trail drops down the steep southern face of the mountain. The main trail (**I**) is the right fork; the left fork leads to another unmarked overlook.

At the bottom of Acadia, the trail crosses Man-of-War Brook. The 100-yard side trip beyond this intersection to the overlook (**J**) is highly recommended. The cascade at the mouth of the brook was a favorite watering spot for ships from many countries until the late 1800s. The steep sides of the sound and the convenient course of the cascade allowed sailors to fill their casks without removing them from shipboard—the only equipment needed was a trough or pipe placed from the upper cascade to the barrel top.

The Acadia Trail may be combined with the Flying Mountain Trail, returning to the Acadia Mountain parking lot via Saint Sauveur Mountain. For this 5-mile loop (see Remarks), bear left at (**K**) onto the trail to Valley Cove.

If you continue along the Acadia Trail, you will join the Man-of-War Brook truck road at an old homestead site (**L**). Only cellar holes and a few apple trees remain (see **#74**). The bark of these trees is peppered with horizontal rows of small round holes pecked over the years by hungry sapsuckers. Members of the woodpecker family of birds, sapsuckers have long, heavy, chisel-like beaks adapted for getting at food buried inside the tough protection of tree bark. Sapsuckers eat the sap that oozes out where they have pierced the cambium layer of the tree; they also feed on insects. You may discover a number of different species of warblers flitting around the branches of the trees. Their beaks are small and slender, useful for picking insects from twigs and foliage. The dark-eyed juncos that frequent the forest floor have short, conical beaks, well adapted for cracking seeds. From the homestead site it is about a mile to Route 102. The woods along the road (**M**) have not been logged or burned for over a century. A few large white pines still tower here (see **#60**). Massive, straight specimens of this species were (and still are) very popular as building material for masts. As in other parts of New England, the straight individuals with a girth of 24 inches or more were blazed with "The King's Broad Arrow," which reserved them for the British navy, a policy not looked upon with favor by the colonists. Those marked trees that did succumb to rebel axes were carefully milled into boards no greater than 23 inches in width, so that poachers were never caught with illegal planks.

Remarks: *The trail is a 3-mile loop, with some steep places that require scrambling. The last mile is an old truck road.*

5-Mile Loop Option: *Just before the Acadia Mountain Trail joins the Man-of-War Brook truck road, take the trail to Valley Cove (1 mile) and Flying Mountain (1⅓ miles). The first part is a rather easy and pleasant hike, through big old cedars full of pileated-woodpecker holes and then through ash groves; in the lower, wetter lands mixed with cedar; on the higher slopes mixed with other conifers.*

Beyond the ashes, the trail winds up and down the talus (loose rock) slope beneath the Eagle Cliffs, and through sections of forest dominated by several different tree associations: beech and yellow birch; red oak; and birch and goosefoot maple. In one area, scarred trunks and branches on living trees and a swath of dead trunks scattered to the water's edge are evidence of a rockfall that occurred during the freezings and thawings of March 1979.

Follow the red arrows, in reverse direction, across the open talus slope. At the south side, look for delicate rock gardens of polypody ferns. From the cove shore, cross the footbridge and follow the Flying Mountain Trail, in the opposite direction to that described in the Flying Mountain text (#90). On the far side of the mountain, at the trailhead, go right on the Valley Cove truck road to the Valley Peak Trail, which begins its ascent of Saint Sauveur through a stand of conifers. Continue up a jumbled slope and over an outcrop ridge with a fine example of horizontal fracturing of granite, which probably occurred when the weight of rock above it was eroded, allowing the granite to expand (see #92). From Valley Peak, proceed to the Saint Sauveur summit via the trail to either the Saint Sauveur parking lot (1¼ miles) or Acadia Mountain (2¼ miles). Return to your car by following trail signs for the Man-of-War truck road and the Acadia Mountain parking lot.

92.

Schoodic Peninsula

Directions: **Schoodic Peninsula, Maine. From Bangor, take U.S. 1A southeast about 27 miles to Ellsworth. Go east on U.S. 1 about 18 miles to West Gouldsboro; turn south (right)**

onto Route 186. Go about 6 miles; at the head of Winter Harbor, follow Route 186 as it turns east (left). About 0.5 mile farther on, turn right onto Schoodic Point Rd. and follow it into the park. (Most of the road within the park goes one way only.)

Ownership: Acadia National Park, National Park Service.

A trip to the Schoodic Peninsula is especially wonderful on a stormy day. In addition to storm beaches and crashing surf, Schoodic includes wide basaltic dikes and the granite cliffs of the Raven's Nest. Large numbers of sea ducks flock to this area, especially in winter. Some of the southernmost stands of jack pines thrive here in the cold climate and rocky soil.

There is no trail along the shore at Schoodic, but there are numerous places to park off the road and walk down to the shore, several of which are mentioned here. Of the four trails to the top of Schoodic Head, the one via the Anvil is described.

Just after you enter the park, the dock at the Frazer Point picnic area, on the right, is a good place from which to look for ducks. Common eider are present year-round; oldsquaw, buffleheads, and goldeneyes arrive in winter from their breeding grounds on the Canadian tundra and the Arctic.

About 1.5 miles beyond the picnic area, just after the 35 mph sign, stop in the dirt pullout on the left. Follow the small footpath on the opposite side of the road down to the Raven's Nest Cliffs (not labeled). The rock that formerly filled the two deep coves had more closely spaced cracks than the surrounding rock, and it was more readily eroded by frost-wedging and wave-induced undercutting and plucking. Eventually, the rocks will be worn away (see **#74**). Notice the white spruces, sculptured by the wind. Find three-toed cinquefoil (a relative of strawberries and roses), black crowberry, and juniper— all tolerant of the exposure and thin soils of this rocky coast.

For those who wish to drive most of the way to the jack pine forests and views on top of Schoodic Head, proceed another ¾ mile and turn left on the old dirt road; bear left at the Y. A short trail leads from the parking lot to the summit. (Note: this dirt road is usually closed in winter.)

At the road junction down near the naval base, bear right to Schoodic Point parking. Walk down onto the storm beach. The fine-grained granite is broken in two major sets of parallel joints, or cracks. One set is long, relatively horizontal, and slightly curved cracks, called *sheeting fractures,* that incline gently toward the sea. This kind of crack often forms in granite when it is relieved of the weight of overlying rocks. In this area, hundreds and perhaps thousands of feet of ancient sedimentary and metamorphic rocks have been eroded away over the millions of years since these rocks were formed. The second set of joints is more vertical, extending deep into the bedrock. Such cracks generally form when granite cools from liquid magma to solid rock or when it is stressed by tectonic movements within the earth (see #83). Here, the combined fractures have joined with frost and wave action to erode great blocks of granite from the ledges. Such ponderous chunks may look as if they will remain quite stationary, yet even they are further rearranged and decomposed during roaring sou'westers.

Examine one of the large bands of dark rock, basaltic dikes, which cross the ledges. These are places where cracks in the lighter-colored granitic rocks were intruded by (filled with) dark-colored molten minerals, which cooled relatively rapidly in contact with the colder surrounding rock, thus assuming a fine-grained structure. Follow the paths of the two intersecting dikes (about 4 and 6 feet wide) opposite the lower parking area. The smaller dike cuts through the larger, indicating that the smaller is the younger of the two. Because basalt rock often becomes more closely jointed than granitic rock, it is more readily eroded, sometimes forming steep-sided chasms in the shoreline. Such chasms often resemble those in areas of closely jointed granite, such as at the Raven's Nest and Thunder Hole (see #95). A major distinguishing feature is that those formed along dikes generally develop rather straight walls along the contact between the dike and the surrounding rock, whereas those formed in severely fractured granite tend to evolve irregular sides.

Notice, too, the pitted surface of much of the ledges. Small indentations in the rock have been enlarged by the chemical weathering action of rainwater that collects in them. Rain mixes with carbon dioxide as it falls through the air and becomes a *weak* solution of carbonic acid. Lightning bolts, volcanic eruptions, forest fires, and the slow bacterial decomposition of organic matter produce nitrogen and sulfur compounds, which also contribute to the general acidity of rain and snow. Industrial wastes, such as smoke from coal-fired power plants, release similar chemicals into the air in great quantities, making our precipitation much more acidic today than it used to be. Early research suggests that numerous life forms in fresh waters in Maine and other localities around the world may be in danger, particularly those living in small, high-elevation ponds of granitic bedrock areas where natural buffering capacities are low. Low-buffered forests and croplands, and the groundwaters and soils that support them, may also be threatened. The sea, with its huge volume and high buffering capacity, is thought to be relatively well protected, though not totally inviolate. Much more research is needed on the topic before we will have a good understanding of the complex processes involved.

Shortly beyond Blueberry Hill picnic area, park in the paved pull-off on the right. The trail to the Anvil (and Schoodic Head) is just ahead, on the left side of the road. Ascend through red and white spruce, birch, and fir. Beyond the cleft, you enter jack-pine territory. The Acadia National Park area is at the southern end of this species' range. Look for cones on the branches. Old ones, farther in on the branches, may still be closed and thus still retain their seeds. Unlike most pines, which shed their seeds when they ripen, this pine tends to shed its seeds only after intense heat (generally from a fire) stimulates the cones to open. This mechanism allows it to take advantage of the bare soil, open space, and abundant sunlight in a newly burned area (see **#87**). Among the jack pines are lush patches of reindeer and antler lichen, sheep laurel, and red spruce.

Descend into a broad notch and then head up the slope of Schoodic Head. Notice the variety of vegetation: short jack pine; larger, gnarly spruces; lichens, juniper, and sheep laurel; alders, herbs, grasses, and ferns; spruce saplings beneath a dense spruce canopy; a barren scree slope of loose, angular fragments of rock (please step *carefully* to avoid excessive erosion). At the summit of Schoodic Head, you are surrounded by jack pines and other small trees, but you are not far from some excellent views: Follow the Ranger Station Rd. trail about a hundred yards for a panorama including the mountainous silhouette of Mount Desert Island, or descend the South Trail a short way to catch a glimpse of peninsula ridges down east. Then, retrace your path to the road again. Follow the Schoodic road out of the park. Bear right onto Route 186. In Prospect Harbor, go left on Route 195, then left on Route 1 near West Gouldsboro, and retrace your route to Bar Harbor.

Remarks: *Round trip from Bar Harbor is close to 90 miles. The hiking trail to Schoodic Head is about 1 mile (one way). The loop from Frazer Point picnic area around Schoodic to Birch Harbor and back to Frazer Point is about 15 miles; it is excellent for bicycling. There are camping facilities at Lamoine State Park, southeast of Ellsworth on Route 184, from mid-May to mid-October. For more detailed information on the geology of Schoodic Point, see* The Geology of Acadia National Park, *by Carleton Chapman.*

93.
Wonderland and
Ship Harbor

Directions: **Mount Desert Island, Maine. Follow directions for #85, but after crossing the causeway, do not bear left on Route 3; instead, go straight on Route 102. Go south about 10 miles to Southwest Harbor; after about 1 mile more, turn left onto Route 102A. Go through Manset; about 1 mile beyond the Seawall Campground (right) and picnic area (left) is the parking for Wonderland.**

Ownership: **Acadia National Park, National Park Service.**

Wonderland and Ship Harbor provide a variety of coastal habitats that are accessible to almost anyone. The two walks (which may be taken separately or combined, as in this description) feature bogs and spruce forests, a rocky coastline, and tidal pools with a variety of marine life. Spring warblers and nesting boreal chickadees are plentiful, as are summer shorebirds, fall and winter ducks, migrating kestrels, and merlins.

Almost immediately as you head down the Wonderland Trail, look for a boggy area on the left (see **#56**). Fragile sphagnum mosses are among the species able to tolerate the acidic, low-nitrogen conditions that are characteristic of these wetlands. The brown color of the water comes from tannins leached from cedars, oaks, and other vegetation—very much like a tea solution.

Further on, pocket communities on open granite slabs offer several examples of succession in miniature: As the amount, fertility, and moisture-holding capacity of the soil increases from edge to center, crustose lichens give way to mosses and reindeer lichen, then sheep laurel and huckleberries, and finally spruce (see **#85**).

Walk on to an old boggy area on the right, where a spruce forest has taken hold. Spruce trees have very shallow root systems, which enable them to live in the thin soils that are typical of much of Mount Desert Island. Deeper-rooted species, which include most hardwoods, cannot survive.

As the trail reaches its highest elevation, open slabs are sprinkled with the curly forms of pitch pines. A white pine on a windy site will generally maintain a single-trunked, though lopsided silhouette, its branches "wind-flagged," or bent away from the strong prevailing winds. A wind-sculptured pitch pine, on the other hand, will assume a rounded and bushy shape.

Descending the shore side of the hill, spruce again becomes dominant. In the cove, on the left as you reach the shore, look for terrestrial and saltwater plants growing adjacently: salt grass and rockweed. The grass has air pockets in it to help keep it from drowning; the alga has a mucilaginous coating to help keep it from drying out. The seaside plantain, also growing within reach of desiccating salt sprays, has evolved thickened, succulent leaves to help maintain its moisture supply.

Where the road splits, go left, through older forests crammed with young spruces. Trees produce an abundance of seeds in order to compensate for the fact that only a few will survive to maturity. Many of the young trees will be shaded out or blown down in storms.

On the ledges and in pools at the end of the point, low tides expose the inhabitants of the area between forest and sea (see **Portland North**). Irish moss and periwinkles are particularly prominent here. Notice the glinting purple iridescence of the Irish moss under water. Some of the periwinkles are not really snails but hermit crabs. These have a very soft tail, adapted over the generations into a curve, which fits perfectly inside the spiral of an empty snail shell. This provides ready-made protection, as long as the growing crab can continue to find larger and larger shells.

Off the tip of the point lies Long Ledge, one of the many "hilltops" that were not quite submerged as the waters from the melting glaciers flowed back into the oceans. From the point, either return via Wonderland Trail to the parking lot or follow the shore around to Ship Harbor. Prowling the shore westward (beware of slippery slime and algae on the rocks), explore the variety of patterns in the beach boulders. Farther on, the coastal "no-man's land" comprises wave-washed ledge, then cobble beach and seawall, then ledge again: even the rocks and the shoreline "adapt" to or are expressions of the forces that created them. After you round the end of Ship Harbor's point, look for a well-worn trail and marker 9. Follow the trail that parallels the shore (you will be heading in the direction opposite to that described in the Ship Harbor Trail booklet; see "Remarks").

At the trail junction, go right a short distance to marker 11, where there are several white spruce with a virus that produces a pot-belly effect. These cankers, galls, and witches' brooms are "infections," of which the white spruce is tolerant (see **#98**).

Return to the trail junction and follow the trail on your right to marker 6. From here, proceed to the Ship Harbor parking lot, and from there to Wonderland parking via the tarred road, heading to the right.

Remarks: *If taken separately, the Wonderland Trail and the Ship Harbor Trail are each 1½ miles; combined they form a 2½-mile loop. Both are fairly easy, over level terrain. Wonderland is an old dirt-and-gravel road, accessible by wheelchair (attendant advised). The shoreline connection between Wonderland and Ship Harbor is rocky beach and broad ledges. A self-guided trail booklet for Ship Harbor is available at the Acadia National Park Visitor Center and at the Seawall Campground.*

94.

Baker Island

Directions: **Off Mount Desert Island, Maine. Follow directions for #85, but after crossing the causeway, do not bear left on Route 3; instead, go straight on Route 102. After about 2 miles, at Town Hill, Route 198 joins Route 102; bear left on Route 198 in another 2 miles when it splits off from Route 102 and heads southeast. About 4 miles farther on, turn right (southwest) on Route 3 to Northwest Harbor. The dock and parking are 1 block east of the town center.**

Ownership: **Acadia National Park, National Park Service.**

This is a very good example of a Maine coastal island and is one of the few accessible to the public. It can be reached only by small private boat, or by the naturalist cruise that sails from Northeast Harbor. The cruise allows close views of coastal birds and marine life, as well as excellent views of Mount Desert Island. Baker Island has trails leading from the shore through beautiful open meadows and spruce forest overlooking the ocean. The homes of early settlers still stand, offering a glimpse of life on the remote island 100 years ago. The island's most striking natural features are the glacially scarred rocks, and Storm Beach on the eastern shore.

As the boat leaves the harbor, many coastal birds of the area can be seen at close range. The double-crested cormorant, great black-backed gull, herring gull (see **#17** and **#77**), and eider duck are all common. An osprey nest can be seen on a large chimney rock off the coast of Sutton Island. The osprey, or sea hawk, hunts fish in the relatively calm waters of the bay during the summer (see **#22, #50,** and **#99**). The rocks and sea cliffs in this area show the effects of both glaciation and erosion by the ocean waters (see **Portland North**). Harbor seals are often seen on the rocky ledges here, and porpoises are occasionally sighted further out to sea.

The shore of Baker Island affords one of the finest views of Mount Desert Island and the entire Mount Desert mountain range. From here it is apparent how the mountains were shaped and sculpted by the glacier 10,000 to 15,000 years ago. As the glacier moved southward, rocks and soil were pulled off the peaks, leaving the southern slopes rough and steep and the northern slopes more smooth and gradual. This process is known as glacial plucking.

The trail across the island rises gradually from the shore through a meadow populated by rugosa rose, serviceberry, beach pea, thistle, blueberry, raspberry, and wild wheat. All of these plants do well in the dry, sandy soil near the beach. The trail passes through a small cemetery into an area with moister soil, where the wild cranberry dominates. After passing an old homestead, the trail proceeds through a field along the edge of the forest where shadbush and spiraea grow along with the cranberry and blueberry. All of the vegetation on the island is comfortable with soil that is both thin and acidic. The forest is almost entirely blue spruce, a species whose root system does not require deep soil.

The trail proceeds through a mature spruce forest and opens onto an area of exposed bedrock where clear evidence of the glacier's presence is visible. Grooves and scrape marks were left when the ice dragged rocks across the granite surface. Shatter marks can be seen in several places where rocks were bounced along the ground, leaving a series of crescent-shaped indentations. Some parts of the rock were polished smooth into small depressions that filled with organic matter which decomposed into soil. Clumps of moss and small spruce seedlings have taken root here, although they will never grow very well due to the scarcity of soil and nutrients. Scattered throughout this area are several large glacial erratics. These rocks, different in structure from the island's native rock, were carried from elsewhere and deposited when the ice melted (see **#85**).

The trail descends to Storm Beach, one of the most impressive geological features along the Maine coast. The thousands of granite boulders were left here by the glacier and have been pounded and moved by the sea ever since. Some geologists believe that the land that was covered by the glacier is rebounding from the weight of the ice. The rocks here illustrate this theory of the land rising. The rocks high up on the shore, away from the water, have been eroded so that they have smoother surfaces than the rocks at the water's edge. Presumably, the high rocks have been exposed longer, having been freed of the glacier's weight earlier than the low rocks; the sharp-featured low rocks are still rising and have been exposed to the sea for a relatively short time. Whether this theory is correct or not, the rocks stand as an example of the immense power of the ocean that has moved, broken, and worn them down for centuries.

Remarks: *The naturalist cruise sails daily from late June to early September. Call (207) 244-3366 for schedules and fares. The round trip, including 2½ hours on the island, takes approximately 4 hours. The trails are clear, and the terrain is relatively easy. It is often cool and windy on the boat, so bring warm clothes.*

95.
The Shore Trail

Directions: **Mount Desert Island, Maine. Follow directions for #85. Enter the park at Hull's Cove and follow signs for the Park Loop Rd. and Ocean Dr., turning left onto the Loop Rd. after about 3 miles. Continue about 8 miles; park at Thunder Hole, about 0.7 mile beyond Sand Beach, on the one-way section of Park Loop Rd.**

Ownership: **Acadia National Park, National Park Service.**

The Shore Trail lies between the Park Loop Rd. and the water's edge, running from Sand Beach to Otter Point. Here the interplay of land, sea, and wind is expressed in tide pools, "blowholes," tumbling cobbles, and seafoam dancing on rocky ledges. From the edge of spruce and fir forests and dense growths of rugosa rose, you can watch seaward for abundant coastal and seabirds or landward for passerines (songbirds) of coniferous, thicket, and deciduous woods.

From the ledges above Thunder Hole, look up and down along the coast. Some rocks, because of their mineral composition and physical structure, are more easily eroded than others. This can be seen at Thunder Hole. Here, the granite ledge is broken by numerous large joints (see **#92**) along which frost and wave action have dislodged chunks of rock, forming the chasm you see below. Wall fragments, which the waves round by bouncing them against the chasm sides, are visible on the bottom at low tide. When the combination of tide and swells is just right, an incoming wave, capturing a pocket of air in the cavern at the back of the chasm and forcing it out, will cause a booming splash. This occurs most often during winter storms. In summer, the best time to check is at mid-tide rising (about 3 hours after low tide), especially when there is a southeast wind. Another good time is at mid-tide falling.

Follow the Shore Trail (no sign) in the same direction as traffic flow on the Loop Rd. The path is lined with aspen, cherry, staghorn sumac (feel its fuzzy branches), white spruce, balsam fir, asters, meadowsweet, and various types of roses. The rugosa rose was imported from Asia as a garden ornamental, popular for its large pink or white flowers that bloom throughout the summer, for its lustrous green foliage that turns orange and scarlet in autumn, and for its large red fruits, or "hips." For centuries, rose hips have been gathered to make tea and jam, and to extract the rich supplies of vitamin C. The hips of the rugosa rose have a large amount of flesh compared to other species and are delicious to eat fresh from the bush. As is evidenced here, the rugosa is no longer restricted to gardens in New England; it has escaped from those confines to seashore thickets, roadsides, and backdune sands.

Notice the sheeting foliation (see **#92**) of the coastal granite slabs and the size of some of the chunks that have been tossed around on shore. The no-man's-land of bare rock is that way for a good reason: winter storm waves pound it unmercifully, allowing little soil to accumulate and only a few small plants with high tolerance of wind and salt to survive. Seaside plantain, or goose's tongue (see **#77**), is a good example. Look for its narrow, thickened leaves growing in sheltered cracks. The younger leaves make a tangy and salty addition for salads.

A little farther along the trail, you overlook a cobble beach surrounded by granite cliffs with nearly perpendicular sets of joints. As blocks of rock are eroded from the cliffs, they become part of the beach (see **#86**), at first as angular chunks and later as rounded boulders, smoothed by tumbling in storm waves. During the 1800s, cobbles such as these were shipped to Boston and other cities further south to be used as paving stones. The chunks on the southern end of the beach, not bounced much yet by the waves, still retain their sharper edges. Just beyond and opposite the Gorham Mountain parking lot, an open ledge offers a view of the cove from the south. The sea-stack at the northern end has been eroded from the cliffs and is now a free-standing pillar.

All along the trail, the shoreline vegetation reflects morphological, or growth-form, modifications demanded by an environment of thin soil and high exposure to the lashing and dehydration of wind and salt spray. Many plants, like the black crowberry, simply grow low, staying close to the ground where winds are less strong. Individuals of bayberry and other old field or roadside species have thicker leaves and tougher cuticles (surfaces) if they live along the shore than if they grow further inland; these adaptations help conserve moisture. White pines may be heavily wind-flagged, their branches trailing out from the trunk on the side away from strong prevailing winds or from the lash of salt spray. Many of the spruces and firs have tiny or dead tops and long green lower branches, so that they maintain a large photosynthetic area yet keep it protected from desiccation and breakage.

Opposite the pull-through parking lot are some pot-bellied spruces. Botanists suspect that a nonlethal viral infection causes the trees to grow these extra tissues. Just beyond, Monument Cove shelters a beautiful boulder beach. Here the material available for beach building is of large size, as compared with the cobbles of the previous cove or the sand of Sand Beach. Only during storms are particles such as these tumbled about and further rounded by waves. At more than 250 feet above sea level on Day Mountain lies another beach with boulders smooth like these, testament to a coastline of another era. Some 11,000 years ago, as glaciers melted away from these shores, the sea level rose so that waves washed the "shore" of Day Mountain. But with the great weight of ice removed from it, the down-pressed crustal rock sprang back up, leaving Day Mountain's boulder beach high and dry, to be invaded by trees and other terrestrial species.

As you continue along the trial, you pass through forests composed mostly of balsam fir and white spruce not burned in 1947 (see **#87**). Grayish-green old-man's-beard dangles from many of the branches. Although it looks a bit like the Spanish moss of southern climates, it is not a close relative; Spanish "moss" (not a true moss) is a relative of the pineapple whereas old-man's-beard is a lichen (see **#88**). Like other lichens, it makes its own food through photosynthesis and uses trees only for anchoring places in the sun. You see it crowding dead branches, not because it has killed them, but rather because leafless branches offer more open space for the lichen to occupy.

This segment of the trail crosses along the top of the Otter Cliffs, tough granitic rocks that have managed to maintain a tall face to the sea. A broad, crowberry-bordered path leads left to the rim of the cliffs. At low tide, voluptuously wave-sculpted rocks are exposed in the cove below. A black guillemot may be diving here, pursuing its prey of small fish and red rock eels by swimming with its wings (see **#82**). Other avian divers along this coast include the double-crested cormorant and the common eider duck, both of which use their feet for underwater locomotion. Watch a cormorant as it swallows a large fish. Birds do not have teeth, so they must swallow their prey whole. A cormorant's long, slender neck bulges as large morsels slide down its throat. In Japan, humans profit from the cormorants' ability to catch fish. A fisherman places a ring around the neck, and a leash on the leg, of each of his birds and then sends them out fishing from his boat. Because of the ring, the cormorant is unable to swallow fish of large size. It returns to the boat, its catch is removed, and it is sent out again. Surprisingly, even though the cormorant spends much of its life diving for food, it does not have the good oil gland typical of most birds and cannot waterproof its feathers well; it gets soggy and must come ashore periodically to dry out. Frequently you see cormorants standing on ledges with their wings outstretched, presumably to dry, although recent study suggests this behavior may be in part thermoregulatory—a way to either gain heat or lose it.

Along the rounded tip of Otter Point, low tide exposes some of the best places for exploring the rocky intertidal zone. Look for roughly horizontal bands of life that appear as the salt waters retreat on a falling tide (see **#96** for an explanation of tides). At the very top, just below the bare rock of no-man's-land, is a dark band called the splash or black zone. It is colored by blue-green "algae" that need to be moistened regularly but not submerged. Blue-greens are some of the earth's most ancient organisms, having appeared on the planet some 3.5 billion years ago. Although for many years they were thought to be close relatives of green algae—hence their former name, blue-green algae—now they are recognized as kin to primitive bacteria and are called *cyanophytes* (*cyano-* = blue; *-phyte* = plant), or simply blue-greens.

Below the black zone is the barnacle zone, the topmost of the intertidal zones where salt waters come and go twice daily. Few kinds of organisms can survive the extremes of temperature, wave pounding, and drought that occur here where the moderating influence of water is absent for 8 to 10 hours at a stretch and where evaporation or rain may change the salinity with dramatic rapidity. Barnacles close the tops of their volcanolike shells with four calcareous plates, retaining enough water inside to keep their gills moist. When the tide comes in, the barnacles open and feed, using bristle-covered legs to strain the "sea soup" for the tiny plant and animal plankton that float there, the center of all intertidal and oceanic food webs. Find some barnacles in a shallow pool. If they are shut, you may be able to fool them into opening and feeding while you watch. Jiggle the water surface gently, pause, and jiggle it again—you are imitating the tide coming in. Pretty soon, at least some of the barnacles will begin kicking their legs out of the top of their shells, like miniature fans.

A bit further toward the water, in an area covered by the sea and left high and dry for fairly equal periods each day, you will find the rockweed zone colonized by olive-brown seaweeds or algae (all seaweeds are algae), also called wrack (see **#100**). Although not bright green, like other algae they do photosynthesize. In the always moist and cool spaces behind the curtains of rockweed you may find smooth periwinkles grazing, dog whelk snails hunting, and little green crabs scavenging. Here, as in the spruce forests above, the living community is made up of photosynthesizers, herbivores, carnivores, and decomposers, participating in similar flows of energy and cyclings of nutrients.

Below the rockweeds are the tide pools and other shoreline areas that remain submerged nearly all the time. Only the lowest monthly tides uncover the top of this section, named for the bushy red Irish moss that fringes it. Anyone who has eaten ice cream, chocolate pudding, or candy bars has eaten Irish moss; it is also used in some brands of beers. In some parts of Maine and New Brunswick this alga is raked from the rocks and processed to extract carrageenan, a food additive for thickening and smoothing. Another red alga of this zone is dulse, which grows in long, graceful, branching tongues. This one is edible right from the sea. You may also find it in its dried, black form, sold in Down East markets and movie theaters.

The kelp zone lies beneath the Irish moss zone, where it is always inundated. The lower tide pools and basins on Otter Point have kelp-lined bottoms. In these deep places, or in ones disconnected from the sea for only short periods, roam creatures that are tolerant of little change in their environment. Look for sea cucumbers, the larger of the blue-eyed hermit crabs (see **#93**), and secretive maned nudibranchs, or sea slugs (see **#101**) with bright red, carpetlike gills.

Come again to this spot at high tide, at night, or next year, and see how this intertidal world has changed since today. For many years, the bottom of the deep basin at the end of the point was packed tightly with sea urchins, and not a blade of kelp could be seen there. One spring, there were no urchins to be found; during the winter months, something, ice perhaps, had wiped out the population. That summer, kelp began to grow in the basin, and today it flourishes. Not too long ago, a few urchins turned up, yet no one knows what the basin's future will bring. Marine biologists have noticed that there is a definite rise in urchin populations in the Gulf of Maine and that great swaths of kelp beds are being mowed down by the active, five-toothed mouths of these spiny creatures. Some researchers suspect that larger lobsters feed in part on small urchins and that this may be an important checking factor on urchin populations. The fact that larger lobsters are almost entirely fished out, at least in the nearshore waters, may account for much of the present urchin abundance.

Climb back up the trail and continue past the Ocean Trail sign into Otter Cove. Bright buoys bob on the water, each indicative of a lobster trap that sits on the bottom below. A color-code system allows each lobsterman to identify the location of his own traps, which he generally checks and rebaits every other day with old, smelly fish—just what lobsters love to eat. Like their cousins the crabs, lobsters participate in the recycling of garbage in the sea. In the past, they did this in tide pools as well, but fishing has almost entirely eliminated them from the intertidal zone.

The Shore Trail ends in disarray as it rises in a number of small spurs to meet the Park Loop Rd. You may either turn around here and return to Thunder Hole by the Shore Trail, or cross the road, enter the parking lot via the car exit, go to the far (eastern) end, turn left at the last parking space, and proceed on an overgrown dirt road. Many trees in this area have blown down over the years, creating brushy habitat with much dead wood, suitable now for deer, woodpeckers, parula warblers, and red squirrels, as well as mountain cranberries, bunchberries, and raspberries. Scramble over and under a number of fallen trees and through dense young spruce to the junction with the tarred Otter Cliff Rd. From here, bird-watchers may want to take a side trip left a few hundred feet to the next junction (**I**), where birch woods, thicket, and spruce-fir forest lie side by side. Such a juxtaposition attracts a high diversity of birds (and other animals), as along the borders between different types of communities an organism can take advantage of food and shelter resources on both sides. Return to the dirt-and-tar junction and continue along the tar road (a right turn if you don't make the side trip). At the stop sign, cross the Park Loop Rd., find the Shore Trail, and go left to Thunder Hole.

Remarks: *This is a 2½-mile walk round-trip, over generally easy terrain. A walk here can be wonderful at any time of year, although from July through early September you may want to walk it early in the morning, since these are the months of heavy traffic on the Park Loop Rd., which in a few sections lies directly adjacent to the trail. For the best tidepooling, try to arrive at Otter Point a little before low tide. Please exercise caution in the intertidal zone; the white encrustations of barnacles are alive and also very sharp; seaweeds, whether in branched or scum form, are slippery. There is a little poison ivy along the shore between Thunder Hole and Monument Cove. The Gorham Mountain hike (see #87) is in this same area and makes a nice combination with the Shore Trail.*

96.

The Bar Harbor Bar

Directions: **Bar Harbor, Maine. Follow directions for #85. Stay on Route 3 about 2 miles beyond the Hull's Cove entrance, then turn left (northeast) onto West St. (there are traffic islands in the intersection). Go 0.3 mile and park on West St. near Bridge St.**

Ownership: **Maine Bureau of Parks and Recreation.**

The Bar Harbor Bar is a rocky tidal bar that stretches between Mount Desert Island and Bar Island. It is a fine place to watch gulls and migrating shorebirds, to hunt for intertidal creatures, and to see the changing water levels of the tides. Plant a stick at the edge of the water on the left-hand (western) side of the bar when you begin your walk and note its relationship to the edge of the water when you return.

The tidal bar begins at the bottom of Bridge St. (a dead end). It is passable for about 5 hours at a time, 2½ hours on either side of the low tide. In the Gulf of Maine, there are two high tides and two low tides each day, each high and low separated by about 6¼ hours. This means that if the low tide on a particular day falls at 10:00 a.m., the next daytime low tide (two low tides later—there will be one at night) will be at about 11:00 a.m., and the next (another two lows hence) at about noon. Tides are generated by gravitational, rotational, and orbital forces of the moon, sun, and earth. A simple model for tides is difficult to create, but it is essentially the following: (a) the earth's gravity, in our part of space the strongest of the three, holds our water and other matter on earth; (b) the relatively weaker gravitational forces of the moon and the sun pull bulges or tides in the earth's water (and in rocks, but these are much smaller because rocks are less plastic than water); (c) tidal bulges occur on the side of the earth nearest the moon or sun *and* on the side of the earth away from those bodies; (d) these tidal bulges move around the earth each day because it is rotating. Bar Harbor Bar passes "under" or closest to the moon once every 25 hours; although the earth rotates once every 24 hours, the moon is also going around us, and it takes us an hour longer than our own day to "catch up" to it. If you stood on Bar Harbor Bar for a 25-hour period, you would see two high and two low tides. Although the moon is much smaller than the sun, it is much closer to us and has the greater effect on our tides.

The variation between high and low tides in this area is about 8 to 12 feet. The highest highs and the lowest lows, called the spring tides, occur when the pulls of the sun and the moon are in the same direction. That happens when the earth, moon, and sun are arranged essentially in a straight line, that is, when we see a full or a new moon. These produce the best lows for tidepooling (see **#80, #93, #95, #100,** and **#101**). The lowest highs and highest lows, called the neap tides, occur when the bulges induced by the moon and the sun are in opposing directions. During these periods, we see the moon at half phases.

If you have been to shores in other places, you may have noticed

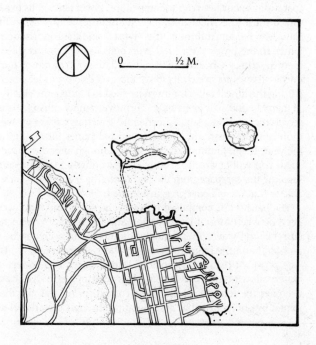

that there is quite a variation in tide patterns worldwide. Parts of Florida have tides of only a few inches, whereas the head of the Bay of Fundy has tides up to 52 feet. Texas has only one high and one low tide each day, whereas some of the islands off the coast of Scotland have four highs and four lows in the same period. This is because the shapes of coastlines, baybottoms, and tidal basins also affect the tides, in some instances overriding the general two-high-and-two-low-per-day pattern. Tides are so complex that the only way we can predict them in a specific location is to observe and record them in that place for a long time.

Walk down onto the bar. Herring gulls (see **#17** and **#77**) are usually quite visible. Often they fly up into the air, drop a mussel, sea urchin (see **#80**), or some other hard-shelled creature, and fly down after it. The gull is trying to break the shell in order to reach the creature inside. Even if the shell lands on hard rock, it usually takes more than one drop to accomplish this.

During the warmer months, you may discover numerous crab carapaces on the bar. If these are unbroken, they are probably molted shells rather than the remains of a gull's dinner. Crabs, like lobsters and shrimp, have hard exoskeletons, which they outgrow periodically. When it molts, a crab literally backs out of its shell, through a space that opens between the upper and lower parts of its exoskeleton. It must lose water from its body in order to do this, so that its claws can be pulled through the "wrists" and the legs through their joints. In the process, the crab even pulls its eyes and its gills out of their coverings! Once out of its old shell, the crab pumps water back into its tissues to stretch its new, soft exoskeleton to its larger size. During the time it takes for this new shell to harden, the crab is quite vulnerable and will often hide. Turn over empty mussel shells and see if you can find a small green crab. Touch its back. You will find more soft ones early in summer, and hard ones during the rest of the year. If you find molted shells soon enough after they have been shed, you will be able to see the eye coverings and, if you carefully separate the carapace from the legs (from the rear edge), you will be able to find the gill coverings inside the hollow shell.

The bar itself is composed of rocks and shells and mud accumulated between Mount Desert Island and Bar Island by the action of currents and waves. It is actually a tombolo, an accretion between an island and the mainland or, as in this case, between two islands (see **#78**). At high tide, it may be buried under some 6 feet of salt water, allowing boats passage back and forth over it. At low tide it becomes the territory of the gulls. During spring and fall, they are joined by shorebirds that are migrating through the area. Before it was widely known that some birds migrate, there were varied explanations for their disappearance in winter, one being that swallows spent the winter in the mud at the bottoms of ponds. The question of why birds migrate has intrigued modern ornithologists for years, for certainly such journeys require the expenditure of great amounts of energy and are full of hazards. For example, (a) a bird may lose as much as one-fifth of its weight in a flight as short as crossing the English Channel; (b) adverse weather such as high winds, storms, or precipitation can slow migration drastically and even kill some birds; (c) most birds that migrate must expend energy reestablishing their breeding territories each year; (d) traveling through unfamiliar territory and areas with little cover increases the potential of predation; and (e) some human activities have been and continue to be significant threats: pollution can affect the health and breeding capabilities of birds (see **#99**); activities such as beach recreation can compete with migrant resting stops; tall lighted structures seem to attract birds, which often fly into them, with fatal results. It sounds like a grim picture, yet birds would not migrate unless the advantages at least balanced the disadvantages. By migrating south, birds can escape harsh climates and lack of winter food supplies. Seeds and rodents may be covered by snow, and insects are only seasonally abundant. In the south, birds have longer daylight hours for winter feeding. Ornithologists suspect that the birds return north in the spring to ensure availability of adequate food supplies for raising young and to take advantage of longer daylight for feeding, a factor that may cut down on the number of days a young bird must remain in the nest, highly vulnerable to predation. In one study, it was found that robins raised in Ohio were fed about 16 hours per day and remained in the nest an average of 13.2 days, whereas robins reared in Alaska were fed about 21 hours per day and stayed in the nest only about 9 days.

How migration evolved is not clear, and a number of theories have been proposed. One of these suggests that the ranges of organisms in general are complex and diverse. Even sedentary animals often use different habitats within their range for different activities, such as feeding, wintering, and breeding. For more mobile animals, these areas can be further apart. Thus, a green frog's use of Witch Hole Pond (see **#89**) mud for winter hibernation and the pond's waters for breeding may be analogous to a greater yellowlegs wintering in Argentina and breeding in northern Canada. At some point that has not been clearly defined, movements between parts of a range cover enough distance to be called migration.

Of the shorebirds that stop over on the Bar Harbor Bar, many are nighttime migrators. If you come down to the bar at night, you may be able to hear them calling as they pass overhead. These birds probably fly during the dark hours so that they can spend the days feeding and resting. Many songbirds that travel at night probably benefit in this way, as well as by being less visible to predators, such as hawks. Hawks rely on the rising air of thermals to help them soar and generally travel by day (see **#41**).

Yellowlegs and ruddy turnstones are among the other visitors to the Bar Harbor Bar. Both species nest in northern Canada and winter from the southern United States to the Southern Hemisphere, the greater yellowlegs as far south as Tierra del Fuego. Although both species use the bar during migration, they feed so differently that they do not compete with each other. The tall, slender yellowlegs tends to feed by probing while wading in the pools. The rather chunky and squat turnstones (with orangy legs and harlequinlike plumage) feed by picking organisms from the seaweeds and from under shells and stones they overturn.

Remarks: *This is a ¾-mile walk over a tidal bar. A wide swath of it is quite compacted and fairly dry, the rest is rather soft and wet. Access is very easy, ideal for families. The entire length of the bar is exposed for about 2½ hours on either side of the low tide. Tidal information is available from the Acadia National Park Visitor Center, the Bar Harbor Chamber of Commerce information station, and various local publications. The bar is a good place for a night walk and even for winter adventures when the wind is not too bitter. The western half of Bar Island is owned by Acadia National Park. Trails pass through old fields and mixed woods. Remember to keep the tide in mind when you explore the island. Another place to walk or hike is the Bar Harbor Shore Path, which follows the shore southeast from the town waterfront parking area. Several boat companies offer trips among the islands around Mount Desert; some are narrated by Acadia National Park naturalists. Check the Acadia naturalist program and individual boat-company schedules. Of special interest are Bob Bowman's whale and seabird cruises aboard the* Island Queen *out of Northeast Harbor, June through September. For some other places on Mount Desert Island to look for migrating birds, see* **Acadia National Park.**

97.
Blagden
Preserve

Directions: **Indian Point, Mount Desert Island, Maine. Follow directions for #85, but after crossing the causeway, do not bear left on Route 3; instead, go straight southeast on Route 102 for about 2 miles. Just before the Town Hill Country Store, turn southwest (right) onto Indian Point Rd. Go 2 miles to the preserve entrance on the right; the sign at the head of the driveway says Indian Point. Register and pick up a map at the caretaker's house.**

Ownership: **The Nature Conservancy.**

The spruce-fir forests of 110-acre Blagden Preserve retain much of the open, parklike character typical of estates that have been purposely manicured. For decades before they donated the land to The Nature Conservancy, the Blagdens removed blowdowns and systematically thinned these woods. At the northwest end of the coastline of the preserve, one can often see seals swimming in the water and basking on offshore ledges at low tide. This is the only place on Mount Desert Island where one is likely to see seals out of water.

Follow the Big Woods Trail to the lower parking area (or drive there on the tarred road). The trail meanders through tall woods (**A**) not burned by the 1947 fire (see **#87**). Wonderful arrays of mosses and lichens (see **#88**), some of the few plants that can tolerate the shady, acidic soil conditions found in many Maine forests, carpet the ground. Among the most fascinating members of these miniature forests are club mosses; British soldiers, with their red "caps"; pixie-cup and reindeer lichens; haircap and sphagnum mosses. The haircap moss is named for the hairy cap that covers its flame-shaped spore case before it sheds the spores. This is the asexual reproductive part of their life cycle. The sexual phase is one of the key factors that ties mosses to wet places. Having neither a flower or other structure to attract insects to carry their male cells, nor pollen that allows those male cells to travel great distances on either air currents or insects, the moss sperm must be able to swim to its female destination: that requires moisture. Among the damp hummocks of moss, look also

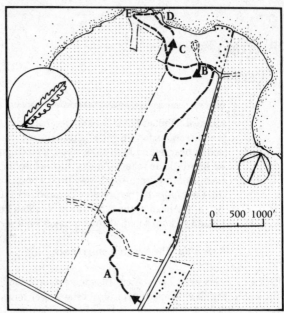

Inset: Sweet fern

for mounds of dirt particles, which slowly grow as the ants that live in them excavate beneath the surface.

Jog left and then right as the trail crosses a private road. If conditions are right, bayberry bushes may scent the air with a sweet, almost peppery aroma. If the odor is not readily apparent, rub your fingers on the shiny leaves. The waxy berries also have this aroma and were very popular in past centuries as an ingredient to mask the unpleasant stench of the tallow used in making household candles. Bayberry is a *diecious* (*di-* for "two," *ecious* for "house") species, male and female structures growing on separate plants. Look for small catkins (clusters of pollen-bearing anthers) on the male plants and small green berries on the female plants. A member of the waxmyrtle family, bayberry is one of the few species other than legumes (bean-family plants) to harbor nitrogen-fixing bacteria on its roots. These tiny organisms perform the vital role of changing gaseous nitrogen from the air, which plants cannot use, into nitrogenous compounds, which plants can absorb.

The Shore Trail begins at the edge of an old orchard (**B**). Not far into the woods, notice the old, but still living, ground-hugging apple tree (see **#74**). The forest in this section is a mixture of coniferous and deciduous trees. There is a large amount of dead debris, and many of the large birches are ragged looking. Trees, like most other organisms, seem to have life· spans. At 80 years, a white birch is old whereas a spruce is but middle-aged. In this stretch of forest, the canopy composition is shifting to a higher and higher concentration of conifers as the birch trees reach the end of their life-spans and die. At the same time, each falling branch and tree opens a new patch of forest floor to colonization by new plants and to more rapid growth of saplings and other plants already established.

Beyond the gravel road (**C**), white spruce becomes very common, since it is more tolerant of shoreline exposure than the red spruce of the inner forests. Another odoriferous inhabitant here is the small woody shrub called sweet fern, a flowering plant, and not a true fern. Its pungent, resinous, scalloped leaves have been used by many peoples for making tea.

The banded rock outcroppings along the shore (**D**) are part of the oldest known rock series on Mount Desert Island—the Ellsworth schists. About 450 million years ago, the sea and land were arranged very differently than the way they are today, and this area was then under water (see **#83**). The sea floor built up with layer upon layer of sediments that gradually consolidated into rock (see **#74**). Notice the variety of rock types included in the "beach." Many of these are from some distance away, and were brought here by the glaciers (see **#85**). The granite ones with very large white-to-pinkish crystals come from bedrock in the Lucerne area, some 30 miles northwest of here.

The west end of the preserve shoreline, just before the private property, is a good spot for seal watching (**E**). Look for gold, brown, or gray figures reclining on the shallow, angled ledges beyond the neck of private property and to the north of the islands. These are harbor seals, "true" seals with no external ear and no ability to use their rear flippers for walking, the way sea lions can. Harbor seals live year-round in the Gulf of Maine, their behavior and habits closely related to the movement of the tides. At high tide, they are usually in the water fishing; at low tide, most of them "haul out" on ledges to sun themselves and sleep. Although they are warm-blooded mammals, seals do not mind being immersed in the cold water for hours at a time. They are protected by thick insulating layers of blubber, which streamline them for swimming as well (see **#53**). As mammals, they must get their oxygen from the air, yet they have been discovered swimming at depths as great as 450 feet! A number of adaptations allow this seemingly phenomenal behavior. A seal exhales before diving, relying entirely on oxygen stored in its blood and muscles for the duration of its dive. Its blood circulation is reduced to vital organs only—heart and brain. Its entire metabolism may also slow down, demanding even less use of oxygen.

Seal populations fluctuate in response to a wide variety of factors, including food availability, predators, access to breeding territories, and diseases. By the early 1900s, harbor seals had been hunted to the brink of extinction in the Gulf of Maine. Places like Seal Harbor and Seal Cove (on the southern side of Mount Desert Island) may have been named, not for an abundance of seals, but because the sight of them in these waters was so exceptional. Federal protection of the past two decades has allowed harbor seals to reestablish substantial herds in the Gulf of Maine.

From the shore, return to the woods as the trail loops back along a fence surrounded by beautiful old white birches. Go left on the gravel road; the parking lot and Big Woods Trail are a few hundred feet away.

Remarks: *This walk is about 2½ miles round-trip, over terrain sloping moderately to the shore. The soft forest sections are often quite damp. Those unable to walk the full distance have the option of driving from the caretaker's house to the lower parking area (**B**). Please respect the private property adjacent to the boundaries of the preserve.*

98.

Schoodic Mountain

Directions: **East Franklin, Maine. From Bangor, take U.S. 1A southeast about 27 miles to Ellsworth. Go east about 13 miles on U.S. 1 to Sullivan; turn north (left) onto Route 200. In 3.6 miles, there is a road on the right between two bridges, which is the trailhead. Park north of the second bridge.**

Ownership: **Private.**

Rearing a prominent, open summit, Schoodic Mountain dominates the head of Frenchman Bay. It offers an interesting perspective of the lumpy form of Mount Desert Island and an opportunity to contemplate the blue waters of the Gulf of Maine, which so much influence the livelihoods of Mainers, human and nonhuman. Its flanks and the lowlands around its base are an invitation to explore adaptations and life-styles of coastal mountain vegetation and wildlife.

The hike begins on the right-hand fork of the paved road between the bridges. At the top of the hill, it turns to dirt, skirting blueberry fields. At the next fork, stay right, following the power lines, through a shrubby swath full of meadowsweet and across a small brook (**A**). On a sunny day, especially after cloudy or rainy weather, you may be lucky enough to see a garter snake on the road edge before it slithers away. Perhaps it will flick out its tongue and wiggle it in the air. This is not a threat; it is simply one way a snake perceives its environment, using a sense akin to a combination of taste and smell. It can also see movement over short distances. It can feel vibrations in the ground and usually glides away before being seen.

Snakes are unjustly maligned, to a great extent because people know very little about them. Although some snakes are poisonous even these can only strike over a distance of about a third the length of their body. For example, if you stand 6 feet away from a 4-foot

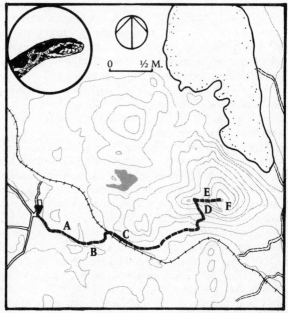

Inset: Eastern milk snake

long rattlesnake, you are perfectly safe. There are no wild poisonous snakes in Maine, except in the southernmost part. The common snakes in this region are the garter, milk, smooth green, red-bellied, and ring-necked snakes, all of them small to medium in size. All snakes can bite, but only poisonous snakes can make you sick. The bite from a garter snake feels like a little pin prick, more startling than painful. Snakes are able to move quite quickly and silently without the aid of legs. This unnerves many people, but it is not in itself dangerous or unnatural, just different from human locomotion. Some snakes, especially milk snakes, like to prowl around in barns— not to drink milk from cows or goats, a myth that gave rise to their name—but to eat young mice and rats. Snakes sometimes reflect light from their scales in a way that makes them look shiny, but they are not slimy. Unless they have been in damp or wet places (garter snakes swim a fair amount), their skin is dry.

Catch a snake, if you can (with your hands, not with a stick, which may hurt it). If you let it crawl from hand to hand, it will very likely calm down. Feel the difference between its back and belly scales. Notice that the belly scales are overlapped from front to back, like a fish's, giving it a bit of traction for forward movement. Look at its eyes. A snake cannot blink—its eyes are covered with a non-movable, clear lid, which is shed with the rest of the skin each time a snake molts. Watch it breathe. It has long, slender lungs. The snake's mouth is one of its most interesting features. The jaws have very stretchy hinging, enabling the snake to swallow prey significantly larger in diameter than its own body. A garter snake commonly eats frogs, toads, tadpoles, salamanders, and earthworms.

Enter mixed woods with Canada mayflower, a common ground-cover species. Near the top of the rise surfaced with old pavement (**B**), look for huckleberry bushes, whose light-green, somewhat shiny leaves have golden, glandular dots all over the bottom side; in June, they have small, reddish, dangling flowers. Some of the bushes have swollen, pinkish "flowers" about ¼ inch in diameter called *galls*. Galls are formed in plant tissues that have been irritated, usually by an insect or a fungus. Commonly, an insect will lay egg(s) on or just beneath the surface of a leaf, bud, stem, or twig. When the larva hatches, it chews its way into the growing part of the plant tissues. It is believed that a secretion from the larva stimulates the growth of the gall tissue, which provides food and protection for the developing insect. Aphids, small flies, and tiny wasps are the most common gall-inducing insects. Galls appear in many forms, from little, pink nubbles on maple leaves to cotton-candy-like masses on rose stems, each shape caused by a particular species on its preferred plant. Here, an insect has been active in the flower buds, causing them to grow abnormally—these swollen buds will not be able to be pollinated and to grow into huckleberries.

Cross the railroad tracks and swing right with the road (**C**). In early spring, many of the new leaves have a purplish or reddish color, especially the wintergreen, sarsaparilla, maple, and oak. Botanists believe that these colors are pigments that protect the young, tender tissues from sun damage, in the same manner that the pigment melanin in human skin helps protect us from sunburn. At this time of year, too, young aspen leaves are covered with short, soft, white hairs. These may help shield the tissues from too much heat and from desiccation. By summertime, all these leaves will be green and virtually hairless.

The large triangular fronds of bracken fern and circular clumps of interrupted fern are common in much of this area. They exhibit two different spore-producing strategies. Bracken-fern sori (spore cases) grow in lines along the curled margins of the pinnae (small, leaflike sections). Interrupted-fern sori dangle on fertile pinnae in the middle of green fronds, "interrupting" them.

At the fork, go left. You will travel close to a mile through the woods, crossing a small brook. Just beyond the stretch of road that is obviously widened and rutted from extended muddy conditions, go left on a narrow, well-beaten path. In about 0.2 mile, you reach the ruins of the fire warden's cabin. From here, follow the left fork of the trail, up a steep hill, and then through shorter, more shrubby woods (**D**), toward the saddle between Schoodic Nubble and the summit of the mountain. White-throated sparrows sing their plaintive *Hey, Sam Peabody, Peabody, Peabody* songs over and over and over again during the spring and summer months. Even for beginners, this is a distinct and readily recognizable bird vocalization. Ornithologists generally divide bird vocalizations into two categories: calls and songs. Calls are brief sounds, usually associated with coordinating nonsexual behaviors, such as flocking, feeding, migrating, and reactions to predators. These sounds seem to be genetically determined rather than learned. Songs tend to be longer utterances, patterned in pitch and rhythm. They are sung mostly during the breeding season, when they seem to serve as substitutes for physical violence in defense of territory, as stimulus for and in synchronizing the reproductive cycle, and as attraction and maintenance mechanisms for pair bonding. Songs are sometimes modified by learning.

Investigators have conducted numerous experiments in order to distinguish the significant features of a bird's song. They have discovered that what seems significant varies from species to species. In white-throated sparrows, ornithologist J. B. Falls determined that "pitch, form, and arrangement of component sounds, and timing of the sounds and the intervals between them" were the important factors. A white-throated sparrow could recognize its neighbor by the first three notes of its song, but a 10 percent change in pitch (achieved by slowing down tape-recorded songs) led to confusion. Falls also discovered that a white-throated sparrow responded more vigorously, that is, in song replies per minute, to the recorded calls of a stranger than to the recorded calls of its neighbor. But when the neighbor's call was sounded from the wrong side of the owner's territory, the bird responded as if the neighbor were a stranger. Although many bird songs have oscillations too rapid for the human ear to distinguish, by listening carefully you may be able to hear differences (minor to us but perhaps gross to the birds) in the songs of the white-throated sparrows on Schoodic Mountain.

From the saddle, the summit trail heads eastward (**E**). Toward the top, cairns and paint marks on the rocks delineate the route. Scars on old wood remain from fires that have burned these slopes (see **#87**). Among the matted juniper, blueberry, chokeberry, three-toed cinquefoil, lichens, and mosses of the open ledges are clumps of golden heather, a low, bushy plant with spreading, needlelike leaves and small, five-petaled, yellow flowers that bloom in late spring and early summer. Although its name implies a relationship to the heather of the Scottish moors, it is in a separate and semidistant family. Golden heather lives in such dry habitats as dunes, pine barrens, and rocks, mainly in maritime Canada and the mountains of New England.

From the summit (**F**) of Schoodic, you look east into the Gouldsboro Hills and Tunk Lake, southwest to the lumpy silhouette of Mount Desert Island, and south into the Gulf of Maine. The gulf is a partially enclosed sea that lies in a shallow basin bounded by Cape Cod, the coast of Maine, Nova Scotia, and Brown's and Georges Banks. The deeper Atlantic is south of the banks, which help keep the warm Gulf Stream current from mixing with the cold waters of the Gulf of Maine. Five big river systems (the Saint John, Penobscot, Kennebec, Piscataqua, and Merrimack) empty into the gulf, making its waters measurably less salty than the Atlantic Ocean and increasing the dissolved and suspended nutrient concentrations, especially adjacent to the rivermouths. These factors combine to make the Gulf of Maine a nursery for many species of saltwater fish, some of which, as adults, roam the larger reaches of the Atlantic (see **#82** and **Cape Cod to Portland**). The great expanse of the Atlantic, and of the world's oceans in general, is biologically much like a desert—for all its vast size, it can support very little biomass. If you were to jump into Frenchman Bay and swim southward across the Gulf of Maine and on into the Atlantic, the water would tend to get increasingly clear as you moved from the thick planktonic soup of the cold northern waters and into the relatively thin soup of the warmer southern waters.

Return to your car by the same route you ascended Schoodic Mountain.

Remarks: *This is a 5¾-mile hike, round trip, the first half of the ascent over gently rising dirt roads, the second half on a steep, rocky trail. It is very nice in early spring (bring insect repellent) and probably best during the fall leaf-change, in late September to early October. November, which is deer-hunting season, is not a good time to visit. In winter you can cross-country ski and snowshoe on the road portion. Other hiking in the area: Lead Mountain, off Route 9, near Beddington, and Peaked Mountain (Chick Hill), off Route 9, east of East Eddington, both described in* Fifty More Hikes in Maine *by Cloe Catlett; Bald Mountain off Route 46, southeast of Dedham, and Tunk Mountain, off Route 182, northeast of Franklin, described in the* AMC Maine Mountain Guide.

99.

Columbia Falls

Glaciomarine Delta

Directions: **Columbia Falls, Maine. From Bangor, take U.S. 1A southeast about 27 miles to Ellsworth. Go east on U.S. 1 about 32 miles to Milbridge, then 8 miles on U.S. 1A back to U.S. 1 at Harrington. Continue east on U.S. 1 for 4.3 miles past this junction; at an intersection with a Poneo Lumber Company sign on the northeast corner, turn north (left). Go up the hill, cross the railroad tracks, and stay right at the fork. You are now on the Centerville Rd. In 2 miles you will come to a junction where a dirt road leaves to the right and a concrete company and another road are on the left. Mileages for the rest of this drive-and-stop trip begin from here—this is mile 0.0. You will continue straight.**

Ownership: **Private.**

This entry does not describe a hike, but rather a pleasant drive with various points of interest. From the 0.0-mile point, the road rises up the gentle slope of the delta. A *delta* is defined as deposits of sediment, in either the ocean or a lake, formed at the mouth of a river.

The name of the triangular-shaped Greek letter *delta* has been applied to these alluvial formations because most of them do have a roughly triangular shape. To identify rising land covered with blueberry barrens as a delta takes at least a second glance and may come as a surprise to many, yet that is precisely what geologists have done north of Columbia Falls. The Columbia Falls Delta is not really as strange a phenomenon as it might seem. Like other deltas, it did form under water, but that water is no longer there today. The Columbia Falls Delta is a *glaciomarine* delta, formed along the contact between ice and sea where a meltwater stream on or in the glacier discharged into the salt water. The story, as far as glaciologists can tell, is as follows. The last ice sheet to cover eastern North America reached its greatest extent southward about 18,000 years ago. Then it began to melt, releasing great amounts of water into the sea and causing the worldwide sea level to rise. Some 13,000 years ago, the glacier margin, retreating in contact with the rising sea, reached the position of the present Maine coast. It continued to retreat inland for another 35 miles or so and then, for unknown reasons, it advanced again about 25 miles, leaving a series of deposits extending from Cherryfield into New Brunswick. Subsequently, the ice sheet melted again, retreating this time to the Arctic. The Columbia Falls Delta was formed some 12,700 years ago, when the second advance of the ice sheet halted.

At the beginning of this drive, there are many large depressions in the surface of the delta, two of which are near the road on the left and the right, at about 0.2 mile (**A**). These are called *kettle holes*. Kettle holes generally form where chunks of ice, deposited by the glacier and buried in sand and gravel, eventually melt. The sand-and-gravel surface collapses into the hole, forming a rounded or oval depression. In the case of the Columbia Falls Delta kettles, glaciologists propose a variation on this creation theory. They suggest that the ice margin was thin and irregular and covered by deltaic sediments. When the ice melted out, the whole layer of sediments collapsed into the rolling and kettle-pocked surface we see today.

Intermixed with a variety of herbs and shrubby plants, lowbush blueberries are the prize of the delta barrens. The sandy-and-gravelly composition of the delta drains extremely well in most places, creating a dry substrate. This is a condition that blueberries tolerate very well but that is not conducive to growing most domestic crops or even most forest tree species. Blueberries have been cultivated in Maine for over a century, the emergent glaciomarine deltas and other sandy glacial outwash deposits of Knox, Hancock, and Washington counties providing prime ground. Ever since the Indians discovered its effects, fire has been used as one way of minimizing competition from taller species and of promoting high production of berries. Much as we might like to think of human management techniques as being beneficial to the managed species, numerous biologists suspect that the increase in blueberry production following burning may be more of a stress-induced response than a response to increased availability of nutrients, a factor we might consider positive.

As you pass through the barrens, you may see long strings staked out in parallel lines, which define strips of field to be harvested. Commercial harvesters use a short-handled, rakelike tool that is much faster than picking by hand.

Late July and August is blueberry time in this part of Maine, and humans are not the only species to observe it. Foxes, coyotes, and ruffed grouse also love to eat the berries, and white-tailed deer and hares often browse the twigs. The lives of osprey and bald eagles that frequent Maine's coasts and lakes have also been affected by these cultivated fields of blueberries. Earlier in this century, DDT and dieldrin/aldrin were sprayed on the blueberries to inhibit infestation of the fruit by insect larvae ("worms"). These chemicals, washed from the plants and leached from the soil, were carried by streams into

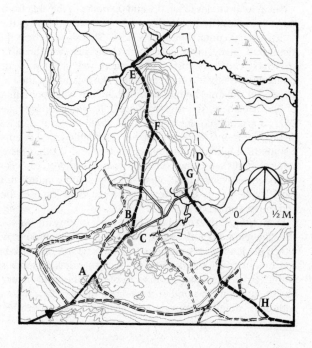

the sea. Through a series of metabolic interactions that are ill understood, a chemical breakdown product called DDE is formed and stored in animal tissues. In fish of the size that eagles and osprey eat, concentrations of DDE can be quite high. Passed on to the birds of prey, this chemical wreaks havoc with their calcium metabolism, causing them to lay thin-shelled eggs, which crack under the weight of the adults when they try to incubate them. Although we have banned most use of DDT and dieldrin/aldrin in the United States, we still export them. Fortunately, most other countries have curtailed use of these pesticides, and worldwide use has dropped. Osprey populations on the East Coast are increasing again. Eagle populations are not doing as well, although their numbers appear to have stabilized. This difference between the two species may be related to the longer life-span of eagles. For a longer period of time, their populations would include a higher percentage of older adults affected by the pesticides. This would slow the resilience of the population. This series of events is a good example of how asking the wrong question leads to discovery of the wrong answer: early testing was done on the effects of DDT on animal physiology rather than on the effects of DDE, which proved to be the important chemical (see **#22** and **#50**).

Pass two dirt roads left at 0.5 and 0.8 mile. In the area from about 1.0 to 1.5 miles (**B**), you can see the north-facing slope of the delta, which was in contact with the glacier. This slope, where the sediments built up against the ice, is much steeper than the distal slope up which you have just driven, where sediments were dropped gradually over a wide area spreading like a fan from the mouth of the glacial stream. The mouth of this stream was approximately at **C**. North of here, the four rounded hills are a lumpy esker (**D**). *Eskers* are sand and gravel deposited along the course of a stream flowing in or on a glacier (see **#66**). Generally an esker appears as a smooth, single ridge of uniform height and width. This esker is atypical in this sense and is called a *headed esker*. You can get several good perspectives on the Columbia Esker if you continue driving to the 3.2-mile point (**E**), where a small gravel pit exposes the sand-and-gravel composition.

From here, turn around and head back southward. At 4.8 miles, (**F**), stay left at the fork. Along the road at **G,** wet pockets, many of which are kettle holes, are colonized by tamarack, alder, red maple, and cottonwood. White pines fringe the better-drained sections, along with cherry and staghorn sumac. In the fall, the reddish, fuzzy clusters of sumac fruits stand at the branch tips like fat candle flames. Although with their hairy surface they look unpalatable, they can be steeped in boiled water to make a fruity tea, which is refreshing hot or cold, especially with a dash of lemon.

Soaring above the barrens spring through fall, you may see a large hawk with a rusty-, or rufous-, colored tail. There is quite a bit of variation in the plumage of these red-tailed hawks, especially in the West. Some of them are very pale and buffy, whereas others are quite dark, almost black. Redtails are classified as *buteos,* a group of large hawks with broad wings and wide, fan-shaped tails. Both of these are good adaptations for soaring, which they habitually do in high, wide circles over open country, where they feed on rodents, hares, small birds, large grasshoppers, and reptiles.

At 5.5 miles stay left. At 6.1 miles the road surface changes to dirt and, in a couple of tenths of a mile more, it suddenly drops down a short hill (**H**). This is a wave-cut terrace, which stretches along the south-facing slope of the delta. The sea level did continue to rise as the glaciers melted, but the land that had been under the ice sheet also began to rise, or rebound (see **Portland North**). If you place an eraser on a sponge and put a brick on top of that, the eraser gets flattened a bit and pressed down into the sponge. When you take the brick off the eraser, it regains its shape and rises as the sponge expands. Similarly, when the weight of the ice was gone from the land surface, the hard crustal rocks expanded again and rose from the softer mantle. Along the coast of Maine, the land happened to rise faster than the sea, and the delta began to emerge above the water. This cliff was eroded by waves that washed that emerging shore. As the sea level continued to drop, that is, in relation to the rising land, a series of beach terraces were formed on the lower levels of the delta slope. On the east side of the road as it descends the steep terrace is a gravel pit where the makeup of this part of the delta is exposed. Sand, gravel, and rocks of numerous granitic and metamorphic compositions are present. On the right-hand side of the pit entrance, there is a good-sized glacial erratic (see **#85**) of coarse-grained light-colored granite. This collection of widely assorted rock types is indicative of the variety of bedrock types north of here. Matching the fragments with the areas from which they were derived helps scientists to chart the movements of the glaciers.

From here, continue down the slope of the delta. At 6.5 miles, the road becomes paved again, and at 11.3 miles, you rejoin Route 1 in Jonesboro.

Remarks: *This driving tour is 6½ miles long over paved and dirt roads. Please respect the fact that it lies on private property; do not wander off the road or pick the blueberries. You may gather them on the mountains at*

Acadia National Park or on other state or federal property. As you are traveling, you may also discover blueberry operations where you can pick your own. A good time to visit the Columbia Falls Delta is in late September and October, after the harvest, when the blueberry leaves turn red and wine-colored. There is a primitive campsite just southwest of Jonesboro at the junction of Routes 1 and 187. Camping is also available at Cobscook Bay State Park, Whiting (May 15 to October 15); Mountain View Campground, East Sullivan (Memorial Day to October); Lamoise State Park, southeast of Ellsworth (May 15 to October 15); Acadia National Park, Mount Desert Island (year-round at Blackwoods Campground).

100.

Petit Manan

Point

Directions: **Steuben, Maine. From Bangor, take U.S. 1A southeast about 27 miles to Ellsworth. Go east on U.S. 1 about 25 miles to Steuben; continue on U.S. 1, passing Dyer Bay Rd. at 2.1 miles, to Pigeon Hill Rd. after another 0.8 miles. Go south (right); at 1.6 miles, stay right at the fork. In another 3.9 miles, the pavement changes to dirt; stay right, entering the Petit Manan Wildlife Refuge. Go 0.1 mile and park in the space on the right.**

Ownership: **Petit Manan Wildlife Refuge, U.S. Fish and Wildlife Service.**

Petit Manan Point is a narrow peninsula jutting southward between Dyer and Pigeon Hill bays in eastern Maine. Connected to the mainland by only a small neck, it is almost an island. Open to the onslaught of storms, its southeastern shores are piled with spectacular seawalls. Low tides expose extensive sand and rock intertidal areas. Old blueberry fields, groves of jack pine, and sections of heath are among its interior features.

Follow the dirt road through the gate, continuing straight past the private drive with the mailbox. Go left on the Shore Trail (**A**), where the vegetation on the left turns to low, shrubby heaths with numerous small quaking aspen. In May and June, when the spring flowers are blooming, you may see numerous very large bumblebees. These

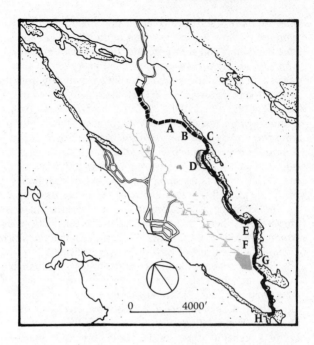

big, early bees are fertilized queens that have spent the winter in subterranean burrows. Watch one as she drinks nectar with her long, strawlike proboscis (mouthpart) or as she gathers pollen and stuffs it into the pollen pouches on her hind legs. Each of these queens will seek out an existing underground cavity in which to start a nest. There she will arrange the pollen she has collected into clumps, lay eggs on top, cover the whole with wax, and then sit on top of it, keeping the eggs warm while they develop. When the larvae hatch, they feed on the pollen for about a week and then pupate, after which they emerge as sterile females that will take care of future broods during the summer. Toward the end of summer, the queen lays eggs that develop into fertile females and males, which leave the nest and mate. These new fertilized queens are the only members of the colony to survive the coming winter; the rest die (see **#73**).

At **B,** you travel through a corridor surrounded by numerous jack pines, which are at the edge of their range here in Maine. In the damp areas just before you reach the shore, you pass tall clumps of cinnamon fern, which has two different types of fronds. The infertile ones are green and leaflike, and grow in a circular clump. The fertile ones are narrow and covered at the upper end by clusters of round spore cases. Growing in the center of the clump in early summer, they stand erect and are a gorgeous, fresh cinnamon color. By mid-summer they are bent over and dark brown.

The trail ends at the shore (**C**). A little way upbay from the cove is a well-kept fish weir (see **#101**). From here, follow the shore to the end of Petit Manan Point. At **D,** Chair Pond lies in a basin behind a large, sea-built wall (seawall) of rounded stones. Storm waves from the open sea to the southeast have sufficient energy to pile these quite high. Rotting piles of seaweeds on top of and on the back side of the seawall indicate that storm waves still overwash the wall, making the pond brackish. Few species live in such ponds. During the spring and fall, you may find whirligig beetles zooming about on the surface of the water, along the quiet edges near the vegetation. These are the adult insects; the larvae live under the water. The whirligig beetle has three rather interesting adaptations, which make its life-style possible: (a) each of its eyes is divided into two parts, one able to see above the surface of the water, the other able to see in the water; (b) its antennae have an organ at their base that can detect minute changes in the angle of the antennae, which are held along the surface of the water, and thereby perceive the rise and fall of surface ripples. These disturbances may be caused by another beetle, a predator, a prey, or the beetle's own movement, bounced back from a stationary object like an echo; and (c) the front pair of the beetle's legs, the only ones visible at the surface, are built for grabbing prey, whereas the other two pairs are flattened, making them good oars for locomotion.

As you walk along the top of the seawall, you may notice numer-ous small, dark creatures that dart quickly down between the stones. Catch one, if you can. Some may be carrying spherical, white egg cases. While these spiders do not use silk for making webs to capture prey (they ambush it from hiding places), they do spin silk for co-coons and lifelines. If your spider will stay still long enough, you may be able to tell which sex it is. Spiders have two body parts and eight legs (which means that they are not insects, which have three body parts and six legs) and two pedipalps or "foot feelers," which are parts of their mouth system. On a female spider, these pedipalps are about the same diameter for their entire length; on a male, they are swollen at the tip, a bit like pointed boxing gloves. The males use their palps for grasping females when they mate.

Also on the tops of many of the seawalls are some extremely lush growths of beach pea, blooming bright purple and magenta in the early summer. Each flower has five petals, the top broad one called the banner, the side two the wings, and the bottom two, which may look like a single petal, the keel. The pistil and stamens are enclosed within the keel. When the flower is ready for pollination, an insect of the right weight settling on the wings of the flower will cause the keel to bend downward, whereupon up pop the stiff pistil and the united stamens. The pistil, taller than the stamens, touches the insect first, picking up any pollen grains the insect brings from other flowers. A split second later, the anthers (pollen sacks) of the stamens brush against the insect, releasing the ripe pollen they contain. (See also **#101**.) If you gently pull down on the keel petals, you can see the pistil and stamens as they pop up.

At Wood Pond (**E**), you may startle black ducks or be able to watch spotted sandpipers wandering, picking up food, and bobbing their hind ends up and down. Notice how short are the cinnamon ferns in this exposed and desiccating environment.

Behind the steep, tall seawall at **F,** there is a wonderfully plush bog. Follow a game path out onto it. One of the rather abundant species here is baked-apple berry, a relative of the blackberry and the raspberry (with five-lobed leaves somewhat reminiscent of red maples). The peach-to-yellow-colored berries are considered delicacies by some, especially in Scandinavia. They are eaten fresh, or made into preserves or "cloudberry" (another of their common names) liqueur. It is one of the peatland species almost entirely restricted to coastal sites. Look also for carnivorous pitcher plants and sundews (see **#89**).

On the sand and rock beaches of Big Pond (**G**) and other coves, you may find large, gray sandpipers called willets. When they fly, a broad white band is exposed on each wing. This is one of the few shorebirds that nests in Maine. The chicks are difficult to see because of their cryptic coloring (see **#79**) and the noisy diversionary tactics of the adults who may perch high in a tree and call your attention away from their chicks on the beach.

At the end of the peninsula (**H**), and at numerous other places along the shore, low tide exposes a broad, low-angle intertidal zone, including large, shallow pools and a few deep crevices. The green-brown tangle of rockweed or wrack is particularly evident. Two genera are represented here: Fucus, the flattened types, often referred to as flat or bladder wrack, and Ascophyllum, the long, stringy type, often called knotted wrack. Both make excellent mulch and fertilizer for gardens. The knotted rockweed commonly has clumps of dark red, filamentous Polysiphonia ("many siphons") attached to it. Although it is red and the rockweed only faintly green, both of these algae photosynthesize, using pigments somewhat different in structure from the bright-green chlorophyll usually associated with the process. Scientist James Lovelock, author of *Gaia: A New Look at*

Life on Earth, suspects that this algae may be a large part of the mechanism by which sulfur is returned to the land from the sea. Polysiphonia produces dimethyl sulfide, a volatile gas that escapes from the sea and is probably blown over landmasses, where it becomes reincorporated in terrestrial ecosystems. Bacteria of the sea floor also have developed this technique, converting toxic substances such as lead, mercury, and arsenic into their volatile methyls. These gases permeate everything, including fish, as they rise through the seawater. Generally, the process of biological methylation involves small-enough amounts that toxic effects are not observed. The disaster in Minamata, Japan, some years ago, though, gives cause for thought. An industry discharged methyl mercury into the sea in quantities that made fish poisonous to humans. Everyone who ate the fish suffered. Many were horribly and painfully crippled, and some died. Although seabed processes of mercury methylation are not thought to function rapidly enough to cause problems, the case may be very different with other substances, such as arsenic. What has been discovered so far suggests that we ought to be cautious about the amounts of metals we dump into the sea—they may indeed affect biological systems.

Before heading back up the shore, check in crevices and behind curtains of seaweed for other intertidal organisms. Whelks are particularly abundant here (see **#101**). Their egg cases look like troops of white-to-purplish rice grains or tiny urns glued to sheltered rock surfaces. Each one contains perhaps a hundred eggs. The first to hatch reportedly feed on the others.

Remarks: *This is approximately a 7-mile hike, round trip. The first mile is on an easily walked trail; the rest is on rocks, stones, and some sand—much of it on rounded fragments, which make it like walking on marbles. Allow a whole day to explore as far as the end of the point. A trip timed with low tide near the middle of the day will allow chances for tidepooling in the greatest variety of areas. Day use only. The season is from mid-April to mid-November. For more information, contact Refuge Manager, Moosehorn National Wildlife Refuge, Box X, Calais, Maine 04619—there is no manager on this site. In August, flocks of whimbrels frequently feed on berries in the heaths of Petit Manan Point. Camping is available at McLellan Park, Milbridge (Washington County–operated), and at Mountainview Campground, East Sullivan (May 25 to October 1). Other sites nearby to visit are the Whaleback, an outstanding example of an esker segment, on Route 9 east of Aurora; Roque Bluffs State Park, including one of Maine's northernmost recreational beaches, about 10 miles southeast of Jonesboro; Fort O'Brien (or Fort Machias) in Machiasport, overlooking large tidal mudflats frequented by shorebirds from late July to September. These three sites are described in Dorcas Miller's* The Maine Coast: A Nature Lover's Guide.

101.

Quoddy Head

Directions: **Lubec, Maine. From Bangor, take U.S. 1A southeast about 27 miles to Ellsworth. Go east on U.S. 1 about 80 miles to Whiting and turn right (east) onto Route 189 as U.S. 1 swings north. Go about 5 miles to West Lubec; from the junction with Route 191, continue east on Route 189 for 4.1 miles. Turn right onto South Lubec Rd. at the sign for Quoddy Head State Park. After 2.6 miles bear left; after another 2 miles, the road forks: the lighthouse is to the left and the state park to the right.**

Ownership: **Maine Bureau of Parks and Recreation.**

Quoddy Head is a windswept peninsula poking out from the easternmost shore of Maine. Tides 20 to 28 feet high (see **#96**) create a large intertidal habitat (see **Portland North**) along the rocky shore, while the narrow neck of the peninsula supports an unusual bog. The walk along the isthmus passes through gnarled coniferous woods and over rocky outcrops. Eiders, irises, and nudibranchs are among the local inhabitants you may discover.

The trail begins at the end of the state-park parking lot. Walk down onto the shore rocks (**A**), which lie below and stretch several hundred yards east of the parking lot. Since this shore is very much exposed to the onslaught of waves, many of the organisms that live here hide in cracks, under rocks, or beneath curtains of seaweed. When the tide is low enough to uncover green-brown curtains and tangles of rockweed, look into some of the crevices and on sheltered rock surfaces. You are likely to find clusters, herds even, of dog whelks. White, almost-black, brown, banded, and sometimes purplish or bright-orange, their oblong short-spired shells vary so much in color that you may think you are finding half a dozen different kinds of snail when really all are of a single species. Some of the color variation seems to be akin to that of hair-color variation in

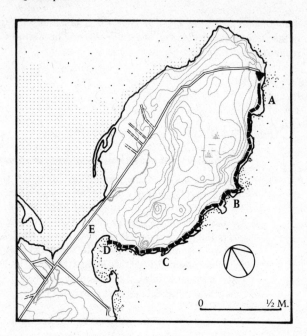

humans, whereas other of the differences seem to be related to what the snails have been eating.

Turn over one of the snails. On the side of its soft, muscular foot, which it uses for "walking" and for holding itself against the force of the waves, is a fingernail-like piece called an operculum. The dog whelk can pull it into the opening of its shell, where, like a trapdoor, it helps to keep moisture in (whelks obtain oxygen from water, even at low tide) and predators out. Also on the bottom, on the end of its shell, there is a groove along which the snail extrudes its tubularly curled mouthparts. Like other snails, the dog whelk has a filelike tongue or radula, but instead of using it for scraping algae off surfaces, the dog whelk uses it (in conjunction with enzymatic secretions) to bore a small, round hole in the side of a mussel or other shelled creature and then to eat the soft body inside. Its secretions have been found useful to humans as well; Phoenicians and American Indians used whelk purpurin for a vivid-purple dye.

Another inhabitant of this area between forest and sea, and one less commonly found than the dog whelk, is the branch-backed nudibranch, or sea slug. Although an animal called a sea slug may not sound like something you would intentionally seek out, discovering the delicate pink beauty of one of these creatures is a wonderful tidepoolers' treat. Like the whelk, it is a member of the group of mollusks called *gastropods* (from the words for "stomach" and "foot"). Lacking the protective shell of its snail relatives, nudibranchs prowl in the deeper parts of the intertidal zone, which are moist or wet throughout the tidal cycle. Anywhere from ⅛ to 1 inch long, here, they dangle behind curtains of algae or crawl across algal or rock surfaces, their "branched backs," or gills, like tiny pink parsley fronds, rocking ever so slightly in a vague tide-pool current. This species reportedly feeds on hydroids, branching, sometimes feathery, marine organisms related to hydra. Hydroids have spring-loaded, stinging cells, which deter some predators but which the branch-backed nudibranch seems to find palatable enough. When the nudibranch feeds on the hydroids, it somehow manages not to pop the stinging cells. Later incorporated into the nudibranch's gills, these cells make its soft body less palatable to would-be predators.

Follow the trail that hugs the shore and bluff-top edges, taking left forks. After passing the upper and lower sections of High Ledge, stay straight (not left) on the main gravelly trail beyond the beach. At Green Point, fork left and go out onto the point (**B**). In late spring and early summer, blue-flag iris display their fancy flowers. The three inner, upright blades of these flowers are the true petals. The three downward-curving, petal-like parts are specialized sepals (the structures that cover the petals of a flower when it is in the bud stage; they are usually green), which not only attract insects but also act as broad landing platforms. Botanists think that the bold veining that crosses the white and yellow-green spots helps guide incoming insects to the sexual parts of the flower, which are located on the purple flap that arches closely above the sepal. The pollinating insect will first bump against the stigmatic surface (the end of the female part of the flower, often sticky) leaving behind pollen it carries from other irises. Further in, under the flap, it will brush against the stamen, picking up pollen from this iris. Many flowers, likely the iris included, have mechanisms by which the pistil can recognize and inhibit the growth process of pollen grains that originate in their own flowers; thus if an insect brushes pollen on the stigmatic surface as it exits this flower, the plant will still have the highest chances of being fertilized by pollen from another iris rather than from itself. These strategies are just a few of the many that plants have evolved in order to maximize the chances of gene recombination from cross-pollination.

Out on the water, common eiders are among the ducks you may see. In summer, look for brown females and young paddling close to shore. You will generally see two or more females and their broods traveling together. At this time of year, the males have gone northward on their molt migration. Because feathers, like clothes, do wear out, all birds go through some form of molting process whereby they shed their old feathers and grow new ones. While songbirds molt their flying feathers gradually, always maintaining the ability to fly, ducks and many other heavy-bodied birds that would have trouble flying if a few of their primary wing feathers were missing, get the process completed all at once. They seek sheltered retreats on the open water where they can be fairly safe during their flightless period. If you were to see them during this time, you might not recognize them, because their body plumage, so striking in males during the rest of the year, is rather drab. This is called *eclipse plumage*. In the fall, after the females have finished rearing the young and have completed their molting, eiders gather together, and you may see groups of hundreds of them "rafting" (floating) offshore.

As you approach Carrying Place Cove, notice the herring weir, a group of tall sticks poking up out of the water (**C**). Until recently, herring fishing in Maine was primarily a coastal operation in which the use of such traps was common. The poles, interlaced with brush, were arranged in relatively shallow water in locations where schools of herring were expected to pass. The idea was that fish, encountering the outer wings of the weir, would follow along the funnel of fencing and end up trapped in the inner pocket of the maze, circling in confusion and not able to find the small opening of the funnel. Today, a netting technique called *purse seining* allows fishermen to capture the fish wherever they happen to be. The purse seine, which can be drawn closed at the bottom, is used to gather fish into a concentrated pocket, from which they can be pumped onboard a carrier vessel. These Maine herring are used to make sardines and kippers. The catch has varied greatly, especially over the last decade, and there has been great debate as to whether this has been due to the regular movements of the fish populations or to overfishing.

The trail ends at Carrying Place Cove (**D**), whose bog is a wonderful example of a coastal raised peatland, which generally has a much more distinctly domed shape than does an interior bog. Such peat lands are especially intriguing because they can change a landscape's topography, reroute streams, elevate water tables, and maintain their own water tables apart from the groundwater table. It seems that this bog originally formed above the reach of tide water, in a shallow depression on the isthmus of Quoddy Head (which probably was a tombolo—see **#78**). Today, as a result of the relative rise in sea level (see **#99**), the sea directly impinges on the north and south sides of the bog. In Carrying Place Cove, the south margin is being overridden by a gravel beach. On the north face, seas and rains have eroded an outstanding vertical escarpment, and it is here that you can probably gain the best insights into the peat land.

Return to your car, and as you head back toward Lubec, make a stop on the narrow neck of the peninsula (**E**), where you can observe the bog cross-section in the road cut and in the bank along the shore. (Note: A state-park parking lot and interpretative sign are planned for this area.) The history revealed here begins with clays, followed by shallow pond or marsh sediments, then the exposed roots of a swamp forest or thicket, and finally the hummocks and hollows of sphagnum and other bog plants that have occasionally been burned by surface fires (see **#56** for bog formation).

Remarks: *This is a 4-mile hike, round trip. The terrain varies from smooth to bumpy. There is camping at Cobscook Bay State Park, on Route 1 north of Whiting, from May 15 to October 15. The tidal mudflats on the northern side of the Quoddy Head peninsula are an excellent place to watch migrating shorebirds.*

102.
Goodall Heath
Trail

Directions: **Baring Unit, Calais, Maine. Take Route 1 north (pass the Edmunds Unit of the Refuge) to Pembroke; then go 6 miles northwest on Route 214 to Hatten's Store (left), at the junction with Charlotte Rd. Turn right and go 7.9 miles. The refuge headquarters and the Woodcock Trail are to the left, and Goodall Heath Rd. is to the right: drive 0.1 mile and park at the fork (no vehicles allowed beyond the gate).**

Ownership: **Moosehorn National Wildlife Refuge.**

Down East near the Canadian border, Moosehorn is one of numerous national wildlife refuges that lie scattered across the United States. Originally established for the protection and management of international migratory waterfowl, their scope has been expanded to include protection for many species of wildlife and plants.

The primary objective at Moosehorn is to develop, test, and demonstrate management techniques for the American woodcock, a squat, brown bird with a long, tough beak. The woodcock is very popular among both hunters and bird-watchers. Particularly spectacular is the spring courtship display of the males, which make a series of buzzing *peent* sounds, then chirping, fly in upward spirals, and finally drop silently back to their singing fields. On the south side of the headquarters road, a short, self-guided nature trail has been routed through woodcock-display territory. The brochure for the walk describes numerous facets of woodcock ecology.

The walk described below is in the Goodall Heath area; it begins on the east side of the tarred road, opposite the headquarters entrance. Although the area is managed primarily for woodcock and nesting waterfowl, the cutting, prescribed-burning, and water-level-regulation techniques that are employed benefit numerous other species, such as deer, moose, bear, muskrat, grouse, bald eagles, and many songbirds. From spring through fall, American woodcock are abundant. Look for them in fields, in cut swaths that are growing into thickets, and particularly in alder groves. Living on alder roots (as they also do on the roots of clover and alfalfa) are bacteria that convert gaseous nitrogen from the air into nitrates and nitrites, which can be used by plants and animals. The enriched soil of damp alder thickets is an excellent habitat for earthworms, which are the primary food of woodcock. Beaverworks are particularly visible here in the several flowages and ponds.

From the fork where you park, follow the left-hand road. At the bottom of the hill, cross the Tyler Flowage (**A**). Already there is sign of beaver: the beautifully arched dam bowed convexly upstream exhibits the architectural capabilities of these animals. Although a baby beaver instinctively knows the basics of dam building, it is through trial and error that it polishes its skills. American beavers were nearly trapped to extinction in the past century in order to satisfy the demand for hats made from their fur. Today they have made a remarkable comeback, and their population at Moosehorn has gradually increased to about three hundred.

Besides protecting the beavers that built it, a pond like the one before you is of benefit to other wildlife. It provides food resources and nesting habitat for ducks and geese, stores water through dry seasons, helps minimize flooding, and is home for many fish and amphibians. In the marshy edges, alders, sedges, pickerelweed, and meadowsweet find a mushy foothold.

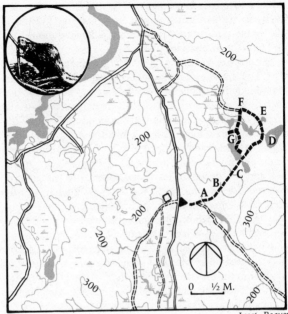

Inset: Beaver

Continue through spruces and more alders, a shadowy young pine forest, deciduous woods, and a cleared opening on the right. Take a side trip left on the Moose Highway at **B**. Named after a Youth Conservation Corps leader who helped clear it, the "highway" penetrates the forest for about 100 yards and emerges into another cut swath that might harbor woodcock or other wildlife. Beginning in the 1940s and continuing today, swaths are cleared for habitat management: the new growth provides high-nutrient forage and ample protective cover for many mammals and birds.

As the forest edge gives way to the Upper Goodall Heath area (**C**), look left for a semicleared but very brushy pathway marked by red plastic flagging. It permits relatively easy access to a rock outcrop from which you can survey the entire environs. Keep an eye open for marsh hawks (northern harriers) soaring low over the vegetation in search of rodents, birds, and large insects (see **#18**).

From the flowage, three beaver lodges are visible. Generally, only one of them is active at a time. Look for the one with the most blond, recently cut sticks. Its occupants are a family group: a pair of adults and their offspring of the last 2 years. Just before the next kits are born (litters average two to six kits), the female will chase everyone else out. Later, only the male and the yearling kits will be allowed to return; the 2-year-olds will have to move to other areas and fend for themselves.

The array of spindly snags emerging from the pond stand as a clue that a young forest previously occupied at least some of this site. It was flooded and killed when the beavers built their dam. Heaths such as sweet gale and cranberries are currently encroaching on the pond's far edge, suggesting that the pond might grow into a bog if the beaver abandon it. Given enough time, a pond in Maine will usually turn into either a meadow or a bog. If the water is not too acidic and if inflowing streams bring sediments that make the pond less and less deep, shallow-pond plants, such as cattails, and then wet-meadow grasses and herbs, such as buttercups, will be able to colonize the area. If the water is acidic, as is common in drainages that are either high in coniferous and oak species, located on granitic bedrock, or receive large amounts of acidic precipitation, and if incoming water seeps slowly, bringing little sediment, sphagnum mosses and other bog plants such as sweet gale and cranberries will be able to grow in the area (see **#56** for more on bog formation).

At the junction, go right to Vose Pond (**D**). Great cormorants are common winter visitors at Moosehorn.

As you continue, notice the groups of long scratches, perpendicularly traversing the roadbed, where beavers dragged sticks from cutting grounds to the water. The beavers eat the bark, leaves, and twigs and use sections of the peeled branches and trunks for building dams and bridges. The woods around this next small flowage are a beaver's paradise: young aspen and birch, near water. A beaver in search of food will go perhaps 100 yards (200 or more, if food is scarce and/or predators absent) from the protection of water. In 15 minutes it can cut down a tree 4 inches in diameter. Here the beaver can work safely, without danger from predators.

The beavers at the Boundary Flowage (**E**) have built their lodge attached to the bank rather than entirely surrounded by water. This seems to be the preference of some individuals. In Europe, beavers commonly live in burrows *in* the banks.

The road junction at **F** is a critter crossing: a well-worn pathway is visible on the banks on either side of the road. Follow the left fork over the Popple Flowage and through a gray squirrel's forest of clumped maples and birches (see **#73** and **#83** for more on squirrels). This section of Maine was heavily logged in the 1800s. In addition, large portions of this unit of the refuge were severely burned in the early 1930s. Maples and birches sprout well from root crowns and, as here, often establish clumped growth patterns.

A wide, grassy swath (right) leads down to the Lower Goodall Heath (**G**). Here, as at all the ponds you have passed on this walk, the water level can be regulated, maintaining inviting conditions for the waterfowl that nest at the refuge: common loons, Canada geese, black ducks, blue- and green-winged teal, wood ducks, common and hooded mergansers, and others.

A right turn at the next junction will head you back toward your car. Strawberries are common on the road edges. Perhaps a goshawk will dart through the woods ahead of you, its long tail ruddering it agilely between the trees. More likely, ravens will croak above you, hoarse reminders that the forest is indeed alert to your passage despite your care to be unobtrusive.

Remarks: *This is a 4-mile hike along fairly level, old dirt roads (which are closed to motor vehicles). Binoculars may be useful. Patience is vital if you want to see wildlife. The fall season is recommended. Bird and mammal lists, self-guided trail brochures, and general refuge information are available at the headquarters. There is camping at Cobscook Bay State Park near the southern unit of the refuge. The walk into the Natural Area along Headquarters Rd. takes you into the older forests on the refuge. The roads overlooking the Magurrewock marshes are a good place to watch for wildlife.*

Glossary

acidic: Containing an abundance of hydrogen ions. Very acidic soils are poor in nutrients.

alga: Any of a large group of primitive and mostly aquatic plants, ranging from tiny one-celled to large multicelled organisms.

basalt: A dark, fine-grained igneous rock formed of solidified lava.

basic: Containing any one substance or a combination of substances that combine with acids to form salts. Slightly basic soils are rich in nutrients and are generally very fertile. Highly basic soils are toxic.

bird of prey: One of the carnivorous birds, such as hawks, owls, and eagles.

bog: A wet, soggy area with little or no drainage.

bottomland: Low-lying ground that may be flooded from time to time.

boulder train: A glacial deposit of large boulders, usually scattered in a fan-shaped pattern; an important indicator of glacial movement.

brackish: A term used to describe water that is somewhat salty but not as salty as seawater.

calcite: A mineral made up of calcium, carbon, and oxygen; also known as *calcium carbonate.*

canopy: An umbrella of trees formed by the tallest trees in a stand.

carnivore: A flesh-eating animal.

cirque: A deep, steep-sided hollow formed on mountainsides by glacial erosion.

climax forest: A forest in which the mix of species is relatively stable over time.

competition: Rivalry of plants or animals for the same resources or habitat.

coniferous: Evergreen and cone-bearing.

deciduous: Shedding leaves annually.

dike: A body of igneous rock imbedded in the structure of surrounding rocks when molten material was forced through cracks to the surface.

disjunct: Set apart from the main distribution of the species.

drumlin: An elongated or oval hill composed of glacial till, lying on an axis parallel to the direction of the ice flow.

ecosystem: The interaction of plants, animals, and their environment.

erosion: The process by which the earth's surface is worn away by water, wind, or waves.

esker: A long, narrow ridge of sand, gravel, and boulders deposited by a stream flowing in a tunnel beneath a stagnant, melting glacier.

fault: A crack in the earth's surface where movement has taken place.

glacial drift: Debris deposited directly by a glacier without being reworked by glacial meltwaters; usually found in jumbled piles in irregular patterns.

glacial erratic: A boulder that has been carried from its point of origin by glacial ice and deposited elsewhere when the ice melted.

glacial scouring: The erosion of rock and soil by moving ice, usually identified by surface polishing and scrape marks.

gneiss: A metamorphic rock with a banded structure due to the separation of dark and light minerals by heat and pressure.

granite: A very common New England rock composed of quartz, feldspar, and other minerals. It is a very durable and coarse igneous rock with the individual mineral grains clearly distinguishable.

habitat: The natural environment of an animal or plant.

herbivore: A plant-eating animal.

humus: Decomposed animal and plant matter that forms the organic portion of soil.

Ice Age: A period from about 10,000 to 2 million years ago during which a large portion of the earth was covered by glaciers; also called the *glacial epoch.*

igneous rock: Rock, such as basalt and granite, that has solidified from a molten state.

impoundment: An artificial pond or lake.

interglacial: Warm periods that occurred between glacial advances when the ice sheets withdrew toward the poles.

intertidal: Pertaining to that part of the shore that lies between the low-tide and the high-tide mark.

kame: A short ridge or hill of stratified glacial drift deposited by meltwaters.

kame terrace: A narrow, level plain of sand and gravel deposited by glacial meltwaters running between a valley wall and a deposit of ice. A kame terrace usually borders a river, stream, or lake.

kettle hole: A bowl-shaped depression formed by a mass of glacial ice that has broken off from a melting glacier and become buried in gravel. When the ice melts, a hole is created. Many bogs are in kettle holes.

larva: The immature, wingless stage of certain insects.

litter: The layer of slightly decomposed plant material on the surface of a forest floor.

magma: Molten material within the earth's crust.

mantle rock: The loose rock and soil lying on top of bedrock, usually deposited by melting glaciers.

marsh: Low, wet land covered by grassy vegetation.

meander: A bend in a river.

metamorphic rock: Sedimentary and igneous rock that has been changed in appearance and composition by heat and pressure.

migration: The rhythmic seasonal movement of certain birds and other animals.

moraine: A deposit of glacial debris. A *terminal moraine* is the deposit of glacial material at the point at which a glacier ceased its advance.

old field: A stage in the succession of cleared land to forest characterized by grasses, flowering plants, and shrubs.

omnivore: A flesh- and plant-eating animal.

outwash plain: A sandy or gravelly plain of glacial debris formed by streams from a melting glacier.

peat: Partially decomposed plant material common to wet areas with poor drainage.

pelagic: Oceanic.

peneplain: A land surface either worn down by erosion or built up by deposits or by upward thrusting of the earth's surface.

photosynthesis: The process by which green plants convert water and carbon dioxide into carbohydrates.

pioneer: One of a number of plants that appear early in the process of succession.

Pleistocene epoch: The geological epoch during which the Ice Age occurred.

runoff: Rainwater, melting snow, or groundwater that drains away across the surface of the ground.

schist: A coarse-grained metamorphic rock with a mostly parallel structure of minerals.

secondary growth: The forest that appears after land has been cleared.

sedimentary rock: Layered rocks formed by sediments of different materials building upon each other.

shorebirds: Species that frequent coastal areas and inland beaches, such as sandpipers, plovers, and oystercatchers.

shrub: A woody perennial plant that usually has several stems and is generally smaller than a tree.

species: A group of related plants or animals that interbreed to produce fertile offspring.

sphagnum: A coarse but soft moss found on bog surfaces; also known as *peat moss.*

succession: The process by which the vegetation of an ecosystem changes over time.

swamp: Low, wet forest that is regularly flooded and poorly drained.

talus: A pile of broken rocks and boulders at the bottom of a cliff.

tannin: Any one of a variety of large, complex molecules contained in most woody plants.

tarn: A small mountain pool or lake.

till: Unstratified glacial drift, consisting mostly of clay, sand, and boulders.

understory: The trees found growing beneath the canopy species and above the shrub layer.

waterfowl: Aquatic birds, including geese, ducks, and swans.

Bibliography

AMC Guide to Mount Washington and the Presidential Range. 1982. Boston: Appalachian Mountain Club.

AMC Field Guide to Mountain Flowers of New England. 1977. Boston: Appalachian Mountain Club.

AMC Maine Mountain Guide. 1976. Boston: Appalachian Mountain Club.

AMC Massachusetts and Rhode Island Trail Guide. 1982. 5th ed. Boston: Appalachian Mountain Club.

AMC New England Canoeing Guide. 1971. 3rd ed. Boston: Appalachian Mountain Club.

AMC River Guide. Vol. 1, Maine. 1980. Boston: Appalachian Mountain Club.

AMC Trail Guide to Mount Desert Island and Acadia National Park. 1975. Boston: Appalachian Mountain Club.

AMC White Mountain Guide. 1979. 22nd ed. Boston: Appalachian Mountain Club.

Appalachian Trail Guide to Maine. 1983. 10th ed. Harpers Ferry, W. Va.: Appalachian Trail Conference.

Appalachian Trail Guide to Massachusetts and Connecticut. 1983. 6th ed. Harpers Ferry, W. Va.: Appalachian Trail Conference.

Appalachian Trail Guide to New Hampshire and Vermont. 1983. 4th ed. Harpers Ferry, W. Va.: Appalachian Trail Conference.

Audubon Society Field Guide to Butterflies. 1981. New York: Alfred A. Knopf.

Audubon Society Field Guide to Fishes, Whales, and Dolphins. 1983. New York: Alfred A. Knopf.

Audubon Society Field Guide to North American Birds: Eastern Region. 1977. New York: Alfred A. Knopf.

Audubon Society Field Guide to North American Mammals. 1980. New York: Alfred A. Knopf.

Audubon Society Field Guide to North American Rocks and Minerals. 1978. New York: Alfred A. Knopf.

Audubon Society Field Guide to Reptiles and Amphibians. 1979. New York: Alfred A. Knopf.

Audubon Society Field Guide to Seashells. 1981. New York: Alfred A. Knopf.

Baldwin, Henry I. 1980. *Monadnock Guide.* 3rd ed. Concord: Society for the Protection of New Hampshire Forests.

Berrill, Michael and Deborah. 1981. *A Sierra Club Naturalist's Guide: The North Atlantic Coast.* San Francisco: Sierra Club Books.

Brady, John, and Brian White. 1983. *Fifty Hikes in Massachusetts.* Woodstock, Vt.: Backcountry Publications.

Brockman, C. Frank. 1979. *Trees of North America.* New York: Golden Press.

Butcher, Russell D. 1977. *Guide to Acadia National Park.* New York: Reader's Digest Press.

Caldwell, Dabney. 1972. *The Geology of Baxter State Park.* Augusta: Maine Geologic Survey.

Carson, Rachel. 1962. *Silent Spring.* New York: Fawcett Books.

Carson, Rachel. 1965. *A Sense of Wonder.* New York: Harper & Row.

Catlett, Cloe. 1980. *Fifty More Hikes in Maine.* Woodstock, Vt.: Backcountry Publications.

Chamberlain, Barbara B. 1964. *These Fragile Outposts.* Garden City, N.Y.: Natural History Press.

Chapman, Carleton A. 1970. *The Geology of Acadia National Park.* Old Greenwich, Conn.: Chatham Press.

Conklin, Philip. 1981. *Islands in Time.* Camden, Maine: Down East Books.

Detels, Pamela, and Janet Harris. 1977. *Canoeing Trips in Connecticut.* Chester, Conn: Globe Pequot Press.

Doane, Daniel. 1983. *Fifty Hikes in the White Mountains.* 3rd rev. ed. Woodstock, Vt.: Backcountry Publications.

Doane, Daniel. 1983. *Fifty More Hikes in New Hampshire.* 2nd ed. Woodstock, Vt.: Backcountry Publications.

Dwilley, Marilyn. 1973. *Spring Wildflowers of New England.* Camden, Maine: Down East Publishing Co.

Eppee, Anne Orth. 1983. *The Amphibians of New England.* Camden, Maine: Down East Books.

Federal Writers Project. 1983. *WPA Guide to Massachusetts.* Reprint ed. New York: Pantheon Books.

Gabler, Ray. 1981. *New England White Water River Guide.* Boston: Appalachian Mountain Club.

Gibson, John. 1983. *Fifty Hikes in Maine.* 2nd ed. Woodstock, Vt.: Backcountry Publications.

Godin, Alfred J. 1977. *Wild Mammals of New England*. Baltimore: Johns Hopkins University Press.

Guide Book of the Long Trail. 1977. 21st ed. Montpelier, Vt.: Green Mountain Club.

Hardy, Gerry and Sue. 1978. *Fifty Hikes in Connecticut*. Woodstock, Vt.: Backcountry Publications.

Harlow, William M. 1957. *Trees of the Eastern and Central United States and Canada*. New York: Dover Publications.

Harper and Row's Complete Field Guide to North American Wildlife: Eastern Edition. 1981. New York: Harper & Row.

Hildebrandt, Barry and Susan. 1979. *Coastal Connecticut: Eastern Region*. Old Saybrook, Conn.: Peregrine Press.

Irland, Lloyd C. 1982. *Wildlands and Woodlots: The Story of New England's Forests*. Hanover, N.H.: University of New England Press.

Johnson, Charles W. 1980. *The Nature of Vermont*. Hanover, N.H.: University of New England Press.

Jorgensen, Neil. 1977. *A Guide to New England's Landscape*. Chester, Conn.: Pequot Press.

Jorgensen, Neil. 1978. *A Sierra Club Naturalist's Guide: Southern New England*. San Francisco: Sierra Club Books.

Kingsbury, John M. 1970. *The Rocky Shore*. Old Greenwich, Conn.: Chatham Press.

Kostecke, Diana M., ed. 1975. *Franconia Notch: An In-Depth Guide*. Concord: Society for the Protection of New Hampshire Forests.

Leopold, Aldo. 1966. *A Sand County Almanac*. New York: Oxford University Press.

Mallett, Sandy. 1978. *A Year with New England's Birds: 25 Field Trips*. Somersworth, N.H.: New Hampshire Publishing Co.

Matthews, L. Harrison. 1978. *The Natural History of the Whale*. New York: Columbia University Press.

Michelin Green Guide to New England. 1982. New Hyde Park, N.Y.: Michelin Guides & Maps.

Miller, Dorcas. 1979. *The Maine Coast: A Nature Lovers Guide*. Charlotte, N.C.: East Woods Press.

Moore, Patrick. 1980. *The Pocket Guide to Astronomy*. New York: Simon & Schuster.

Morrison, Samuel Eliot. 1960. *The Story of Mount Desert Island, Maine*. Boston: Little, Brown & Co.

Murie, Claus J. 1975. *A Field Guide to Animal Tracks*. Boston: Houghton Mifflin Co.

Perry, John and Jane Greverus. 1980. *The Random House Guide to Natural Areas of the Eastern United States*. New York: Random House.

Peterson, Roger Tory. 1980. *A Field Guide to The Birds of Eastern and Central North America*. 4th ed. Boston: Houghton Mifflin Co.

Pierson, Elizabeth and Jan. 1981. *A Birder's Guide to the Coast of Maine.* Camden, Maine: Down East Books.

Preston, Philip, and Jonathan Kannau. 1979. *White Mountains West.* Ashland, N.H.: Waumbek Books.

Proctor, Noble S. 1978. *Twenty-Five Birding Areas in Connecticut.* Chester, Conn.: Globe Pequot Press.

Rand McNally Campground and Trailer Park Guide: Eastern Edition. 1983. New York: Rand McNally & Co.

Randall, Peter E. 1983. *Mount Washington: A Guide and Short History.* Camden, Maine: Down East Books.

Riley, Laura and William. 1979. *Guide to the National Wildlife Refuges.* Garden City, N.Y.: Doubleday & Co., Anchor Press.

Robbins, Braun and Zim. 1966. *Birds of North America.* New York: Western Publishing Co.

Roberts, Mervin F. 1977. *The Tidemarsh Guide.* New York: E. P. Dutton.

Roth, Charles E. 1982. *The Wildlife Observer Guidebook.* Englewood Cliffs, N.J.: Prentice-Hall.

Sandlier, Hugh and Heather. 1983. *Short Walks on Cape Cod and the Vineyard.* Chester, Conn.: Globe Pequot Press.

Steele, Frederick L. 1982. *At Timberline: A Nature Guide to the Mountains of the Northeast.* Boston: Appalachian Mountain Club.

Stokes, Donald W. 1976. *A Guide to Nature in Winter: Northeast and North Central America.* Boston: Little, Brown & Co.

Stokes, Donald W. 1979. *A Guide to the Behavior of Common Birds.* Boston: Little, Brown & Co.

Stokes, Donald W. 1983. *A Guide to Observing Insect Lives.* Boston: Little, Brown & Co.

Strabler, Arthur N. 1966. *A Geologist's View of Cape Cod.* Garden City, N.Y.: Natural History Press.

Thompson, Betty Flanders. 1977. *The Changing Face of New England.* Boston: Houghton Mifflin Co.

Weber, Ken. 1978. *25 Walks in Rhode Island.* Somersworth, N.H.: New Hampshire Publishing Co.

Maps

Delorme's Map and Guide of Baxter State Park and Katahdin. 1982. Freeport, Maine: Delorme Publishing Co.

Illustrated Map of the Maine Coast. 1982. Freeport, Maine: Delorme Publishing Co.

Maine Atlas and Gazetteer. 1982. Freeport, Maine: Delorme Publishing Co.

New Hampshire Atlas and Gazetteer. 1982. Freeport, Maine: Delorme Publishing Co.

Rand McNally Road Atlas: United States/Canada/Mexico. 1982. New York: Rand McNally Co.

Trail Map and Guide to the White Mountain National Forest. 1982. Freeport, Maine: Delorme Publishing Co.

Vermont Atlas and Gazetteer. 1982. Freeport, Maine: Delorme Publishing Co.

Index

Except for bird species, of which every citation is included, the index lists only those plant and animal species that are significantly mentioned or described in detail. *Italic* figures refer to major discussions; **boldface** figures refer to site numbers.

A Note
About the Authors

Stephen Kulik is a writer living in rural Massachusetts who works in the energy and environmental fields.

Pete Salmansohn is a naturalist at the National Audubon Society Camp in Maine, and has taught in Rhode Island, Connecticut, New York, and Oregon.

Matthew Schmidt is a free-lance writer from Massachusetts who has written about travel and history in New England for several regional publications.

Heidi Welch is a naturalist and environmental educator living in Maine who has worked for both the National Park Service and the National Audubon Society in Maine, and at the Yosemite Institution in California.

Notes

342

1533x9